AF753520

UNITED STATES

US FEDERAL MARYTIME COMMISSION HANDBOOK

STRATEGIC INFORMATION, REGULATIONS, CONTACTS

International Business Publications, USA
Washington, DC USA

UNITES STATES

US FEDERAL MARYTIME COMMISSION HANDBOOK

STRATEGIC INFORMATION, REGULATIONS, CONTACTS

UPDATED ANNUALLY

We express our sincere appreciation to all government agencies and international organizations which provided information and other materials for this handbook

Cover Design: **International Business Publications, USA**

International Business Publications, USA. *has used its best efforts in collecting, analyzing and preparing data, information and materials for this unique handbook. Due to the dynamic nature and fast development of the economy and business environment, we cannot warrant that all information herein is complete and accurate. IBP does not assume and hereby disclaim any liability to any person for any loss or damage caused by possible errors or omissions in the handbook.*
This handbook is for individual use only. Use this handbook for any other purpose, included but not limited to reproducing and storing in a retrieval system by any means, electronic, photocopying or using the addresses or other information contained in this handbook for any commercial purposes requires a special written permission from the publisher.

2016 Edition Updated Reprint International Business Publications, USA
ISBN 1-4387-5435-3

For additional analytical, business and investment opportunities information,
please contact Global Investment & Business Center, USA
at (703) 370-8082. Fax: (703) 370-8083. E-mail: ibpusa3@gmail.com
Global Business and Investment Info Databank - www.ibpus.com

Printed in the USA

For additional analytical, business and investment opportunities information,
please contact Global Investment & Business Center, USA
at (703) 370-8082. Fax: (703) 370-8083. E-mail: ibpusa3@gmail.com
Global Business and Investment Info Databank - www.ibpus.com

UNITED STATES
US FEDERAL MARYTIME COMMISSION HANDBOOK
STRATEGIC INFORMATION, REGULATIONS, CONTACTS

TABLE OF CONTENTS

For additional analytical, business and investment opportunities information, please contact Global Investment & Business Center, USA at (703) 370-8082. Fax: (703) 370-8083. E-mail: ibpusa3@gmail.com Global Business and Investment Info Databank - www.ibpus.com

For additional analytical, business and investment opportunities information, please contact Global Investment & Business Center, USA at (703) 370-8082. Fax: (703) 370-8083. E-mail: ibpusa3@gmail.com Global Business and Investment Info Databank - www.ibpus.com

STRATEGIC AND DEVELOPMENT PROFILES

Capital	Washington, D.C. 38°53′N 77°01′W38.883°N 77.017°W
Largest city	New York City 40°43′N 74°00′W40.717°N 74.000°W
Official languages	None at federal level
Recognised regional languages	List
National language	English
Demonym	American
Government	Federal presidential constitutional republic
- President	Barack Obama
- Vice President	Joe Biden
- Speaker of the House	John Boehner
- Chief Justice	John Roberts
Legislature	Congress
- Upper house	Senate
- Lower house	House of Representatives
Independence from Great Britain	
- Declared	July 4, 1776
- Recognized	September 3, 1783
- Constitution	June 21, 1788
- Current Statehood	August 21, 1959
Area	
- Total	9,857,306 km^2 (3rd) 3,805,927 sq mi
- Water (%)	2.23
Population	
- 2014 estimate	319,435,700 (3rd)
- Density	34.2/km^2 (180th) 88.6/sq mi
GDP (PPP)	2013 estimate
- Total	$16.768 trillion (1st)
- Per capita	$53,001 (9th)
GDP (nominal)	2013 estimate
- Total	$16.768 trillion (1st)
- Per capita	$53,001 (9th)
Gini (2012)	36.9 medium ·
HDI (2013)	0.914 very high · 5th
Currency	United States dollar ($) (USD)
Time zone	(UTC−5 to −10)
- Summer (DST)	(UTC−4 to −10
Drives on the	right

Calling code	+1
ISO 3166 code	US
Internet TLD	.us .gov .mil .edu

The **United States of America** (**USA** or **U.S.A.**) , commonly referred to as the **United States** (**US** or **U.S.**) , **America**, and sometimes **the States**, is a federal republic consisting of 50 states and a federal district. The 48 contiguous states and Washington, D.C., are in central North America between Canada and Mexico. The state of Alaska is located in the northwestern part of North America and the state of Hawaii is an archipelago in the mid-Pacific. The country also has five populated and nine unpopulated territories in the Pacific and the Caribbean. At 3.80 million square miles (9.85 million km^2) and with around 318 million people, the United States is the world's third- or fourth-largest country by total area and third-largest by population. It is one of the world's most ethnically diverse and multicultural nations, the product of large-scale immigration from many countries. The geography and climate of the United States is also extremely diverse, and it is home to a wide variety of wildlife.

Paleo-Indians migrated from Eurasia to what is now the U.S. mainland around 15,000 years ago, with European colonization beginning in the 16th century. The United States emerged from 13 British colonies located along the Atlantic seaboard. Disputes between Great Britain and these colonies led to the American Revolution. On July 4, 1776, as the colonies were fighting Great Britain in the American Revolutionary War, delegates from the 13 colonies unanimously issued the Declaration of Independence. The war ended in 1783 with the recognition of independence of the United States from the Kingdom of Great Britain, and was the first successful war of independence against a European colonial empire. The current Constitution was adopted on September 17, 1787. The first ten amendments, collectively named the Bill of Rights, were ratified in 1791 and designed to guarantee many fundamental civil rights and freedoms.

Driven by the doctrine of manifest destiny, the United States embarked on a vigorous expansion across North America throughout the 19th century. This involved displacing native tribes, acquiring new territories, and gradually admitting new states. During the second half of the 19th century, the American Civil War ended legal slavery in the country.

By the end of that century, the United States extended into the Pacific Ocean, and its economy began to soar. The Spanish–American War and World War I confirmed the country's status as a global military power. The United States emerged from World War II as a global superpower, the first country to develop nuclear weapons, the only country to use them in warfare, and as a permanent member of the United Nations Security Council. The end of the Cold War and the dissolution of the Soviet Union left the United States as the sole superpower.

The United States is a developed country and has the world's largest national economy.

The economy is fueled by an abundance of natural resources and high worker productivity. While the U.S. economy is considered post-industrial, it continues to be one of the world's largest manufacturers. The country accounts for 37% of global military spending, being the world's foremost economic and military power, a prominent political and cultural force, and a leader in scientific research and technological innovations

STRATEGIC PROFILE

Background:	The United States became the world's first modern democracy after its break with Great Britain (1776) and the adoption of a constitution (1789) . During the 19th

	century, many new states were added to the original 13 as the nation expanded across the North American continent and acquired a number of overseas possessions. The two most traumatic experiences in the nation's history were the Civil War (1861-65) and the Great Depression of the 1930s. Buoyed by victories in World Wars I and II and the end of the Cold War in 1991, the US remains the world's most powerful nation-state. The economy is marked by steady growth, low unemployment and inflation, and rapid advances in technology.

GEOGRAPHY

Location:	North America, bordering both the North Atlantic Ocean and the North Pacific Ocean, between Canada and Mexico
Geographic coordinates:	38 00 N, 97 00 W
Map references:	North America
Area:	total: 9,629,091 sq km land: 9,158,960 sq km water: 470,131 sq km note: includes only the 50 states and District of Columbia
Area - comparative:	about one-half the size of Russia; about three-tenths the size of Africa; about one-half the size of South America (or slightly larger than Brazil) ; slightly larger than China; about two and one-half times the size of Western Europe
Land boundaries:	total: 12,248 km border countries: Canada 8,893 km (including 2,477 km with Alaska) , Cuba 29 km (US Naval Base at Guantanamo Bay) , Mexico 3,326 km note: Guantanamo Naval Base is leased by the US and thus remains part of Cuba

Coastline:	19,924 km
Maritime claims:	contiguous zone: 24 NM continental shelf: not specified exclusive economic zone: 200 NM territorial sea: 12 NM

For additional analytical, business and investment opportunities information, please contact Global Investment & Business Center, USA at (703) 370-8082. Fax: (703) 370-8083. E-mail: ibpusa3@gmail.com Global Business and Investment Info Databank - www.ibpus.com

For additional analytical, business and investment opportunities information, please contact Global Investment & Business Center, USA at (703) 370-8082. Fax: (703) 370-8083. E-mail: ibpusa3@gmail.com
Global Business and Investment Info Databank - www.ibpus.com

Climate:	mostly temperate, but tropical in Hawaii and Florida, arctic in Alaska, semiarid in the great plains west of the Mississippi River, and arid in the Great Basin of the southwest; low winter temperatures in the northwest are ameliorated occasionally in January and February by warm chinook winds from the eastern slopes of the Rocky Mountains
Terrain:	vast central plain, mountains in west, hills and low mountains in east; rugged mountains and broad river valleys in Alaska; rugged, volcanic topography in Hawaii

Elevation extremes:	lowest point: Death Valley -86 m highest point: Mount McKinley 6,194 m
Natural resources:	coal, copper, lead, molybdenum, phosphates, uranium, bauxite, gold, iron, mercury, nickel, potash, silver, tungsten, zinc, petroleum, natural gas, timber
Land use:	arable land: 19% permanent crops: 0% permanent pastures: 25% forests and woodland: 30% other: 26%
Irrigated land:	207,000 sq km
Natural hazards:	tsunamis, volcanoes, and earthquake activity around Pacific Basin; hurricanes along the Atlantic and Gulf of Mexico coasts; tornadoes in the midwest and southeast; mud slides in California; forest fires in the west; flooding; permafrost in northern Alaska, a major impediment to development
Environment - current issues:	air pollution resulting in acid rain in both the US and Canada; the US is the largest single emitter of carbon dioxide from the burning of fossil fuels; water pollution from runoff of pesticides and fertilizers; very limited natural fresh water resources in much of the western part of the country require careful management; desertification
Environment - international agreements:	party to: Air Pollution, Air Pollution-Nitrogen Oxides, Antarctic-Environmental Protocol, Antarctic-Marine Living Resources, Antarctic Seals, Antarctic Treaty, Climate Change, Desertification, Endangered Species, Environmental Modification, Marine Dumping, Marine Life Conservation, Nuclear Test Ban, Ozone Layer Protection, Ship Pollution, Tropical Timber 83, Tropical Timber 94, Wetlands, Whaling signed, but not ratified: Air Pollution-Persistent Organic Pollutants, Air Pollution-Volatile Organic Compounds, Biodiversity, Climate Change-Kyoto Protocol, Hazardous Wastes
Geography - note:	world's third-largest country (after Russia and Canada)

PEOPLE

Population:	278,058,881
Age structure:	0-14 years: 21.12% (male 30,034,674; female 28,681,253) 15-64 years: 66.27% (male 91,371,753; female 92,907,199)

	65 years and over: 12.61% (male 14,608,948; female 20,455,054)
Population growth rate:	0.9%
Birth rate:	14.2 births/1,000 population
Death rate:	8.7 deaths/1,000 population
Net migration rate:	3.5 migrant(s) /1,000 population
Sex ratio:	at birth: 1.05 male(s) /female under 15 years: 1.05 male(s) /female 15-64 years: 0.98 male(s) /female 65 years and over: 0.71 male(s) /female total population: 0.96 male(s) /female
Infant mortality rate:	6.76 deaths/1,000 live births
Life expectancy at birth:	total population: 77.26 years male: 74.37 years female: 80.05 years
Total fertility rate:	2.06 children born/woman
HIV/AIDS - adult prevalence rate:	0.61%
HIV/AIDS - people living with HIV/AIDS:	850,000
HIV/AIDS - deaths:	20,000
Nationality:	noun: American(s) adjective: American
Ethnic groups:	white 83.5%, black 12.4%, Asian 3.3%, Amerindian 0.8% note: a separate listing for Hispanic is not included because the US Census Bureau considers Hispanic to mean a person of Latin American descent (especially of Cuban, Mexican, or Puerto Rican origin) living in the US who may be of any race or ethnic group (white, black, Asian, etc.)
Religions:	Protestant 56%, Roman Catholic 28%, Jewish 2%, other 4%, none 10%
Languages:	English, Spanish (spoken by a sizable minority)
Literacy:	definition: age 15 and over can read and write total population: 97% male: 97%

For additional analytical, business and investment opportunities information, please contact Global Investment & Business Center, USA at (703) 370-8082. Fax: (703) 370-8083. E-mail: ibpusa3@gmail.com Global Business and Investment Info Databank - www.ibpus.com

	female: 97%

GOVERNMENT

Country name:

conventional long form: United States of America
conventional short form: United States
abbreviation: US or USA

Government type:

constitution-based federal republic; strong democratic tradition

Capital:

name: Washington, DC
geographic coordinates: 38 53 N, 77 02 W
time difference: UTC-5 (during Standard Time)
daylight saving time: +1hr, begins second Sunday in March; ends first Sunday in November
note: the 50 United States cover six time zones

Administrative divisions:

50 states and 1 district*; Alabama, Alaska, Arizona, Arkansas, California, Colorado, Connecticut, Delaware, District of Columbia*, Florida, Georgia, Hawaii, Idaho, Illinois, Indiana, Iowa, Kansas, Kentucky, Louisiana, Maine, Maryland, Massachusetts, Michigan, Minnesota, Mississippi, Missouri, Montana, Nebraska, Nevada, New Hampshire, New Jersey, New Mexico, New York, North Carolina, North Dakota, Ohio, Oklahoma, Oregon, Pennsylvania, Rhode Island, South Carolina, South Dakota, Tennessee, Texas, Utah, Vermont, Virginia, Washington, West Virginia, Wisconsin, Wyoming

Dependent areas:

American Samoa, Baker Island, Guam, Howland Island, Jarvis Island, Johnston Atoll, Kingman Reef, Midway Islands, Navassa Island, Northern Mariana Islands, Palmyra Atoll, Puerto Rico, Virgin Islands, Wake Island
note: from 18 July 1947 until 1 October 1994, the US administered the Trust Territory of the Pacific Islands; it entered into a political relationship with all four political entities: the Northern Mariana Islands is a commonwealth in political union with the US (effective 3 November 1986) ; the Republic of the Marshall Islands signed a Compact of Free Association with the US (effective 21 October 1986) ; the Federated States of Micronesia signed a Compact of Free Association with the US (effective 3 November 1986) ; Palau concluded a Compact of Free Association with the US (effective 1 October 1994)

Independence:

4 July 1776 (declared) ; 3 September 1783 (recognized by Great Britain)

National holiday:

Independence Day, 4 July (1776)

Constitution:

previous 1781 (Articles of Confederation and Perpetual Union) ; latest drafted July - September 1787, submitted to the Congress of the Confederation 20 September 1787, submitted for states' ratification 28 September 1787, ratification completed by nine states 21 June 1788, effective 4 March 1789; amended many times, last in 1992 (2014)

Legal system:

common law system based on English common law at the federal level; state legal systems based on common law except Louisiana, which is based on Napoleonic civil code; judicial review of legislative acts

International law organization participation:

withdrew acceptance of compulsory ICJ jurisdiction in 2005; withdrew acceptance of ICCt jurisdiction in 2002

Suffrage:

18 years of age; universal

Executive branch:

chief of state: President Barack H. OBAMA (since 20 January 2009) ; Vice President Joseph R. BIDEN (since 20 January 2009) ; note - the president is both chief of state and head of government
head of government: President Barack H. OBAMA (since 20 January 2009) ; Vice President Joseph R. BIDEN (since 20 January 2009)
cabinet: Cabinet appointed by the president with Senate approval
elections: president and vice president elected on the same ticket by a college of representatives who are elected directly from each state; president and vice president serve four-year terms (eligible for a second term) ; election last held 6 November 2012 (next to be held on 8 November 2016)
election results: Barack H. OBAMA reelected president; percent of popular vote - Barack H. OBAMA 50.6%, Mitt ROMNEY 47.9%, other 1.5%;

Legislative branch:

bicameral Congress consists of the Senate (100 seats, 2 members elected from each state by popular vote to serve six-year terms; one-third elected every two years) and the House of Representatives (435 seats; members directly elected by popular vote to serve two-year terms)
elections: Senate - last held on 6 November 2012 (next to be held on 4 November 2014) ; House of Representatives - last held on 4 November 2014

For additional analytical, business and investment opportunities information, please contact Global Investment & Business Center, USA at (703) 370-8082. Fax: (703) 370-8083. E-mail: ibpusa3@gmail.com Global Business and Investment Info Databank - www.ibpus.com

Judicial branch:

highest court(s) : US Supreme Court (consists of 9 justices - the chief justice and 8 associate justices)
note - The US court system consists of the federal court system and the state court systems; although each court system is responsible for hearing certain types of cases, neither is completely independent of the other, and the systems often interact
judge selection and term of office: president nominates, and with the advice and consent of the Senate, appoints Supreme Court justices; justices appointed for life
subordinate courts: Courts of Appeal (includes the US Court of Appeal for the Federal District and 12 regional appeals courts) ; 94 federal district courts in 50 states and territories

Political parties and leaders:

Democratic Party [Debbie Wasserman SCHULTZ]
Green Party
Libertarian Party [Mark HINKLE]
Republican Party [Reince PRIEBUS]

Political pressure groups and leaders:

environmentalists; business groups; labor unions; churches; ethnic groups; political action committees or PACs; health groups; education groups; civic groups; youth groups; transportation groups; agricultural groups; veterans groups; women's groups; reform lobbies

International organization participation:

ADB (nonregional member) , AfDB (nonregional member) , ANZUS, APEC, Arctic Council, ARF, ASEAN (dialogue partner) , Australia Group, BIS, BSEC (observer) , CBSS (observer) , CD, CE (observer) , CERN (observer) , CICA (observer) , CP, EAPC, EAS, EBRD, EITI (implementing country) , FAO, FATF, G-20, G-5, G-7, G-8, G-10, IADB, IAEA, IBRD, ICAO, ICC (national committees) , ICRM, IDA, IEA, IFAD, IFC, IFRCS, IGAD (partners) , IHO, ILO, IMF, IMO, IMSO, Interpol, IOC, IOM, ISO, ITSO, ITU, ITUC (NGOs) , MIGA, MINUSMA, MINUSTAH, MONUSCO, NAFTA, NATO, NEA, NSG, OAS, OECD, OPCW, OSCE, Pacific Alliance (observer) , Paris Club, PCA, PIF (partner) , SAARC (observer) , SELEC (observer) , SICA (observer) , SPC, UN, UNCTAD, UNESCO, UNHCR, UNITAR, UNMIL, UNMISS, UNRWA, UNSC (permanent) , UNTSO, UPU, WCO, WHO, WIPO, WMO, WTO, ZC

Flag description:

13 equal horizontal stripes of red (top and bottom) alternating with white; there is a blue rectangle in the upper hoist-side corner bearing 50 small, white, five-pointed stars arranged in nine offset horizontal rows of six stars (top and bottom) alternating with rows of five stars; the 50 stars represent the 50 states, the 13 stripes represent the 13 original colonies; the blue stands for loyalty, devotion, truth, justice, and friendship; red symbolizes courage, zeal, and fervency, while white denotes purity and rectitude of conduct; commonly referred to by its nickname of Old Glory

For additional analytical, business and investment opportunities information, please contact Global Investment & Business Center, USA at (703) 370-8082. Fax: (703) 370-8083. E-mail: ibpusa3@gmail.com Global Business and Investment Info Databank - www.ibpus.com

note: the design and colors have been the basis for a number of other flags, including Chile, Liberia, Malaysia, and Puerto Rico

National symbol(s) :

bald eagle

National anthem:

name: "The Star-Spangled Banner"

lyrics/music: Francis Scott KEY/John Stafford SMITH
note: adopted 1931; during the War of 1812, after witnessing the successful American defense of Fort McHenry in Baltimore following British naval bombardment, Francis Scott KEY wrote the lyrics to what would become the national anthem; the lyrics were set to the tune of "The Anacreontic Song"; only the first verse is sung

ECONOMY

The US has the largest and most technologically powerful economy in the world, with a per capita GDP of $49,800. In this market-oriented economy, private individuals and business firms make most of the decisions, and the federal and state governments buy needed goods and services predominantly in the private marketplace. US business firms enjoy greater flexibility than their counterparts in Western Europe and Japan in decisions to expand capital plant, to lay off surplus workers, and to develop new products. At the same time, they face higher barriers to enter their rivals' home markets than foreign firms face entering US markets. US firms are at or near the forefront in technological advances, especially in computers and in medical, aerospace, and military equipment; their advantage has narrowed since the end of World War II. The onrush of technology largely explains the gradual development of a "two-tier labor market" in which those at the bottom lack the education and the professional/technical skills of those at the top and, more and more, fail to get comparable pay raises, health insurance coverage, and other benefits.

Since 1975, practically all the gains in household income have gone to the top 20% of households. Since 1996, dividends and capital gains have grown faster than wages or any other category of after-tax income. Imported oil accounts for nearly 55% of US consumption. Crude oil prices doubled between 2001 and 2006, the year home prices peaked; higher gasoline prices ate into consumers' budgets and many individuals fell behind in their mortgage payments. Oil prices climbed another 50% between 2006 and 2008, and bank foreclosures more than doubled in the same period.

Besides dampening the housing market, soaring oil prices caused a drop in the value of the dollar and a deterioration in the US merchandise trade deficit, which peaked at $840 billion in 2008. The sub-prime mortgage crisis, falling home prices, investment bank failures, tight credit, and the global economic downturn pushed the United States into a recession by mid-2008. GDP contracted until the third quarter of 2009, making this the deepest and longest downturn since the Great Depression.

To help stabilize financial markets, in October 2008 the US Congress established a $700 billion Troubled Asset Relief Program (TARP) . The government used some of these funds to purchase equity in US banks and industrial corporations, much of which had been returned to the government by early 2011. In January 2009 the US Congress passed and President Barack OBAMA signed a bill providing an additional $787 billion fiscal stimulus to be used over 10 years - two-thirds on additional spending and one-third on tax cuts - to create jobs and to help the economy recover. In 2010 and 2011, the federal budget deficit reached nearly 9% of GDP. In 2012 the federal government reduced the growth of spending and the deficit shrank to 7.6% of GDP.

Wars in Iraq and Afghanistan required major shifts in national resources from civilian to military purposes and contributed to the growth of the budget deficit and public debt. Through 2011, the direct costs of the wars totaled nearly $900 billion, according to US government figures. US revenues from taxes and other sources are lower, as a percentage of GDP, than those of most other countries. In March 2010, President OBAMA signed into law the Patient Protection and Affordable Care Act, a health insurance reform that was designed to extend coverage to an additional 32 million American citizens by 2016, through private health insurance for the general population and Medicaid for the impoverished. Total spending on health care - public plus private - rose from 9.0% of GDP in 1980 to 17.9% in 2010. In July 2010, the president signed the DODD-FRANK Wall Street Reform and Consumer Protection Act, a law designed to promote financial stability by protecting consumers from financial abuses, ending taxpayer bailouts of financial firms, dealing with troubled banks that are "too big to fail," and improving accountability and transparency in the financial system - in particular, by requiring certain financial derivatives to be traded in markets that are subject to government regulation and oversight.

In December 2012, the Federal Reserve Board (Fed) announced plans to purchase $85 billion per month of mortgage-backed and Treasury securities in an effort to hold down long-term interest rates, and to keep short term rates near zero until unemployment drops below 6.5% or inflation rises above 2.5%. In late 2013, the Fed announced that it would begin scaling back long-term bond purchases to $75 billion per month in January 2014 and reduce them further as conditions warranted; the Fed, however, would keep short-term rates near zero so long as unemployment and inflation had not crossed the previously stated thresholds. Long-term problems include stagnation of wages for lower-income families, inadequate investment in deteriorating infrastructure, rapidly rising medical and pension costs of an aging population, energy shortages, and sizable current account and budget deficits.

GDP (purchasing power parity) :

$16.72 trillion (2013 est.)
country comparison to the world: 1
$16.47 trillion (2012 est.)
$16.02 trillion (2011 est.)
note: data are in 2013 US dollars

GDP (official exchange rate) :

$16.72 trillion (2013 est.)

GDP - real growth rate:

1.6% (2013 est.)
country comparison to the world: 157
2.8% (2012 est.)

1.8% (2011 est.)

GDP - per capita (PPP) :

$52,800 (2013 est.)
country comparison to the world: 14
$52,400 (2012 est.)
$51,400 (2011 est.)
note: data are in 2013 US dollars

Gross national saving:

13.5% of GDP (2013 est.)
country comparison to the world: 116
12.5% of GDP (2012 est.)
11.4% of GDP (2011 est.)

GDP - composition, by end use:

household consumption: 68.6%
government consumption: 18.6%
investment in fixed capital: 15.3%
investment in inventories: 0.4%
exports of goods and services: 13.4%
imports of goods and services: -16.3%
(2013 est.)

GDP - composition, by sector of origin:

agriculture: 1.1%
industry: 19.5%
services: 79.4%
(2013 est.)

Agriculture - products:

wheat, corn, other grains, fruits, vegetables, cotton; beef, pork, poultry, dairy products; fish; forest products

Industries:

highly diversified, world leading, high-technology innovator, second largest industrial output in world; petroleum, steel, motor vehicles, aerospace, telecommunications, chemicals, electronics, food processing, consumer goods, lumber, mining

Industrial production growth rate:

2.5% (2013 est.)
country comparison to the world: 115

Labor force:

155.4 million
country comparison to the world: 4
note: includes unemployed (2013 est.)

Labor force - by occupation:

farming, forestry, and fishing: 0.7%
manufacturing, extraction, transportation, and crafts: 20.3%
managerial, professional, and technical: 37.3%
sales and office: 24.2%
other services: 17.6%
note: figures exclude the unemployed
(2009)

Unemployment rate:

7.3% (2013 est.)
country comparison to the world: 79
8.1% (2012 est.)

Population below poverty line:

15.1% (2010 est.)

Household income or consumption by percentage share:

lowest 10%: 2%
highest 10%: 30% (2007 est.)

Distribution of family income - Gini index:

45 (2007)
country comparison to the world: 41
40.8 (1997)

Budget:

revenues: $2.849 trillion
expenditures: $3.517 trillion
note: for the US, revenues exclude social contributions of approximately $1.0 trillion; expenditures exclude social benefits of approximately $2.3 trillion (2013 est.)

Taxes and other revenues:

17% of GDP
country comparison to the world: 182
note: excludes contributions for social security and other programs; if social contributions were added, taxes and other revenues would amount to approximately 22% of GDP (2013

est.)

Budget surplus (+) or deficit (-) :

-4% of GDP (2013 est.)
country comparison to the world: 142

Public debt:

71.8% of GDP (2013 est.)
country comparison to the world: 36
70% of GDP (2012 est.)
note: data cover only what the United States Treasury denotes as "Debt Held by the Public," which includes all debt instruments issued by the Treasury that are owned by non-US Government entities; the data include Treasury debt held by foreign entities; the data exclude debt issued by individual US states, as well as intra-governmental debt; intra-governmental debt consists of Treasury borrowings from surpluses in the trusts for Federal Social Security, Federal Employees, Hospital Insurance (Medicare and Medicaid) , Disability and Unemployment, and several other smaller trusts; if data for intra-government debt were added, "Gross Debt" would increase by about one-third of GDP

Fiscal year:

1 October - 30 September

Inflation rate (consumer prices) :

1.5% (2013 est.)
country comparison to the world: 40
2.1% (2012 est.)

Central bank discount rate:

0.5% (31 December 2010)
country comparison to the world: 137
0.5% (31 December 2009)

Commercial bank prime lending rate:

3.3% (31 December 2013 est.)
country comparison to the world: 167
3.25% (31 December 2012 est.)

Stock of narrow money:

$2.612 trillion (31 December 2013 est.)
country comparison to the world: 4
$2.311 trillion (31 December 2012 est.)

Stock of broad money:

$12.99 trillion (31 December 2011 est.)
country comparison to the world: 3
$12.07 trillion (31 December 2010 est.)

Stock of domestic credit:

$16.97 trillion (31 December 2013 est.)
country comparison to the world: 2
$16.17 trillion (31 December 2012 est.)

Market value of publicly traded shares:

$18.67 trillion (31 December 2012 est.)
country comparison to the world: 1
$15.64 trillion (31 December 2011)
$17.14 trillion (31 December 2010 est.)

Current account balance:

-$360.7 billion (2013 est.)
country comparison to the world: 193
-$440.4 billion (2012 est.)

Exports:

$1.575 trillion (2013 est.)
country comparison to the world: 3
$1.561 trillion (2012 est.)

Exports - commodities:

agricultural products (soybeans, fruit, corn) 9.2%, industrial supplies (organic chemicals) 26.8%, capital goods (transistors, aircraft, motor vehicle parts, computers, telecommunications equipment) 49.0%, consumer goods (automobiles, medicines) 15.0%

Exports - partners:

Canada 18.9%, Mexico 14%, China 7.2%, Japan 4.5% (2012)

Imports:

$2.273 trillion (2013 est.)
country comparison to the world: 2
$2.303 trillion (2012 est.)

Imports - commodities:

agricultural products 4.9%, industrial supplies 32.9% (crude oil 8.2%) , capital goods 30.4% (computers, telecommunications equipment, motor vehicle parts, office machines, electric power machinery) , consumer goods 31.8% (automobiles, clothing, medicines, furniture, toys)

Imports - partners:

China 19%, Canada 14.1%, Mexico 12%, Japan 6.4%, Germany 4.7% (2012)

Reserves of foreign exchange and gold:

$150.2 billion (31 December 2012 est.)
country comparison to the world: 19
$148 billion (31 December 2011 est.)

Debt - external:

$15.68 trillion (31 December 2012 est.)
country comparison to the world: 2
$15.51 trillion (31 December 2011)
note: approximately 4/5ths of US external debt is denominated in US dollars; foreign lenders have been willing to hold US dollar denominated debt instruments because they view the dollar as the world's reserve currency

Stock of direct foreign investment - at home:

$2.815 trillion (31 December 2013 est.)
country comparison to the world: 1
$2.651 trillion (31 December 2012 est.)

Stock of direct foreign investment - abroad:

$4.854 trillion (31 December 2013 est.)
country comparison to the world: 1
$4.453 trillion (31 December 2012 est.)

Exchange rates:

British pounds per US dollar: 0.6324 (2012 est.) , 0.624 (2011 est.) , 0.6472 (2010) , 0.6175 (2009) , 0.5302 (2008)
Canadian dollars per US dollar: (2013 est.) , 1.001 (2012 est.) , 0.9895 (2011 est) , 1.0302 (2010 est.) , 1.1431 (2009) , 1.0364 (2008)
Chinese yuan per US dollar: (2012 est.) , 6.311 (2012 est.) , 6.4615 (20111 est.) , 6.7703 (2010 est.) , 6.8314 (2009) , 6.9385 (2008)
euros per US dollar: 0.7838 (2012 est.) , 0.7185 (2011 est.) , 0.755 (2010 est.) , 0.7198 (2009) , 0.6827 (2008)
Japanese yen per US dollar: 79.42 (2012 est.) , 79.81 (2011 est.) , 87.78 (2010) , 93.57 (2009) , 103.58 (2008)

ENERGY

Electricity - production:

4.099 trillion kWh
country comparison to the world: 2

Electricity - consumption:

3.886 trillion kWh
country comparison to the world: 2

Electricity - exports:

12 billion kWh
country comparison to the world: 19

Electricity - imports:

59.26 billion kWh
country comparison to the world: 1

Electricity - installed generating capacity:

1.039 billion kW
country comparison to the world: 2

Electricity - from fossil fuels:

75.3% of total installed capacity
country comparison to the world: 101

Electricity - from nuclear fuels:

9.7% of total installed capacity
country comparison to the world: 18

Electricity - from hydroelectric plants:

7.6% of total installed capacity
country comparison to the world: 119

Electricity - from other renewable sources:

5.3% of total installed capacity
country comparison to the world: 45

Crude oil - production:

For additional analytical, business and investment opportunities information, please contact Global Investment & Business Center, USA at (703) 370-8082. Fax: (703) 370-8083. E-mail: ibpusa3@gmail.com Global Business and Investment Info Databank - www.ibpus.com

11.11 million bbl/day
country comparison to the world: 2

Crude oil - exports:

41,640 bbl/day
country comparison to the world: 47

Crude oil - imports:

9.213 million bbl/day
country comparison to the world: 1

Crude oil - proved reserves:

20.68 billion bbl
country comparison to the world: 13

Refined petroleum products - production:

18.45 million bbl/day
country comparison to the world: 1

Refined petroleum products - consumption:

18.84 million bbl/day
country comparison to the world: 1

Refined petroleum products - exports:

2.311 million bbl/day
country comparison to the world: 2

Refined petroleum products - imports:

2.58 million bbl/day
country comparison to the world: 2

Natural gas - production:

681.4 billion cu m
country comparison to the world: 1

Natural gas - consumption:

689.9 billion cu m
country comparison to the world: 1

For additional analytical, business and investment opportunities information,
please contact Global Investment & Business Center, USA
at (703) 370-8082. Fax: (703) 370-8083. E-mail: ibpusa3@gmail.com
Global Business and Investment Info Databank - www.ibpus.com

Natural gas - exports:

45.84 billion cu m
country comparison to the world: 8

Natural gas - imports:

88.77 billion cu m
country comparison to the world: 3

Natural gas - proved reserves:

9.459 trillion cu m
country comparison to the world: 5

Carbon dioxide emissions from consumption of energy:

5.491 billion Mt

COMMUNICATIONS

Telephones - main lines in use:

139 million
country comparison to the world: 2

Telephones - mobile cellular:

310 million
country comparison to the world: 3

Telephone system:

general assessment: a large, technologically advanced, multipurpose communications system
domestic: a large system of fiber-optic cable, microwave radio relay, coaxial cable, and domestic satellites carries every form of telephone traffic; a rapidly growing cellular system carries mobile telephone traffic throughout the country
international: country code - 1; multiple ocean cable systems provide international connectivity; satellite earth stations - 61 Intelsat (45 Atlantic Ocean and 16 Pacific Ocean) , 5 Intersputnik (Atlantic Ocean region) , and 4 Inmarsat (Pacific and Atlantic Ocean regions)

Broadcast media:

4 major terrestrial TV networks with affiliate stations throughout the country, plus cable and satellite networks, independent stations, and a limited public broadcasting sector that is largely supported by private grants; overall, thousands of TV stations broadcasting; multiple national radio networks with many affiliate stations; while most stations are commercial, National Public Radio (NPR) has a network of some 600 member stations; satellite radio available; overall, nearly 15,000 radio stations operating

For additional analytical, business and investment opportunities information, please contact Global Investment & Business Center, USA at (703) 370-8082. Fax: (703) 370-8083. E-mail: ibpusa3@gmail.com Global Business and Investment Info Databank - www.ibpus.com

Internet country code:

.us

Internet hosts:

505 million (2012) ; note - the US Internet total host count includes the following top level domain host addresses: .us, .com, .edu, .gov, .mil, .net, and .org
country comparison to the world: 1

Internet users:

245 million (2009)
country comparison to the world: 2

TRANSPORTATION

Airports:

13,513
country comparison to the world: 1

Airports - with paved runways:

total: 5,054
over 3,047 m: 189
2,438 to 3,047 m: 235
1,524 to 2,437 m: 1,478
914 to 1,523 m: 2,249
under 914 m: 903

Airports - with unpaved runways:

total: 8,459
over 3,047 m: 1
2,438 to 3,047 m: 6
1,524 to 2,437 m: 140
914 to 1,523 m: 1,552
under 914 m:
6,760

Heliports:

5,287

Pipelines:

natural gas 1,984,321 km; petroleum products 240,711 km

For additional analytical, business and investment opportunities information, please contact Global Investment & Business Center, USA at (703) 370-8082. Fax: (703) 370-8083. E-mail: ibpusa3@gmail.com Global Business and Investment Info Databank - www.ibpus.com

Railways:

total: 224,792 km
country comparison to the world: 1
standard gauge: 224,792 km 1.435-m gauge

Roadways:

total: 6,586,610 km
country comparison to the world: 1
paved: 4,304,715 km (includes 76,334 km of expressways)
unpaved: 2,281,895 km

Waterways:

41,009 km (19,312 km used for commerce; Saint Lawrence Seaway of 3,769 km, including the Saint Lawrence River of 3,058 km, is shared with Canada)
country comparison to the world: 5

Merchant marine:

total: 393
country comparison to the world: 26
by type: barge carrier 6, bulk carrier 55, cargo 51, carrier 2, chemical tanker 30, container 84, passenger 18, passenger/cargo 56, petroleum tanker 35, refrigerated cargo 3, roll on/roll off 27, vehicle carrier 26
foreign-owned: 85 (Australia 1, Bermuda 5, Denmark 31, France 4, Germany 5, Malaysia 2, Norway 17, Singapore 16, UK 4)
registered in other countries: 794 (Antigua and Barbuda 7, Australia 2, Bahamas 109, Belgium 1, Bermuda 26, Canada 10, Cayman Islands 57, Comoros 2, Cyprus 5, Georgia 1, Greece 8, Honduras 1, Hong Kong 44, Indonesia 2, Ireland 2, Isle of Man 1, Italy 23, Liberia 53, Malta 34, Marshall Islands 200, Netherlands 16, Norway 10, Panama 90, Portugal 4, Saint Kitts and Nevis 1, Saint Vincent and the Grenadines 18, Singapore 36, South Korea 8, Togo 1, UK 14, Vanuatu 2, unknown 6)

Ports and terminals:

cargo ports (tonnage) : Baton Rouge, Corpus Christi, Hampton Roads, Houston, Long Beach, Los Angeles, New Orleans, New York, Plaquemines, Tampa, Texas City
container port(s) (TEUs) : Hampton Roads (1,918,029) , Houston (1,866,450) , Long Beach (6,061,091) , Los Angeles (7,940,511) , New York/New Jersey (5,503,485) , Oakland (2,342,504) , Savannah (2,944,678) , Seattle (2,033,535) (2011)
cruise departure ports (passengers) : Miami (2,032,000) , Port Everglades (1,277,000) , Port Canaveral (1,189,000) , Seattle (430,000) , Long Beach (415,000) (2009)
oil terminals: LOOP terminal, Haymark terminal

MILITARY

Military branches:

United States Armed Forces: US Army, US Navy (includes Marine Corps) , US Air Force,

US Coast Guard; note - Coast Guard administered in peacetime by the Department of Homeland Security, but in wartime reports to the Department of the Navy

Military service age and obligation:

18 years of age (17 years of age with parental consent) for male and female voluntary service; no conscription; maximum enlistment age 42 (Army) , 27 (Air Force) , 34 (Navy) , 28 (Marines) ; service obligation 8 years, including 2-5 years active duty (Army) , 2 years active (Navy) , 4 years active (Air Force, Marines) ; DoD is eliminating prohibitions restricting women from assignments in units smaller than brigades or near combat units

Manpower available for military service:

males age 16-49: 73,270,043
females age 16-49: 71,941,969

Manpower fit for military service:

males age 16-49: 60,620,143
females age 16-49: 59,401,941

Manpower reaching militarily significant age annually:

male: 2,161,727
female: 2,055,685

Military expenditures:

4.35% of GDP
country comparison to the world: 9
4.75% of GDP (2011)
4.35% of GDP (2010)

TRANSNATIONAL ISSUES

Disputes - international:

the US has intensified domestic security measures and is collaborating closely with its neighbors, Canada and Mexico, to monitor and control legal and illegal personnel, transport, and commodities across the international borders; abundant rainfall in recent years along much of the Mexico-US border region has ameliorated periodically strained water-sharing arrangements; 1990 Maritime Boundary Agreement in the Bering Sea still awaits Russian Duma ratification; Canada and the United States dispute how to divide the Beaufort Sea and the status of the Northwest Passage but continue to work cooperatively to survey the Arctic continental shelf; The Bahamas and US have not been able to agree on a maritime boundary; US Naval Base at Guantanamo Bay is leased from Cuba and only mutual agreement or US abandonment of the area can terminate the lease; Haiti claims US-administered Navassa Island; US has made no territorial claim in Antarctica (but has reserved the right to do so) and does not recognize the claims of any other states; Marshall Islands claims Wake Island; Tokelau included American Samoa's Swains Island among the islands listed in its 2006 draft constitution

Refugees and internally displaced persons:

refugees (country of origin) : the US admitted 69,926 refugees during FY2013 including:

For additional analytical, business and investment opportunities information, please contact Global Investment & Business Center, USA at (703) 370-8082. Fax: (703) 370-8083. E-mail: ibpusa3@gmail.com Global Business and Investment Info Databank - www.ibpus.com

19,488 (Iraq) ; 16,299 (Burma) ; 9,134 (Bhutan) ; 7,608 (Somalia) ; 4,205 (Cuba) ; 2,578 (Iran) ; 1,824 (Eritrea)

Illicit drugs:

world's largest consumer of cocaine (shipped from Colombia through Mexico and the Caribbean) , Colombian heroin, and Mexican heroin and marijuana; major consumer of ecstasy and Mexican methamphetamine; minor consumer of high-quality Southeast Asian heroin; illicit producer of cannabis, marijuana, depressants, stimulants, hallucinogens, and methamphetamine; money-laundering center

US MARYTIME COMMISSION - STRATEGIC INFORMATION

BASIC INFORMATION

The **United States Maritime Commission** (**MARCOM**) was an independent executive agency of the U.S. federal government that was created by the Merchant Marine Act of 1936, passed by Congress on June 29, 1936, and replaced the United States Shipping Board which had existed since World War I. It was intended to formulate a merchant shipbuilding program to design and build five hundred modern merchant cargo ships to replace the World War I vintage vessels that comprised the bulk of the United States Merchant Marine, and to administer a subsidy system authorized by the Act to offset the cost differential between building in the U.S. and operating ships under the American flag. It also formed the United States Maritime Service for the training of seagoing ship's officers to man the new fleet.

The purpose of the Maritime Commission was multifold as described in the Merchant Marine Act's Declaration of Policy. The first role was to formulate a merchant shipbuilding program to design and then have built over a ten-year period 500 modern fast merchant cargo ships which would replace the World War I-vintage vessels which made up the bulk of the U.S. Merchant Marine prior to the Act. Those ships were intended to be chartered (leased) to U.S. shipping companies for their use in the foreign seagoing trades for whom they would be able to offer better and more economical freight services to their clients. The ships were also intended to serve as a reserve naval auxiliary force in the event of armed conflict which was a duty the U.S. merchant fleet had often filled throughout the years since the Revolutionary War. The second role given to the Maritime Commission was to administer a subsidy system authorized by the Act which would offset the differential is cost between both building in the U.S. and operating ships under the American flag. Another function given to the Commission involved the formation of the U.S. Maritime Service for the training of seagoing ship's officers to man the new fleet. The actual licensing of officers and seamen still resided with the Bureau of Marine Inspection and Navigation.

President Roosevelt nominated Joseph P. Kennedy first head of the Commission. Kennedy held that position until February 1938 when he left to become US Ambassador to Great Britain. After Kennedy's departure, the chairmanship was assumed by Rear Admiral Emory S. Land, USN (ret.) , who had been the head of U.S. Navy's Bureau of Construction and Repair prior to his appointment to the Commission on the behest of the President and where he had been a deputy commissioner since the founding of the body. The other four members of the Commission in the years before the beginning of World War II were a mix of retired naval officers and men from disciplines of law and business. The man most notable in the group Land brought to the Commission was Commander Howard L. Vickery, USN, who, like Land, was a naval officer closely involved in the construction of new Navy vessels. Vickery became responsible for overseeing the Commission's shipbuilding functions including the design and construction of the ships, developing shipyards to build them and companies to manufacture the complicated and highly specialized ship's machinery. As World War II drew closer, Vickery was very much at the forefront of putting into place the Emergency Shipbuilding Program which man like Henry J. Kaiser were so instrumental in developing into an industry which would perform some of the greatest feats of wartime industrial production ever previously witnessed and never since matched.

For additional analytical, business and investment opportunities information, please contact Global Investment & Business Center, USA at (703) 370-8082. Fax: (703) 370-8083. E-mail: ibpusa3@gmail.com Global Business and Investment Info Databank - www.ibpus.com

As a symbol of the rebirth of the U.S. Merchant Marine and Merchant Shipbuilding under the Merchant Marine Act, the first vessel contracted for was SS *America*, which was owned by the United States Line and operated in the passenger liner and cruise service during 1940-1. Upon the U.S. entry into World War II, *America* was requisitioned by the U.S. Navy and became USS *West Point.* In the prewar years, several dozen other merchant ships were built for the Commission under its original 500 ship Long Range Shipbuilding Program but it wasn't until the late fall of 1940 the critical importance of the Commission to the defense of the lifeline to Great Britain and to the national mobilization for war became apparent when the beginnings of the Emergency Shipbuilding program were laid. Together, all the Maritime Commission's shipbuilding program became known as Ships for Victory and great pride was taken in it by the many thousands of ordinary citizens went to work in the shipyards and joined the ranks of the shipbuilding workforce.

From 1939 through the end of World War II, the Maritime Commission funded and administered the largest and most successful merchant shipbuilding effort in world history, producing thousands of ships, including Liberty ships, Victory ships, and others, notably Type C1, Type C2, Type C3, Type C4 freighters and T2 tankers. Most of the C2s and C3s were converted to Navy auxiliaries, notably attack cargo ships, attack transports, and escort aircraft carriers and many of the tankers became fleet replenishment oilers. The Commission also was tasked with the construction of many hundred "military type" vessels such as Landing Ship, Tank (LST) s and *Tacoma*-class frigates and large troop transports. By the end of the war, U.S. shipyards working under Maritime Commission contracts had built a total of 5,777 oceangoing merchant and naval ships.

In early 1942 both the training and licensing was transferred to the U.S. Coast Guard for administration, but then late in the fall of 1942, the Maritime Service was transferred to the newly created War Shipping Administration which itself was created for the purpose of overseeing the operation of the fleet of merchant ships being built by the Emergency Program for the needs of the U.S. Armed Services. The WSA was added to the list of wartime agencies created within the Roosevelt Administration and was intended to relieve the already full plate of responsibilities of the Commission, yet they shared the same Chairman in Admiral Land and so worked very closely together.

With the end of World War II, both the Emergency and Long Range shipbuilding programs were terminated as there were far too many merchant vessels now for the Nation's peacetime needs. In 1946, the Merchant Ship Sales Act was passed to sell off a large portion of the ships previously built during the war to commercial buyers, both domestic and foreign. This facilitated the rebuilding of the fleets of both allied nations such as Great Britain, Norway and Greece which had lost a majority of their prewar vessels to the Battles of the Atlantic and Mediterranean Sea. Although not sold outright to nations that were enemies during the war, U.S. merchant ships helped nations such as Japan, which had lost many hundreds of its merchant vessels to the Allies' submarine offensive in the western Pacific, recover their merchant shipping capacity via the loan of vessels and the carrying of relief cargoes to war ravaged Europe. Ships were also used in both the rebuilding programs under the Marshall Plan and the transport of food aid sent during the desperate winter of 1945-46 when famine loomed large over much of the European continent. For the next 25 years, in ports all around the world one could find dozens of ships which had been built during the war but which now were used in peace. Many of those same ships continued to sail until the early 1980s but most had been sold for scrap in the 1960s and 1970s as more modern designs were developed and more efficient slow speed diesel engines introduced to replace the steamships which predominated those built by the Commission during the war years.

For additional analytical, business and investment opportunities information, please contact Global Investment & Business Center, USA at (703) 370-8082. Fax: (703) 370-8083. E-mail: ibpusa3@gmail.com Global Business and Investment Info Databank - www.ibpus.com

Ships not disposed of through the Ship Sales Act were placed into one of eight National Defense Reserve Fleet(NDRF) sites maintained on the Atlantic, Pacific and Gulf coasts. On several occasions in the postwar years ships in the reserve fleets were activated for both military and humanitarian aid missions. The last major mobilization of the NDRF came during the Vietnam War. Since then, a smaller fleet of ships called the Ready Reserve Force has been mobilized to support both humanitarian and military missions.

The last major shipbuilding project undertaken by the Commission was to oversee the design and construction of the super passenger liner SS *United States* which was intended to be both a symbol of American technological might and maritime predominance but also could be quickly converted into the world's fastest naval troop transport.

The Maritime Commission was abolished on 24 May 1950, and its functions were divided between the U.S. Federal Maritime Commission which was responsible for regulating shipping trades and trade routes and the United States Maritime Administration, which was responsible for administering the construction and operating subsidy programs, maintaining NDRF, and operating the U.S. Merchant Marine Academy which had been built and opened during World War II and which continues to be funded and operated today as one of the five Federal Service Academies.

GENERAL INQUIRIES

The FMC welcomes general inquiries pertaining to foreign waterborne commerce. The staff will respond directly, or, alternatively, refer the questioner to the proper source of information. For more information, contact the Office of Consumer Complaints:

Voice: (202) 523-5807
Fax: (202) 523-0014
e-mail: complaints@fmc.gov

Maritime Commission, Federal, a regulatory agency charged with protecting the interests of shippers, carriers, and passengers sailing under the U.S. flag. The Commission investigates anticompetitive practices in the maritime transport business and reviews the records of service contracts and rates. It issues licenses to ocean transportation intermediaries to guard against unqualified, insolvent, or dishonest companies; requires companies to maintain bonds against financial loss; and ensures that passenger cruise operations take financial responsibility when found liable for personal injury, death, or nonperformance of a voyage.

Today's Federal Maritime Commission is a fragment of a once huge network of government agencies created by legislation including the Shipping Act of 1916 and the Merchant Marine Acts of 1920 and 1936. On the eve of World War I, with American ships carrying only 2 percent of the nation's foreign trade, policymakers moved to reverse the nation's vulnerability to shortages in vital supplies. With the help of massive government subsidies, by the end of world War II the United States had one of the largest maritime fleets in the world and U.S. merchant ships carried 60 percent of the world's tonnage.

In the decades after the war, U.S.-flagged shipping began a continuing decline as air traffic took over passenger service previously provided by ocean liners, containerization technology made managing cargo more efficient, and U.S.-owned ships transferred registration to foreign countries such as Liberia to avoid higher costs associated with U.S. regulation.

In 1950 the U.S. Maritime Commission, which had presided over the fleet's buildup, was dismantled and its responsibilities shifted to the Maritime Administration and the Federal Maritime Board. In 1961 the Board was renamed the Federal Maritime Commission and its non-regulatory responsibilities were given to the Maritime Administration. Regulatory provisions of the Shipping Act of 1984 and the Ocean Shipping Reform Act of 1998 reflect the recent era of diminished government involvement in the ocean transportation industry.

The Federal Maritime Commission (FMC) was established in 1961 as an independent government agency, responsible for the regulation of shipping in the foreign trades of the United States. The Commission's five members are appointed by the President with the advice and consent of the Senate. The FMC is headquartered at 800 North Capitol Street, N.W., Washington, D.C. 20573, with five Area Representatives around the nation.

The FMC: • Regulates certain activities of international shipping lines (called "ocean common carriers") , marine terminals operators, and ocean transportation intermediaries (OTIs) who operate in the

U.S. foreign commerce

- Oversees the financial responsibility of cruise ship lines and other passenger ship operators, to ensure they have the resources to pay compensation for personal injuries or non-performance
- Monitors the laws and practices of foreign governments which could have a discriminatory or otherwise adverse impact on the U.S. shipping industry and U.S. maritime trade, and administers bilateral trade sanctions to persuade foreign governments to remove adverse conditions
- Enforces special regulatory requirements applicable to shipping lines owned or controlled by foreign governments (so-called "controlled carriers")
- Reviews and regulates agreements between shipping lines and/or marine terminals (which enjoy statutory immunity from the antitrust laws) and service contracts between shipping lines and their customers
- Licenses and regulates ocean transportation intermediaries in the U.S., and ensures all maintain evidence of financial responsibility. These intermediaries include freight forwarders, who make bookings and process paperwork for shipper customers (roughly analogous to a travel agent for freight) , and "non-vessel-operating common carriers", who act as resellers of space on shipping lines' vessels.

FUNCTIONS

x Protects shippers, carriers and others engaged in the foreign commerce of the U.S. from restrictive rules and regulations of foreign governments and from the practices of foreign-flag carriers that have an adverse effect on shipping in U.S. trades;

x Investigates, upon its own motion or upon filing of a complaint, discriminatory, unfair, or unreasonable rates, charges, classifications, and practices of ocean common carriers, terminal operators, and freight forwarders operating in the foreign commerce of the U.S.;

x Receives agreements among ocean common carriers or marine terminal operators and monitors them to assure that they are not substantially anticompetitive or otherwise violative of the Shipping Act of 1984;

For additional analytical, business and investment opportunities information, please contact Global Investment & Business Center, USA at (703) 370-8082. Fax: (703) 370-8083. E-mail: ibpusa3@gmail.com Global Business and Investment Info Databank - www.ibpus.com

x Reviews tariff publications under the access and accuracy standards of the Shipping Act of 1984.

ORGANIZATION AND LEADERSHIP

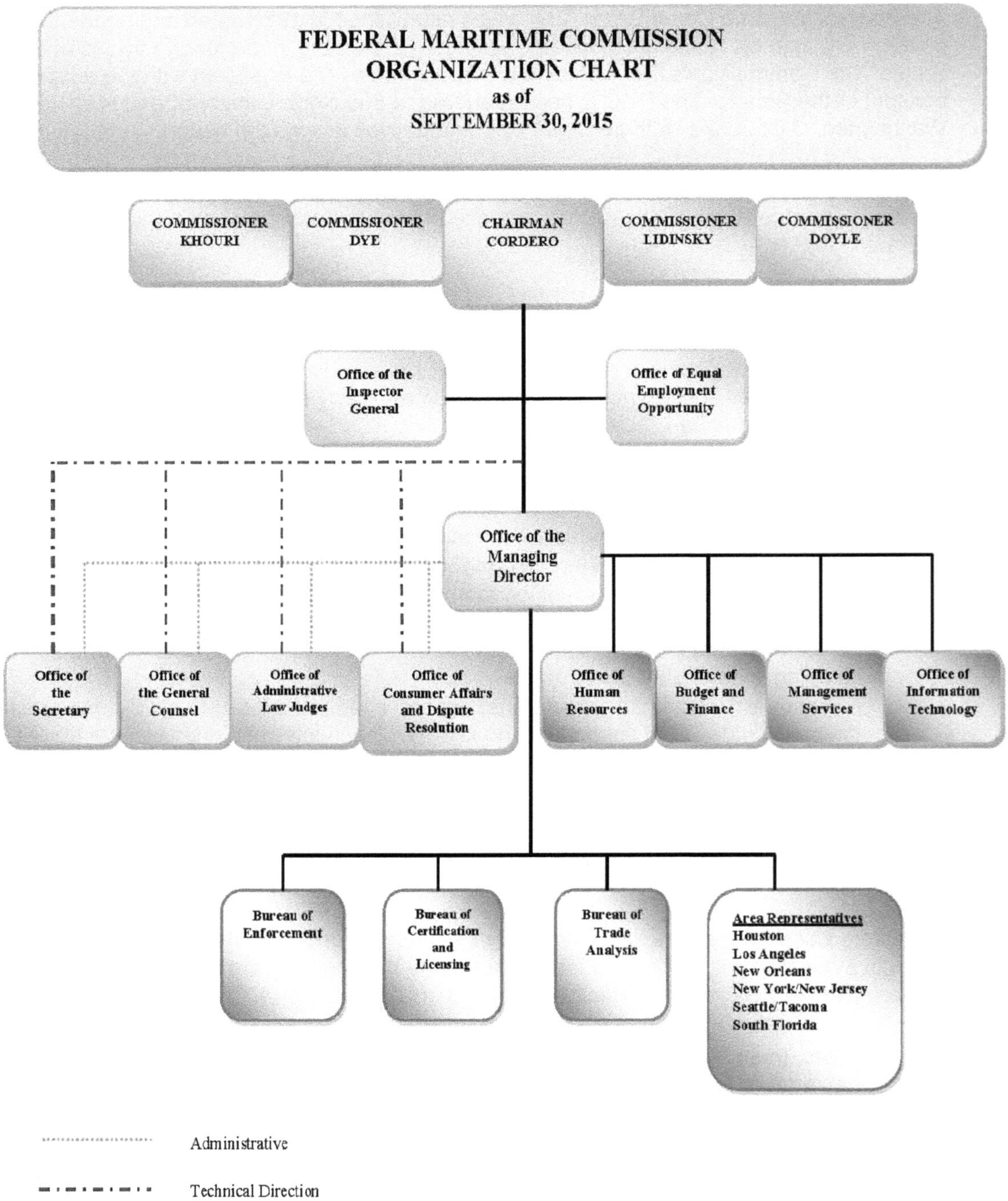

x Regulates rates, charges, classifications, rules, and regulations contained in tariffs of carriers controlled by foreign governments and operating in U.S. trades to ensure that such matters are just and reasonable;

x Licenses U.S.-based international ocean ocean transportation intermediaries;

x Requires bonds of U.S. & foreign based OTIs ; and

x Issues passenger vessel certificates showing evidence of financial responsibility of vessel owners or charterers to pay judgments for personal injury or death or to repay fares for the nonperformance of a voyage or cruise.

The FMC's jurisdiction encompasses many facets of the maritime industry. However, it has no jurisdiction over vessel operations, navigation, vessel construction, vessel documentation, vessel inspection, licensing of seafaring personnel, maintenance of navigational aids or dredging. These activities are handled by other federal, state and local agencies.

The principal shipping statutes administered by the FMC are the Shipping Act of 1984 (46 USC app. 1710 et seq) , the Foreign Shipping Practices Act of 1988 (46 USC app. 1701 et seq) , and section 19 of the Merchant Marine Act, 1920 (46 USC app. 876) . The FMC's regulations are published in 46 CFR 500 et seq.

LEADERSHIP

The Commission is composed of five Commissioners appointed for 5-year terms by the President with the advice and consent of the Senate. Not more than three members of the Commission may belong to the same political party. The President designates one of the Commissioners to serve as Chairman. The Chairman is the agency's chief executive and administrative officer. As such, the Chairman has exclusive authority over agency personnel matters, organization and supervision, distribution of business, and use of funds for administrative purposes.

The Chairman and the other four Commissioners are responsible for making decisions and determinations in the disposition of docketed cases, and ensuring the efficient, equitable, and expeditious resolution of all other matters arising under statutes administered by the Commission.

COMMISSIONERS

Chairman Mario Cordero

Chief of Staff: Mary T. Hoang
Counsel: Rachit J. Choksi
Senior Advisor – Legislative/Public Affairs: John K. DeCrosta

Commissioner Mario CorderoContact
Phone: 202-523-5911
E-mail: mcordero@fmc.gov

Chairman Mario Cordero of Long Beach, California, was designated Chairman of the Federal Maritime Commission (FMC) by President Barack Obama on April 1, 2013. Prior to being designated Chairman, Mr. Cordero served as an FMC Commissioner. He was initially nominated to the Commission by President Obama on September 17, 2010, and he was confirmed by the Senate on April 14, 2011. Chairman Cordero was first sworn in as an FMC Commissioner on June 3, 2011, for a term set to expire on June 30, 2014. He was reconfirmed on October 8th 2015, for a term set to expire on June 30, 2019. In his role as Chairman, Mr. Cordero brings with him over thirty years of private legal practice and decades of public service – including serving eight years on the Board of Harbor Commissioners for the Port of Long Beach (POLB) .

Prior to serving at the federal level, Chairman Cordero was very active in the Long Beach Maritime Community. Initially appointed by the then-Mayor of Long Beach and confirmed by the Long Beach City Council in 2003. While a POLB Commissioner, Chairman Cordero spearheaded the Port of Long Beach's pioneering Green Port Policy, a policy aimed at reconciling economic growth and environmental stewardship to achieve long-term, sustainable port development. During his years serving on the Port of Long Beach's managing body; he served as both a Vice-President and President. He also used his time and leadership position on the POLB to educate the public about the importance of a robust Port, an effort that included new and expanded community outreach initiatives.

Maritime Environmental Committee
Message from FMC Chairman Mario Cordero

Chairman's Earth Day Award

MEC Events

Concurrent with his leadership positions on the POLB, Chairman Cordero took an active role in the American Association of Port Authorities (AAPA) , a multi-national trade association representing more than 130 public port authorities throughout the United States, Canada, the Caribbean, and Latin America. Notably, Chairman Cordero served on the Executive Board for the AAPA's Latin American delegation. In this role, he led efforts to develop cohesive policies for greater cooperation, increased trade, and joint-growth across the combined North American and Latin American footprint.

Actively seeking to share the knowledge and opportunity he gained with his education, Chairman Cordero tries to find time to teach. In the past, he has served as adjunct professor for the Long Beach City College, where he taught political science. The Chairman earned his Bachelor of Science in Political Science degree from California State University, Long Beach, and he subsequently earned his Juris Doctor from the University of Santa Clara.

On September 29, 2015, Chairman Mario Cordero accepted the Connie Award in recognition of the Chairman's leadership and dedication to the containerized shipping industry. Established by the Containerization & Intermodal Institute in 1972, the Connie Award honors the achievements of those who have contributed to the evolution of the industry.

Commissioner William P. Doyle

Counsel: Patrick W. Parsons
Contact
Phone: 202-523-5723
E-mail: pparsons@fmc.gov

On January 1, 2013, the United States Senate confirmed President Barack Obama's nomination of William P. Doyle of York, Pennsylvania as a Commissioner of the Federal Maritime Commission. He was nominated to another term by President Obama on January 29, 2015, and unanimously confirmed by the U.S. Senate on March 23, 2015

Commissioner Doyle served over a decade as officer in the U.S. Merchant Marine as a marine engineer aboard numerous classes of vessels. Combined, Commissioner Doyle has over 20 years of experience in the transportation industry, including both the maritime and energy sectors. Throughout his career, he has held several senior executive positions in the industry.

Internationally, Commissioner Doyle participates on certain bilateral shipping matters with other countries. Commissioner Doyle represents the FMC at the annual U.S.-China Bilateral Maritime Consultations where he meets with officials from the People's Republic of China regarding maritime shipping matters such as tax policies affecting U.S. interests in the U.S.-China trade. Further, he managed the most recent update to the 2012 FMC Study of U.S. Inland Containerized Cargo Moving Through Canadian and Mexican Seaports. This study examines the impacts and the extent to which the U.S. Harbor Maintenance Tax (HMT) , and other U.S. policies may incentivize container cargo to shift from U.S. West Coast ports to Canadian and Mexican ports. Last year Commissioner Doyle surveyed construction sites for the Panama Canal's third set of locks. The Canal is major transit point for FMC-regulated vessel operating common carriers and a critical component to international oceanborne commerce to and from the U.S.

At the FMC, Commissioner Doyle has worked with his fellow Commissioners to adjudicate a backlog of cases filed with the Commission; the Commission now resolves over 90% of its cases within two years. Commissioner Doyle has also voiced strong support for natural gas as a marine fuel, especially with regard to meeting international environmental standards (MARPOL Annex VI Emission Control Areas) . Commissioner Doyle is a vocal proponent of the development of U.S. natural gas resources and its impact on the U.S. energy and transportation landscape in helping to improve U.S. energy security while spurring economic development and job creation around the country.

Prior to being sworn in as Commissioner, Commissioner Doyle was Chief-of-Staff of the Marine Engineers' Beneficial Association. There, Commissioner Doyle managed the organization's interests before federal, state, and local elected and administrative bodies. He was the Association's leader in business development, legislative strategies, contract negotiations, and provided counsel and guidance to the executive board.

For additional analytical, business and investment opportunities information, please contact Global Investment & Business Center, USA at (703) 370-8082. Fax: (703) 370-8083. E-mail: ibpusa3@gmail.com Global Business and Investment Info Databank - www.ibpus.com

Previous to his role as Chief-of-Staff, Commissioner Doyle served in an executive management role as the Director of Permits, Scheduling, and Compliance with the Office of the Federal Coordinator for Alaska Natural Gas Transportation Projects. There, he managed and directed the permitting and regulatory coordination of 24 federal agencies, numerous State of Alaska agencies, and both federal and provincial agencies of Canada. Additionally, the Commissioner acted as lead negotiator for the U.S. Government in securing cost recovery agreements with private sector national and multinational companies.

Prior to his FMC appointment, Commissioner Doyle had been appointed to boards and committees under both the Obama and Bush Administrations, including:

Representative on U.S. delegation for the United States on the bilateral trade delegation for the U.S. – Canada Energy Consultative Mechanism meetings, where bilateral energy trade issues were explored for strengthening the largest bilateral energy relationship in the world;

Representative of the U.S. in the annual coordination meeting between the U.S. Pipeline and Hazardous Materials Safety Administration and Canada's National Energy Board;

Selected by the U.S. Department of State to participate in an international shale gas workshop to assess international resources, supply options, and market conditions;

Served a two-year term as a liaison on the Labor Advisory Committee to the U.S. Trade Representative, and in this capacity, the Commissioner assisted the Committee in soliciting and obtaining advice from various industries, agricultural concerns, environmental stakeholders, labor groups, and other non-governmental organizations throughout the trade policy process; and

Appointed and served for four years as a Board Member on the United States Department of Labor's Advisory Committee on Apprenticeship.

Commissioner William P. Doyle was born in Boston, Massachusetts and raised in Weymouth. He is a 1992 graduate of the Massachusetts Maritime Academy, where he earned a Bachelor of Science in Marine Engineering. As a cadet, he worked in the Quincy, Massachusetts shipyard breaking out vessels for Operations Desert Shield and Desert Storm. Upon graduation from Mass Maritime, he began sailing as an officer in the U.S. Merchant Marine. As a U.S. Merchant Marine Officer from 1992 to 2002, Commissioner Doyle's shipboard experience included serving aboard ammunition ships in and around Diego Garcia, car carriers servicing Europe and the Pacific Rim, tanker vessels, and in the U.S. Maritime Administration's U.S. Ready Reserve Force Fleet. While still serving in the U.S. Merchant Marine, Commissioner Doyle entered law school at Widener University School of Law in Harrisburg, Pennsylvania. Throughout law school, Commissioner Doyle worked his summer and winter breaks serving aboard Pre-positioning ships in South Carolina, delivering jet fuel to Haifa, Israel, and transporting liquid-sulfur between ports along the Gulf Coast of the United States.

Commissioner Daniel B. Maffei

Counsel: Zoraya B. De La Cruz
Contact
E-mail: zdelacruz@fmc.gov

Commissioner Daniel B. Maffei, of New York, was nominated to serve on the Federal Maritime Commission (FMC) by President Barack Obama on November 19, 2015, confirmed by the United States Senate on June 29, 2016, and appointed by the President on July 18, 2016.

A native of Syracuse, New York, Commissioner Maffei's career in government spans more than twenty years. He served two terms as a member of the United States House of Representatives from 2009 to 2011 and from 2013 to 2015. Immediately prior to being sworn in at the FMC, Commissioner Maffei was a Senior Fellow at the Center for the Study of the Presidency and Congress and served briefly as a Senior Advisor at the United States Department of Commerce.

Commissioner Maffei's time in Congress included service on the House Armed Services Committee, House Financial Services Committee, and House Judiciary Committee. His priority on the Armed Services Committee was to improve the military's capacity to defend the country from terrorist and cyber threats. He worked on several provisions in the 2013 and 2014 armed services authorization bills to support and promote new and better technologies. On the Financial Services Committee, he focused on consumer protection and helped improve and pass, with increased bipartisan support, the Credit Cardholder's Bill of Rights of 2009, a law that took important steps to level the playing field between customers and card issuers. Commissioner Maffei also served on the House Committee on Science and Technology and was Ranking Member of its Oversight Subcommittee.

While serving in Congress, Commissioner Maffei's Central New York district included the Port of Oswego, the first U.S. port of call and deepwater port on the Great Lakes. Working closely with Representative Richard L. Hanna and New York's Senators, he was able to secure vital funding to improve the port's rail link and the resources to better dredge the port.

In between his two terms, Commissioner Maffei was a Senior Fellow at Third Way, LLC, a Senior Policy Advisor at Manatt, Phelps, Phillips LLP, and a visiting faculty member at the New York State College of Environmental Science and Forestry. From 2006 to 2008, Mr. Maffei was the Senior Vice President of Corporate Development for Pinnacle Capital Management, LLC, in Syracuse.

From 1998 to 2004, Commissioner Maffei worked on the Democratic staff of the House Ways and Means Committee as Press Secretary and Communications Director, and he was also Senior Policy Advisor for the Committee from 2004 to 2005. He was Press Secretary for United States Senator Daniel Patrick Moynihan from 1997 to 1998 and was Press Secretary for United States Senator Bill Bradley in 1996.

Commissioner Maffei received his bachelor's degree from Brown University and holds master's degrees from the Columbia University Graduate School of Journalism and Harvard University's John F. Kennedy School of Government.

Commissioner Rebecca F. Dye

Counsel: Robert M. Blair
Contact
Phone: (202) 523-5715
E-mail: rdye@fmc.gov

Commissioner Rebecca F. Dye, of North Carolina, was nominated by President George W. Bush on June 13, 2002 and was confirmed by the United States Senate on November 14, 2002. She was nominated to her second term by President Bush on July 12, 2005 and confirmed by the Senate on July 22, 2005. She was nominated to her third term, which expires on June 30, 2015, by President Barack Obama and confirmed by the Senate on April 14, 2011. On May 26, 2016, Commissioner Dye was nominated by President Obama and confirmed by the Senate on June 29, 2016, for a term expiring June 30, 2020.

Prior to her appointment to the FMC, Commissioner Dye was Counsel to the Transportation and Infrastructure Committee of the U.S. House of Representatives. She held that position from 1995 until 2002. As Counsel, she provided advice to Members of Congress on issues pertaining to commercial shipping, international maritime agreements, oil pollution, maritime safety and law enforcement, the Federal budget process and Federal financing.

Commissioner Dye comes to the Commission with an extensive background in maritime matters. She began her Federal career as a commissioned officer and attorney in the Coast Guard's Office of the Chief Counsel, then served as a law instructor at the Coast Guard Academy. After two years as an attorney at the U.S. Maritime Administration, she joined the staff of the former Committee on Merchant Marine and Fisheries, and served there as Minority Counsel from 1987 to 1995.

Commissioner Dye graduated from the University of North Carolina at Chapel Hill in 1974, and earned a law degree from the University of North Carolina at Chapel Hill in 1977.

Commissioner Michael A. Khouri

Counsel: John A. Moran

Contact
Phone: 202-523-5712
E-mail: mkhouri@fmc.gov

Michael A. Khouri of Kentucky is serving in his third term with the Federal Maritime Commission. He was first nominated by President Obama and confirmed by the U.S. Senate in December, 2009, was re-nominated and confirmed for a full five year term in November, 2011, and was re-nominated and confirmed for his current term in June, 2016.

Commissioner Khouri is a forty-five year veteran in the maritime industry from positions held in marine vessel operations, legal and executive positions. He also served on the boards of directors at the Waterways Council, Inc. and the American Waterways Operators Association.

Mr. Khouri began his career as a deck crewman for Paducah, KY-based Crounse Corp., where he worked up in rank with service in the engine room and then into the wheelhouse as Pilot and Captain, earning his U.S. Merchant Marine Officer's License as Master and First Class Pilot on Steam and Motor Vessels. He then served for twenty-three years with American Commercial Lines, the largest U.S. inland marine company, holding executive positions including General Counsel & Secretary, Senior Vice President for Law & Corporate Affairs, and Senior Vice President for Transportation Services-marine operations. Khouri then joined MERS/Economy Boat, serving as President & COO before moving home to Louisville to join the law firm of Pedley & Gordinier.

In 1971, Mr. Khouri received his BA in Economics from Tulane University, and in 1980, his JD from the Brandeis School of Law-University of Louisville. He is also a graduate of the Harvard Business School's Advanced Management Program.

STRATEGIC GOALS AND FUNCTIONS

The Federal Maritime Commission (FMC or Commission) is an independent agency responsible for the regulation of oceanborne transportation in the foreign commerce of the United States for the benefit of U.S. exporters, importers, and the U.S. consumer.

The FMC's **Mission** is:

•To foster a fair, efficient and reliable international ocean transportation system and to protect the public from unfair and deceptive practices.

The FMC's **Vision** is:

•Fairness and Efficiency in the U.S. Maritime Commerce.

STRATEGIC GOAL 1

Maintain an efficient and competitive international ocean transportation system.

The FMC ensures competitive and efficient ocean transportation services for the shipping public by:

•Reviewing and monitoring agreements among ocean common carriers and marine terminal operators (MTOs) serving the U.S. foreign oceanborne trades to ensure that they do not cause substantial increases in transportation costs or decreases in transportation services;

•Maintaining and reviewing confidentially filed service contracts and Non-Vessel-Operating Common Carrier (NVOCC) Service Arrangements to guard against detrimental effects to shipping;

•Providing a forum for exporters, importers, and other members of the shipping public to obtain relief from ocean shipping practices or disputes that impede the flow of commerce;

•Ensuring common carriers' tariff rates and charges are published in private, automated tariff systems and electronically available;

•Monitoring rates, charges, and rules of government-owned or –controlled carriers to ensure they are just and reasonable; and

•Taking action to address unfavorable conditions caused by foreign government or business practices in U.S. foreign shipping trades.

STRATEGIC GOAL 2

Protect the shipping public from unlawful, unfair and deceptive ocean transportation practices and resolve shipping disputes.

The FMC protects the public from financial harm, and contributes to the integrity and security of the U.S. supply chain and transportation system by:

•Helping resolve disputes involving shipment of cargo, personal or household goods, or disputes between cruise vessel operators and passengers;

•Investigating and ruling on complaints regarding rates, charges, classifications, and practices of common carriers, MTOs, and Ocean Transportation Intermediaries (OTIs) , that violate the Shipping Act;

•Licensing OTIs with appropriate character and adequate financial responsibility;

•Identifying and holding regulated entities accountable for mislabeling cargo shipped to or from the United States; and

•Ensuring that cruise lines maintain financial responsibility to pay claims for personal injury or death, and to reimburse passengers when their cruise fails to sail.

STATUTORY AUTHORITY

The principal statutes administered by the Commission, now codified in Title 46 of the U.S. Code at sections 40101 through 44106, are:

•The Shipping Act of 1984, as amended by the Ocean Shipping Reform Act of 1998 (Shipping Act)

For additional analytical, business and investment opportunities information, please contact Global Investment & Business Center, USA at (703) 370-8082. Fax: (703) 370-8083. E-mail: ibpusa3@gmail.com Global Business and Investment Info Databank - www.ibpus.com

•The Foreign Shipping Practices Act of 1988 (FSPA)

•Section 19 of the Merchant Marine Act, 1920 (1920 Act)

•Sections 2 and 3 of Pub. L. No. 89-777, 80 Stat.1350

EFFICIENCY AND COMPETITION

Strategic Goal 1

Maintaining an efficient and competitive international ocean transportation system and enhancing liner trade through the use of various types of agreement authority is a primary function of the Commission. An efficient and competitive transportation system facilitates commerce, economic growth, and job creation. Competition among participants in U.S. liner trades fosters competitive rates and encourages a variety of service offerings for the benefit of U.S. exporters and importers, and ultimately consumers.

The Shipping Act allows competitors to meet and discuss (and in some cases agree on) certain business issues, but first they must file a written agreement with the Commission. The Commission reviews agreements using traditional antitrust law and economic models to evaluate the potential competitive impact of a proposed agreement before it may go into effect. The initial review and analysis of a proposed agreement and subsequent monitoring of the members' activities under the agreement, should it become effective, are designed to identify and guard against possible abuse of the filed authority, avoid unreasonable increases in transportation costs or decreases in transportation services, and address other activities prohibited by the Shipping Act.

The Shipping Act is itself a federal competition law applicable to the industry of international liner shipping. It contains provisions similar to those found in the Sherman Act of 1890, the 1914 Clayton Act, and the Robinson-Patman Act of 1936 concerning various prohibitions of discriminatory or unfair business practices and standards regarding business combinations. The Shipping Act creates a separate regulatory regime from antitrust under which collective carrier or MTO activity is both evaluated when the agreement is initially filed and closely monitored thereafter for any adverse impact on competition in the trade.

So long as the regulated entities comply with the statutory and regulatory proscriptions of the Act, then the other federal antitrust statutes generally do not apply. Conversely, if a regulated entity violates the Shipping Act, they would be subject to penalties set forth in the Act, and may under certain circumstances be subject to investigation and prosecution under the full array of federal antitrust statutes.

Agreement Filings and Review

Under Sections 4 and 5 of the Shipping Act, all agreements by or among ocean common carriers to fix rates or conditions of service, pool cargo revenue, allot ports or regulate sailings, limit or regulate the volume or character of cargo (or passengers) to be carried, control or prevent competition, or engage in exclusive or preferential arrangements, are required to be filed with the Commission. Except for certain exempted categories, agreements among MTOs, and agreements among one or more MTOs and one or more ocean common carriers also must be filed with the Commission. Generally, an agreement becomes effective 45 days after filing, unless the Commission requests additional information to evaluate the competitive impact of the

For additional analytical, business and investment opportunities information, please contact Global Investment & Business Center, USA at (703) 370-8082. Fax: (703) 370-8083. E-mail: ibpusa3@gmail.com Global Business and Investment Info Databank - www.ibpus.com

agreement. All agreements filed with the Commission are reviewed pursuant to the standard set forth in section 6(g) of the Shipping Act, 46 U.S.C. § 41307(b) (1) . Effective agreements are exempt from U.S. antitrust laws, and instead subject to Shipping Act restrictions and Commission oversight.

In fiscal year 2015, the Commission received 258 agreement filings, an increase of 38 percent over the previous year. This was the largest number of agreements filed (both new agreements and amendments to existing agreements) during a 12 month period since 2006.

Types of Carrier Agreements

Conference agreements are distinguished from all other types of agreements because they allow members to collectively discuss, agree, and fix freight rates and practices.

Rate discussion agreements (RDAs) also focus on rate matters, but unlike conferences, any consensus on rates is non-binding on the members.

Operational agreements do not contain authority to discuss or fix rates. They include vessel-sharing agreements (VSAs) , joint service agreements (JSAs) , cooperative working agreements (CWAs) , and discussion agreements.

- VSAs typically authorize some level of service cooperation with the goal of reducing an individual line's operating costs.
- Under JSAs, two or more carriers operate a combined service under a single name in a specified trading area.
- Many CWAs deal with unique operational considerations relating to acquisitions, sharing of administrative services, or internet portal management. Other CWAs include agency, sailing, trans-shipment, and equipment interchange (including chassis pooling) agreements.
- Discussion agreements allow members to discuss matters of mutual interest other than rates. Typically, these agreements focus on macro-economic, regulatory, safety or security issues.

MTO agreements are agreements between MTOs (operated by both public and private entities) that provide facilities, services, and labor for the interchange of cargo and passengers between land and ocean carriers, and for the receipt and delivery of cargo from shippers and consignees.

Conference or price-fixing agreements have become largely irrelevant to U.S. liner shipping, particularly in light of the periodic excess capacity conditions in U.S. liner trades. No new carrier

For additional analytical, business and investment opportunities information, please contact Global Investment & Business Center, USA at (703) 370-8082. Fax: (703) 370-8083. E-mail: ibpusa3@gmail.com Global Business and Investment Info Databank - www.ibpus.com

conference agreement has been filed with the Commission in 15 years. The three remaining conferences cover only U.S. military or government cargoes. At this time, no changes in the membership or activities of these conferences are anticipated.

While the number of RDAs on file with the Commission have declined 60 percent over the last 5 years from 36 to 22 agreements, RDAs remain the primary pricing forum in U.S. trade lanes.

At the end of the fiscal year, operational agreements accounted for 93 percent of all carrier agreements on file. VSAs account for the vast majority in this category - 90 percent, and 84 percent of all carrier agreements on file during FY 2015.

A broad view of the types of agreements filed during the past year shows a trend towards greater cooperation among carriers and MTOs under cooperative working agreements to provide transportation services and address concerns with cargo movement. In addition, operational cooperation among carriers under VSAs and CWAs jumped during the fiscal year with 26 new agreements filed.

Significant filings of this type involve some of the largest carriers and cover multiple geographic regions, including a new cooperative arrangement among CMA CGM, China Shipping Container Line (CSCL) , and the United Arab Shipping Company (known as the "Ocean 3 Alliance") ; and the addition of Evergreen to the CKYH Alliance. Cooperation between members of different carrier alliances also expanded under new or amended agreements, most likely necessitated by increasingly larger vessels that require multiple participating carriers to optimize vessel capacity utilization.

The inception of what could prove to be a period of consolidation within the liner shipping industry emerged during the fiscal year. Hapag Lloyd and Hamburg Sud completed their purchases of the liner shipping assets of Chilean Compañía Sud Americana de Vapores (CSAV) and Compañía Chilena de Navegación Interoceánica S.A. (CCNI) . In addition, at the close of the fiscal year, preliminary discussions regarding a new merger between COSCO and CSCL were emerging, and the proposed purchase of APL by CMA CGM was separately being explored.

In addition to the substantial number of agreement filings related to container shipping in 2015, slot charter agreements among Roll On-Roll Off (RO/RO) carriers grew significantly. A number of RO/RO carriers developed global slot charter agreements to allow more efficient and rapid access to space for the movement of vehicles and other RO/RO cargo. This trend is expected to continue.

Two new MTO agreements of significance were filed during the fiscal year. The Ports of Seattle and Tacoma formed the Northwest Seaport Alliance allowing the two competing ports to act as a single entity for marketing and infrastructure development, jointly operate container facilities, and jointly discuss rates. The Pacific Ports Operational Improvements Agreement authorizes the Ocean Carrier Equipment Management Association, the West Coast MTO Agreement, and most vessel-operating common carriers and MTOs serving U.S. West Coast ports to discuss and exchange information, and reach agreement on measures to address congestion and improve operations at U.S. West Coast port facilities. Prior to and at the time of filing this agreement, port congestion was particularly severe at the Ports of Los Angeles and Long Beach.

Competitive Impact and Monitoring

For additional analytical, business and investment opportunities information, please contact Global Investment & Business Center, USA at (703) 370-8082. Fax: (703) 370-8083. E-mail: ibpusa3@gmail.com Global Business and Investment Info Databank - www.ibpus.com

While systematically monitoring ocean common carrier and MTO activities and commercial conditions in the U.S. foreign trades, the Commission took the following specific measures to assess the competitive impact of certain agreements. Notable during the fiscal year were the relatively high number of unique or "special" reporting requirements developed by the Commission for several new agreements or amended agreements where the market share of the parties and/or the expansive operational cooperation contemplated under the agreement warranted heightened oversight.

Pacific Ports Operational Improvements Agreement: This new agreement allows carriers and MTOs to jointly discuss and reach agreement on measures to address congestion at U.S. West Coast ports. To complete a competitive impact analysis and establish appropriate monitoring requirements, the Commission issued a Section 15 Order to obtain certain commercial information from the agreement parties related to terminal operations. The Commission's review also included evaluation of information received from the agreement parties in response to questions raised by staff and Commissioners during the review period; removal of agreement authority to address Commission concerns, including proposed authority to impose fees and charges on third parties; and consideration of public comments received on the Agreement.

The Los Angeles and Long Beach Port Infrastructure and Environmental Programs Cooperative Working Agreement: The agreement was amended to allow the two neighboring ports to jointly discuss and reach agreement on measures aimed at expediting the flow of containers through the ports. Under its agreement monitoring program, the Commission reviews reports of activities authorized by this amendment.

West Coast MTO Agreement: Expanding on previous monitoring efforts, during the fiscal year the Commission commenced a more in-depth examination of the activities conducted by the parties to assess their potential competitive impact including examining complaints received regarding the PierPass program under the agreement.

Oakland MTO Agreement: The Commission issued a Request for Additional Information (RFAI) regarding a proposed amendment to establish OAKPASS, a program that would allow MTOs to offer Saturday gate access. The cost of providing these extra gates would be recovered by imposing a fee on shippers and truckers using the Monday through Friday daytime gates. Responses to the RFAI will permit the Commission to conduct an in-depth analysis of the proposed program under the section 6(g) standard of the Shipping Act, to address public comments received, and to establish appropriate monitoring requirements, if warranted.

Port of Seattle/Port of Tacoma Alliance Agreement: This new agreement allows the two ports to jointly operate, through the Northwest Seaport Alliance, container and other cargo facilities to help improve the competitiveness of the Puget Sound gateway. Special ongoing monitoring requirements were developed and imposed on the agreement parties to assist the Commission in monitoring the competitive impact of the agreement.

The COSCON/KL/YMUK/HANJIN/ELJSA (CKYHE) Slot Allocation and Sailing Agreement: Evergreen joined a pre-existing vessel sailing alliance among COSCO, K Line, Yang Ming and Hanjin covering multiple geographic regions. Following a competitive impact analysis of the amended agreement, special reporting requirements were issued and tailored to the specific authority contained in this operational agreement.

Consolidated Chassis Management Pool Agreement: The Commission continued to closely monitor new developments and the availability of chassis equipment under the agreement as ocean carriers divest themselves of their chassis fleets and discontinue providing chassis service.

For additional analytical, business and investment opportunities information, please contact Global Investment & Business Center, USA at (703) 370-8082. Fax: (703) 370-8083. E-mail: ibpusa3@gmail.com Global Business and Investment Info Databank - www.ibpus.com

Transpacific Stabilization Agreement (TSA) : Under the terms of the 2003 settlement agreement between the Commission and the TSA parties, biannual meetings are conducted with representatives of the TSA to review and closely examine major developments in the liner trade between the U.S. and Asia. Under the Commission's ongoing agreement monitoring program, TSA is also required to file regular reports on its members' commercial performance and activities in the trade.

Tariffs, Service Contracts, NSAs, & MTO Schedules

Tariffs

The Shipping Act requires common carriers and conferences to publish their tariffs containing rates, charges, rules, and practices, electronically in private systems. For ease of public access, the Commission publishes the web addresses of those tariffs on its website. At the close of the fiscal year, 5,500 tariff location addresses were posted. Of that number, 5,163 tariff addresses were for NVOCCs.

The Commission provides regulatory relief, allowing licensed and foreign registered NVOCCs to "opt out" of the requirement to file rate tariffs providing they use NVOCC Negotiated Rate Arrangements (NRAs) exclusively. At the end of the fiscal year, nearly 1,800 NVOCCs had filed prominent notices or a rule in their respective tariff indicating that they had invoked the exemption – up 98 percent from 900 in FY 2014. It is anticipated that NVOCCs will continue to take advantage of this opportunity, thereby significantly reducing the number of rate tariffs that the Commission must review to ensure compliance with applicable regulations.

Service Contracts

Service contracts are an alternative to transportation of cargo under tariff rates. Between 90 and 95 percent of the total cargo moving in the U.S. liner trades moves under service contracts, not tariffs. Service contracts enable the parties to tailor transportation services and rates to their commercial and operational needs and to keep these arrangements confidential. During the fiscal year, the Commission received 51,109 new service contracts, compared to 44,208 in fiscal year 2014; and 653,315 contract amendments, compared to 573,208 in fiscal year 2014.

NVOCC Service Arrangements (NSAs)

Commission rules allow NVOCCs to offer transportation services pursuant to individually negotiated, confidential service arrangements with customers, rather than under a published tariff. For the first time since NSAs became available for use, the number of NSAs filed during the fiscal year plummeted 41 percent. This significant reduction in NSA filings was the result of one of the largest volume filers discontinuing the use of NSAs during the fiscal year. Of the 1,780 NVOCCs registered with the Commission to file NSAs, only 244 (about 13 percent) have done so. Those 244 NSA users represent approximately 4 percent of all registered NVOCCs.

Marine Terminal Schedules

An MTO may make available to the public a schedule of rates, regulations, and practices, including limitations of liability for cargo loss or damage, pertaining to receiving, delivering, handling, or storing property at its marine terminal. Any such schedule made available to the public shall be enforceable by an appropriate court as an implied contract without proof of actual knowledge of its provisions. During the fiscal year, 266 MTOs filed Form FMC-1, which reports

For additional analytical, business and investment opportunities information, please contact Global Investment & Business Center, USA at (703) 370-8082. Fax: (703) 370-8083. E-mail: ibpusa3@gmail.com Global Business and Investment Info Databank - www.ibpus.com

the electronic location of an MTO's terminal schedule, with 158 MTOs electing to voluntarily publish their actual terminal schedules. The internet addresses of these MTO terminal schedules are posted on the Commission's website.

Port Congestion

International trade through U.S. ports now accounts for one-third of our nation's economic output (GDP) and this figure is expected to reach two-thirds by 2030. International trade supports U.S. jobs, and in 2010 (the latest available data) nearly 25 percent of all U.S. manufacturing and agricultural jobs were supported by U.S. exports. Because international trade and GDP are thoroughly linked, modern efficient ports are essential to facilitate international trade and to maintain a healthy and vibrant U.S. economy. Maintaining the efficiency and effectiveness of America's global supply chains is exceptionally important to the nation's continued economic vitality. Unfortunately, congestion at ports and other points in the nation's intermodal system has become a serious risk factor to the growth of the American economy and its competitive position in the world economy.

During the latter part of fiscal year 2014 and extending into FY 2015, the Commission hosted discussion forums around the country to hear firsthand the port congestion problems that ports, their customers, and other partners in the U.S. intermodal system were facing as a result of problems brought on by contemporary developments in liner shipping. Four separate one-day public listening sessions were held in different regions of the country, each lead by at least one FMC Commissioner. Forums were held in Los Angeles, Baltimore, New Orleans and Charleston.

The sessions were extremely well attended and, at most venues, there was standing room only. The energetic discussions that took place were transcribed and posted on the Commission's website along with public comments submitted on the port congestion issue. By the time the fourth forum concluded in early November 2014, over one thousand pages of transcripts had been compiled. Participants gave detailed accounts of what they saw as the chief causes of congestion in several of the nation's major container ports, came with reports of new solutions being applied, and shared new ideas. The Commission's dispute resolution specialists also participated in the Baltimore and Charleston port forums and rendered assistance to parties seeking to resolve port congestion related demurrage and per diem disputes in 250 matters.

Building on these efforts, the Chairman made addressing the challenges of port congestion his top priority for calendar year 2015. Several examples of supply chain participants cooperating and working together under the authority of the Shipping Act were reflected in a number of cooperative working agreements filed in 2015 that had as their central focus, improving port productivity, innovation and efficiency. (A description of these agreements is found in the *Efficiency and Competition* section of this Report) .

By and large, participants at the FMC-organized port forums recognized that long-term fixes to the system's infrastructure issues are needed, but they also saw an urgent need for short-term solutions. Following the port congestion forums, to address some of the shorter-term issues identified, the FMC publically released two staff reports. The first dealt with congestion costs in the form of substantial demurrage and detention fees being incurred unavoidably by cargo interests. This study was fast-tracked to address voluminous complaints heard leading up to, during, and continuing after, the forums. Entitled, "*Rules, Rates, and Practices Relating to Detention, Demurrage, and Free Time for Containerized Imports and Exports Moving Through Selected United States Ports*" the report detailed possible actions ocean carriers, terminal operators, and port authorities can take to help minimize congestion and attendant demurrage and detention fees, and noted possible actions that cargo interests and motor carriers can take. It

For additional analytical, business and investment opportunities information, please contact Global Investment & Business Center, USA at (703) 370-8082. Fax: (703) 370-8083. E-mail: ibpusa3@gmail.com Global Business and Investment Info Databank - www.ibpus.com

also identified possible actions the Commission could take concerning free time, detention and demurrage practices.

The second report, "*U.S. Container Port Congestion & Related International Supply Chain Issues: Causes, Consequences & Challenges*," organized and further developed stakeholders' discussions at the port forums around seven major themes that emerged – investment and planning; chassis availability and related issues; vessel and terminal operations; port drayage and truck-turn-time; extended gate hours, PierPASS and congestion pricing; and collaboration and communication. It also addressed current and possible future challenges caused by congestion at U.S. port gateways, and commented on the causes and effects of congestion in order to encourage further discourse on potential solutions.

As the fiscal year drew to a close, plans were being laid to ensure the FMC remains engaged with this serious issue. Ports and terminal operators will be challenged in the foreseeable future to find ways to accommodate bigger ships and larger container exchanges per visit, likely resulting in occasional chassis dislocations, trucking shortages, and local congestion.

International Cooperation

Global Regulatory Summit Part II

Maritime regulators from the United States, the People's Republic of China, and the European Commission met and conferred in Brussels, Belgium, in June 2015 to consider the evolving international maritime landscape. Officials discussed their differing regulatory frameworks and the potential effects of carrier cooperation on international trade. The EU delegation was led by Cecilio Madero Villarejo, the Deputy Director General for Antitrust, and Mr. Hubert de Broca, Head of Unit, Directorate General for Competition, Antitrust-Transport, Post and Other Services; and the Chinese delegation was led by Mr. Li Hongyin, Deputy Director-General, Bureau of Water Transport, Ministry of Transport. FMC Chairman Mario Cordero led the U.S. delegation.

OECD

The FMC's General Counsel participated in a discussion at the Organisation for Economic Co-operation and Development (OECD) on the topic of "Competition Issues in Liner Shipping." The Working Group was organized by the Directorate for Financial and Enterprise Affairs, Competition Committee. The General Counsel discussed the developments in the ocean shipping industry since 1984, and the regulatory oversight of the segment to ensure robust competition.

U.S.-Japan Bilateral Maritime Meeting

September 2015, Chairman Cordero and FMC Chief of Staff participated in a U.S.-Japan Bilateral Maritime Meeting, hosted by the Japanese Ministry of Transport in Tokyo, Japan. Maritime Administrator Paul Jaenichen headed the U.S. Delegation. U.S. and Japanese officials discussed many mutual issues and shared insights on the global maritime landscape. Officials discussed such topics as the global alliances, the Panama Canal expansion, environmental issues, liquefied natural gas (LNG) -fueled vessels, port development, anti-piracy measures, and education efforts aimed at increasing visibility of the maritime industry. Participants agreed that coordination on these maritime issues is valuable for promoting mutual interests in international ocean transportation and commerce.

Trade In Services Agreement Negotiations

For additional analytical, business and investment opportunities information, please contact Global Investment & Business Center, USA at (703) 370-8082. Fax: (703) 370-8083. E-mail: ibpusa3@gmail.com Global Business and Investment Info Databank - www.ibpus.com

On behalf of the Commission, the OGC acted as a maritime technical advisor to two ongoing trade negotiations, Trade in Services Agreement (TiSA) and Transatlantic Trade and Investment Partnership (T-TIP) .

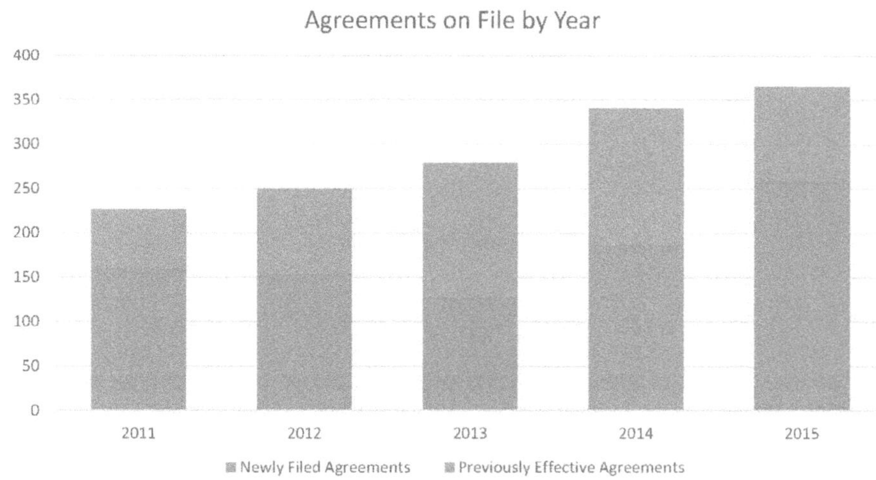

No new conference or price fixing agreement has been filed in 15 years.

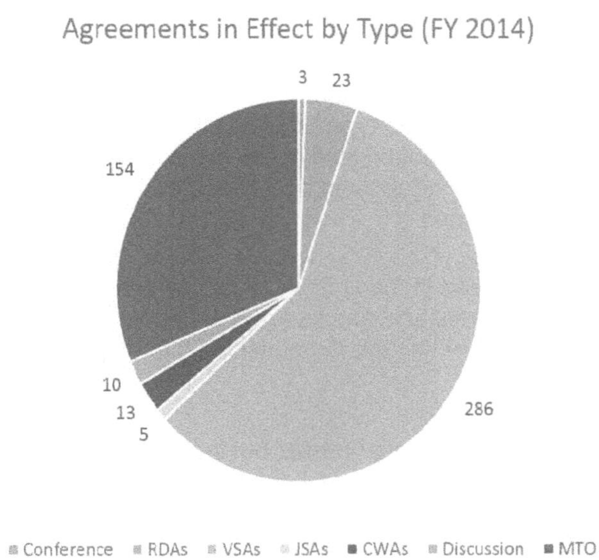

Service Contracts and NSAs filed in 2015

••

Newly filed service contracts: 51,109

••

Amendments to service contracts: 653,315

••

Newly filed NSAs: 901

••

Amendments to NSAs: 1,790

Protecting the Public

Strategic Goal 2

The FMC engages in a variety of activities that protect the public from financial harm, including licensing and registering of ocean transportation intermediaries; helping resolve disputes about the shipment of goods or the carriage of passengers; investigating and prosecuting unreasonable or unjust practices, and ruling on private party complaints alleging Shipping Act violations. These activities contribute to the integrity and security of the nation's import and export supply chains and ocean transportation system. In addition, the FMC ensures that passenger vessel operators maintain proper financial coverage to reimburse cruise passengers in the event their cruise is cancelled or to cover liability in the event of death or injury at sea.

Licensing

Ocean Transportation Intermediaries are transportation middlemen for cargo moving in the U.S.-foreign oceanborne trades. There are two types: NVOCCs and ocean freight forwarders (OFFs) . An NVOCC is a common carrier that holds itself out to the public to provide ocean transportation, issues its own house bill of lading or equivalent document, but does not operate the vessel by which ocean transportation is provided.

An ocean freight forwarder domiciled in the U.S. arranges for the transportation of cargo with a common carrier on behalf of shippers and processes documents related to those shipments. Both NVOCCs and OFFs must be licensed by the Commission if they are located in the U.S. and must establish financial responsibility.

NVOCCs doing business in the U.S.-foreign trades but located outside the U.S. (foreign NVOCCs) may choose to become FMC-licensed, but are not required to do so. If not licensed under the FMC's program, foreign-based NVOCCs must register with the Commission and establish financial responsibility.

NVOCCs wishing to serve in the U.S.-China trade may file an Optional Rider for Additional NVOCC Financial Responsibility, to meet the Chinese government's financial responsibility requirements. This rider adds additional financial liability to meet the bond aggregate amount of $125,000.

The rider amount is available to pay fines and penalties for activities in the U.S.-China trades imposed by the Chinese government. This rider is accepted as a convenience to the U.S. During the fiscal year, 50 China Bond Riders were received and 23 were terminated. At the close of the fiscal year, 440 U.S. NVOCCs had China Bond Riders.

Revisions to Licensing Rules

On October 10, 2014 the Commission published a Notice of Proposed Rulemaking (NPR) , 79 FR 61544, significantly amending its regulations governing OTIs for the first time since it promulgated implementing regulations under the Ocean Shipping Reform Act of 1998, Public Law 105-258, 112 Stat. 1902 (OSRA) . The proposed rule was published following an ANPR published in May 2013. After considering extensive comments submitted to the ANPR, the proposed rule was revised to address commenters concerns and adapt to changing industry conditions, improve regulatory oversight, improve transparency, streamline FMC business processes, and reduce regulatory burdens on the industry. Among other revisions, most significantly the rule proposed to:

require licenses and registrations be renewed every three years;

require the FMC to develop a user-friendly, online renewal process;

require common carriers to verify OTI licenses and registrations, tariff publication and financial responsibility, and that the Commission develop a single location for such verifications on its website; and

provide for a new expedited hearing procedure to streamline the current procedures for denial, revocation, or suspension of an OTI license.

At the close of the fiscal year, the Commission was preparing to consider and vote on a draft Final Rule to be implemented in FY 2016.

Leveraging Technology

Improving service delivery through technology is a critical priority for the FMC. Due to historical budgetary constraints, the FMC had been unable to migrate from its legacy applications and aging architecture. While the Commission's budget remains lean, it is committed to establishing a more robust IT infrastructure. The Commission's multi-year strategy, encompassed in the FMC's Information Technology Capital Plan, will enhance its cybersecurity efforts and better manage current and future business demands.

The cornerstone of the Commission's IT upgrade effort is development and implementation of its Enterprise Content Management (ECM) platform, designed to capture, manage, store, preserve, and deliver information supporting key Commission processes. The ECM will enhance both internal and external interface with its electronic systems and databases and will eliminate duplicate data entry that is inherent in the current legacy systems.

In FY 2015, the FMC completed a cloud migration of its in-house file server based data management system. In addition, all Commission employee workstations were upgraded to the latest Microsoft operating system and Office 365. A cloud-based training solution was procured to give all employees access to high quality, job-relevant, training courses as well as eBooks and audio books. By leveraging these cloud services, the Commission is better able to support the President's policy on Enhancing Workplace Flexibilities and Work-Life Programs by extending telework to a greater number of employees.

For additional analytical, business and investment opportunities information, please contact Global Investment & Business Center, USA at (703) 370-8082. Fax: (703) 370-8083. E-mail: ibpusa3@gmail.com Global Business and Investment Info Databank - www.ibpus.com

The Commission also upgraded its server hardware to improve the operating efficiency of the internal and external applications used by FMC staff and the maritime industry. In addition, the Commission launched its disaster recovery site to support access to critical applications in the event of an emergency.

Passenger Vessel Program

The Commission administers the passenger vessel operator program as described under 46 U.S.C. §§ 44102-44103, which requires evidence of financial responsibility for vessels that have berth or stateroom accommodations for 50 or more passengers and embark passengers at U.S. ports and territories. Certificates of performance cover financial responsibility used to reimburse passengers in the event their cruise is cancelled. Certificates of casualty are required to cover liability that may occur for death or injury to passengers or other persons on voyages to or from U.S. ports.

At the close of the fiscal year, 223 vessels owned by 48 passenger vessel operators were certified under the Commission's program. The combined evidence of financial responsibility for nonperformance of transportation for all cruise vessels in the program is $590 million. Under the Commission's program, $750 million in aggregate financial responsibility for casualty coverage is evidenced. In FY 2015, 18 new performance certificates and 19 casualty certificates were issued. No reimbursements for unperformed cruises were necessary under the FMC's program during the fiscal year.

On April 2, 2015 the maximum coverage requirement increased to $30 million per cruise line with an adjustment to the cap thereafter every two years based on the Consumer Price Index for All Urban Consumers (CPI-U) .

The Commission offers information and guidance to the cruising public on passenger rights and obligations regarding monies paid to cruise lines that fail to perform voyages, as well as other cruise difficulties such as itinerary changes. A new cruise brochure was designed and published during the fiscal year that provides information and resources to help passengers avoid problems that may commonly arise during a cruise vacation. This brochure was widely distributed to travel agents and associations, and other federal agencies working in partnership with the Commission to educate and protect the cruising public.

Consumer Affairs and Education

Dispute Resolution

Through its Office of Consumer Affairs and Dispute Resolution Services (CADRS) , the Commission provides alternative dispute resolution (ADR) , *ombuds*, and mediation services, to assist parties in resolving international ocean shipping disputes, including a Rapid Response Team especially focused on addressing problems exporters may encounter. Such services are available to the shipping public at any stage of a dispute, regardless of whether litigation has been filed at the FMC or another jurisdictional forum. The Commission's ADR services help parties avoid the expense and delay inherent in litigation, and facilitate the flow of U.S. foreign commerce. During the fiscal year, the FMC:

> Closed 574 *ombuds* matters: 152 household goods matters; 328 cargo other than household goods matters; 93 cruise matters; and 1 other Shipping Act matter.

For additional analytical, business and investment opportunities information, please contact Global Investment & Business Center, USA at (703) 370-8082. Fax: (703) 370-8083. E-mail: ibpusa3@gmail.com Global Business and Investment Info Databank - www.ibpus.com

Provided mediation services in 5 matters.

Collaborated with Miami-Dade Consumer Protection to render assistance to consumers whose shipments were in jeopardy after tendering shipments and payment to an unlicensed OTI that deposited the cargo with a licensed OTI, but failed to tender freight. CADRS negotiated with the licensed entity to ship the cargo to destination at no further cost to consumers.

With the Commission's Area Representatives (ARs) , actively assisted individual cargo owners victimized by the shutdown of a major household goods company operating to Central America. As a result of this effort, many cargo owners were able to locate and retrieve their personal effects from warehouses in various port areas.

Published an informational article on the importance of using FMC-licensed and bonded OTIs in *The Compass*, a trade association publication for the Florida Yacht Brokers Association.

Presented to various industry and consumer trade associations regarding regulatory compliance, best practices, and the use of alternative dispute resolution to resolve regulatory and commercial ocean transportation disputes.

Area Representatives

Area Representatives represent the FMC at regional field offices located in Southern California, South Florida, New Orleans, New York, Houston and Seattle. They resolve complaints and disputes between parties involved in international oceanborne shipping (often coordinating with CADRS staff) , investigate alleged violations of the shipping statutes, and participate in local maritime industry groups. ARs provide advice and guidance to the shipping public, collect and analyze information of regulatory significance, and assess industry conditions.

During the fiscal year, ARs were actively involved in reaching out to the public, consumer groups, trade associations, and other government agencies to achieve regulatory compliance and protection for the shippers of household goods and personal effects. The ARs were instrumental in the publication of public service announcements (PSAs) for each major port area, warning consumers against the use of unlawful transportation providers and intermediaries. They also made presentations to interested industry audiences in their regions, explaining OTI licensing requirements, proposed changes to the Commission's OTI rules on bonding and license renewals, and OTI compliance with tariff filing requirements and provisions applicable to NRAs.

Enforcement, Audits and Penalties

The Commission's Bureau of Enforcement (BOE) and the ARs investigated and prosecuted possible illegal practices in many trade lanes, including the Transpacific, North Atlantic, Middle East, South American and Caribbean trades. These market-distorting activities included various forms of unfiled agreements, rebates and absorptions, misdescription of commodities, and unlawful use of service contracts, as well as carriage of cargo by and for untariffed and unbonded NVOCCs.

At the beginning of the fiscal year, 10 enforcement cases were pending final resolution by BOE, the Bureau was party to 4 formal proceedings, and there were 14 matters pending for which BOE was providing internal legal advice. The ARs referred 18 investigative matters to BOE for enforcement action or informal compromise; 17 were compromised and settled, administratively closed, or referred for formal proceedings; and 11 enforcement cases were pending resolution at fiscal year's end. Three formal proceedings were initiated; 4 formal proceedings were completed; and 3 were pending at the end of the fiscal year.

Major investigations undertaken or completed during the fiscal year addressed VOCCs seeking to operate pursuant to agreements that were not filed with the Commission, as well as deceptive or fraudulent practices of certain OTIs operating in the China-U.S. inbound trades. Of note, BOE's efforts in pursuing inquiries regarding certain car carriers in the Japan/South Korea/China-U.S. trade, Europe-U.S. trade and in other U.S. trades, culminated in an additional $135,000 settlement with Siem Car Carriers AS relating to unfiled carrier agreements. Penalties of $537,500 were also compromised with United Arab Shipping Co. with respect to allegations of unlawful rebates paid in the U.S.-Middle East trades. Civil penalties were also pursued in several noteworthy formal proceedings before the Commission's Administrative Law Judges that are summarized in the *Formal Investigations* section of this report.

Cumulatively, the Commission collected $2 million in penalties in FY 2015. Most of these investigations were resolved informally, some with compromise settlements and civil penalties. A list of parties and penalties can be found in Appendix D.

BOE's compliance audit program, conducted from headquarters primarily by mail, e-mail and telephone, reviews the operations of licensed OTIs to assist them in complying with the statutory requirements and the Commission's rules and regulations. The audit program also reviews entities holding themselves out as VOCCs, where there is no indication of actual vessel operations. At the beginning of the fiscal year, 14 audits were pending. During the fiscal year, 183 audits were commenced, 163 audits were completed (including audits carried over from fiscal year 2014) , and 34 remained pending at the close of the fiscal year.

Inter-Agency Cooperation

The Commission works regularly with a number of other federal, state, and local transportation and law enforcement agencies, either through established memoranda of understanding (MOU) or collaborations to address specific transportation related issues or incidents in both the U.S. domestic shipping arena and international liner shipping.

CADRS advanced the MOU between the FMC and the Federal Motor Carrier Safety Administration (FMCSA) through continued participation in the FMCSA's Moving Fraud Task Force and Moving Fraud Partnership initiatives. CADRS staff also participated in FMCSA's Moving Season Kickoff Event, giving a panel presentation on cooperative efforts and innovations to protect consumers against international moving fraud.

Interaction between BOE, the ARs, and Customs and Border Patrol (CBP) on the exchange of investigative information continues to be beneficial to all parties. Cooperation with CBP included staff interactions and joint field operations to investigate entities suspected of violating both agencies' statutes or regulations. Such cooperation also has included local police and other government entities, including the U.S. Attorney's Office, Federal Bureau of Investigation (FBI) , and Immigration and Customs Enforcement (ICE) , when necessary.

BOE completed its third year under a formal MOU with the Census Bureau, U.S. Department of Commerce, providing FMC with access to the Census' Automated Export System (AES) database. The completed MOU accommodates Census' ongoing concerns for data security by limiting such use of confidential U.S. export shipment data only for FMC law enforcement

For additional analytical, business and investment opportunities information, please contact Global Investment & Business Center, USA at (703) 370-8082. Fax: (703) 370-8083. E-mail: ibpusa3@gmail.com Global Business and Investment Info Databank - www.ibpus.com

purposes. BOE also commenced membership in the Homeland Security Investigations-led National Intellectual Property Rights Coordination Center (IPR Center) , a partnership of 21 Federal and international agencies targeting intellectual property- and trade-related crimes.

The ARs continued to work closely with a number of law enforcement agencies, including local police jurisdictions in New York, New Jersey, South Florida and Houston, in matters relating to international shipping, such as the export of stolen motor vehicles. They also participated in various enforcement initiatives sponsored by Federal law enforcement agencies: the U.S. Department of Justice, Alcohol, Tobacco and Firearms (ATF) ; FBI; the Department of Homeland Security (including CBP and ICE) ; the Joint Terrorism Task Force (JTTF) ; Department of Commerce; Coast Guard; Export-Import Bank; and the FMCSA. These activities included criminal and civil investigations of entities licensed or regulated by the Commission, interdiction of illicit imports and exports, consultation on carrier practices, procedures and documentation relating to shipping and international trade, and coordinated action seeking to protect the shipping public from deceptive and unfair practices.

Three AR offices participated in a large multi-agency strike force operation, jointly led by the Coast Guard and CBP, which included a dozen federal agencies and numerous local police jurisdictions engaged in the inspection of hundreds of intermodal ocean containers at port terminals in New York/New Jersey to uncover violations of safety, cargo declaration and licensing regulations.

Licensing Activity in FY 2015

New OTI applications accepted: 376
Amended applications accepted: 314
New OTI licenses issued: 250
Amended licenses issued: 100
Licenses revoked: 293
Licenses voluntarily surrendered: 72

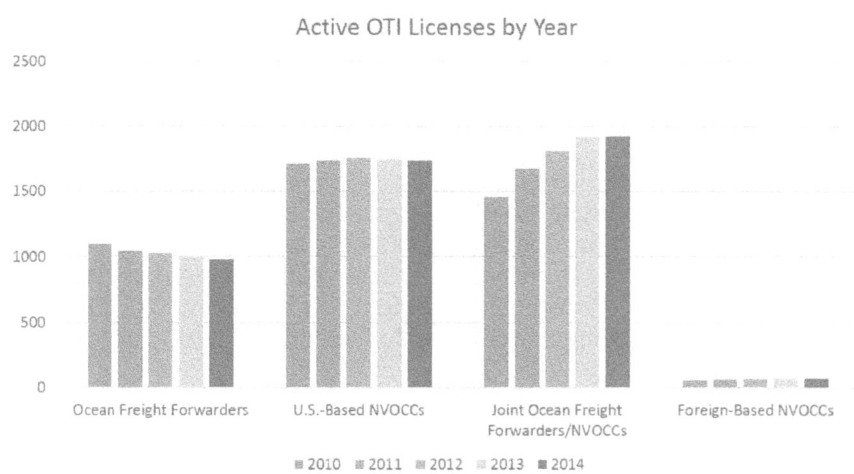

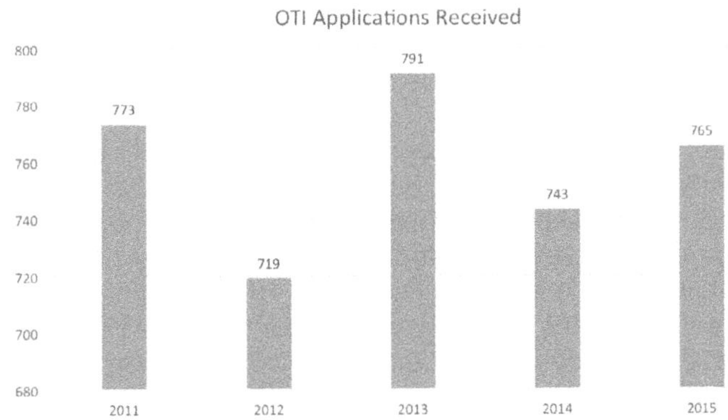

PVO Program Participants

48 PVOs are certified under the Commission's program
223 vessels are certified
19 new Casualty Certificates issued in FY 2015
18 new Performance Certificates issued in FY 2015

PVO Program Coverage

$590 million aggregate evidence of financial responsibility for nonperformance

$750 million aggregate evidence of financial responsibility for casualty

DEVELOPMENTS IN MAJOR U.S. FOREIGN TRADES

Worldwide

The world's container trade expanded by 3 percent in fiscal year 2015 compared to a more robust growth rate of 5 percent in 2014. As the fiscal year came to a close, 243 containerships lay idle, representing 4 percent of the total fleet capacity measured in TEUs (twenty-foot equivalent container units) . In contrast, 131 ships or 1 percent of the containership capacity lay idle at the end of fiscal year 2014.

The world's container shipping industry remained as concentrated during fiscal year 2015 as it had been in prior years. The top three container operators controlled 38 percent of the world's containership capacity; the top five controlled 47 percent; and the top ten controlled nearly 64 percent. A.P. Moller-Maersk A/S (15 percent) , Mediterranean Shipping Company SA (13 percent) and CMA CGM S.A. (9 percent) continued to hold the top three positions in terms of vessel capacity deployed.

Container volumes in the U.S. liner trades expanded by 2 percent to 31.5 million TEUs, compared to 31 million last year. The U.S. share of the world's container trades was nearly 17 percent. U.S. container imports continued to grow, expanding 6 percent to 20 million TEUs, compared to a revised figure of 18.8 million in 2014. This was the second consecutive year that U.S. imports surpassed the record of 18.6 million reached in fiscal year 2007. U.S. container exports lost ground decreasing 5 percent to nearly 11.5 million TEUs. As a result, the U.S. container imbalance continued to worsen; for every 100 loaded containers exported from the U.S., 175 were imported, compared to 156 imported in fiscal year 2014.

For additional analytical, business and investment opportunities information, please contact Global Investment & Business Center, USA at (703) 370-8082. Fax: (703) 370-8083. E-mail: ibpusa3@gmail.com
Global Business and Investment Info Databank - www.ibpus.com

The world's containership fleet continued to expand with nominal capacity growing by approximately 9 percent. At the end of the fiscal year, 5,143 containerships, with a total fleet capacity of 19.7 million TEUs, were available to serve the world's container trades and there were orders worldwide for 511 new containerships with an aggregate capacity of 4.1 million TEUs – an increase of 21 percent over the existing fleet capacity. Vessels with nominal capacities exceeding 10,000 TEUs comprised 22 percent of the existing containership fleet capacity and 73 percent of the orderbook fleet capacity at year-end, reflecting the increasing size of containerships being ordered.

Asia

In terms of container cargo volumes, Asia remains our largest trading region. In fiscal year 2015, Asia was responsible for 62 percent of U.S. container trade volumes (exports and imports combined) . Northeast Asia accounted for 53 percent of all U.S. container cargo from this region and Southeast Asia accounted for nearly 10 percent. Roughly 69 percent of all U.S. container imports originated from Asia and the region received 51 percent of all U.S. container exports. Nearly half of all containers originating from or destined to Northeast and Southeast Asia are handled at the Ports of Los Angeles and Long Beach.

The U.S. imported 13.7 million TEUs of merchandise from Asia, which is a 6 percent increase over the previous fiscal year. On the export side, the U.S. sent nearly 5.9 million TEUs of goods to Asia, a decrease of 7 percent over the last year.

The *Transpacific Stabilization Agreement*, a 15-member discussion agreement with voluntary pricing authority is the major agreement in the transpacific trade. TSA covers the inbound and outbound transpacific container trade lanes, and its geographic scope also includes parts of the Indian Subcontinent (Bangladesh, Pakistan and Sri Lanka, but not India) . During the fiscal year, TSA's share of the U.S. inbound and outbound Asia container trades was approximately 90 and 91 percent, respectively.

Australia and Oceania

The Oceania trade includes the nations and territories of Australia, New Zealand, Papua New Guinea, Western Samoa, and other South Pacific islands. As in many of the U.S. liner trades, the increase in the value of the U.S. dollar against foreign currencies affected the container cargo market making U.S. exports less attractive. Compared to the preceding fiscal year, U.S. container exports to the region declined by 4 percent, while imports to the U.S. jumped nearly 10 percent. Notwithstanding the decline in U.S. exports to this region, container exports continued to exceed imports by a ratio of 1.37 to 1. Meat and wine, the top commodities from the region, accounted for nearly 36 percent of the total import cargo volume. The top two carriers, Hamburg Sud and ANL Singapore Pte. Ltd. (a subsidiary of CMA CGM) , moved close to 50 percent of the total liner cargo volume in each trade direction. As parties to the Trans-Pacific Partnership, if ratified, trade in container cargo between the U.S. and Australia and New Zealand will likely benefit from the reduction or elimination of tariffs and quotas on many products.

Two main rate discussion agreements cover the trade between the U.S. and Australia and New Zealand. Seven carriers with a combined market share of 80 percent participate in the *United States/Australasia Discussion Agreement* covering the outbound trade; and five carriers with a combined market share of 94 percent participate in the *Australia and New Zealand-United States Discussion Agreement* covering the inbound trade. All carriers serving the trade provide direct service through vessel sharing and space charter agreements.

For additional analytical, business and investment opportunities information, please contact Global Investment & Business Center, USA at (703) 370-8082. Fax: (703) 370-8083. E-mail: ibpusa3@gmail.com Global Business and Investment Info Databank - www.ibpus.com

Papua New Guinea, Western Samoa, and other South Pacific islands are served by five carriers operating under the *Pacific Islands Discussion Agreement*. Collectively these carriers hold a market share of 76 percent.

Indian Subcontinent and Middle East

The Indian Subcontinent and Middle East regions together accounted for over 6 percent of total U.S. container volumes in fiscal year 2015. U.S. container trade with the Indian Subcontinent alone (exports and imports combined) grew 7 percent over last year, while the container market between the U.S. and Middle East (exports and imports combined) grew by nearly 3 percent.

The U.S. imported 801,000 TEUs from the Indian Subcontinent and 201,000 TEUs from the Middle East - 10 percent and 15 percent increases respectively over the prior fiscal year. The U.S. exported 458,000 TEUs to the Indian Subcontinent and 578,000 TEUs to the Middle East, an increase of almost 3 percent and a decrease of slightly more than 1 percent, respectively, over the preceding fiscal year.

In this region, TSA is the rate discussion agreement covering part of the U.S. inbound and outbound container trades. Its geographic scope covers the Indian Subcontinent countries of Bangladesh, Pakistan, and Sri Lanka, but not India or the Middle East. For the fiscal year, TSA's market share for imports from and exports to this trade region were 86 and 89 percent, respectively. There are no other rate discussion agreements covering the trades between the U.S. and India or the Middle East.

North Europe

During the fiscal year, the strength of the U.S. dollar against European currencies affected container cargo growth in the U.S. liner trade with North Europe. Compared to the preceding period, container exports to North Europe declined by nearly 6 percent, while container imports to the U.S. rose by nearly 9 percent. In both trade directions, half of the containers were moved by the top three ocean carriers, which in ranking order were MSC, Hapag Lloyd, and Maersk Line. The deployment of vessel capacity expanded by over 30 percent in each trade direction, and the average vessel capacity utilization rate during the fiscal year reportedly was 91 percent inbound and 64 percent outbound. Freight rates in the stronger inbound direction were reported to range between $1,500 and $2,000 per container, while outbound rates remained depressed at $1,200 per container and below.

A number of significant changes to services offered in the trade are worth noting. In January 2015, UASC entered the trade through a new vessel sharing arrangement with CMA CGM and Hamburg Sud under the *CMA CGM/HSDG/UASC Vessel Sharing Agreement*. Together the three carriers deploy 15 vessels in a weekly pendulum service between ports in North Europe, the U.S. Atlantic, and Asia. In May 2015, independent of its alliance with Maersk Line, MSC introduced a new weekly loop service with eight vessels operating between ports in North Europe and the U.S. Pacific Coast through the Panama Canal. Jointly, MSC and Maersk Line added a fourth weekly loop service with four vessels between U.S. Atlantic and North Europe ports under their alliance, the *Maersk/MSC Vessel Sharing Agreement*. Similarly, members of the *G6 Alliance Agreement* introduced a fourth weekly loop service with four vessels operating in the transatlantic trade. Both groups of carriers announced that their new weekly loop services would be suspended for the winter slack season until April 2016. In August 2015, CMA CGM also temporarily suspended its Liberty Bridge service, which it operated with four vessels in a weekly transatlantic loop.

Mediterranean

For additional analytical, business and investment opportunities information, please contact Global Investment & Business Center, USA at (703) 370-8082. Fax: (703) 370-8083. E-mail: ibpusa3@gmail.com Global Business and Investment Info Databank - www.ibpus.com

After a strong rebound in both trade directions during last fiscal year, conditions in the container cargo market were mixed in the U.S./Mediterranean trade during fiscal year 2015. U.S. container exports tumbled nearly 12 percent, while container imports from the region grew 4 percent. Import containers exceeded export containers by a ratio of 2 to 1. The top imported commodities included wine, furniture and ceramic tiles. Paper, cotton and wood pulp were among the top U.S. export commodities. MSC and Hapag Lloyd moved about half of the total container cargo in each trade direction.

In terms of service changes, in January 2015, CMA CGM terminated its weekly loop service and entered into a vessel sharing arrangement with UASC, Hanjin Shipping Co., and CSCL under the *Hanjin/UASC/CMA CGM/CSCL Vessel Sharing and Slot Charter Agreement*. Together these carriers deploy 12 vessels in a weekly pendulum service operating between ports in the Indian Subcontinent, Middle East, Mediterranean and the U.S. Atlantic Coast via the Suez Canal. In April 2015, CMA CGM independently initiated a new weekly loop service with six vessels between U.S. Gulf and Mediterranean ports and later added three more vessels to expand the service to ports in the Caribbean and South America. Under their alliance, MSC and Maersk Line consolidated their service strings into two weekly loop services between ports in the Mediterranean and the U.S. Atlantic and Gulf, respectively, and two pendulum services between ports in the Mediterranean, Asia, and the U.S. Pacific Coast. By the end of the fiscal year, vessel capacity deployed was reduced by 8 percent in the outbound direction and increased by 7 percent in the inbound direction.

Africa

The Republic of South Africa is the largest U.S. liner trading nation on the continent, accounting for about 25 percent of the total container cargo. The volume of container cargo shipped between the U.S. and all nations in Africa (exports and imports combined) fell 6 percent during the fiscal year. Compared to the preceding year, U.S. exports to Africa dropped nearly 10 percent, while imports from the continent grew almost 4 percent. Notwithstanding the drop in U.S. exports to this region during the fiscal year, U.S. container exports continued to substantially exceed imports. For every container moving inbound, 2.4 containers moved outbound. The major export commodities remained unchanged and included automobiles (mostly used) , poultry, and grocery products, while cocoa bean and citrus fruit were among the top import commodities.

Almost 70 percent of the container cargo in the trade was carried by MSC and Maersk Line (including Maersk Line's subsidiary, Safmarine) . Under the *Southern Africa Agreement*, MSC and Maersk Line share space on each other's ships in the America Express (AMEX) service between the U.S. Atlantic Coast and the Republic of South Africa with calls at Cape Town, Port Elizabeth, and Durban.

Latin America

Central America and the Caribbean

U.S. export cargo volumes to Central America increased by nearly 5 percent to 611,000 TEUs, while U.S. import cargo volumes decreased by almost 4 percent to 751,100 TEUs. Paper and paperboard (including waste paper) accounted for the largest share of U.S. containerized exports. Other major export commodities included fabrics, yarns, and raw cotton. Grocery products, used automobiles and apparel were also significant exports. Fresh fruit made up the majority of all U.S. imports from the region with bananas accounting for close to three quarters of all fresh fruit shipped to the U.S. The second largest commodity imported from this region was clothing and apparel.

For additional analytical, business and investment opportunities information, please contact Global Investment & Business Center, USA at (703) 370-8082. Fax: (703) 370-8083. E-mail: ibpusa3@gmail.com Global Business and Investment Info Databank - www.ibpus.com

Five of the largest regional carriers in the U.S./Central America trade participated in the *Central America Discussion Agreement* (CADA) : Seaboard Marine, Crowley Latin America Services, King Ocean Services, Dole Ocean Cargo Express, and Great White Fleet Liner Service Ltd.

In the liner trade between the U.S. and the Caribbean, U.S. exports, mainly consisting of food, consumer goods, and manufactured products increased almost 8 percent to 512,000 TEUs. Imports to the U.S. decreased nearly 3 percent to approximately 166,000 TEUs.

Carriers operating in the U.S./Caribbean trade participated in three rate discussion agreements covering discrete trades: (1) the *Aruba Bonaire and Curacao Discussion Agreement*, (2) the *Bermuda Discussion Agreement*, and (3) the *Caribbean Shipowners Association*.

South America

U.S. containerized trade with South America (exports and imports combined) was nearly 2 million TEUs during the fiscal year, relatively unchanged from the previous year. U.S. exports to the region slightly exceeded U.S. imports. In addition to general merchandise, other top export commodities to South America included auto parts, petroleum resins, chemical woodpulp, and polymers. On the U.S. import side, bananas/plantains, sawn wood, coffee, plywood, and granite were the commodities moving in greatest volume.

Several carriers providing service to the West Coast of South America are members of the *West Coast of South America Discussion Agreement* (WCSADA) . Previously, the membership of WCSADA consisted of eight regional and four global carriers. However, as a result primarily of mergers and acquisitions, by fiscal year's end WCSADA membership had dwindled to seven, including three regional carriers (Seaboard Marine, Trinity Shipping, and King Ocean Services) and four global carriers (CMA CGM, Hamburg Sud, Hapag Lloyd, and MSC) .

In addition to service from members of WCSADA, a number of independent carriers serve the trade including Dole Ocean Cargo Express and Great White Fleet, that mainly transport proprietary cargo such as fresh fruits and vegetables. WCSADA also faces competition from Nippon Yusen Kaisha Line, Maersk Line, Evergreen, Mitsui O.S.K. Line, and Zim, that often use transshipment hubs in Mexico, Panama, and the Caribbean. Several regional carriers also serve the trade and compete for cargo. There were no active rate discussion agreements in the trade between the U.S. and the East Coast of South America.

Worldwide

Worldwide container trade expanded only 3% vs. a 5% growth rate last year.

New signs of global vessel overcapacity indicated as number of container ships that lay idle nearly doubled at year's end.

The world's top 3 operators controlled 38% of the worldwide vessel capacity.

U.S. LINER TRADES

Container volumes in the U.S. liner trades (imports and exports combined) grew for the 6th consecutive year.

U.S. container imbalance worsened this FY with imports continuing to outpace U.S. exports; a 5% drop in U.S. exports further widened the gap.

Nearly 70% of all U.S. containerized imports are from Asia; and more than half of all U.S. containerized exports are shipped to Asia.

Top 3 carriers carry over half the cargo shipped in the U.S./North Europe trade.

The trade gap between imports/exports shipped in the U.S./Central America and the Caribbean trade narrowed by almost 30% the FY.

Top Twenty U.S. Liner Cargo Trading Partners

Pursuant to the Foreign Shipping Practices Act (FSPA) , the FMC must include in its annual report to Congress "a list of the twenty foreign countries which generated the largest volume of oceanborne liner cargo for the most recent calendar year in bilateral trade with the United States." 46 U.S.C. § 306 (b) (1) .

The Journal of Commerce's *Port Import Export Reporting Service* (PIERS) database was used to derive the Commission's list of top-twenty trading partners. The most recent complete calendar year for which data are available is 2014. The table on the next page lists the twenty foreign countries that generated the largest volume of oceanborne liner cargo in bilateral trade with the United States in 2014. The figures in the table represent each country's total U.S. liner imports and exports combined in thousands of loaded TEUs.

For calendar year 2014, there was a 3 percent year-to-year increase in bilateral trade with the United States' top-twenty liner trading partners. The top-twenty liner cargo trading partners has remained the same since 2009. For the second year in a row, several changes in ranking occurred among the top-twenty countries. India rose above Vietnam in the rankings to occupy 6th place, reflecting a year-to-year liner volume increase of over 12 percent. Belgium and Luxembourg also rose in the rankings to 9th place, trading places with Brazil which slipped to 10th place. Brazil was one of five countries that experienced lower liner cargo volumes (the others being Japan, Hong Kong, Malaysia and Honduras) . The lower volume of liner cargo trade with Malaysia and Honduras enabled Chile to climb above them, rising two places in the listing to 17th place. (Although Hong Kong reverted to Chinese control in July 1997, PIERS continues to report data separately for Hong Kong because it is a major transshipment center) .

Top Twenty U.S. Liner Cargo Trading Partners (CY 2014)

Rank	Country	TEUs (000)
1	China (PRC)	11,861
2	Japan	1,409
3	South Korea	1,329
4	Taiwan (ROC)	1,134
5	Germany	930
6	India	885
7	Vietnam	877
8	Hong Kong	697
9	Belgium & Luxembourg	622

For additional analytical, business and investment opportunities information, please contact Global Investment & Business Center, USA at (703) 370-8082. Fax: (703) 370-8083. E-mail: ibpusa3@gmail.com Global Business and Investment Info Databank - www.ibpus.com

10	Brazil	589
11	Indonesia	576
12	Italy	553
13	Thailand	514
14	Netherlands	500
15	United Kingdom	435
Rank	Country	TEUs (000)
16	Guatemala	410
17	Chile	361
18	Malaysia	342
19	Honduras	335
20	Australia	332

India, Belgium & Luxembourg, and Chile climbed up in the rankings while Vietnam, Brazil, Malaysia and Honduras slipped down the rankings.

Foreign Shipping Practices Act

The Commission has the authority to address restrictive foreign shipping practices under section 19 of the Merchant Marine Act of 1920 and the Foreign Shipping Practices Act of 1988. Section 19 empowers the Commission to make rules and regulations governing shipping in the foreign trade to adjust or meet conditions unfavorable to shipping. The FSPA directs the Commission to address adverse conditions that affect U.S. carriers in foreign trade and that do not exist for foreign carriers in the United States.

The Commission, both through Commission action and through its Office of the General Counsel (OGC) , informally pursued several matters involving potentially restrictive foreign practices. This included interpretations of existing legislation, foreign legislation and administrative law, and regulations of non-domestic carriers' terminal handling charges. No formal FSPA action by the Commission was necessary.

Controlled Carriers

A controlled carrier is an ocean common carrier that is, or whose operating assets are, owned or controlled directly or indirectly by a foreign government. The Shipping Act provides that no controlled carrier may maintain rates or charges in its tariffs or service contracts that are below a level that is just and reasonable, nor may any such carrier establish, maintain, or enforce unjust or unreasonable classifications, rules or regulations in those tariffs or service contracts. In addition, tariff rates, charges, classifications, rules, or regulations of a controlled carrier may not, without special permission of the Commission, become effective sooner than the 30th day after the date of publication. The Commission's staff monitors U.S. and foreign trade press and other information sources to identify controlled carriers and any unjust or unreasonable controlled carrier activity that might require Commission action. In fiscal year 2015, five controlled carriers operated in the U.S. trades:

1. American President Lines, Ltd. and APL Co., Pte. – Republic of Singapore

2. COSCO Container Lines Company, Ltd. - People's Republic of China

3. China Shipping Container Lines Co., Ltd. and China Shipping Container Lines (Hong Kong) Company, Ltd. - People's Republic of China

4. Hainan P.O. Shipping Co., Ltd. – People's Republic of China

5. United Arab Shipping Co. SAG – State of Qatar

Formal Investigations, Private Complaints and Litigation

Adjudicative proceedings before the Commission are commenced by the filing of a complaint, or by order of the Commission upon petition, or upon its own motion. Types of docketed proceedings include:

Private complaints: Any person may file a formal complaint alleging violations of specific sections of the Shipping Act found at 46 U.S.C. Chapter 411. Formal complaints are generally assigned to an Administrative Law Judge (ALJ) who issues an initial decision which is reviewed by the Commission.

Small claims complaints: For claims of $50,000 or less, an informal complaint may be filed. The complaint is handled by a settlement officer for resolution using informal procedures that do not tend to include discovery or motions practice.

Investigative proceedings: The Commission may investigate the activities of ocean common carriers, OTIs, MTOs, and other persons to ensure effective compliance with the statutes and regulations administered by the Commission. Formal orders of investigation and hearing are assigned to an ALJ for an initial decision and maybe reviewed by the Commission.

In FY 2015, 9 new private party complaints were filed and 1 new formal investigation was instituted. The Office of Administrative Law Judges (OALJ) issued 12 initial decisions, including 2 partial dismissals, 2 initial decisions on default, 5 initial decisions approving settlement, and 1 voluntary dismissal. The Commission issued 7 notices finalizing the ALJ's decisions in private complaint cases and 3 notices finalizing the ALJ's decisions in formal investigations. Two docket matters were adjudicated in the Commission's favor during the fiscal year in United States Courts of Appeals by the Office of General Counsel.

The following summarizes the results of docketed proceedings concluded during FY 2015 by the ALJs and the Commission.

FORMAL INVESTIGATIONS

Oceanic Bridge International, Inc. – Possible Violations of Section 10(a) (1) of the Shipping Act of 1984 [Docket No. 14-02]

On February 21, 2014, the Commission issued an Order of Investigation and Hearing to determine whether Oceanic Bridge violated section 10(a) (1) of the Shipping Act, 46 U.S.C. § 41102(a) , by knowingly and willfully obtaining ocean transportation at less than the rates and charges otherwise applicable by accessing services contracts on which it was not a signatory or named affiliate. Oceanic Bridge did not file an answer, respond to an order to show cause, or respond to BOE's motion for decision on default. On October 21, 2014, the ALJ issued an Initial Decision on Default finding that Oceanic Bridge violated section 10(a) (1) on 49 shipments and

For additional analytical, business and investment opportunities information, please contact Global Investment & Business Center, USA at (703) 370-8082. Fax: (703) 370-8083. E-mail: ibpusa3@gmail.com Global Business and Investment Info Databank - www.ibpus.com

assessing a civil penalty of $392,000. On November 21, 2014, the Commission issued a Notice Not to Review and the decision became administratively final.

Metro Freight Services, Inc. d/b/a Maritime Express Lines – Possible Violations of Section 19(e) (3) of the Shipping Act of 1984 and 46 C.F.R. Part 515, LLC, [Docket No. 14-13]

On September 29, 2014, the Commission issued an Order of Investigation and Hearing to determine whether respondent Metro Freight Services, Inc. d/b/a Maritime Express Lines (Metro Freight) , a licensed OTI, violated the Shipping Act, 46 U.S.C. § 40904(c) , by failing to notify the Commission promptly after the death of its qualifying individual ("QI") and failing to seek and obtain approval of a replacement QI and whether it violated the Act by receiving freight forwarder compensation from a common carrier for shipments in which Metro Freight had a direct or indirect beneficial interest. On February 19, 2015, the ALJ issued an Initial Decision approving the settlement agreement between the BOE and Metro Freight. On March 23, 2015, the Commission issued a Notice Not to Review and the decision became administratively final.

Huntington International, Inc., JC Horizon Ltd., and Judy Lee – Possible Violations of Sections 10(a) (1) and 19 of the Shipping Act of 1984 [Docket No. 14-05]

On June 4, 2014, the Commission issued an Order of Investigation and Hearing to determine: (1) whether Huntington International, previously licensed as an OTI violated provisions of the Shipping Act, 46 U.S.C. §§ 40901, 40902, 40904, § 41102(a) , and 46 C.F.R. Part 515, by continuing to operate as an OTI after its license had been revoked, by collecting freight forwarder compensation on shipments in which Judy Lee, an officer and director of the company, had a beneficial interest, and by sharing compensation with JC Horizon and Judy Lee; and (2) whether JC Horizon and Judy Lee violated 46 U.S.C. § 41102(a) by knowingly and willfully obtaining ocean transportation at less than the rates and charges that would otherwise apply by directing Huntington International to pay to Respondents monies derived from freight forwarder compensation paid by ocean common carriers that transported Respondent JC Horizon's shipments. On July 7, 2014, Respondents Judy Lee and JC Horizon filed an Answer denying the allegations, asserting affirmative defenses, and filing a counterclaim under the Equal Access to Justice Act. Respondent Huntington International did not enter an appearance in this proceeding. On September 10, 2014, the ALJ issued an Initial Decision granting BOE's motion to dismiss claims against Huntington International with prejudice and approving a settlement agreement with a $300,000 monetary payment from the remaining respondents. On October 15, 2014 the Commission issued a Notice Not to Review and the decision became administratively final.

Private Complaints

Yakov Kobel and Victor Berkovich v. Hapag-Lloyd A.G., HapagLloyd America, Inc., Limco Logistics, Inc., and International TLC, Inc. [Docket No. 10-06]

This proceeding was initiated by a complaint filed with the Commission on July 6, 2010, alleging that Respondents violated various sections of the Shipping Act. After discovery, an evidentiary hearing, and briefing, on February 14, 2012, an Initial Decision was issued dismissing the complaint. On July 12, 2013, the Commission issued an Order Vacating Initial Decision In Part and Remanding for Further Proceedings. On July 30, 2014, the ALJ issued an Initial Decision on remand finding that the Respondents violated 46 U.S.C. § 41102(c) of the Shipping Act, and ordering that the Respondents be jointly and severally liable to the Complainants for a reparation award of $126,072. On August 12, 2014, the Commission served a notice that it would review the decision. Exceptions to the ALJ's decision were filed on September 22, 2014. On May 26, 2015, the Commission entered an order imposing liability on several respondents, including Limco

For additional analytical, business and investment opportunities information, please contact Global Investment & Business Center, USA at (703) 370-8082. Fax: (703) 370-8083. E-mail: ibpusa3@gmail.com Global Business and Investment Info Databank - www.ibpus.com

Logistics, Inc., and International TLC, Inc. Limco requested that the Commission reconsider its decision. At the end of the fiscal year, the matter was pending before the Commission.

Maher Terminals, LLC v. The Port Authority of New York and New Jersey [Docket No. 12 02]

On March 30, 2012, Maher Terminals, LLC, filed a complaint alleging that the Port Authority of New York and New Jersey ("PANYNJ") violated the Shipping Act, 46 U.S.C. §§ 41102(c) , 41106(2) , 41106(3) , and 41106(1) , because PANYNJ: (a) has and continues to fail to establish, observe, and enforce just and reasonable regulations and practices relating to or connected with receiving, handling, storing or delivering property; (b) gave and continues to give an undue or unreasonable prejudice or disadvantage with respect to Maher and gave and continues to give an undue or unreasonable preference or advantage with respect to Maersk, APM, MSC, PNCT, NYCT, and Global, and other marine container terminal operators and ocean carriers; (c) has and continues to unreasonably refuse to deal or negotiate with Maher; and (d) has and continues to agree with another marine terminal operator or common carrier to boycott and/or unreasonably discriminate in the provision of terminal services to a common carrier. PANYNJ filed a motion to dismiss arguing that the proceeding should be dismissed for a number of reasons, including failure to plead a plausible violation of the Shipping Act. On January 30, 2015, the ALJ issued an Initial Decision granting the motion to dismiss, which dismissed all pending claims in the proceeding. Maher filed exceptions to the Initial Decision and the proceeding is pending before the Commission.

Streak Products, Inc., and SYX Distribution, Inc. v. UTi, United States, Inc. [Docket No. 13-04]

On April 12, 2013, Streak, a shipper, filed a complaint alleging that UTi violated three sections of the Shipping Act: (1) 46 U.S.C. § 41104(2) by charging Streak rates greater than those stated in its published tariff; (2) 46 U.S.C. § 41104(4) by charging Streak rates greater than those it charged other shippers; and (3) 46 U.S.C. § 40501 by failing to keep open to public inspection in its tariff system tariffs showing all its rates, charges, classifications, rules, and practices between all points or ports on its own route and any through transportation route that has been established. Leave was granted to amend the Complaint to include Streak's affiliate SYX Distribution. On September 10, 2014, the ALJ entered an Initial Decision approving the parties' Confidential Settlement Agreement and General Release. On October 15, 2014 the Commission issued a Notice Not to Review and the ALJ's decision became administratively final.

Global Link Logistics, Inc. v. Hapag-Lloyd AG [Docket No. 13-07]

On September 10, 2013, Global Link, an NVOCC, filed a Complaint alleging that Hapag Lloyd, a VOCC, violated the Shipping Act, 46 U.S.C. §§ 41102(c) , 41104(3) , and 41104(10) when it refused to renegotiate rates established by a service contract during the life of the contract. Hapag Lloyd moved to dismiss the Complaint for failure to state a claim. On April 17, 2014, the ALJ issued an Initial Decision granting the motion to dismiss, holding that the Complaint failed to state a claim of violation of the Act. On May 27, 2014, Global Link filed exceptions to the Initial Decision. On April 14, 2015 the Commission issued an Order approving a settlement agreement between the parties and the proceeding was dismissed.

Edaf Antillas, Inc. v. Crowley Caribbean Logistics, LLC; IFS International Forwarding, S.L.; and IFS Neutral Maritime Services [Docket No. 14-04]

For additional analytical, business and investment opportunities information, please contact Global Investment & Business Center, USA at (703) 370-8082. Fax: (703) 370-8083. E-mail: ibpusa3@gmail.com Global Business and Investment Info Databank - www.ibpus.com

On April 28, 2014, Edaf Antillas filed a complaint with the Commission alleging that Respondents violated the Shipping Act by permitting non-compliant cargo to be placed in a container with compliant cargo causing delay of Edaf Antillas's shipment and by failing to correct the problem in a timely manner after the container arrived in Puerto Rico. On November 6, 2014, the ALJ granted a motion to dismiss in part, but found that the Complaint stated a claim that Respondents failed to establish, observe, and enforce just and reasonable regulations and practices relating to or connected with receiving, handling, storing, or delivering property in violation of 46 U.S.C. § 41102(c) . On December 8, 2014, the Commission issued a Notice Not to Review the dismissal.

Complainant Edaf Antillas failed to file its brief on the merits, and the ALJ issued an order to show cause to which Edaf Antillas did not respond. On April 15, 2015, the ALJ issued an Initial Decision dismissing the proceeding for failure to prosecute. The Initial Decision also addressed the applicability of a new provision in the Shipping Act permitting an award of attorney fees to a prevailing party. On May 18, 2015, the Commission issued a Notice Not to Review the dismissal. Prevailing Respondents filed petitions for attorney fees to be decided by the ALJ pursuant to 46 C.F.R. § 502.254.

Santa Fe Discount Cruise Parking, Inc., d/b/a EZ Cruise Parking, Lighthouse Parking, Inc., and Sylvia Robledo d/b/a 81st Dolphin Parking v. The Board of Trustees of the Galveston Wharves and the Galveston Port Facilities Corporation [Docket No. 14-06]

Respondents operate the cruise terminal at the Port of Galveston. Complainants operate parking facilities near the Port where they provide parking for passengers who embark on cruises from the cruise terminal. As part of their service, Complainants provide transportation to the Port. On June 16, 2014, Complainants filed a complaint alleging that Respondents' tariff imposing charges on Complainants' shuttles transporting passengers to and from the terminal violated three sections of the Shipping Act. On November 21, 2014, the ALJ granted Respondents' motion to dismiss claims under two sections of the Act, but denied dismissal of claims under 46 U.S.C. § 41106(2) , finding that the Complaint stated a claim that Respondents gave an undue or unreasonable preference or advantage or imposed an undue or unreasonable prejudice or disadvantage with respect to Complainants. On December 23, 2014, the Commission issued a Notice Not to Review the partial dismissals and the decision became administratively final. At the close of FY 2015, the ALJ's Initial Decision on the remaining claim was pending.

Econocaribe Consolidators, Inc. v. Amoy International, LLC, [Docket No. 14-10]

On August 11, 2014, Econocaribe Consolidators, Inc. filed a complaint alleging that Respondent Amoy International, LLC violated numerous sections of the Shipping Act and Commission regulations in connection with shipment of auto parts detained by Chinese customs. On September 9, 2014, Amoy filed its Answer denying the allegations. The parties engaged in discovery, filed numerous motions, and briefed the merits of the proceeding. The parties eventually reached a settlement agreement that they submitted for approval. On September 2, 2015, the ALJ issued an Initial Decision Approving Joint Settlement and Granting Motion to Dismiss. The time to file exceptions or for the Commission to review to the decision had not expired at the close of FY 2015.

Mark Barr v. Ocean Trade Lines, Inc. [Docket No. 14-14]

On November 13, 2014, Mark Barr filed a complaint alleging that Ocean Trade Lines violated the Shipping Act, 46 U.S.C. §§ 41102(c) , 41104(2) , 41104(3) , and 41104(4) , by failing to publish a tariff and to adhere to tariff publishing requirements and by failing to adhere to just, reasonable,

For additional analytical, business and investment opportunities information, please contact Global Investment & Business Center, USA at (703) 370-8082. Fax: (703) 370-8083. E-mail: ibpusa3@gmail.com Global Business and Investment Info Databank - www.ibpus.com

and non-discriminatory practices regarding its cancellation and refund policies with respect to international ocean transport of Complainant's yacht. On November 19, 2014, the Commission's BOE filed a motion seeking leave to intervene. On February 19, 2015, the ALJ issued an Initial Decision approving the settlement agreement. On March 23, 2015, the Commission issued a Notice Not to Review and the decision became administratively final.

Baltic Auto Shipping, Inc. v. Michael Hitrinov a/k/a Michael Khitrinov and Empire Unite Lines Co., Inc. [Docket No. 14-16]

On November 28, 2014, Baltic filed a complaint alleging that on several thousand shipments between November 2007 and January 2012, Empire, an NVOCC, violated several sections of the Shipping Act, 46 U.S.C. §§ 41102, 41104, 40501, and 46 C.F.R. Part 515, by charging rates not set forth in a tariff, charging Baltic rates greater than rates charged other shippers, and by failing to provide Baltic with shipping documents. Baltic sought a reparation award. All shipments began and almost all were delivered more than three years before Baltic filed its complaint. Empire moved for a summary decision dismissing the claim for a reparation award, arguing that the claim was barred by the statute of limitations. On September 15, 2015, the ALJ held that based on the material facts not in dispute, Baltic's claims accrued more than three years before Baltic filed the complaint and were barred. It was also determined that no other relief was warranted, and the complaint was dismissed. The time to file exceptions to the decision had not expired at the close of FY 2015.

Okoye Christian Ogochukwu v. Emeka Onyechi d/b/a Donem International, LLC, [Docket No. 1945(F)]

Complainant alleged violations of the Shipping Act, 46 U.S.C. 41102(c) , related to shipment of nine pieces of medical equipment to Nigeria. Respondent received the equipment in Africa, but would not release it to Complainant's consignee until storage fees were paid. On April 8, 2015, the ALJ issued an initial decision approving a settlement between the parties. On May 11, 2015, the Commission issued a Notice Not to Review the dismissal and the decision became administratively final.

Smartstone Private Limited v. General Noli USA, Inc. and Savino Del Bene Freight Forwarders (India) PVT LTD [Docket No. 1946(F)]

On August 5, 2014, Smartstone Private Limited filed an informal complaint against General Noli USA, Inc. and Savino Del Bene Freight Forwarders (India) Pvt. Ltd. The complaint alleged that Respondents violated the Shipping Act, 46 U.S.C. §§ 41102(c) , and 41106(2) . Smartstone asserted that the Respondents released a shipment of granite slabs shipped from Bangalore, India, to Houston, Texas, without obtaining the original bill of lading. In their Answer, Respondents denied the allegations in the complaint and raised 14 affirmative defenses. On July 16, 2015, a joint motion seeking approval of a settlement agreement, dismissal of the complaint, a stay of the briefing schedule, and a confidential settlement agreement were filed by the parties. On July 22, 2015, an Initial Decision Approving Proposed Settlement Agreement was issued. On August 24, 2015, the Commission issued a Notice Not to Review and the decision became administratively final.

ShemiTrans, LLC v. Rose Containerline, Inc. [Docket No. 1950(F)]

On May 18, 2015, ShemiTrans filed a small claims complaint alleging violation of the Shipping Act, 46 U.S.C. § 41102(c) . Rose Containerline filed an objection to small claims adjudication. ShemiTrans then filed a request to dismiss the proceeding voluntarily. The Chief

For additional analytical, business and investment opportunities information, please contact Global Investment & Business Center, USA at (703) 370-8082. Fax: (703) 370-8083. E-mail: ibpusa3@gmail.com Global Business and Investment Info Databank - www.ibpus.com

Judge assigned the proceeding to an ALJ for formal adjudication. On July 9, 2015, the ALJ granted the request for voluntary dismissal. On August 11, 2015, the Commission issued a Notice Not to Review and the decision became administratively final.

Litigation

The following docket matters were litigated during the fiscal year in United States Courts of Appeals by the OGC on behalf of the Commission.

Chief Cargo Services, Inc. v. Federal Maritime Commission, [Docket No. 10-08], United States Court of Appeals for the Second Circuit

On November 1, 2013, Chief Cargo Services, Inc., filed a petition for review of the Commission's Order in FMC Docket 10-08, Bimsha International v. Chief Cargo Services, Inc. & Kaiser Apparel, Inc., upholding the ALJ's initial decision holding that by the release of three shipping containers, without requiring presentation of the original bills of lading, Chief Cargo failed to fulfill its obligations as an NVOCC, thereby violating section 10(d) (1) of the Shipping Act, 46 U.S.C. § 41102(c) . The ALJ also ordered Chief Cargo to "cease and desist releasing cargo without requiring presentation of an original bill of lading." On April 24, 2014, Chief Cargo filed its Joint Appendix, Brief, and Special Appendix. Chief Cargo questioned the jurisdiction of the Commission to hear and adjudicate Bimsha's claim of violations of the Shipping Act; argued that the Commission improperly found violations of the Shipping Act; and argued that the Commission improperly issued a cease and desist order. On June 20, 2014, the Commission and the United States filed a joint brief. Oral Argument was held on September 30, 2014, and the Second Circuit handed down an opinion affirming the Commission, and denying the petition on October 2, 2015.

The Auction Block Co. v. City of Homer, [Docket No. 12-03], United States Court of Appeals for Ninth Circuit

On April 2, 2012, Complainants, the Auction Block Company (Auction Block) and Harbor Leasing, LLC (Harbor Leasing) filed a complaint with the Commission against Respondents, The City of Homer (City) and the Port of Homer (Port) , alleging violations of the Shipping Act, 46 U.S.C. §§ 40101 et seq. Complainants alleged that the City and Port were MTOs that violated the Shipping Act through unreasonable prejudice or preference, refusal to deal, and unfair practices, 46 U.S.C. §§ 41106(2) -(3) , 41102(c) . In a May 20, 2013 Initial Decision, the ALJ dismissed all of Complainants' claims against Respondents with prejudice, finding that the Commission lacked jurisdiction. On August 12, 2014, the Commission upheld the Initial Decision of the ALJ dismissing Auction Block's complaint for lack of jurisdiction. On August 22, 2014 the Auction Block Company filed a Petition for Review of the Commission Order with the United States Court of Appeals for the Ninth Circuit. The Ninth Circuit heard oral argument in May 2015, and issued a decision affirming the Commission and denying the petition three weeks later.

Kawasaki Kisen Kaisha, Ltd. v. The Port Authority of New York and New Jersey [Docket No. 11-12], United States Court of Appeals for the District of Columbia Circuit

On August 5, 2011, nine vessel-operating common carriers filed a complaint alleging that the Port Authority of New York and New Jersey (PANYNJ) violated the Shipping Act by imposing a cargo facility charge. Eight complainants withdrew from the proceeding, leaving only Kawasaki Kisen Kaisha, Ltd. ("K" Line) . On February 5, 2014, the ALJ dismissed the Complaint because "K" Line willfully failed to provide discovery. On March 31, 2014, "K" Line filed exceptions to the dismissal, and the Commission entered an order affirming the dismissal on November 20, 2014. "K" Line filed a Petition for Review in the

For additional analytical, business and investment opportunities information,
please contact Global Investment & Business Center, USA
at (703) 370-8082. Fax: (703) 370-8083. E-mail: ibpusa3@gmail.com
Global Business and Investment Info Databank - www.ibpus.com

United States Court of Appeals for the District of Columbia Circuit. With the briefing deadline pending, "K" Line withdrew the petition.

Lisa Anne Cornell and G. Ware Cornell, Jr. v. Princess Cruise Lines, Ltd. (Corp) , Carnival plc, and Carnival Corporation, [Docket No. 13-02], United States Court of Appeals for the District of Columbia Circuit

On January 30, 2013, complainants filed a complaint alleging that Respondent cruise ship lines refused to permit them to sail on their cruise ships in violation of section 10(b) (10) of the Act, 46 U.S.C. § 41104(10) . The controversy stemmed from a dispute over a refund of money paid to a fine arts auction company that operates on the cruise ships after Lisa Cornell cancelled a purchase of works of art. Complainants had been involved in litigation for several years in Florida courts with the auction company, an affiliate of the cruise lines. Respondents filed a motion to dismiss or alternatively for summary judgment. On July 23, 2013, the ALJ issued a summary Initial Decision dismissing most claims, but found that respondent Princess violated section 10(b) (10) and entered a cease and desist order. The ALJ found that Complainants did not meet their burden of offering evidence that they had suffered actual injury as a result of the violation. On August 14, 2013, both parties filed exceptions to the decision. On August 28, 2014, the Commission issued an Order reversing in part, affirming in part, and vacating in part the Initial Decision and dismissing the complaint with prejudice on the ground that Princess Cruise Lines and other respondents did not violate the Shipping Act. The Complainants filed a Petition for Review in the D.C. Circuit, and the parties filed briefs. Oral argument was scheduled for October 2, 2015. At the end of the fiscal year, the matter was pending before the D.C. Circuit.

Maher Terminals, Inc. v. The Port Authority of New York and New Jersey [Docket No. 08-03], United States Court of Appeals for the District of Columbia Circuit

Maher leases land and facilities at the Elizabeth Port Authority Marine Terminal from the Port Authority of New York and New Jersey (PANYNJ) for use as a marine terminal. On June 3, 2008, Maher filed a complaint alleging that PANYNJ violated the Shipping Act, 46 U.S.C. §§ 41106(2) and (3) and 41102(c) , because PANYNJ: (a) gave and continues to give an undue or unreasonable prejudice or disadvantage with respect to Maher as compared to APM Terminals North America, Inc. (APM) , another marine terminal operator; (b) gave and continues to give an undue or unreasonable preference or advantage with respect to APM; (c) continues unreasonably to refuse to deal or negotiate with Maher; and (d) continues to fail to establish, observe, and enforce just and reasonable regulations and practices relating to or connected with receiving, handling, storing, or delivering property. In January 2013, the Commission granted partial summary judgment to the Port, finding that some of Maher's requested relief was barred by the Commission's statute of limitations. Maher appealed this decision to the United States Court of Appeals for the D.C. Circuit. The Commission's OGC filed a motion to dismiss, and the D.C. Circuit dismissed the appeal in June 2013. The Commission subsequently denied Maher's motion for reconsideration of the summary judgment order, and again successfully defended its decision before the D.C. Circuit, which dismissed Maher's second appeal for lack of jurisdiction in July 2014, by granting the Commission's motion to dismiss. While the summary judgment issue was pending on appeal, the ALJ rejected Maher's claims on the merits in an Initial Decision dated April 25, 2014 determining that PANYNJ did not violate the Act and dismissed Maher's claims. The Commission issued a decision affirming the ALJ December 17, 2014. The claimants filed a Petition for Review in the D.C. Circuit in February 2015. The parties filed briefs, and at the end of the fiscal year, the matter was still pending before the D.C. Circuit.

Procedural Rule Updates

The Commission updated several of its procedural rules this year concerning proceeding and information requests at the Commission.

Dismissals of Actions, Final Rule, Docket No. 14-12 (79 FR 76901)

The Commission amended its rules governing dismissals of actions by complainants, by order of the presiding officer, and by respondents when complainant fails to prosecute to reflect the Commission's intent to adhere to its long-standing policy of reviewing settlements by adding language to clarify that when a voluntary dismissal is based on a settlement agreement, the agreement must be submitted for approval by the Commission.

Service of Private Party Complaints and Documents Containing Confidential Materials, Direct Final Rule, Docket No. 15-01 (80 FR 14318)

The Commission amended its rules to clarify instructions to parties in proceedings concerning service of documents and filing of confidential documents.

Access to Commission Information and Records; Freedom of Information Act, Direct Final Rule, Docket No. 15-05 (80 FR 52638)

The Commission amended its regulations governing access to Commission information and records and its regulations implementing the Freedom of Information Act to update and revise procedures for processing FOIA requests, to modify the criteria for a FOIA request to qualify for expedited processing, and to extend the administrative appeal deadline.

Time and Service in Adjudicatory Proceedings, Direct Final Rule, Docket No. 15-09 (80 FR 57305)

The Commission amended its rules concerning time and service in adjudicative proceedings to improve consistency across various processes and increase efficiency for parties to proceedings.

Attorneys Fees, Notice of Proposed Rulemaking, Docket No. 15-06 (80 FR 38153)

The Commission proposed to amend its rules governing the award of attorney fees in Shipping Act complaint proceedings, and its regulations related to Commissioner terms and vacancies. The propose changes would implement amendments made by the Howard Coble Coast Guard and Maritime Transportation Act of 2014.

For additional analytical, business and investment opportunities information, please contact Global Investment & Business Center, USA at (703) 370-8082. Fax: (703) 370-8083. E-mail: ibpusa3@gmail.com Global Business and Investment Info Databank - www.ibpus.com

FEDERAL MARITIME COMMISSION STRATEGIC PLAN FISCAL YEARS 2014-2018

This 2014-2018 Strategic Plan. replaces and updated the 2010-2015 Strategic Plan. OMB is requiring all federal agencies to prepare strategic plans for the 2014-2018 time period in an effort to coordinate planning across the federal government. This plan retains previous strategic goals one and two, as well as a section on the Administrative Strategies in support of Agency Objectives. This latter section was established for administrative support functions such as human resources, information technology and financial management. Each of these important functions is subject to its own stringent planning and measuring regimes pursuant to various laws and executive mandates. Those related plans support this strategic plan and are referenced and described herein. This plan sets goals and objectives for each fiscal year through 2018 and contains targets and measures linked to objectives via strategies. It should be noted that for the most part the target measures for 2013 and the out years are below the actual 2012 performance. This is for two reasons. The first is that the 2012 actuals were markedly higher than the prior years' thus belying the trend. Secondly, the trend forecasts of achievable targets were lowered to account for anticipated reductions in staff resources due to fiscal austerity. These objectives, strategies, targets, and measures drive the agency's budgetary process. This strategic plan conforms with the spirit and letter of the *GPRA Modernization Act of 2010*; OMB Circular A-11 *Preparation of Submission of Strategic Plans, and Annual Program Performance Reports*; and Executive Order 13450 – *Improving Government Program Performance.*

SUMMARY OF STRATEGIC GOALS, OBJECTIVES, AND PERFORMANCE MEASURES

STRATEGIC GOAL 1: Maintain an efficient and competitive international ocean transportation system.

OBJECTIVE 1: Enhance efficiency in the trades through the use of asset sharing authority under the Shipping Act of 1984.

Performance Measure: Percentage share of U.S. containerized cargo moving on other agreement parties' vessels in major U.S. trades.	2012 Actual	2013 Target	2014 Target	2015 Target	2016 Target	2017 Target	2018 Target
N/A 1	39%	39.5%	40%	40.5%	41%	41.5%	

STRATEGIC GOAL 2: Protect the public from unlawful, unfair and deceptive ocean transportation practices and resolve shipping disputes.

OBJECTIVE 1: Identify and take action to end unlawful, unfair and deceptive practices.

Performance Measure: Percentage of enforcement actions taken under the Shipping of 1984 Act success-fully resolved through favorable judgment, settlement, issuance of default judgment, or compliance letter or notice.	2012 Actual	2013 Target	2014 Target	2015 Target	2016 Target	2017 Target	2018 Target
	77.5%	76.5%	77%	77.5%	77.5%	77.5%	88%

For additional analytical, business and investment opportunities information, please contact Global Investment & Business Center, USA at (703) 370-8082. Fax: (703) 370-8083. E-mail: ibpusa3@gmail.com Global Business and Investment Info Databank - www.ibpus.com

OBJECTIVE 2: Prevent public harm through licensing and financial responsibility requirements.

Performance Measure: Percentage of decisions on completed OTI license applications rendered within 60 calendar days of receipt, facilitating lawful operation of OTIs with the appropriate character and experience.	2012 Actual	2013 Target	2014 Target	2015 Target	2016 Target	2017 Target	2018 Target
	75%	75%	75%	75%	75%	75%	90.2%
Performance Measure: Percentage of cruise line operators examined during the year that have the full financial coverage required by regulation to protect against loss from non-performance or casualty.	2012 Actual	2013 Target	2014 Target	2015 Target	2016 Target	2017 Target	2018 Target
	93%	94%	95%	95%	95%	95%	100%

OBJECTIVE 3: Enhance public awareness of agency resources, remedies and regulatory requirements through education and outreach.

Performance Measure: Percentage of key Commission issuances, orders and reports are available through the Commission's website within 5 working days of receipt.	2012 Actual	2013 Target	2014 Target	2015 Target	2016 Target	2017 Target	2018 Target
	76%	76%	78%	80%	82%	84%	79%

OBJECTIVE 4: Impartially resolve international shipping disputes through alternative dispute resolution and adjudication.

Performance Measure: Number of cases opened and closed each fiscal year using ombuds and ADR services assisting consumers to recover goods or funds.	2012 Actual	2013 Target	2014 Target	2015 Target	2016 Target	2017 Target	2018 Target
893	800	825	825	825	850	850	
Performance Measure: Percentage of formal complaints or Commission initiated orders of investigation completed within two years of filing or Commission initiation.	2012 Actual	2013 Target	2014 Target	2015 Target	2016 Target	2017 Target	2018 Target
	56%	58%	58%	60%	62%	64%	73%

For additional analytical, business and investment opportunities information, please contact Global Investment & Business Center, USA at (703) 370-8082. Fax: (703) 370-8083. E-mail: ibpusa3@gmail.com Global Business and Investment Info Databank - www.ibpus.com

FMC STRATEGIC PLAN FISCAL YEARS 2014-2018

STRATEGIC GOAL 1 - MAINTAIN AN EFFICIENT AND COMPETITIVE INTERNATIONAL OCEAN TRANSPORTATION SYSTEM.

The Federal Maritime Commission (FMC) or (Commission) is responsible for the regulation of oceanborne transportation in the foreign commerce of the United States pursuant to the provisions of the Shipping Act of 1984 (Shipping Act) . A stated policy objective of the Shipping Act is "to promote the growth and development of United States exports through competitive and efficient ocean transportation and by placing a greater reliance on the marketplace." The Commission's oversight of carrier and terminal operator antitrust immunity, as part of a non-discriminatory regulatory process, works to provide an efficient and economic transportation system in the ocean commerce of the United States. In addition, the Commission addresses unfavorable conditions affecting U.S. carriers in U.S. oceanborne trades when such conditions do not exist for foreign carriers.

Following the global economic downturn and during this time of recovery, the Commission's oversight is of key importance. Efficiency and competition in the transportation system are essential to the re-growth of trade and the creation of jobs.

OBJECTIVE 1: ENHANCE EFFICIENCY IN THE TRADES THROUGH THE USE OF ASSET SHARING AUTHORITY UNDER THE SHIPPING ACT OF 1984.

The agency will achieve this objective through a number of strategies (as indicated below) aimed at using its statutory authority in a fair and expeditious manner to readily permit use of asset sharing agreements.

The FMC is also charged with protecting the shipping public, and ultimately American exporters and consumers, from possible abuse of the limited antitrust immunity granted by Congress to international liner carriers and domestic marine terminal operators under the Shipping Act. In addition, the FMC is responsible, under the Foreign Shipping Practices Act of 1988, for investigating whether laws, rules, regulations or practices of foreign governments, or the practices of foreign carriers result in the existence of unfavorable conditions in U.S. trades.

The Shipping Act requires that vessel operating common carriers (VOCCs) and marine terminal operators (MTOs) that wish to establish agreements that would benefit from antitrust immunity file copies of their agreements with the FMC. FMC staff review these proposed agreements when they are initially filed, and before they take effect. The FMC allows agreements to proceed when they do not cause competitive harm. The FMC is authorized, pursuant to section 6(g) of the Shipping Act, to seek appropriate injunction relief against any agreement which is likely to result in a reduction in competition of the sort that could be expected to unreasonably raise transportation costs or reduce transportation service.

The Shipping Act and implementing regulations also authorize the FMC to require that agreement parties (a) provide accompanying information needed to assess certain categories of agreements upon request; (b) file certain standard types of reports —including quarterly economic data and/or minutes of meetings held by the agreement parties — depending on the authorities sought in the agreement; and (c) submit special informational reports, if the FMC requires them, once the agreement comes into effect. These reporting requirements, and the economic data and information about agreement activities they provide, allow the FMC to initially evaluate, and

For additional analytical, business and investment opportunities information, please contact Global Investment & Business Center, USA at (703) 370-8082. Fax: (703) 370-8083. E-mail: ibpusa3@gmail.com Global Business and Investment Info Databank - www.ibpus.com

continue to monitor on an on-going basis, the conduct of the parties to VOCC and MTO agreements with limited antitrust immunity.

In recent years, the FMC has seen an increase in operational VOCC and MTO agreements, many of which allow cooperation to improve efficiency, allow sustainable growth, or respond to new or imminent environmental regulations. The FMC gives consideration to likely efficiency, sustainability, and environmental benefits when evaluating their net impact on competition, transportation cost, and transportation service.

Under the Foreign Shipping Practices Act of 1988 (FSPA) , the Commission can address adverse conditions affecting U.S. carriers in the U.S. oceanborne trades, when such conditions do not exist for foreign carriers or others providing maritime or maritime-related services in the U.S. Section 9 of the Shipping Act also charges the Commission with regulating the rates, charges, and rules of foreign government-owned or -controlled carriers to ensure that they are just and reasonable.

1. Strategies

The Commission's performance measure tracking the use of asset sharing agreements will be achieved through the following strategies. These strategies cover a broad range of Commission activities, all using agency resources to foster the purposes of the Shipping Act, particularly with regard to the asset sharing agreements under this objective:

- Review initial agreements and amendments, including any additional information requested by the FMC, to determine the likelihood that the agreement parties could engage in substantially anti-competitive conduct with respect to transportation costs or services.

- Review, on a regular, on-going basis, the data and information provided in standard reports and special reporting measures to assess the existence or likelihood of substantially anti-competitive conduct or unfavorable trade conditions.

- Initiate meetings with representatives of the FMC's various stakeholder industries to help determine whether anti-competitive behavior or unfavorable trade conditions exist in U.S. trades.

- Conduct research studies on current competition issues with respect to U.S. trades.

- Actively monitor for and record the presence of all foreign controlled carriers in U.S. trades, and regularly review their pricing practices.

- Obtain information via inquiries and/or complaints about conduct or conditions that impede the efficient movement of cargo.

- Ensure competitive conditions in the U.S. foreign oceanborne trades by working with agreement parties on an informal basis to negotiate changes in agreements that raise competitive concerns.

- Preserve competition and efficiency in ocean transportation by seeking appropriate injunctive relief under section 6 of the Shipping Act for agreements likely, by a reduction in competition, to produce an unreasonable reduction in transportation service or an unreasonable increase in transportation cost.

• Assess, acknowledge and promote environmentally sustainable shipping practices and environmentally protective agreement activities.

• Address disruptions in the ocean transportation marketplace by investigating carrier and marine terminal operator violations of the Shipping Act.

• Take action under the FSPA to address adverse conditions affecting U.S. carriers in the U.S. oceanborne trades, when such conditions do not exist for foreign carriers or others providing maritime or maritime-related services in the U.S.

• Make rules and regulations, pursuant to the 1920 Act, affecting shipping in the foreign trade not in conflict with law in order to adjust or meet general or special conditions unfavorable to shipping in the foreign trade.

• Ensure timely action on formal proceedings undertaken to protect competition.

• Maintain an electronic library, accessible from the FMC's website, of agreement documents so as to allow interested parties to easily search for and download those documents.

2. Five-Year Performance Measure

• Percentage share of U.S. containerized cargo moving on other agreement parties' vessels in major U.S. trades.

STRATEGIC GOAL 2 – Protect the public from unlawful, unfair and deceptive ocean transportation practices and resolve shipping disputes.

The FMC has jurisdiction over activities of ocean carriers and marine terminal operators in a variety of their commercial activities in international ocean commerce. The FMC has a wide variety of responsibilities in protecting the shipping public from financial harm.

Those responsibilities include the licensing of ocean transportation intermediaries that serve U.S. trades; assisting the public in the resolution of informal complaints related to the shipment of goods or to passenger vessel cruises; the identification and prosecution of unreasonable or unjust practices by carrier or marine terminals; and the investigation and satisfaction of formal complaints alleging violation of the Shipping Act. To carry out its broad mission, the FMC uses various means including monitoring, investigation, education, enforcement, and ombuds services.

The Commission, and its regional area representatives, also have a role in the education of the public and of industry groups involved in U.S. international trade with respect to their rights and/or responsibilities under the Shipping Act – including informing them of available Commission resources that might be of use to them.

OBJECTIVE 1: IDENTIFY AND TAKE ACTION TO END UNLAWFUL, UNFAIR AND DECEPTIVE PRACTICES.

For additional analytical, business and investment opportunities information, please contact Global Investment & Business Center, USA at (703) 370-8082. Fax: (703) 370-8083. E-mail: ibpusa3@gmail.com Global Business and Investment Info Databank - www.ibpus.com

This objective will be met through agency strategies including gathering intelligence, monitoring OTI activity, audits, effective prosecution and dealing with complaints on violations.

The FMC is responsible for ensuring that individual carriers and marine terminal operators, as well as those permitted by agreement to act in concert, treat shippers and other members of the shipping public fairly by not engaging in prohibited acts set out in the Shipping Act. In the effort to identify such practices, the FMC maintains a visible presence amongst regulated entities, collects intelligence in a variety of ways and exchanges intelligence with other regulatory and law enforcement agencies.

In order to ensure compliance with laws and regulations under the jurisdiction of the FMC, various formal and informal actions may be taken by the Commission. Formal investigations are initiated when violations are discovered, though often the Commission enters into settlement agreements ending violative activities.

1. Strategies

The following strategies are specifically aimed at achieving the five year performance measure of successfully resolving enforcement actions through various means.

- Gather intelligence through visible and accessible presence in the regulated community in order to identify unlicensed OTIs and other violations.

- Monitor advertising in print, television, radio and online to identify illegal practices.

- Gather information related to potential unlicensed OTIs.

- Receive and respond to complaints regarding egregious violations and practices.

- Identify subjects who offer, advertise or provide passage on vessels having berths or staterooms to accommodate 50 or more passengers and have not met FMC financial requirements.

- Audit ocean carriers and OTIs based upon information received and on a random basis.

- Exchange information and liaise with other federal, state and local investigative and regulatory agencies and bureaus.

- Review tariffs for accessibility and accuracy.

- Investigate allegations of unlawful, unfair and deceptive practices.

- Efficiently prosecute alleged violations of the Shipping Act.

- Reach voluntary agreement with alleged violators to cease unlawful, unfair and deceptive practices.

- Respond to inquiries regarding complaint history of transportation providers and advise consumer of means to protect themselves.

For additional analytical, business and investment opportunities information, please contact Global Investment & Business Center, USA at (703) 370-8082. Fax: (703) 370-8083. E-mail: ibpusa3@gmail.com Global Business and Investment Info Databank - www.ibpus.com

2. Five-Year Performance Measures

- Percentage of enforcement actions taken under the Shipping Act successfully resolved through favorable judgment, settlement, issuance of default judgment, or compliance letter or notice.

OBJECTIVE 2: PREVENT PUBLIC HARM THROUGH LICENSING AND FINANCIAL RESPONSIBILITY REQUIREMENTS.

To prevent public harm the Commission has developed the following four strategies: OTI licensing, issuing PVO certificates, monitoring PVO unearned passenger revenue and updating bond and coverage amounts.

The FMC licenses and regulates ocean transportation intermediaries (OTIs) , including ocean freight forwarders and NVOCCs, and ensures that OTIs have sufficient financial responsibility. As well, the FMC issues certificates to owners and operators of passenger vessels (PVOs) that have evidenced financial responsibility to satisfy liability incurred for nonperformance of voyages and for death or injury to passengers and other persons.

1. Strategies

The following strategies support the Commission's five year performance measures of tracking the expeditious review of OTI licensing applications and assuring cruise line operator compliance with FMC financial responsibility requirements.

- License OTIs with the requisite character, experience and financial responsibility.

- Issue PVO certificates to cruise line operators that have met regulatory requirements for proof of financial responsibility.

- Monitor PVO unearned passenger revenue (UPR) reports and conduct on-site review of PVOs' UPR receipts.

- Review and update OTI bonds and coverage amount.

2. Five-Year Performance Measures

- Percentage of decisions on completed OTI license applications rendered within 60 calendar days, facilitating lawful operation of OTIs with the appropriate character and experience requirements.

- Percentage of cruise line operators examined during the year that have the full financial coverage required by regulation to protect against loss from non-performance or casualty.

OBJECTIVE 3: ENHANCE PUBLIC AWARENESS OF AGENCY RESOURCES, REMEDIES AND REGULATORY REQUIREMENTS THROUGH EDUCATION AND OUTREACH.

For additional analytical, business and investment opportunities information, please contact Global Investment & Business Center, USA at (703) 370-8082. Fax: (703) 370-8083. E-mail: ibpusa3@gmail.com Global Business and Investment Info Databank - www.ibpus.com

The Commission developed various educational and outreach strategies in support of this objective in assuring that the public is fully aware of their regulatory responsibilities and how the agency can be of service to them.

Protection of the public requires knowledge on the part of regulated parties and users of their services as to FMC regulatory requirements. As well, the public needs to be well informed of the services offered by the FMC and the remedies available in the event of noncompliance, injury or unresolved disputes.

1. Strategies

The following strategies aimed at enhancing public awareness include a specific focus on the performance measure of posting certain actions on the agency website within 5 days.

- Maintain an accessible presence in local regulated communities.
- Proactively educate regulated parties of regulatory requirements.
- Maintain VOCC and NVOCC tariff location information on the agency website.
- Emphasize OTI requirements to new licensees by letter.
- Promote awareness of FMC licensing and financial requirements.
- Make available to the public key documents in all Commission formal proceedings through the Commission website.
- Create and produce brochures to educate industry and public about FMC requirements and services.
- Promote general awareness of resources available through Commission's website.
- Continuously expand and update information available to the public through the website, including list of licensed OTIs.

2. Five -Year Performance Measures

- Percentage of key Commission issuances, orders and reports that are available through the Commission's website within 5 working days of receipt.

OBJECTIVE 4: IMPARTIALLY RESOLVE INTERNATIONAL SHIPPING DISPUTES THROUGH ALTERNATIVE DISPUTE RESOLUTION AND ADJUDICATION.

The following strategies carry out this objective of fostering ADR and adjudication as an efficient and least costly and contentious means of resolving shipping disputes. These strategies concern *ombuds* services, facilitating ADR, arbitration, and timely conduct of proceedings.

The Commission has several means by which the public or entities in the shipping industry may seek resolution of disputes or complaints. The Commission provides *ombuds* services to assist parties in resolving complaints informally through its office of Consumer Affairs and Dispute

For additional analytical, business and investment opportunities information, please contact Global Investment & Business Center, USA at (703) 370-8082. Fax: (703) 370-8083. E-mail: ibpusa3@gmail.com Global Business and Investment Info Databank - www.ibpus.com

Resolution and its Area Representatives. Formal complaints of alleged Shipping Act violations may be filed for adjudication by an

administrative law judge. Parties may seek the assistance of a trained neutral at any stage in a formal proceeding or in the first instance for resolution using ADR processes.

1. Strategies

The principle measure capturing the effectiveness of these strategies is the number of cases using *ombuds* and ADR services. The strategies were developed to encourage the use of such services and bring about timely resolution of disputes.

- Provide *ombuds* services to informally resolve passenger vessel, household goods and other shipper complaints.

- Encourage the use of and provide facilitative ADR services to parties who request services of a trained neutral in resolving disputes and shipping problems that affect international ocean shipping.

- Adjudicate disputes under the jurisdiction of the agency through the administrative law judge (ALJ) , with the possibility of appeal to the Commission, use of settlement officers and through arbitration.

- Timely conduct Commission proceedings so that litigants and industry can adjust behavior accordingly.

2. Five -Year Performance Measures

- Number of cases opened and closed each fiscal year using *ombuds* and ADR services assisting consumers to recover goods or funds.

- Percentage of formal complaints or Commission initiated orders of investigation will be completed within two years of filing or Commission initiation

Administrative Strategies in Support of Agency Objectives

In pursuing its strategic goals of maintaining an efficient and competitive international transportation system and protecting the shipping public from unlawful, unfair and deceptive ocean transportation practices, the FMC recognizes the critical importance of providing effective, performance-oriented management and of ensuring that all resources allocated to its mission are wisely employed. Separate but linked plans and measurement mechanisms are in place for human capital, information technology and financial management at the Commission.

The Commission's ability to carry out its mission and serve its customers depends on having a well-trained, highly skilled, and flexible workforce. Critical to accomplishing the agency mission is a commitment to the principles of Equal Employment Opportunity (EEO) , diversity and the implementation of EEO policies and objectives to enhance the quality of our work life and productivity of our workforce. The Commission's Office of Equal Employment Opportunity effectively carries out this mission.

For additional analytical, business and investment opportunities information, please contact Global Investment & Business Center, USA at (703) 370-8082. Fax: (703) 370-8083. E-mail: ibpusa3@gmail.com Global Business and Investment Info Databank - www.ibpus.com

The Commission's Human Capital Plan (for FY 2012 – 2017) aligns our human capital with our operational, information technology, and support processes in order to develop a performance-based organization. FMC's Human Capital Accountability Plan guides human capital decisions using data-driven information and results-oriented planning techniques. It will ensure human capital needs are carefully considered as part of the Commission's strategic planning and budgeting processes and will contribute to our mission success by monitoring and evaluating the progress and results of human capital goals, programs, and activities.

Planning is ongoing for use of information technology (IT) resources necessary to drive accomplishment of the Commission's strategic goals. Upon the publication of this plan in final, the Commission will have in place a 2014-2018 IRM Strategic Plan. The Commission is committed to an integrated approach to IT capital planning and investment control — both of which are driven by the Commission's Strategic Plan and its need to meet mission objectives in an efficient, transparent, and effective manner. Information technology planning is driven by programmatic needs of the Commission.

Financial systems are monitored and audited annually as required by the Federal Manager's Financial Integrity Act of 1982, the Chief Financial Officers Act of 1990 (CFO Act) , as amended, and the Government Management Reform Act (GMRA) of 1994 and reported annually through the Performance and Accountability Report. The Federal Managers' Financial Integrity Act (FMFIA) of 1996 requires that agencies establish controls that reasonably ensure that obligations and costs comply with applicable law; assets are safeguarded against waste, loss, unauthorized use, or misappropriation; and revenues and expenditures are properly recorded and accounted for. It requires the agency head to provide an assurance statement of the adequacy of management controls and conformance of financial systems with Government standards. As well, the CFO Act mandates annual audits of the Commission's internal controls systems. The Commission is committed to maintaining an unqualified audit opinion on audits of its Annual

Financial Statements. Further, the Commission is committed to addressing matters identified through the Financial Statement Audits involving internal controls and operations considered material weaknesses. By carefully and closely monitoring all of its operational programs, personnel needs, planning processes, financial and procurement practices, and vital support activities, the agency strives to ensure that its strategic goals are not only being met – but being advanced in ways that make the most productive, efficient, and sustainable use of the scarce resources with which it has been entrusted.

1. Strategies

The FMC realizes the critical importance of the administrative component of the agency in support of agency strategic goals, objectives and performance measures. The following strategies addressing budget, planning, human resources, procurement and IT were developed to assure an effective administrative support program within the FMC.

- Develop annual budget directly linked to strategic and annual performance plans for submission to the Congress and OMB.

- Annually measure performance as established in the strategic plan and assess the efficacy of performance measures for preparation of the annual performance plan.

- Identify and alleviate current and future skill gaps by fostering human resources management principles, including recruitment and placement, position classification and pay administration, occupational safety and health, employee assistance, employee

For additional analytical, business and investment opportunities information, please contact Global Investment & Business Center, USA at (703) 370-8082. Fax: (703) 370-8083. E-mail: ibpusa3@gmail.com Global Business and Investment Info Databank - www.ibpus.com

relations, workforce discipline, performance management and incentive awards, employee benefits, career transition, retirement, employee development and training, personnel security, and equal employment opportunity.

• Promote economy and efficiency by detecting waste, fraud and abuse in the agency's programs via auditing agency operations.

• Increase energy efficiency by implementing environmental programs throughout agency operations, including reducing green house gases, recycling waste and conservation of resources.

• Ensure program compliance with various rules and regulations regarding such areas as forms clearance, Paperwork Reduction, Small Business Paperwork Reduction Act, and other federally required reports and submissions.

• Execute financial management policies and programs, manage agency appropriations, administer internal control systems for agency funds, travel and cash management, and coordinate with contractors who provide accounting and payroll services.

• Monitor performance to ensure the agency's program operations are effectively, efficiently, and sustainably supported via telecommunications, procurement of administrative goods and services, property management, space, printing and

copying, mail and records services, facilities and equipment maintenance, and transportation.

• Provide guidance to staff regarding administrative matters, including procurement, personnel and contracting issues.

• Utilize technology and IT expertise to streamline the agency's work processes and enhance the productivity and efficiency of the workforce to support the needs of the Commission.

Factors Affecting the Achievement of Goals

The FMC is a small agency that has established considerable in-house expertise in the legal, economic and organizational aspects of international liner shipping and the inter-modal movement of ocean cargo. That expertise allows the FMC to effectively pursue its goals of maintaining a competitive international ocean transportation system and protecting the public from unlawful, unfair and deceptive practices efficiently at a very modest cost to the taxpayer and with a minimum regulatory burden on stakeholder industries.

A significant challenge facing the agency is the potential reduction in its operating budget. Given that the predominant portion of the agency's costs is salaries, reductions in payroll through attrition or furloughs (as is the case in FY 2013) may be inevitable. The agency will continue to be seriously hampered in making necessary IT improvements.

In spite of the above fiscal austerity, the agency will need to maintain its relevant expertise through the recruitment, training and retention of highly qualified attorneys, economists, industry specialists, and information technology experts. The importance of the recruitment and retention

For additional analytical, business and investment opportunities information, please contact Global Investment & Business Center, USA at (703) 370-8082. Fax: (703) 370-8083. E-mail: ibpusa3@gmail.com Global Business and Investment Info Databank - www.ibpus.com

issue is likely to increase as the agency's experienced personnel reach retirement age, and in the face of competition from other federal agencies seeking to replace their retiring personnel.

Addressing the use of information technologies is one way in which the FMC is able to do more with less. The increasing importance of information technologies results not only from its contribution to the agency's ability to collect and process information more efficiently and accurately, but also because of the agency's need to keep up with the electronic-business practices of the industries it regulates. Greater use of information technology also helps make many of the aspects of licensing, certification and information filing simpler and easier to accomplish for the agency's stakeholders. IT is critical to the maintenance and effective use of various key agency databases.

The security of agency databases and confidential business reports and associated documents filed with the FMC has received increasing attention in recent years. Enhanced and extended applications of information technologies helps ensure that security.

The FMC regulates international ocean liner transportation, and is also involved, through its regulation of marine terminal operators, with aspects of the intermodal movement of ocean cargo in the U.S. In addition, foreign-based ocean transportation intermediaries are subject to statutory bonding requirements under FMC jurisdiction. To the extent that there are changes in the regulatory treatment of international liner operations by foreign governments, as was the case in Europe beginning in late 2008 with the FMC's publication of its *Study of the 2008 Repeal of the Liner Conference Exemption from European Union Competition Law*, the agency will continue to monitor such changes and the likely effect of such changes on U.S. trades. Over time, and depending on their actual impacts, regulatory changes in other regions could also provide a possible impetus for a review of U.S. statutes or regulations on liner shipping. Consequently, FMC analyses of possible future proposals for statutory revisions may be required.

Finally, in recent years the FMC has witnessed the filing of new types of agreements -- especially marine terminal agreements -- that address nontraditional issues such as traffic congestion, environmental mitigation proposals, terminal operational efficiencies, and infrastructure funding. These nontraditional agreements tend to involve industries (drayage trucking and rail service) , operations (pooling of chassis) , and issues (air pollution, public health, infrastructure finance) that require the development, by agency staff, of additional information sources and areas of expertise. Not infrequently, these nontraditional agreements have potentially significant pricing and service consequences. To the extent that the filing of nontraditional agreements increases in coming years – which seems to be the likely trend – they will continue to weigh heavily on the agency's limited resources.

PROGRAM EVALUATION

In general, the FMC will continue to evaluate its programs, both that address industry competition and those designed to protect the public from unlawful, unfair and deceptive practices, to ensure that they focus on the areas of greatest concern as determined by the analysis of required and special reporting requirements, stakeholder outreach discussions, and informal complaints. In addition, the agency will evaluate the extent to which its compliance activities are effectively addressing identified problem areas, and will implement any changes needed to improve compliance targeting.

The FMC will periodically review its initial agreement review process and on-going monitoring programs to determine whether the current reporting requirements continue to provide adequate information in light of changing industry conduct and new types of agreements being filed. In

For additional analytical, business and investment opportunities information,
please contact Global Investment & Business Center, USA
at (703) 370-8082. Fax: (703) 370-8083. E-mail: ibpusa3@gmail.com
Global Business and Investment Info Databank - www.ibpus.com

particular, the process for monitoring non-traditional agreements, and ensuring oversight of agreement implementation activities, will be assessed.

Taking into account the discussions with stakeholder industries, the agency will regularly assess which research study topics likely will best address the competitive effects, in the U.S. trades, of changing industry operations and business practices, foreign government regulatory changes, and controlled carrier activity.

The agency will, on an on-going basis, continue to assess the effectiveness of its auditing, investigatory and information gathering procedures with respect to unlawful, unfair and deceptive transportation practices. Particular attention will be given to ways to efficiently and accurately identify, and take appropriate compliance action with respect to, unlicensed ocean transportation intermediaries, including foreign-based intermediaries.

Educational and stakeholder outreach activities will be tracked and periodically evaluated to ensure their effectiveness in reaching targeted audiences on specific topics. Possible alternative activities and approaches will be considered as part of each periodic evaluation. These evaluations will also include the educational material provided via the FMC website.

For additional analytical, business and investment opportunities information, please contact Global Investment & Business Center, USA at (703) 370-8082. Fax: (703) 370-8083. E-mail: ibpusa3@gmail.com Global Business and Investment Info Databank - www.ibpus.com

IMPORTANT LAWS AND REGULATIONS

STATUTES

Statute	Former Citation	New Codification
Shipping Act of 1984	46 App. U.S.C. §§ 1701 – 1719	46 U.S.C. §§ 40101 - 41309
Foreign Shipping Practices Act of 1988	46 App. U.S.C. § 1710a	46 U.S.C. §§ 42301 - 42307
Section 19 of the Merchant Marine Act, 1920	46 App. U.S.C. § 876	46 U.S.C. §§ 42101 - 42109
Public Law 89-777 (Financial Responsibility for Death or Injury to Passenger and for Nonperformance of Voyage)	46 App. U.S.C. §§ 817d - 817e	46 U.S.C. §§ 44101 - 44106

CHAPTER 401—GENERAL

Sec. 40101. Purposes. 40102. Definitions. 40103. Administrative exemptions. 40104. Reports filed with the Commission.

§ 40101. Purposes

The purposes of this part are to—

(1) establish a nondiscriminatory regulatory process for the common carriage of goods by water in the foreign commerce of the United States with a minimum of government intervention and regulatory costs;

(2) provide an efficient and economic transportation system in the ocean commerce of the United States that is, insofar as possible, in harmony with, and responsive to, international shipping practices;

(3) encourage the development of an economically sound and efficient liner fleet of vessels of the United States capable of meeting national security needs; and

(4) promote the growth and development of United States exports through competitive and efficient ocean transportation and by placing a greater reliance on the marketplace.

§ 40102. Definitions

In this part:

(1) AGREEMENT.—The term "agreement"—

(A) means a written or oral understanding, arrangement, or association, and any modification or cancellation thereof; but

(B) does not include a maritime labor agreement.

(2) ANTITRUST LAWS.—The term “antitrust laws” means—

(A) the Sherman Act (15 U.S.C. 1 et seq.) ;

(B) sections 73 and 74 of the Wilson Tariff Act (15 U.S.C. 8, 9) ;

(C) the Clayton Act (15 U.S.C. 12 et seq.) ;

(D) the Act of June 19, 1936 (15 U.S.C. 13, 13a, 13b, 21a) ;

(E) the Federal Trade Commission Act (15 U.S.C. 41 et seq.) ;

(F) the Antitrust Civil Process Act (15 U.S.C. 1311 et seq.) ; and

(G) Acts supplementary to those Acts.

(3) ASSESSMENT AGREEMENT.—The term “assessment agreement” means an agreement, whether part of a collective bargaining agreement or negotiated separately, to the extent the agreement provides for the funding of collectively bargained fringe-benefit obligations on other than a uniform worker-hour basis, regardless of the cargo handled or type of vessel or equipment used.

(4) BULK CARGO.—The term “bulk cargo” means cargo that is loaded and carried in bulk without mark or count.

(5) CHEMICAL PARCEL-TANKER.—The term “chemical parcel-tanker” means a vessel that has—

(A) a cargo-carrying capability consisting of individual cargo tanks for bulk chemicals that—

(i) are a permanent part of the vessel; and

(ii) have segregation capability with piping systems to permit simultaneous carriage of several bulk chemical cargoes with minimum risk of cross-contamination; and

(B) a valid certificate of fitness under the International Maritime Organization Code for the Construction and Equipment of Ships Carrying Dangerous Chemicals in Bulk.

(6) COMMON CARRIER.—The term “common carrier”—

(A) means a person that—

(i) holds itself out to the general public to provide transportation by water of passengers or cargo between the United States and a foreign country for compensation;

(ii) assumes responsibility for the transportation from the port or point of receipt to the port or point of destination; and

For additional analytical, business and investment opportunities information, please contact Global Investment & Business Center, USA at (703) 370-8082. Fax: (703) 370-8083. E-mail: ibpusa3@gmail.com Global Business and Investment Info Databank - www.ibpus.com

(iii) uses, for all or part of that transportation, a vessel operating on the high seas or the Great Lakes between a port in the United States and a port in a foreign country; but

(B) does not include a carrier engaged in ocean transportation by ferry boat, ocean tramp, or chemical parcel-tanker, or by vessel when primarily engaged in the carriage of perishable agricultural commodities—

(i) if the carrier and the owner of those commodities are wholly-owned, directly or indirectly, by a person primarily engaged in the marketing and distribution of those commodities; and

(ii) only with respect to the carriage of those commodities.

(7) CONFERENCE.—The term “conference”—

(A) means an association of ocean common carriers permitted, pursuant to an approved or effective agreement, to engage in concerted activity and to use a common tariff; but

(B) does not include a joint service, consortium, pooling, sailing, or transshipment agreement.

(8) CONTROLLED CARRIER.—The term “controlled carrier” means an ocean common carrier that is, or whose operating assets are, directly or indirectly, owned or controlled by a government, with ownership or control by a government being deemed to exist for a carrier if—

(A) a majority of the interest in the carrier is owned or controlled in any manner by that government, an agency of that government, or a public or private person controlled by that government; or

(B) that government has the right to appoint or disapprove the appointment of a majority of the directors, the chief operating officer, or the chief executive officer of the carrier.

(9) DEFERRED REBATE.—The term “deferred rebate” means a return by a common carrier of any freight money to a shipper, where the return is—

(A) consideration for the shipper giving all or any portion of its shipments to that or any other common carrier over a fixed period of time;

(B) deferred beyond the completion of the service for which it was paid; and

(C) made only if the shipper has agreed to make a further shipment with that or any other common carrier.

(10) FOREST PRODUCTS.—The term “forest products” includes lumber in bundles, rough timber, ties, poles, piling, laminated beams, bundled siding, bundled plywood, bundled core stock or veneers, bundled particle or fiber boards, bundled hardwood, wood pulp in rolls, wood pulp in unitized bales, and paper and paper board in rolls or in pallet or skid-sized sheets.

(11) INLAND DIVISION.—The term “inland division” means the amount paid by a common carrier to an inland carrier for the inland portion of through transportation offered to the public by the common carrier.

For additional analytical, business and investment opportunities information, please contact Global Investment & Business Center, USA at (703) 370-8082. Fax: (703) 370-8083. E-mail: ibpusa3@gmail.com Global Business and Investment Info Databank - www.ibpus.com

(12) INLAND PORTION.—The term "inland portion" means the charge to the public by a common carrier for the non-ocean portion of through transportation.

(13) LOYALTY CONTRACT.—The term "loyalty contract" means a contract with an ocean common carrier or agreement providing for—

(A) a shipper to obtain lower rates by committing all or a fixed portion of its cargo to that carrier or agreement; and

(B) a deferred rebate arrangement.

(14) MARINE TERMINAL OPERATOR.—The term "marine terminal operator" means a person engaged in the United States in the business of providing wharfage, dock, warehouse, or other terminal facilities in connection with a common carrier, or in connection with a common carrier and a water carrier subject to subchapter II of chapter 135 of title 49.

(15) MARITIME LABOR AGREEMENT.—The term "maritime labor agreement"—

(A) means—

(i) a collective bargaining agreement between an employer subject to this part, or a group of such employers, and a labor organization representing employees in the maritime or stevedoring industry;

(ii) an agreement preparatory to such a collective bargaining agreement among members of a multiemployer bargaining group; or

(iii) an agreement specifically implementing provisions of such a collective bargaining agreement or providing for the formation, financing, or administration of a multi-employer bargaining group; but

(B) does not include an assessment agreement.

(16) NON-VESSEL-OPERATING COMMON CARRIER.—The term "non-vessel-operating common carrier" means a common carrier that—

(A) does not operate the vessels by which the ocean transportation is provided; and

(B) is a shipper in its relationship with an ocean common carrier.

(17) OCEAN COMMON CARRIER.—The term "ocean common carrier" means a vessel-operating common carrier.

(18) OCEAN FREIGHT FORWARDER.—The term "ocean freight forwarder" means a person that—

(A) in the United States, dispatches shipments from the United States via a common carrier and books or otherwise arranges space for those shipments on behalf of shippers; and

(B) processes the documentation or performs related activities incident to those shipments.

For additional analytical, business and investment opportunities information, please contact Global Investment & Business Center, USA at (703) 370-8082. Fax: (703) 370-8083. E-mail: ibpusa3@gmail.com Global Business and Investment Info Databank - www.ibpus.com

(19) OCEAN TRANSPORTATION INTERMEDIARY.—The term "ocean transportation intermediary" means an ocean freight forwarder or a non-vessel-operating common carrier.

(20) SERVICE CONTRACT.—The term "service contract" means a written contract, other than a bill of lading or receipt, between one or more shippers, on the one hand, and an individual ocean common carrier or an agreement between or among ocean common carriers, on the other, in which—

(A) the shipper or shippers commit to providing a certain volume or portion of cargo over a fixed time period; and

(B) the ocean common carrier or the agreement commits to a certain rate or rate schedule and a defined service level, such as assured space, transit time, port rotation, or similar service features.

(21) SHIPMENT.—The term "shipment" means all of the cargo carried under the terms of a single bill of lading.

(22) SHIPPER.—The term "shipper" means—

(A) a cargo owner;

(B) the person for whose account the ocean transportation of cargo is provided;

(C) the person to whom delivery is to be made;

(D) a shippers' association; or

(E) a non-vessel-operating common carrier that accepts responsibility for payment of all charges applicable under the tariff or service contract.

(23) SHIPPERS' ASSOCIATION.—The term "shippers' association" means a group of shippers that consolidates or distributes freight on a nonprofit basis for the members of the group to obtain carload, truckload, or other volume rates or service contracts.

(24) THROUGH RATE.—The term "through rate" means the single amount charged by a common carrier in connection with through transportation.

(25) THROUGH TRANSPORTATION.—The term "through transportation" means continuous transportation between origin and destination for which a through rate is assessed and which is offered or performed by one or more carriers, at least one of which is a common carrier, between a United States port or point and a foreign port or point.

§ 40103. Administrative exemptions

(a) IN GENERAL.—The Federal Maritime Commission, on application or its own motion, may by

order or regulation exempt for the future any class of agreements between persons subject to this part or any specified activity of those persons from any requirement of this part if the Commission finds that the exemption will not result in substantial reduction in competition or be detrimental to

For additional analytical, business and investment opportunities information, please contact Global Investment & Business Center, USA at (703) 370-8082. Fax: (703) 370-8083. E-mail: ibpusa3@gmail.com Global Business and Investment Info Databank - www.ibpus.com

commerce. The Commission may attach conditions to an exemption and may, by order, revoke an exemption.

(b) OPPORTUNITY FOR HEARING.—An order or regulation of exemption or revocation of an exemption may be issued only if the Commission has provided an opportunity for a hearing to interested persons and departments and agencies of the United States Government.

§ 40104. Reports filed with the Commission

(a) IN GENERAL.—The Federal Maritime Commission may require a common carrier or an officer, receiver, trustee, lessee, agent, or employee of the carrier to file with the Commission a periodical or special report, an account, record, rate, or charge, or a memorandum of facts and transactions related to the business of the carrier. The report, account, record, rate, charge, or memorandum shall be made under oath if the Commission requires, and shall be filed in the form and within the time prescribed by the Commission.

(b)

CONFERENCE MINUTES.—Conference minutes required to be filed with the Commission under this section may not be released to third parties or published by the Commission.

CHAPTER 403—AGREEMENTS

Sec. 40301. Application. 40302. Filing requirements. 40303. Content requirements. 40304. Commission action. 40305. Assessment agreements. 40306. Nondisclosure of information. 40307. Exemption from antitrust laws.

§ 40301. Application

(a) OCEAN COMMON CARRIER AGREEMENTS.—This part applies to an agreement between or among ocean common carriers to—

(1) discuss, fix, or regulate transportation rates, including through rates, cargo space accommodations, and other conditions of service;

(2) pool or apportion traffic, revenues, earnings, or losses;

(3) allot ports or regulate the number and character of voyages between ports;

(4) regulate the volume or character of cargo or passenger traffic to be carried;

(5) engage in an exclusive, preferential, or cooperative working arrangement between themselves or with a marine terminal operator;

(6) control, regulate, or prevent competition in international ocean transportation; or

(7) discuss and agree on any matter related to a service contract.

For additional analytical, business and investment opportunities information, please contact Global Investment & Business Center, USA at (703) 370-8082. Fax: (703) 370-8083. E-mail: ibpusa3@gmail.com Global Business and Investment Info Databank - www.ibpus.com

(b) MARINE TERMINAL OPERATOR AGREEMENTS.—This part applies to an agreement between or among marine terminal operators, or between or among one or more marine terminal operators and one or more ocean common carriers, to—

(1) discuss, fix, or regulate rates or other conditions of service; or

(2) engage in exclusive, preferential, or cooperative working arrangements, to the extent the agreement involves ocean transportation in the foreign commerce of the United States.

(c) ACQUISITIONS.—This part does not apply to an acquisition by any person, directly or indirectly, of any voting security or assets of any other person.

(d) MARITIME LABOR AGREEMENTS.—This part does not apply to a maritime labor agreement. However, this subsection does not exempt from this part any rate, charge, regulation, or practice of a common carrier that is required to be set forth in a tariff or is an essential term of a service contract, whether or not the rate, charge, regulation, or practice arises out of, or is otherwise related to, a maritime labor agreement.

(e) ASSESSMENT AGREEMENTS.—This part (except sections 40305 and 40307(a)) does not apply to an assessment agreement.

§ 40302. Filing requirements

(a) IN GENERAL.—A true copy of every agreement referred to in section 40301(a) or (b) of this title shall be filed with the Federal Maritime Commission. If the agreement is oral, a complete memorandum specifying in detail the substance of the agreement shall be filed.

(b) EXCEPTIONS.—Subsection (a) does not apply to—

(1) an agreement related to transportation to be performed within or between foreign countries; or

(2) an agreement among common carriers to establish, operate, or maintain a marine terminal in the United States.

(c) REGULATIONS.—The Commission may by regulation prescribe the form and manner in which an agreement shall be filed and any additional information and documents necessary to evaluate the agreement.

§ 40303. Content requirements

(a) OCEAN COMMON CARRIER AGREEMENTS.—

(1) RESTRICTIONS.—An ocean common carrier agreement may not—

(A) prohibit or restrict a member of the agreement from engaging in negotiations for a service contract with a shipper;

(B) require a member of the agreement to disclose a negotiation on a service contract, or the terms of a service contract, other than those terms required to be published under section 40502(d) of this title; or

(C) adopt mandatory rules or requirements affecting the right of an agreement member to negotiate and enter into a service contract.

(2) VOLUNTARY GUIDELINES.—An ocean common carrier agreement may provide authority to adopt voluntary guidelines relating to the terms and procedures of an agreement member's service contracts if the guidelines explicitly state the right of members of the agreement not to follow the guidelines. Any guidelines adopted shall be submitted confidentially to the Federal Maritime Commission.

(b) CONFERENCE AGREEMENTS.—Each conference agreement must—

(1) state its purpose;

(2) provide reasonable and equal terms for admission and readmission to conference membership for any ocean common carrier willing to serve the particular trade or route;

(3) permit any member to withdraw from conference membership on reasonable notice without penalty;

(4) at the request of any member, require an independent neutral body to police fully the obligations of the conference and its members;

(5) prohibit the conference from engaging in conduct prohibited by section 41105(1) or (3) of this title;

(6) provide for a consultation process designed to promote—

(A) commercial resolution of disputes; and

(B) cooperation with shippers in preventing and eliminating malpractices;

(7) establish procedures for promptly and fairly considering requests and complaints of shippers; and

(8) provide that—

(A) any member of the conference may take independent action on a rate or service item on not more than 5 days' notice to the conference; and

(B) except for an exempt commodity not published in the conference tariff, the conference will include the new rate or service item in its tariff for use by that member, effective no later than 5 days after receipt of the notice, and by any other member that notifies the conference that it elects to adopt the independent rate or service item on or after its effective date, in lieu of the existing conference tariff provision for that rate or service item.

(c) INTERCONFERENCE AGREEMENTS.—Each agreement between carriers not members of the same conference must provide the right of independent action for each carrier. Each agreement between conferences must provide the right of independent action for each conference.

(d) VESSEL SHARING AGREEMENTS.—

(1) IN GENERAL.—An ocean common carrier that is the owner, operator, or bareboat, time, or slot charterer of a liner vessel documented under section 12103 or 12111(c) of this title may agree with an ocean common carrier described in paragraph (2) to which it charters or subcharters the vessel or space on the vessel that the charterer or subcharterer may not use or make available space on the vessel for the carriage of cargo reserved by law for vessels of the United States.

(2) CARRIER DESCRIBED.—An ocean common carrier described in this paragraph is one that is not the owner, operator, or bareboat charterer for at least one year of liner vessels of the United States that are eligible to be included in the Maritime Security Fleet Program and are enrolled in an Emergency Preparedness Program under chapter 531 of this title.

§ 40304. Commission action

(a) NOTICE OF FILING.—Within 7 days after an agreement is filed, the Federal Maritime Commission shall transmit a notice of the filing to the Federal Register for publication.

(b) PRELIMINARY REVIEW AND REJECTION.—After preliminary review, the Commission shall reject an agreement that it finds does not meet the requirements of sections 40302 and 40303 of this title. The Commission shall notify in writing the person filing the agreement of the reason for rejection.

(c) REVIEW AND EFFECTIVE DATE.—Unless rejected under subsection (b) , an agreement (other than an assessment agreement) is effective—

(1) on the 45th day after filing, or on the 30th day after notice of the filing is published in the Federal Register, whichever is later; or

(2) if additional information or documents are requested under subsection (d) —

(A) on the 45th day after the Commission receives all the additional information and documents; or

(B) if the request is not fully complied with, on the 45th day after the Commission receives the information and documents submitted and a statement of the reasons for noncompliance with the request.

(d) REQUEST FOR ADDITIONAL INFORMATION.—Before the expiration of the period specified in subsection (c) (1) , the Commission may request from the person filing the agreement any additional information and documents the Commission considers necessary to make the determinations required by this section.

(e) MODIFICATION OF REVIEW PERIOD.—

(1) SHORTENING.—On request of the party filing an agreement, the Commission may shorten a period specified in subsection (c) , but not to a date that is less than 14 days after notice of the filing of the agreement is published in the Federal Register.

For additional analytical, business and investment opportunities information, please contact Global Investment & Business Center, USA at (703) 370-8082. Fax: (703) 370-8083. E-mail: ibpusa3@gmail.com Global Business and Investment Info Databank - www.ibpus.com

(2) EXTENSION.—The period specified in subsection (c) (2) may be extended only by the United States District Court for the District of Columbia in a civil action brought by the Commission under section 41307(c) of this title.

(f) FIXED TERMS.—The Commission may not limit the effectiveness of an agreement to a fixed term.

§ 40305. Assessment agreements

(a) FILING REQUIREMENT.—An assessment agreement shall be filed with the Federal Maritime Commission and is effective on filing.

(b) COMPLAINTS.—If a complaint is filed with the Commission within 2 years after the date of an assessment agreement, the Commission shall disapprove, cancel, or modify the agreement, or an assessment or charge pursuant to the agreement, that the Commission finds, after notice and opportunity for a hearing, to be unjustly discriminatory or unfair as between carriers, shippers, or ports. The Commission shall issue its final decision in the proceeding within one year after the date the complaint is filed.

(c) ADJUSTMENTS OF ASSESSMENTS AND CHARGES.—To the extent that the Commission finds under subsection (b) that an assessment or charge is unjustly discriminatory or unfair as between carriers, shippers, or ports, the Commission shall adjust the assessment or charge for the period between the filing of the complaint and the final decision by awarding prospective credits or debits to future assessments and charges. However, if the complainant has ceased activities subject to the assessment or charge, the Commission may award reparations.

§ 40306. Nondisclosure of information

Information and documents (other than an agreement) filed with the Federal Maritime Commission under this chapter are exempt from disclosure under section 552 of title 5 and may not be made public except as may be relevant to an administrative or judicial proceeding. This section does not prevent disclosure to either House of Congress or to a duly authorized committee or subcommittee of Congress.

§ 40307. Exemption from antitrust laws

(a) IN GENERAL.—The antitrust laws do not apply to—

(1) an agreement (including an assessment agreement) that has been filed and is effective under this chapter;

(2) an agreement that is exempt under section 40103 of this title from any requirement of this part;

(3) an agreement or activity within the scope of this part, whether permitted under or prohibited by this part, undertaken or entered into with a reasonable basis to conclude that it is—

(A) pursuant to an agreement on file with the Federal Maritime Commission and in effect

when the activity takes place; or

For additional analytical, business and investment opportunities information, please contact Global Investment & Business Center, USA at (703) 370-8082. Fax: (703) 370-8083. E-mail: ibpusa3@gmail.com Global Business and Investment Info Databank - www.ibpus.com

(B) exempt under section 40103 of this title from any filing or publication requirement of this part;

(4) an agreement or activity relating to transportation services within or between foreign countries, whether or not via the United States, unless the agreement or activity has a direct, substantial, and reasonably foreseeable effect on the commerce of the United States;

(5) an agreement or activity relating to the foreign inland segment of through transportation that is part of transportation provided in a United States import or export trade;

(6) an agreement or activity to provide wharfage, dock, warehouse, or other terminal facilities outside the United States; or

(7) an agreement, modification, or cancellation approved before June 18, 1984, by the Commission under section 15 of the Shipping Act, 1916, or permitted under section 14b of that Act, and any properly published tariff, rate, fare, or charge, or classification, rule, or regulation explanatory thereof implementing that agreement, modification, or cancellation.

(b) EXCEPTIONS.—This part does not extend antitrust immunity to—

(1) an agreement with or among air carriers, rail carriers, motor carriers, or common carriers by water not subject to this part relating to transportation within the United States;

(2) a discussion or agreement among common carriers subject to this part relating to the inland divisions (as opposed to the inland portions) of through rates within the United States;

(3) an agreement among common carriers subject to this part to establish, operate, or maintain a marine terminal in the United States; or

(4) a loyalty contract.

(c) RETROACTIVE EFFECT OF DETERMINATIONS.—A determination by an agency or court that results in the denial or removal of the immunity to the antitrust laws under subsection (a) does not remove or alter the antitrust immunity for the period before the determination.

(d) RELIEF UNDER CLAYTON ACT.—A person may not recover damages under section 4 of the Clayton Act (15 U.S.C. 15) , or obtain injunctive relief under section 16 of that Act (15 U.S.C. 26) , for conduct prohibited by this part.

CHAPTER 405—TARIFFS, SERVICE CONTRACTS, REFUNDS, AND WAIVERS

Sec. 40501. General rate and tariff requirements. 40502. Service contracts. 40503. Refunds and waivers.

§ 40501. General rate and tariff requirements

(a) AUTOMATED TARIFF SYSTEM.—

(1) IN GENERAL.—Each common carrier and conference shall keep open to public inspection in an automated tariff system, tariffs showing all its rates, charges, classifications, rules, and practices between all points or ports on its own route and on any through transportation route that

For additional analytical, business and investment opportunities information, please contact Global Investment & Business Center, USA at (703) 370-8082. Fax: (703) 370-8083. E-mail: ibpusa3@gmail.com Global Business and Investment Info Databank - www.ibpus.com

has been established. However, a common carrier is not required to state separately or otherwise reveal in tariffs the inland divisions of a through rate.

(2) EXCEPTIONS.—Paragraph (1) does not apply with respect to bulk cargo, forest products, recycled metal scrap, new assembled motor vehicles, waste paper, or paper waste.

(b) CONTENTS OF TARIFFS.—A tariff under subsection (a) shall—

(1) state the places between which cargo will be carried;

(2) list each classification of cargo in use;

(3) state the level of compensation, if any, of any ocean freight forwarder by a carrier or conference;

(4) state separately each terminal or other charge, privilege, or facility under the control of the carrier or conference and any rules that in any way change, affect, or determine any part or the total of the rates or charges;

(5) include sample copies of any bill of lading, contract of affreightment, or other document evidencing the transportation agreement; and

(6) include copies of any loyalty contract, omitting the shipper's name.

(c) ELECTRONIC ACCESS.—A tariff under subsection (a) shall be made available electronically to any person, without time, quantity, or other limitation, through appropriate access from remote locations. A reasonable fee may be charged for such access, except that no fee may be charged for access by a Federal agency.

(d) TIME-VOLUME RATES.—A rate contained in a tariff under subsection (a) may vary with the volume of cargo offered over a specified period of time.

(e) EFFECTIVE DATES.—

(1) INCREASES.—A new or initial rate or change in an existing rate that results in an increased cost to a shipper may not become effective earlier than 30 days after publication. However, for good cause, the Federal Maritime Commission may allow the rate to become effective sooner.

(2) DECREASES.—A change in an existing rate that results in a decreased cost to a shipper may become effective on publication.

(f) MARINE TERMINAL OPERATOR SCHEDULES.—A marine terminal operator may make available to the public a schedule of rates, regulations, and practices, including limitations of liability for cargo loss or damage, pertaining to receiving, delivering, handling, or storing property at its marine terminal. Any such schedule made available to the public is enforceable by an appropriate court as an implied contract without proof of actual knowledge of its provisions.

(g) REGULATIONS.—

**For additional analytical, business and investment opportunities information,
please contact Global Investment & Business Center, USA
at (703) 370-8082. Fax: (703) 370-8083. E-mail: ibpusa3@gmail.com
Global Business and Investment Info Databank - www.ibpus.com**

(1) IN GENERAL.—The Commission shall by regulation prescribe the requirements for the accessibility and accuracy of automated tariff systems established under this section. The Commission, after periodic review, may prohibit the use of any automated tariff system that fails to meet the requirements established under this section.

(2) REMOTE TERMINALS.—The Commission may not require a common carrier to provide a remote terminal for electronic access under subsection (c) .

(3) MARINE TERMINAL OPERATOR SCHEDULES.—The Commission shall by regulation prescribe the form and manner in which marine terminal operator schedules authorized by this section shall be published.

§ 40502. Service contracts

(a) IN GENERAL.—An individual ocean common carrier or an agreement between or among ocean common carriers may enter into a service contract with one or more shippers subject to the requirements of this part.

(b) FILING REQUIREMENTS.—

(1) IN GENERAL.—Each service contract entered into under this section by an individual ocean common carrier or an agreement shall be filed confidentially with the Federal Maritime Commission.

(2) EXCEPTIONS.—Paragraph (1) does not apply to contracts regarding bulk cargo, forest products, recycled metal scrap, new assembled motor vehicles, waste paper, or paper waste.

(c) ESSENTIAL TERMS.—Each service contract shall include—

(1) the origin and destination port ranges;

(2) the origin and destination geographic areas in the case of through intermodal movements;

(3) the commodities involved;

(4) the minimum volume or portion;

(5) the line-haul rate;

(6) the duration;

(7) service commitments; and

(8) the liquidated damages for nonperformance, if any.

(d) PUBLICATION OF CERTAIN TERMS.—When a service contract is filed confidentially with the Commission, a concise statement of the essential terms specified in paragraphs (1) , (3) , (4) , and

For additional analytical, business and investment opportunities information, please contact Global Investment & Business Center, USA at (703) 370-8082. Fax: (703) 370-8083. E-mail: ibpusa3@gmail.com Global Business and Investment Info Databank - www.ibpus.com

(6) of subsection (c) shall be published and made available to the general public in tariff format.

(e) DISCLOSURE OF CERTAIN TERMS.—

(1) DEFINITIONS.—In this subsection, the terms "dock area" and "within the port area" have the same meaning and scope as in the applicable collective bargaining agreement between the requesting labor organization and the carrier.

(2) DISCLOSURE.—An ocean common carrier that is a party to or is otherwise subject to a collective bargaining agreement with a labor organization shall, in response to a written request by the labor organization, state whether it is responsible for the following work at a dock area or within a port area in the United States with respect to cargo transportation under a service contract:

(A) The movement of the shipper's cargo on a dock area or within the port area or to or from railroad cars on a dock area or within the port area.

(B) The assignment of intraport carriage of the shipper's cargo between areas on a dock or within the port area.

(C) The assignment of the carriage of the shipper's cargo between a container yard on a dock area or within the port area and a rail yard adjacent to the container yard.

(D) The assignment of container freight station work and container maintenance and repair work performed at a dock area or within the port area.

(3) WITHIN REASONABLE TIME.—The common carrier shall provide the information described in paragraph (2) to the requesting labor organization within a reasonable period of time.

(4) EXISTENCE OF COLLECTIVE BARGAINING AGREEMENT.—This subsection does not require the disclosure of information by an ocean common carrier unless there exists an applicable and otherwise lawful collective bargaining agreement pertaining to that carrier. A disclosure by an ocean common carrier may not be deemed an admission or an agreement that any work is covered by a collective bargaining agreement. A dispute about whether any work is covered by a collective bargaining agreement and the responsibility of an ocean common carrier under a collective bargaining agreement shall be resolved solely in accordance with the dispute resolution procedures contained in the collective bargaining agreement and the National Labor Relations Act (29 U.S.C. 151 et seq.) , and without reference to this subsection.

(5) EFFECT UNDER OTHER LAWS.—This subsection does not affect the lawfulness or unlawfulness under this part or any other Federal or State law of any collective bargaining agreement or element thereof, including any element that constitutes an essential term of a service contract.

(f) REMEDY FOR BREACH.—Unless the parties agree otherwise, the exclusive remedy for a breach of a service contract is an action in an appropriate court. The contract dispute resolution forum may not be controlled by or in any way affiliated with a controlled carrier or by the government that owns or controls the carrier.

§ 40503. Refunds and waivers

For additional analytical, business and investment opportunities information, please contact Global Investment & Business Center, USA at (703) 370-8082. Fax: (703) 370-8083. E-mail: ibpusa3@gmail.com Global Business and Investment Info Databank - www.ibpus.com

The Federal Maritime Commission, on application of a carrier or shipper, may permit a common carrier or conference to refund a portion of the freight charges collected from a shipper, or to waive collection of a portion of the charges from a shipper, if—

(1) there is an error in a tariff, a failure to publish a new tariff, or an error in quoting a tariff, and the refund or waiver will not result in discrimination among shippers, ports, or carriers;

(2) the common carrier or conference, before filing an application for authority to refund or waive any charges for an error in a tariff or a failure to publish a tariff, has published a new tariff setting forth the rate on which the refund or waiver would be based; and

(3) the application for the refund or waiver is filed with the Commission within 180 days from the date of shipment.

CHAPTER 407—CONTROLLED CARRIERS

§ 40701. Rates

(a) IN GENERAL.—A controlled carrier may not—

(1) maintain a rate or charge in a tariff or service contract, or charge or assess a rate, that is below a just and reasonable level; or

(2) establish, maintain, or enforce in a tariff or service contract a classification, rule, or regulation that results, or is likely to result, in the carriage or handling of cargo at a rate or charge that is below a just and reasonable level.

(b) COMMISSION PROHIBITION.—The Federal Maritime Commission, at any time after notice and opportunity for a hearing, may prohibit the publication or use of a rate, charge, classification, rule, or regulation that a controlled carrier has failed to demonstrate is just and reasonable.

(c) BURDEN OF PROOF.—In a proceeding under this section, the burden of proof is on the controlled carrier to demonstrate that its rate, charge, classification, rule, or regulation is just and reasonable.

(d) VOIDNESS.—A rate, charge, classification, rule, or regulation that has been suspended or prohibited by the Commission is void and its use is unlawful.

§ 40702. Rate standards

(a) DEFINITION.—In this section, the term "constructive costs" means the costs of another carrier, other than a controlled carrier, operating similar vessels and equipment in the same or a similar trade.

(b) STANDARDS.—In determining whether a rate, charge, classification, rule, or regulation of a controlled carrier is just and reasonable, the Federal Maritime Commission—

For additional analytical, business and investment opportunities information, please contact Global Investment & Business Center, USA at (703) 370-8082. Fax: (703) 370-8083. E-mail: ibpusa3@gmail.com Global Business and Investment Info Databank - www.ibpus.com

(1) shall take into account whether the rate or charge that has been published or assessed, or that would result from the pertinent classification, rule, or regulation, is below a level that is fully compensatory to the controlled carrier based on the carrier's actual costs or constructive costs; and

(2) may take into account other appropriate factors, including whether the rate, charge, classification, rule, or regulation is—

(A) the same as, or similar to, those published or assessed by other carriers in the same trade;

(B) required to ensure movement of particular cargo in the same trade; or

(C)

required to maintain acceptable continuity, level, or quality of common carrier service to or from affected ports.

§ 40703. Effective date of rates

Notwithstanding section 40501(e) of this title and except for service contracts, a rate, charge, classification, rule, or regulation of a controlled carrier may not become effective, without special permission of the Federal Maritime Commission, until the 30th day after publication.

§ 40704. Commission review

(a) REQUEST FOR JUSTIFICATION.—On request of the Federal Maritime Commission, a controlled carrier shall file with the Commission, within 20 days of the request, a statement of justification that sufficiently details the carrier's need and purpose for an existing or proposed rate, charge, classification, rule, or regulation and upon which the Commission may reasonably base a determination of its lawfulness.

(b) DETERMINATION.—Within 120 days after receipt of information requested under subsection (a) , the Commission shall determine whether the rate, charge, classification, rule, or regulation may be unjust and unreasonable.

(c) SHOW CAUSE ORDER.—Whenever the Commission is of the opinion that a rate, charge, classification, rule, or regulation published or assessed by a controlled carrier may be unjust and unreasonable, the Commission shall issue an order to the controlled carrier to show cause why the rate, charge, classification, rule, or regulation should not be prohibited.

(d) SUSPENSION PENDING DETERMINATION.—

(1) NOT YET EFFECTIVE.—Pending a determination of the lawfulness of a rate, charge, classification, rule, or regulation in a proceeding under subsection (c) , the Commission may suspend the rate, charge, classification, rule, or regulation at any time before its effective date.

(2) ALREADY EFFECTIVE.—If a rate, charge, classification, rule, or regulation has already become effective, the Commission, on issuance of an order to show cause, may suspend the rate, charge, classification, rule, or regulation on at least 30 days' notice to the controlled carrier.

For additional analytical, business and investment opportunities information, please contact Global Investment & Business Center, USA at (703) 370-8082. Fax: (703) 370-8083. E-mail: ibpusa3@gmail.com Global Business and Investment Info Databank - www.ibpus.com

(3) MAXIMUM SUSPENSION.—A period of suspension under this subsection may not exceed 180 days.

(e) REPLACEMENT DURING SUSPENSION.—Whenever the Commission has suspended a rate, charge, classification, rule, or regulation under this section, the controlled carrier may publish a new rate, charge, classification, rule, or regulation to take effect immediately during the suspension in lieu of the suspended rate, charge, classification, rule, or regulation. However, the Commission may reject the new rate, charge, classification, rule, or regulation if the Commission believes it is unjust and unreasonable.

§ 40705. Presidential review of Commission orders

(a) TRANSMISSION TO PRESIDENT.—The Federal Maritime Commission shall transmit to the President, concurrently with publication thereof, each order of suspension or final order of prohibition issued under section 40704 of this title.

(b) PRESIDENTIAL REQUEST AND COMMISSION ACTION.—Within 10 days after receipt or the effective date of a Commission order referred to in subsection (a) , the President, in writing, may request the Commission to stay the effect of the order if the President finds that the stay is required for reasons of national defense or foreign policy. The reasons shall be specified in the request. The Commission shall immediately grant the request by issuing an order in which the President's request shall be described. During a stay, the President shall, whenever practicable, attempt to resolve the matter by negotiating with representatives of the applicable foreign governments.

§ 40706. Exceptions

This chapter does not apply to—

(1) a controlled carrier of a foreign country whose vessels are entitled by a treaty of the United States to receive national or most-favored-nation treatment; or

(2) a trade served only by controlled carriers.

CHAPTER 409—OCEAN TRANSPORTATION INTERMEDIARIES

Sec. 40901. License requirement. 40902. Financial responsibility. 40903. Suspension or revocation of license. 40904. Compensation by common carriers.

§ 40901. License requirement

(a) IN GENERAL.—A person in the United States may not act as an ocean transportation intermediary unless the person holds an ocean transportation intermediary's license issued by the Federal Maritime Commission. The Commission shall issue a license to a person that the Commission determines to be qualified by experience and character to act as an ocean transportation intermediary.

(b) EXCEPTION.—A person whose primary business is the sale of merchandise may forward shipments of the merchandise for its own account without an ocean transportation intermediary's license.

§ 40902. Financial responsibility

(a) IN GENERAL.—A person may not act as an ocean transportation intermediary unless the person furnishes a bond, proof of insurance, or other surety—

(1) in a form and amount determined by the Federal Maritime Commission to insure financial responsibility; and

(2) issued by a surety company found acceptable by the Secretary of the Treasury.

(b) SCOPE OF FINANCIAL RESPONSIBILITY.—A bond, insurance, or other surety obtained under this section—

(1) shall be available to pay any penalty assessed under section 41109 of this title or any order for reparation issued under section 41305 of this title;

(2) may be available to pay any claim against an ocean transportation intermediary arising from its transportation-related activities—

(A) with the consent of the insured ocean transportation intermediary and subject to review by the surety company; or

(B) when the claim is deemed valid by the surety company after the ocean transportation intermediary has failed to respond to adequate notice to address the validity of the claim; and

(3) shall be available to pay any judgment for damages against an ocean transportation intermediary arising from its transportation-related activities, if the claimant has first attempted to resolve the claim under paragraph (2) and the claim has not been resolved within a reasonable period of time.

(c) REGULATIONS ON COURT JUDGMENTS.—The Commission shall prescribe regulations for the purpose of protecting the interests of claimants, ocean transportation intermediaries, and surety companies with respect to the process of pursuing claims against ocean transportation intermediary bonds, insurance, or sureties through court judgments. The regulations shall provide that a judgment for monetary damages may not be enforced except to the extent that the damages claimed arise from the transportation-related activities of the insured ocean transportation intermediary, as defined by the Commission.

(d)

RESIDENT AGENT.—An ocean transportation intermediary not domiciled in the United States shall designate a resident agent in the United States for receipt of service of judicial and administrative process, including subpoenas.

§ 40903. Suspension or revocation of license

(a)

FAILURE TO MAINTAIN QUALIFICATIONS OR TO COMPLY.—The Federal Maritime Commission, after notice and opportunity for a hearing, shall suspend or revoke an ocean

For additional analytical, business and investment opportunities information, please contact Global Investment & Business Center, USA at (703) 370-8082. Fax: (703) 370-8083. E-mail: ibpusa3@gmail.com Global Business and Investment Info Databank - www.ibpus.com

transportation intermediary's license if the Commission finds that the ocean transportation intermediary—

(1)

is not qualified to provide intermediary services; or

(2)

willfully failed to comply with a provision of this part or with an order or regulation of the Commission.

(b)

FAILURE TO MAINTAIN BOND, PROOF OF INSURANCE, OR OTHER SURETY.—The Commission may revoke an ocean transportation Intermediary's license for failure to maintain a bond, proof of insurance, or other surety as required by section 40902(a) of this title.

§ 40904. Compensation by common carriers

(a)

CERTIFICATION OF LICENSE AND SERVICES.—A common carrier may compensate an ocean freight forwarder for a shipment dispatched for others only when the ocean freight forwarder has certified in writing that it holds an ocean transportation intermediary's license (if required under section 40901 of this title) and has—

(1)

engaged, booked, secured, reserved, or contracted directly with the carrier or its agent for space aboard a vessel or confirmed the availability of the space; and

(2)

prepared and processed the ocean bill of lading, dock receipt, or other similar document for the shipment.

(b)

DUAL COMPENSATION.—A common carrier may not pay compensation for services described in subsection (a) more than once on the same shipment.

(c)

BENEFICIAL INTEREST SHIPMENTS.—An ocean freight forwarder may not receive compensation from a common carrier for a shipment in which the ocean freight forwarder has a direct or indirect beneficial interest. A common carrier may not knowingly pay compensation on that shipment.

For additional analytical, business and investment opportunities information, please contact Global Investment & Business Center, USA at (703) 370-8082. Fax: (703) 370-8083. E-mail: ibpusa3@gmail.com Global Business and Investment Info Databank - www.ibpus.com

(d)

LIMITS ON AUTHORITY OF CONFERENCE OR GROUP.—A conference or group of two or more ocean common carriers in the foreign commerce of the United States that is authorized to agree on the level of compensation paid to an ocean freight forwarder may not—

(1)

deny a member of the conference or group the right, upon notice of not more than 5 days, to take independent action on any level of compensation paid to an ocean freight forwarder; or

(2)

agree to limit the payment of compensation to an ocean freight forwarder to less than 1.25 percent of the aggregate of all rates and charges applicable under a tariff and assessed against the cargo on which the services of the ocean freight forwarder are provided.

CHAPTER 411—PROHIBITIONS AND PENALTIES

§ 41101. Joint ventures and consortiums

In this chapter, a joint venture or consortium of two or more common carriers operating as a single entity is deemed to be a single common carrier.

§ 41102. General prohibitions

(a)

OBTAINING TRANSPORTATION AT LESS THAN APPLICABLE RATES.—A person may not knowingly and willfully, directly or indirectly, by means of false billing, false classification, false weighing, false report of weight, false measurement, or any other unjust or unfair device or means, obtain or attempt to obtain ocean transportation for property at less than the rates or charges that would otherwise apply.

(b)

OPERATING CONTRARY TO AGREEMENT.—A person may not operate under an agreement required to be filed under section 40302 or 40305 of this title if—

(1)

the agreement has not become effective under section 40304 of this title or has been rejected, disapproved, or canceled; or

(2)

the operation is not in accordance with the terms of the agreement or any modifications to the agreement made by the Federal Maritime Commission.

(c)

PRACTICES IN HANDLING PROPERTY.—A common carrier, marine terminal operator, or ocean transportation intermediary may not fail to establish, observe, and enforce just and reasonable regulations and practices relating to or connected with receiving, handling, storing, or delivering property.

§ 41103. Disclosure of information

(a)

PROHIBITION.—A common carrier, marine terminal operator, or ocean freight forwarder, either alone or in conjunction with any other person, directly or indirectly, may not knowingly disclose, offer, solicit, or receive any information concerning the nature, kind, quantity, destination, consignee, or routing of any property tendered or delivered to a common carrier, without the consent of the shipper or consignee, if the information—

(1)

may be used to the detriment or prejudice of the shipper, the consignee, or any common carrier; or

(2)

may improperly disclose its business transaction to a competitor.

(b)

EXCEPTIONS.—Subsection (a) does not prevent providing the information—

(1)

in response to legal process;

(2)

to the Federal Maritime Commission or an agency of the United States Government; or

(3)

For additional analytical, business and investment opportunities information, please contact Global Investment & Business Center, USA at (703) 370-8082. Fax: (703) 370-8083. E-mail: ibpusa3@gmail.com Global Business and Investment Info Databank - www.ibpus.com

to an independent neutral body operating within the scope of its authority to fulfill the policing obligations of the parties to an agreement effective under this part.

(c)

DISCLOSURE FOR DETERMINING BREACH OR COMPILING STATISTICS.—An ocean common carrier that is a party to a conference agreement approved under this part, a receiver, trustee, lessee, agent, or employee of the carrier, or any other person authorized by the carrier to receive information—

(1)

may give information to the conference or any person or agency designated by the conference, for the purpose of—

(A)

determining whether a shipper or consignee has breached an agreement with the conference or its member lines;

(B)

determining whether a member of the conference has breached the conference agreement; or

(C)

compiling statistics of cargo movement; and

(2)

may not prevent the conference or its designee from soliciting or receiving information for any of those purposes.

§ 41104. Common carriers

A common carrier, either alone or in conjunction with any other person, directly or indirectly, may not—

(1)

allow a person to obtain transportation for property at less than the rates or charges established by the carrier in its tariff or service contract by means of false billing, false classification, false weighing, false measurement, or any other unjust or unfair device or means;

(2)

provide service in the liner trade that is—

For additional analytical, business and investment opportunities information, please contact Global Investment & Business Center, USA at (703) 370-8082. Fax: (703) 370-8083. E-mail: ibpusa3@gmail.com
Global Business and Investment Info Databank - www.ibpus.com

(A)

not in accordance with the rates, charges, classifications, rules, and practices contained in a tariff published or a service contract entered into under chapter 405 of this title, unless excepted or exempted under section 40103 or 40501(a) (2) of this title; or

(B)

under a tariff or service contract that has been suspended or prohibited by the Federal Maritime Commission under chapter 407 or 423 of this title;

(3)

retaliate against a shipper by refusing, or threatening to refuse, cargo space accommodations when available, or resort to other unfair or unjustly discriminatory methods because the shipper has patronized another carrier, or has filed a complaint, or for any other reason;

(4)

for service pursuant to a tariff, engage in any unfair or unjustly discriminatory practice in the matter of—

(A)

rates or charges;

(B)

cargo classifications;

(C)

cargo space accommodations or other facilities, with due regard being given to the proper loading of the vessel and the available tonnage;

(D)

loading and landing of freight; or

(E)

adjustment and settlement of claims;

(5)

for service pursuant to a service contract, engage in any unfair or unjustly discriminatory practice in the matter of rates or charges with respect to any port;

For additional analytical, business and investment opportunities information, please contact Global Investment & Business Center, USA at (703) 370-8082. Fax: (703) 370-8083. E-mail: ibpusa3@gmail.com Global Business and Investment Info Databank - www.ibpus.com

(6)

use a vessel in a particular trade for the purpose of excluding, preventing, or reducing competition by driving another ocean common carrier out of that trade;

(7)

offer or pay any deferred rebates;

(8)

for service pursuant to a tariff, give any undue or unreasonable preference or advantage or impose any undue or unreasonable prejudice or disadvantage;

(9)

for service pursuant to a service contract, give any undue or unreasonable preference or advantage or impose any undue or unreasonable prejudice or disadvantage with respect to any port;

(10)

unreasonably refuse to deal or negotiate;

(11)

knowingly and willfully accept cargo from or transport cargo for the account of an ocean transportation intermediary that does not have a tariff as required by section 40501 of this title and a bond, insurance, or other surety as required by section 40902 of this title; or

(12)

knowingly and willfully enter into a service contract with an ocean transportation intermediary that does not have a tariff as required by section 40501 of this title and a bond, insurance, or other surety as required by section 40902 of this title, or with an affiliate of such an ocean transportation intermediary.

§ 41105. Concerted action

A conference or group of two or more common carriers may not—

(1)

boycott or take any other concerted action resulting in an unreasonable refusal to deal;

(2)

engage in conduct that unreasonably restricts the use of intermodal services or technological innovations;

For additional analytical, business and investment opportunities information, please contact Global Investment & Business Center, USA at (703) 370-8082. Fax: (703) 370-8083. E-mail: ibpusa3@gmail.com Global Business and Investment Info Databank - www.ibpus.com

(3)

engage in any predatory practice designed to eliminate the participation, or deny the entry, in a particular trade of a common carrier not a member of the conference, a group of common carriers, an ocean tramp, or a bulk carrier;

(4)

negotiate with a non-ocean carrier or group of non-ocean carriers (such as truck, rail, or air operators) on any matter relating to rates or services provided to ocean common carriers within the United States by those non-ocean carriers, unless the negotiations and any resulting agreements are not in violation of the antitrust laws and are consistent with the purposes of this part, except that this paragraph does not prohibit the setting and publishing of a joint through rate by a conference, joint venture, or association of ocean common carriers;

(5)

deny in the export foreign commerce of the United States compensation to an ocean freight forwarder or limit that compensation to less than a reasonable amount;

(6)

allocate shippers among specific carriers that are parties to the agreement or prohibit a carrier that is a party to the agreement from soliciting cargo from a particular shipper, except as—

(A)

authorized by section 40303(d) of this title;

(B)

required by the law of the United States or the importing or exporting country; or

(C)

agreed to by a shipper in a service contract;

(7)

for service pursuant to a service contract, engage in any unjustly discriminatory practice in the matter of rates or charges with respect to any locality, port, or person due to the person's status as a shippers' association or ocean transportation intermediary; or

(8)

for service pursuant to a service contract, give any undue or unreasonable preference or advantage or impose any undue or unreasonable prejudice or disadvantage with respect

For additional analytical, business and investment opportunities information, please contact Global Investment & Business Center, USA at (703) 370-8082. Fax: (703) 370-8083. E-mail: ibpusa3@gmail.com Global Business and Investment Info Databank - www.ibpus.com

to any locality, port, or person due to the person's status as a shippers' association or ocean transportation intermediary.

§ 41106. Marine terminal operators

A marine terminal operator may not—

(1)

agree with another marine terminal operator or with a common carrier to boycott, or unreasonably discriminate in the provision of terminal services to, a common carrier or ocean tramp;

(2)

give any undue or unreasonable preference or advantage or impose any undue or unreasonable prejudice or disadvantage with respect to any person; or

(3)

unreasonably refuse to deal or negotiate.

§ 41107. Monetary penalties

(a)

IN GENERAL.—A person that violates this part or a regulation or order of the Federal Maritime Commission issued under this part is liable to the United States Government for a civil penalty. Unless otherwise provided in this part, the amount of the penalty may not exceed $5,000 for each violation or, if the violation was willfully and knowingly committed, $25,000 for each violation. Each day of a continuing violation is a separate violation.

(b)

LIEN ON CARRIER'S VESSELS.—The amount of a civil penalty imposed on a common carrier under this section constitutes a lien on the vessels operated by the carrier. Any such vessel is subject to an action in rem to enforce the lien in the district court of the United States for the district in which it is found.

§ 41108. Additional penalties

(a)

SUSPENSION OF TARIFFS.—For a violation of section 41104(1) , (2) , or (7) of this title, the Federal Maritime Commission may suspend any or all tariffs of the common carrier, or that common carrier's right to use any or all tariffs of conferences of which it is a member, for a period not to exceed 12 months.

(b)

For additional analytical, business and investment opportunities information, please contact Global Investment & Business Center, USA at (703) 370-8082. Fax: (703) 370-8083. E-mail: ibpusa3@gmail.com Global Business and Investment Info Databank - www.ibpus.com

OPERATING UNDER SUSPENDED TARIFF.—A common carrier that accepts or handles cargo for carriage under a tariff that has been suspended, or after its right to use that tariff has been suspended, is liable to the United States Government for a civil penalty of not more than $50,000 for each shipment.

(c)

FAILURE TO PROVIDE INFORMATION.—

(1)

PENALTIES.—If the Commission finds, after notice and opportunity for a hearing, that a common carrier has failed to supply information ordered to be produced or compelled by subpoena under section 41303 of this title, the Commission may—

(A)

suspend any or all tariffs of the carrier or the carrier's right to use any or all tariffs of conferences of which it is a member; and

(B)

request the Secretary of Homeland Security to refuse or revoke any clearance required for a vessel operated by the carrier, and when so requested, the Secretary shall refuse or revoke the clearance.

(2) DEFENSE BASED ON FOREIGN LAW.—If, in defense of its failure to comply with a subpoena or discovery order, a common carrier alleges that information or documents located in a foreign country cannot be produced because of the laws of that country, the Commission shall immediately notify the Secretary of State of the failure to comply and of the allegation relating to foreign laws. On receiving the notification, the Secretary of State shall promptly consult with the government of the nation within which the information or documents are alleged to be located for the purpose of assisting the Commission in obtaining the information or documents.

(d) IMPAIRING ACCESS TO FOREIGN TRADE.—If the Commission finds, after notice and opportunity for a hearing, that the action of a common carrier, acting alone or in concert with another person, or a foreign government has unduly impaired access of a vessel documented under the laws of the United States to ocean trade between foreign ports, the Commission shall take action that it finds appropriate, including imposing any of the penalties authorized by this section. The Commission also may take any of the actions authorized by sections 42304 and 42305 of this title.

(e) SUBMISSION OF ORDER TO PRESIDENT.—Before an order under this section becomes effective, it shall be submitted immediately to the President. The President, within 10 days after receiving it, may disapprove it if the President finds that disapproval is required for reasons of national defense or foreign policy.

§ 41109. Assessment of penalties

(a) GENERAL AUTHORITY.—Until a matter is referred to the Attorney General, the Federal Maritime Commission may, after notice and opportunity for a hearing, assess a civil penalty

For additional analytical, business and investment opportunities information, please contact Global Investment & Business Center, USA at (703) 370-8082. Fax: (703) 370-8083. E-mail: ibpusa3@gmail.com Global Business and Investment Info Databank - www.ibpus.com

provided for in this part. The Commission may compromise, modify, or remit, with or without conditions, a civil penalty.

(b) FACTORS IN DETERMINING AMOUNT.—In determining the amount of a civil penalty, the Commission shall take into account the nature, circumstances, extent, and gravity of the violation committed and, with respect to the violator, the degree of culpability, history of prior offenses, ability to pay, and other matters justice may require.

(c) EXCEPTION.—A civil penalty may not be imposed for conspiracy to violate section 41102(a) or 41104(1) or (2) of this title or to defraud the Commission by concealing such a violation.

(d) PROHIBITED BASIS OF PENALTY.—The Commission or a court may not order a person to pay the difference between the amount billed and agreed upon in writing with a common carrier or its agent and the amount set forth in a tariff or service contract by that common carrier for the transportation service provided.

(e) TIME LIMIT.—A proceeding to assess a civil penalty under this section must be commenced within 5 years after the date of the violation.

(f) REVIEW OF CIVIL PENALTY.—A person against whom a civil penalty is assessed under this section may obtain review under chapter 158 of title 28.

(g) CIVIL ACTIONS TO COLLECT.—If a person does not pay an assessment of a civil penalty after it has become final or after the appropriate court has entered final judgment in favor of the Commission, the Attorney General at the request of the Commission may seek to collect the amount assessed in an appropriate district court of the United States. The court shall enforce the order of the Commission unless it finds that the order was not regularly made and duly issued.

CHAPTER 413—ENFORCEMENT

Sec. 41301. Complaints. 41302. Investigations. 41303. Discovery and subpoenas. 41304. Hearings and orders. 41305. Award of reparations. 41306. Injunctive relief sought by complainants. 41307. Injunctive relief sought by the Commission. 41308. Enforcement of subpoenas and orders. 41309. Enforcement of reparation orders.

§ 41301. Complaints

(a) IN GENERAL.—A person may file with the Federal Maritime Commission a sworn complaint alleging a violation of this part, except section 41307(b) (1) . If the complaint is filed within 3 years after the claim accrues, the complainant may seek reparations for an injury to the complainant caused by the violation.

(b) NOTICE AND RESPONSE.—The Commission shall provide a copy of the complaint to the person named in the complaint. Within a reasonable time specified by the Commission, the person shall satisfy the complaint or answer it in writing.

(c) IF COMPLAINT NOT SATISFIED.—If the complaint is not satisfied, the Commission shall investigate the complaint in an appropriate manner and make an appropriate order.

§ 41302. Investigations

For additional analytical, business and investment opportunities information, please contact Global Investment & Business Center, USA at (703) 370-8082. Fax: (703) 370-8083. E-mail: ibpusa3@gmail.com Global Business and Investment Info Databank - www.ibpus.com

(a) IN GENERAL.—The Federal Maritime Commission, on complaint or its own motion, may investigate any conduct or agreement that the Commission believes may be in violation of this part. The Commission may by order disapprove, cancel, or modify any agreement that operates in violation of this part.

(b) EFFECTIVENESS OF AGREEMENT DURING INVESTIGATION.—Unless an injunction is issued under section 41306 or 41307 of this title, an agreement under investigation by the Commission remains in effect until the Commission issues its order.

(c) DATE FOR DECISION.—Within 10 days after the initiation of a proceeding under this section or section 41301 of this title, the Commission shall set a date by which it will issue its final decision. The Commission by order may extend the date for good cause.

(d) SANCTIONS FOR DELAY.—If, within the period for final decision under subsection (c) , the Commission determines that it is unable to issue a final decision because of undue delay caused by a party to the proceeding, the Commission may impose sanctions, including issuing a decision adverse to the delaying party.

(e) REPORT.—The Commission shall make a written report of every investigation under this part in which a hearing was held, stating its conclusions, decisions, findings of fact, and order. The Commission shall provide a copy of the report to all parties and publish the report for public information. A published report is competent evidence in a court of the United States.

§ 41303. Discovery and subpoenas

(a) IN GENERAL.—In an investigation or adjudicatory proceeding under this part—

(1) the Federal Maritime Commission may subpoena witnesses and evidence; and

(2) a party may use depositions, written interrogatories, and discovery procedures under regulations prescribed by the Commission that, to the extent practicable, shall conform to the Federal Rules of Civil Procedure (28 App. U.S.C.) .

(b) WITNESS FEES.—Unless otherwise prohibited by law, a witness is entitled to the same fees and mileage as in the courts of the United States.

§ 41304. Hearings and orders

(a) OPPORTUNITY FOR HEARING.—The Federal Maritime Commission shall provide an opportunity for a hearing before issuing an order relating to a violation of this part or a regulation prescribed under this part.

(b) MODIFICATION OF ORDER.—The Commission may reverse, suspend, or modify any of its orders.

(c) REHEARING.—On application of a party to a proceeding, the Commission may grant a rehearing of the same or any matter determined in the proceeding. Except by order of the Commission, a rehearing does not operate as a stay of an order.

(d) PERIOD OF EFFECTIVENESS.—An order of the Commission remains in effect for the period specified in the order or until suspended, modified, or set aside by the Commission or a court of competent jurisdiction.

§ 41305. Award of reparations

(a) DEFINITION.—In this section, the term "actual injury" includes the loss of interest at commercial rates compounded from the date of injury.

(b) BASIC AMOUNT.—If the complaint was filed within the period specified in section 41301(a) of this title, the Federal Maritime Commission shall direct the payment of reparations to the complainant for actual injury caused by a violation of this part, plus reasonable attorney fees.

(c) ADDITIONAL AMOUNTS.—On a showing that the injury was caused by an activity prohibited by section 41102(b) , 41104(3) or (6) , or 41105(1) or (3) of this title, the Commission may order the payment of additional amounts, but the total recovery of a complainant may not exceed twice the amount of the actual injury.

(d) DIFFERENCE BETWEEN RATES.—If the injury was caused by an activity prohibited by section 41104(4) (A) or (B) of this title, the amount of the injury shall be the difference between the rate paid by the injured shipper and the most favorable rate paid by another shipper.

§ 41306. Injunctive relief sought by complainants

(a) IN GENERAL.—After filing a complaint with the Federal Maritime Commission under section 41301 of this title, the complainant may bring a civil action in a district court of the United States to enjoin conduct in violation of this part.

(b) VENUE.—The action must be brought in the judicial district in which—

(1) the Commission has brought a civil action against the defendant under section 41307(a) of this title; or

(2) the defendant resides or transacts business, if the Commission has not brought such an action.

(c) REMEDIES BY COURT.—After notice to the defendant, and a showing that the standards for granting injunctive relief by courts of equity are met, the court may grant a temporary restraining order or preliminary injunction for a period not to exceed 10 days after the Commission has issued an order disposing of the complaint.

(d) ATTORNEY FEES.—A defendant prevailing in a civil action under this section shall be allowed reasonable attorney fees to be assessed and collected as part of the costs of the action.

§ 41307. Injunctive relief sought by the Commission

(a) GENERAL VIOLATIONS.—In connection with an investigation under section 41301 or 41302 of this title, the Federal Maritime Commission may bring a civil action to enjoin conduct in violation of this part. The action must be brought in the district court of the United States for any judicial district in which the defendant resides or transacts business. After notice to the defendant,

For additional analytical, business and investment opportunities information, please contact Global Investment & Business Center, USA at (703) 370-8082. Fax: (703) 370-8083. E-mail: ibpusa3@gmail.com Global Business and Investment Info Databank - www.ibpus.com

and a showing that the standards for granting injunctive relief by courts of equity are met, the court may grant a temporary restraining order or preliminary injunction for a period not to exceed 10 days after the Commission has issued an order disposing of the issues under investigation.

(b) REDUCTION IN COMPETITION.—

(1) ACTION BY COMMISSION.—If, at any time after the filing or effective date of an agreement under chapter 403 of this title, the Commission determines that the agreement is likely, by a reduction in competition, to produce an unreasonable reduction in transportation service or an unreasonable increase in transportation cost, the Commission, after notice to the person filing the agreement, may bring a civil action in the United States District Court for the District of Columbia to enjoin the operation of the agreement. The Commission's sole remedy with respect to an agreement likely to have such an effect is an action under this subsection.

(2) REMEDIES BY COURT.—In an action under this subsection, the court may issue—

(A) a temporary restraining order or a preliminary injunction; and

(B) a permanent injunction after a showing that the agreement is likely to have the effect described in paragraph (1) .

(3) BURDEN OF PROOF AND THIRD PARTIES.—In an action under this subsection, the burden of proof is on the Commission. The court may not allow a third party to intervene.

(c) FAILURE TO PROVIDE INFORMATION.—If a person filing an agreement, or an officer, director, partner, agent, or employee of the person, fails substantially to comply with a request for the submission of additional information or documents within the period provided in section 40304(c) of this title, the Commission may bring a civil action in the United States District Court for the District of Columbia. At the request of the Commission, the Court—

(1) may order compliance;

(2) shall extend the period specified in section 40304(c) (2) of this title until there has been substantial compliance; and

(3) may grant other equitable relief that the court decides is appropriate.

(d) REPRESENTATION.—The Commission may represent itself in a proceeding under this section in—

(1) a district court of the United States, on notice to the Attorney General; and

(2) a court of appeals of the United States, with the approval of the Attorney General.

§ 41308. Enforcement of subpoenas and orders

(a) CIVIL ACTION.—If a person does not comply with a subpoena or order of the Federal Maritime Commission, the Attorney General, at the request of the Commission, or an injured party, may seek enforcement in a district court of the United States having jurisdiction over the

For additional analytical, business and investment opportunities information, please contact Global Investment & Business Center, USA at (703) 370-8082. Fax: (703) 370-8083. E-mail: ibpusa3@gmail.com Global Business and Investment Info Databank - www.ibpus.com

parties. If, after hearing, the court determines that the subpoena or order was regularly made and duly issued, the court shall enforce the subpoena or order.

(b) TIME LIMIT ON BRINGING ACTIONS.—An action under this section to enforce an order of the Commission must be brought within 3 years after the date the order was violated.

§ 41309. Enforcement of reparation orders

(a) CIVIL ACTION.—If a person does not comply with an order of the Federal Maritime Commission for the payment of reparation, the person to whom the award was made may seek enforcement of the order in a district court of the United States having jurisdiction over the parties.

(b) PARTIES AND SERVICE OF PROCESS.—All parties in whose favor the Commission has made an award of reparation by a single order may be joined as plaintiffs, and all other parties in the order may be joined as defendants, in a single action in a judicial district in which any one plaintiff could maintain an action against any one defendant. Service of process against a defendant not found in that district may be made in a district in which any office of that defendant is located or in which any port of call on a regular route operated by that defendant is located. Judgment may be entered for any plaintiff against the defendant liable to that plaintiff.

(c) NATURE OF REVIEW.—In an action under this section, the findings and order of the Commission are prima facie evidence of the facts stated in the findings and order.

(d) COSTS AND ATTORNEY FEES.—The plaintiff is not liable for costs of the action or for costs of any subsequent stage of the proceedings unless they accrue on the plaintiff's appeal. A prevailing plaintiff shall be allowed reasonable attorney fees to be assessed and collected as part of the costs of the action.

(e) TIME LIMIT ON BRINGING ACTIONS.—An action under this section to enforce an order of the Commission must be brought within 3 years after the date the order was violated.

CHAPTER 423—FOREIGN SHIPPING PRACTICES

Sec. 42301. Definitions. 42302. Investigations. 42303. Information requests. 42304. Action against foreign carriers. 42305. Refusal of clearance and entry. 42306. Submission of determinations to President. 42307. Review of regulations and orders.

§ 42301. Definitions

(a) DEFINED IN PART A.—In this chapter, the terms "common carrier", "marine terminal operator", "ocean common carrier", "ocean transportation intermediary", "shipper", and "shippers' association" have the meaning given those terms in section 40102 of this title.

(b) OTHER DEFINITIONS.—In this chapter:

(1) FOREIGN CARRIER.—The term "foreign carrier" means an ocean common carrier a majority of whose vessels are documented under the laws of a foreign country.

For additional analytical, business and investment opportunities information, please contact Global Investment & Business Center, USA at (703) 370-8082. Fax: (703) 370-8083. E-mail: ibpusa3@gmail.com Global Business and Investment Info Databank - www.ibpus.com

(2) MARITIME SERVICES.—The term “maritime services” means port-to-port transportation of cargo by vessels operated by an ocean common carrier.

(3) MARITIME-RELATED SERVICES.—The term “maritime-related services” means intermodal operations, terminal operations, cargo solicitation, agency services, ocean transportation intermediary services and operations, and all other activities and services integral to total transportation systems of ocean common carriers and their foreign domiciled affiliates for themselves and others.

(4) UNITED STATES CARRIER.—The term “United States carrier” means an ocean common carrier operating vessels documented under the laws of the United States.

(5) UNITED STATES OCEANBORNE TRADE.—The term “United States oceanborne trade” means the carriage of cargo between the United States and a foreign country, whether directly or indirectly, by an ocean common carrier.

§ 42302. Investigations

(a) IN GENERAL.—The Federal Maritime Commission shall investigate whether any laws, rules, regulations, policies, or practices of a foreign government, or any practices of a foreign carrier or other person providing maritime or maritime-related services in a foreign country, result in the existence of conditions that—

(1) adversely affect the operations of United States carriers in United States oceanborne trade; and

(2) do not exist for foreign carriers of that country in the United States under the laws of the United States or as a result of acts of United States carriers or other persons providing maritime or maritime-related services in the United States.

(b) INITIATION OF INVESTIGATION.—An investigation under subsection (a) may be initiated by the Commission on its own motion or on the petition of any person, including another component of the United States Government.

(c) TIME FOR DECISION.—The Commission shall complete an investigation under this section and render a decision within 120 days after it is initiated. However, the Commission may extend this 120-day period for an additional 90 days if the Commission is unable to obtain sufficient information to determine whether a condition specified in subsection (a) exists. A notice providing an extension shall state clearly the reasons for the extension.

§ 42303. Information requests

(a) IN GENERAL.—To further the purposes of section 42302(a) of this title, the Federal Maritime Commission may order any person (including a common carrier, shipper, shippers' association, ocean transportation intermediary, or marine terminal operator, or an officer, receiver, trustee, lessee, agent or employee thereof) to file with the Commission any periodic or special report, answers to questions, documentary material, or other information the Commission considers necessary or appropriate. The Commission may require the response to any such order to be made under oath. The response shall be provided in the form and within the time specified by the Commission.

(b) SUBPOENAS.—In an investigation under section 42302 of this title, the Commission may subpoena witnesses and evidence.

(c) NONDISCLOSURE.—Notwithstanding any other provision of law, the Commission may determine that any information submitted to it in response to a request under this section, or otherwise, shall not be disclosed to the public.

§ 42304. Action against foreign carriers

(a) IN GENERAL.—Subject to section 42306 of this title, whenever the Federal Maritime Commission, after notice and opportunity for comment or hearing, determines that the conditions specified in section 42302(a) of this title exist, the Commission shall take such action to offset those conditions as it considers necessary and appropriate against any foreign carrier that is a contributing cause, or whose government is a contributing cause, to those conditions. The action may include—

(1) limitations on voyages to and from United States ports or on the amount or type of cargo carried;

(2) suspension, in whole or in part, of any or all tariffs and service contracts, including an ocean common carrier's right to use any or all tariffs and service contracts of conferences in United States trades of which it is a member for any period the Commission specifies;

(3) suspension, in whole or in part, of an ocean common carrier's right to operate under any agreement filed with the Commission, including any agreement authorizing preferential treatment at terminals, preferential terminal leases, space chartering, or pooling of cargo or revenue with other ocean common carriers; and

(4) a fee not to exceed $1,000,000 per voyage.

(b) CONSULTATION.—The Commission may consult with, seek the cooperation of, or make recommendations to other appropriate agencies of the United States Government prior to taking any action under subsection (a) .

§ 42305. Refusal of clearance and entry

Subject to section 42306 of this title, whenever the Federal Maritime Commission determines that the conditions specified in section 42302(a) of this title exist, then at the request of the Commission—

(1) the Secretary of Homeland Security shall refuse the clearance required by section 60105 of this title to a vessel of a foreign carrier that is identified by the Commission under section 42304 of this title; and

(2) the Secretary of the department in which the Coast Guard is operating shall—

(A) deny entry, for purposes of oceanborne trade, of a vessel of a foreign carrier that is identified by the Commission under section 42304 of this title, to a port or place in the United States or the navigable waters of the United States; or

For additional analytical, business and investment opportunities information, please contact Global Investment & Business Center, USA at (703) 370-8082. Fax: (703) 370-8083. E-mail: ibpusa3@gmail.com Global Business and Investment Info Databank - www.ibpus.com

(B) detain the vessel at the port or place in the United States from which it is about to depart for another port or place in the United States.

§ 42306. Submission of determinations to President

Before a determination under section 42304 of this title becomes effective or a request is made under section 42305 of this title, the determination shall be submitted immediately to the President. The President, within 10 days after receiving it, may disapprove it in writing, setting forth the reasons for the disapproval, if the President finds that disapproval is required for reasons of national defense or foreign policy.

§ 42307. Review of regulations and orders

A regulation or final order of the Federal Maritime Commission under this chapter is reviewable exclusively in the same forum and in the same manner as provided in section 2342(3) (B) of title 28.

CHAPTER 421—REGULATIONS AFFECTING SHIPPING IN FOREIGN TRADE

Sec. 42101. Regulations of the Commission. 42102. Regulations of other agencies. 42103. No preference to Government-owned vessels. 42104. Information, witnesses, and evidence. 42105. Disclosure to public. 42106. Other actions to remedy unfavorable conditions. 42107. Refusal of clearance and entry. 42108. Penalty for operating under suspended tariff or service contract. 42109. Consultation with other agencies.

§ 42101. Regulations of the Commission

(a) UNFAVORABLE CONDITIONS.—To further the objectives and policy set forth in section 50101 of this title, the Federal Maritime Commission shall prescribe regulations affecting shipping in foreign trade, not in conflict with law, to adjust or meet general or special conditions unfavorable to shipping in foreign trade, whether in a particular trade or on a particular route or in commerce generally, including intermodal movements, terminal operations, cargo solicitation, agency services, ocean transportation intermediary services and operations, and other activities and services integral to transportation systems, and which arise out of or result from laws or regulations of a foreign country or competitive methods, pricing practices, or other practices employed by owners, operators, agents, or masters of vessels of a foreign country.

(b) INITIATION OF REGULATION.—A regulation under subsection (a) may be initiated by the Commission on its own motion or on the petition of any person, including another component of the United States Government.

§ 42102. Regulations of other agencies

(a) REQUEST TO AGENCY.—To further the objectives and policy set forth in section 50101 of this title, the Federal Maritime Commission shall request the head of a department, agency, or instrumentality of the United States Government to suspend, modify, or annul any existing regulations, or to make new regulations, affecting shipping in the foreign trade, except regulations relating to the Public Health Service, the Consular Service, or the inspection of vessels.

(b) PRIOR REVIEW AND APPROVAL.—A department, agency, or instrumentality of the Government may not prescribe a regulation affecting shipping in the foreign trade (except a

For additional analytical, business and investment opportunities information, please contact Global Investment & Business Center, USA at (703) 370-8082. Fax: (703) 370-8083. E-mail: ibpusa3@gmail.com Global Business and Investment Info Databank - www.ibpus.com

regulation affecting the Public Health Service, the Consular Service, or the inspection of vessels) until the regulation has been submitted to the Commission for its approval and final action has been taken by the Commission or the President.

(c) SUBMISSION TO PRESIDENT.—If the head of a department, agency, or instrumentality of the Government refuses to comply with a request under subsection (a) or objects to a decision of the Commission under subsection (b) , the Commission or the head of the department, agency, or instrumentality may submit the facts to the President. The President may establish, suspend, modify, or annul the regulation.

§ 42103. No preference to Government-owned vessels

A regulation may not give a vessel owned by the United States Government a preference over a vessel owned by citizens of the United States and documented under the laws of the United States.

§ 42104. Information, witnesses, and evidence

(a) ORDER TO SUPPLY INFORMATION.—In carrying out section 42101 of this title, the Federal Maritime Commission may order any person (including a common carrier, tramp operator, bulk operator, shipper, shippers' association, ocean transportation intermediary, or marine terminal operator, or an officer, receiver, trustee, lessee, agent, or employee thereof) to file with the Commission a report, answers to questions, documentary material, or other information the Commission considers necessary or appropriate. The Commission may require the response to any such order to be made under oath. The response shall be provided in the form and within the time specified by the Commission.

(b) SUBPOENAS AND DISCOVERY.—In carrying out section 42101 of this title, the Commission may—

(1) subpoena witnesses and evidence; and

(2) authorize a party to use depositions, written interrogatories, and discovery procedures that, to the extent practicable, conform to the Federal Rules of Civil Procedure (28 App. U.S.C.) .

(c) WITNESS FEES.—Unless otherwise prohibited by law, and subject to funds being appropriated, a witness in a proceeding under section 42101 of this title is entitled to the same fees and mileage as in the courts of the United States.

(d) PENALTIES.—For failure to supply information ordered to be produced or compelled by subpoena under this section, the Commission may—

(1) after notice and opportunity for a hearing, suspend tariffs and service contracts of a common carrier or the common carrier's right to use tariffs of conferences and service contracts of agreements of which it is a member; or

(2) assess a civil penalty of not more than $5,000 for each day that the information is not provided.

(e) ENFORCEMENT.—If a person does not comply with an order or subpoena of the Commission under this section, the Commission may seek enforcement in a district court of the

For additional analytical, business and investment opportunities information, please contact Global Investment & Business Center, USA at (703) 370-8082. Fax: (703) 370-8083. E-mail: ibpusa3@gmail.com Global Business and Investment Info Databank - www.ibpus.com

United States having jurisdiction over the parties. If, after hearing, the court determines that the order or subpoena was regularly made and duly issued, the court shall enforce the order or subpoena.

§ 42105. Disclosure to public

Notwithstanding any other provision of law, the Federal Maritime Commission may refuse to disclose to the public a response or other information submitted to it under this chapter.

§ 42106. Other actions to remedy unfavorable conditions

If the Federal Maritime Commission finds that conditions unfavorable to shipping in foreign trade as described in section 42101 of this title exist, the Commission may—

(1) limit voyages to and from United States ports or the amount or type of cargo carried;

(2) suspend, in whole or in part, tariffs and service contracts for carriage to or from United States ports, including a common carrier's right to use tariffs of conferences and service contracts of agreements in United States trades of which it is a member for any period the Commission specifies;

(3) suspend, in whole or in part, an ocean common carrier's right to operate under any agreement filed with the Commission, including any agreement authorizing preferential treatment at terminals, preferential terminal leases, space chartering, or pooling of cargo or revenue with other ocean common carriers;

(4) impose a fee not to exceed $1,000,000 per voyage; or

(5) take any other action the Commission finds necessary and appropriate to adjust or meet any condition unfavorable to shipping in the foreign trade of the United States.

§ 42107. Refusal of clearance and entry

At the request of the Federal Maritime Commission—

(1) the Secretary of Homeland Security shall—

(A) refuse the clearance required by section 60105 of this title to a vessel of a country that is named in a regulation prescribed by the Commission under section 42101 of this title; and

(B) collect any fees imposed by the Commission under section 42106(4) of this title; and

(2) the Secretary of the department in which the Coast Guard is operating shall—

(A) deny entry, for purposes of oceanborne trade, of a vessel of a country that is named in a regulation prescribed by the Commission under section 42101 of this title, to a port or place in the United States or the navigable waters of the United States; or

(B) detain the vessel at the port or place in the United States from which it is about to depart for another port or place in the United States.

For additional analytical, business and investment opportunities information, please contact Global Investment & Business Center, USA at (703) 370-8082. Fax: (703) 370-8083. E-mail: ibpusa3@gmail.com Global Business and Investment Info Databank - www.ibpus.com

§ 42108. Penalty for operating under suspended tariff or service contract

A common carrier that accepts or handles cargo for carriage under a tariff or service contract that has been suspended under section 42104(d) (1) or 42106(2) of this title, or after its right to use another tariff or service contract has been suspended under those provisions, is liable to the United States Government for a civil penalty of not more than $50,000 for each day that it is found to be operating under a suspended tariff or service contract.

§ 42109. Consultation with other agencies

The Federal Maritime Commission may consult with, seek the cooperation of, or make recommendations to other appropriate agencies of the United States Government prior to taking any action under this chapter.

CHAPTER 441—EVIDENCE OF FINANCIAL RESPONSIBILITY FOR PASSENGER TRANSPORTATION

§ 44101. Application

This chapter applies to a vessel that—

(1) has berth or stateroom accommodations for at least 50 passengers; and

(2) boards passengers at a port in the United States.

§ 44102. Financial responsibility to indemnify passengers for nonperformance of transportation

(a) FILING REQUIREMENT.—A person in the United States may not arrange, offer, advertise, or provide transportation on a vessel to which this chapter applies unless the person has filed with the Federal Maritime Commission evidence of financial responsibility to indemnify passengers for nonperformance of the transportation.

(b) SATISFACTORY EVIDENCE.—To satisfy subsection (a) , a person must file—

(1) information the Commission considers necessary; or

(2) a copy of a bond or other security, in such form as the Commission by regulation may require.

(c) AUTHORIZED ISSUER OF BOND.—If a bond is filed, it must be issued by a bonding company authorized to do business in the United States.

§ 44103. Financial responsibility to pay liability for death or injury

For additional analytical, business and investment opportunities information, please contact Global Investment & Business Center, USA at (703) 370-8082. Fax: (703) 370-8083. E-mail: ibpusa3@gmail.com Global Business and Investment Info Databank - www.ibpus.com

(a) GENERAL REQUIREMENT.—The owner or charterer of a vessel to which this chapter applies shall establish, under regulations prescribed by the Federal Maritime Commission, financial responsibility to meet liability for death or injury to passengers or other individuals on a voyage to or from a port in the United States.

(b) AMOUNTS.—

(1) IN GENERAL.—The amount of financial responsibility required under subsection (a) shall be based on the number of passenger accommodations as follows:

(A) $20,000 for each of the first 500 passenger accommodations.

(B) $15,000 for each additional passenger accommodation between 501 and 1,000.

(C) $10,000 for each additional passenger accommodation between 1,001 and 1,500.

(D) $5,000 for each additional passenger accommodation over 1,500.

(2) MULTIPLE VESSELS.—If the owner or charterer is operating more than one vessel subject to this chapter, the amount of financial responsibility shall be based on the number of passenger accommodations on the vessel with the largest number of passenger accommodations.

(c) AVAILABILITY TO PAY JUDGMENT.—The amount determined under subsection (b) shall be available to pay a judgment for damages (whether less than or more than $20,000) for death or injury to a passenger or other individual on a voyage to or from a port in the United States.

(d) MEANS OF ESTABLISHING.—Financial responsibility under this section may be established

by one or more of the following if acceptable to the Commission:

(1) Insurance.

(2) Surety bond issued by a bonding company authorized to do business in the United States.

(3) Qualification as a self-insurer.

(4) Other evidence of financial responsibility.

§ 44104. Civil penalty

A person that violates section 44102 or 44103 of this title is liable to the United States Government for a civil penalty of not more than $5,000, plus $200 for each passage sold, to be assessed by the Federal Maritime Commission. The Commission may remit or mitigate the penalty on terms the Commission considers proper.

§ 44105. Refusal of clearance

The Secretary of Homeland Security shall refuse the clearance required by section 60105 of this title, at the port or place of departure from the United States, of a vessel that is subject to this

For additional analytical, business and investment opportunities information, please contact Global Investment & Business Center, USA at (703) 370-8082. Fax: (703) 370-8083. E-mail: ibpusa3@gmail.com Global Business and Investment Info Databank - www.ibpus.com

chapter and does not have evidence issued by the Federal Maritime Commission of compliance with sections 44102 and 44103 of this title.

§ 44106. Conduct of proceedings

Part A of this subtitle applies to proceedings conducted by the Federal Maritime Commission under this chapter."

MARITIME COMMISSION FAQ

When do Administrative Law Judges get involved?

When a person files a formal complaint and does not request an informal small claims procedure, or the other party does not agree to the procedure, the Complaint is assigned to an Administrative Law Judge (ALJ) .

Do I need an attorney if my case is assigned to an ALJ?

No, this can be done with or without an attorney.

What are the ALJ authorized to do?

The ALJ is authorized under the Commission's rules to conduct conferences and hearings so that the Commission can decide the matter in the most speedy and inexpensive way possible, depending upon the nature of the dispute, its complexity, the number of parties involved, etc.

How do the ALJ assist parties in settling disputes?

The ALJ may:

-Refer the dispute to a Commission Mediator

-Issue an initial decision promptly

-Establish a procedure to gather necessary evidence

-Allow parties to review each others' evidence

-Proceed to a hearing

What is a hearing?

A hearing resembles a courtroom trial in which witnesses will testify under oath and be cross-examined. However, such a hearing is a last resort when efforts to settle the dispute with the help of the Commission's mediators have not succeeded or the ALJ cannot issue an early decision because the facts are disputed and a more fully developed evidentiary record is required.

Can I appeal the ALJ's initial decision?

**For additional analytical, business and investment opportunities information,
please contact Global Investment & Business Center, USA
at (703) 370-8082. Fax: (703) 370-8083. E-mail: ibpusa3@gmail.com
Global Business and Investment Info Databank - www.ibpus.com**

Yes, either side can appeal the ALJ's "initial decision" to the full Commission, which cannot be done under the "small claims" procedure.

What agreements are required to be filed with the Commission?

Generally, agreements by and among ocean common carriers that provide for the fixing of rates, charges and other conditions of service; the pooling of revenues; the fixing of sailing schedules; the sharing of vessel space; the regulating of competition; the discussion of service contract matters; or any exclusive, preferential, cooperative working arrangement between carriers or with or among marine terminal operators are subject to filing. Pricing agreements between and among marine terminal operators or between marine terminal operators and ocean common carriers are also required to be filed. 46 C.F.R. § 535.201.

How do I file an agreement with the Commission?

Agreements subject to filing are to be submitted to the Secretary of the Commission at its Washington DC Office, 800 North Capitol Street, NW, Washington, DC 20573. Along with the original signed copy of the agreement, the parties are to submit seven extra copies of the agreement and the appropriate filing fee. 46 CFR § 535.401(g) . Certain agreements require the submission of an Information Form, see 46 C.F.R. 535.501 for applicability.

What is an Information Form?

Commission regulations require that most types of ocean common carrier agreements (including those that have the authority to discuss tariffs, any kind of rate or charge, capacity rationalization, joint service, pooling or service contracts) , unless they are low market share agreements (defined at 46 CFR 535.311) submit an Information Form. 46

C.F.R. § 535.503; 46 C.F.R. § 535.201(a) .

The Information Form collects and organizes service and economic data of the proposed agreement. 46 C.F.R. 535 Appendix A.

How do I get a copy of an agreement?

Contact the Bureau of Trade Analysis' Office of Agreements by phone (202) 523-5796, by fax (202) 523-4372, or via email tradeanalysis@fmc.gov. Copies of agreements involving ocean common carriers may also be downloaded from the FMC website.

Can I get a list of agreements by carrier, type, and geographic region?

The Bureau of Trade Analysis' Office of Agreements can provide listings of agreements indexed by various means, including individual carrier name, the type of agreement, and by geographic region, such as Asia, North Europe, and the Indian Subcontinent. The Commission can also provide a complete list of all conference agreements.

How do I find out if an agreement has been filed?

You may contact the Bureau of Trade Analysis' Office of Agreements as indicated above.

For additional analytical, business and investment opportunities information, please contact Global Investment & Business Center, USA at (703) 370-8082. Fax: (703) 370-8083. E-mail: ibpusa3@gmail.com Global Business and Investment Info Databank - www.ibpus.com

What is a Form FMC-1?

Form FMC-1 is an Internet-based electronic form to collect tariff location addresses and other specific organizational information of conferences, ocean common carriers, OTIs and MTOs. The information is entered directly into the FMC-1 Form on-line via the Internet. The Commission's Rules governing Form FMC-1 are located under 46 CFR § 520.3(d) and (e) for vessel-operating-common carriers/conferences and 46 CFR § 525.3(f) for marine terminal operators. Electronic submission of the Form FMC-1 data is mandatory under Commission Rules. The system processes the information collected in the electronic form and posts the carriers, ocean transportation intermediaries, conferences, and marine terminal operators' tariff location addresses on the Carriers' List located on the Commission homepage. The Commission uses the information collected to access the actual tariff publication and review for compliance with Commission rules and regulations. The public uses the Carriers' List to locate carriers' tariff location addresses to access tariff publications, and to verify OTI/NVOCC status as set forth under 46 CFR § 515.27(d) . Click Here To File a Form FMC-1 For assistance completing the form, please click the HELP button in the upper right-hand corner of the form or contact the Commission on 202-523-5856.

Is Form FMC-1 required regarding tariff(s) ?

Yes. Each common carrier (including NVOCCs) and conference shall notify the Bureau of Trade Analysis, prior to the commencement of common carrier service pursuant to a published tariff, of its organization number, home office address, name and telephone number of firm's representative, the location of its tariffs, and the publisher, if any, used to maintain its tariffs, by electronically submitting Form FMC-1 via the Commission's website at www.fmc.gov. 46 CFR § 520.3(d) .

How are changes submitted to Form FMC-1?

Any changes to the FMC-1 information shall be immediately transmitted to the Bureau of Trade Analysis. § 520.3(d) . The filer's changes can be entered electronically from the View Carrier-OTI List, File FMC-1 main menu, select "Edit an Existing FMC-1 Form, via the Commission's website, www.fmc.gov.

How do I obtain an Organization Number?

The Commission's staff will provide a unique organization number to a new entity operating as a common carrier or conference in the U.S. foreign commerce. 46 CFR § 520.3(d) . When an organization changes its name, a new Organization Number is assigned. The filer completes an "Initial" FMC-1 Form submission and may leave the Organization Number field blank. A number will be assigned by the FMC staff.

Who must publish a common carrier tariff?

Each vessel operating common carrier, non-vessel-operating common carrier, and conference, except with regard to bulk cargo, forest products, recycled metal scrap, new assembled motor vehicles, waste paper, and paper waste. 46 CFR § 520.3(a) .

What must be included in a tariff?

Rates, charges, classifications, rules, and practices between all points or ports on a carrier's or conference's own route and on any through transportation route that has been established. Also, content requirements for some provisions in a tariff are the following: places between which cargo will be carried; level of ocean transportation intermediary compensation; each terminal or other charge...; sample copies of bills of lading; any tariff rules; organization record; commodity descriptions; commodity index; tariff rate items; shippers and requests. 46 CFR § 520.4.

What types of services are exempt from tariff publication requirements?

Equipment interchange agreements between common carriers subject to part 520 and inland carriers where such agreements are not referred to in carriers' tariffs and do not affect the tariff rates, charges or practices of the carriers; and terminal barge operators in Pacific Slope states barging containers and containerized cargo by barge between points in the U.S. in certain instance - 46 CFR § 520.13(b) (1) , (2) , and (3) . Tanker services and non-regularly scheduled liner services, such as with tramp vessel operations.

Does the exemption from tariff publication for certain cargo types such as bulk cargo, forest products, etc., apply equally to both ocean common carriers (VOCC) and non-vessel-operating common carriers (NVOCC) ?

Yes.

How do I access a carrier or conference automated tariff system?

Go to the Commission's website, www.fmc.gov, Click on View Carrier-OTI List/File FMC-1, Click Here to Proceed, Click on View Carrier List, Click on tab for FMC 1 VOCC, or FMC-1 OTI/NVOCC for "accepted filings", Scroll down the list alphabetically to carrier's name desired, obtain from the Location of Tariff(s) column the carrier's tariff location address, then logon to the Internet using the tariff location address to find the carrier's tariff publication in the carrier's automated tariff system ("CATS") . Some CATS may require that you register to obtain a logon and password to access the system. In addition, a reasonable charge may be assessed to access a CATS system.

When do I file a special permission application?

Where there may be good cause shown to permit a common carrier to deviate from the provisions of rules governing tariffs under part 520, e.g., for issuance of effective dates on less than the statutory notice under the Commission's rules; or typographical or clerical errors in tariff publication that cause defective tariff material. 46 CFR § 520.14(a) and (b) .

How do I correct a clerical error in a tariff?

An application for special permission ("SP") may be submitted, in letter form in duplicate, to the Bureau of Trade Analysis, accompanied with a filing fee of $172/$195. The application must contain: Organization name, number and trade name of the conference or carrier; tariff number and title; and the rate, commodity, or rules related to the application, and the special circumstances which the applicant believes constitutes good cause to depart from the requirements of the Commission's rules under 46 C.F.R. Part 520, Carrier Automated Tariffs. Should the authority sought under the SP application be granted and assigned a Special Case number, implementation of the authority granted by the Commission must be used in its entirety, including the prompt publishing of the material for which permission was requested. The

For additional analytical, business and investment opportunities information, please contact Global Investment & Business Center, USA at (703) 370-8082. Fax: (703) 370-8083. E-mail: ibpusa3@gmail.com Global Business and Investment Info Databank - www.ibpus.com

Applicants shall use the special case number assigned by the Commission. 46 CFR § 520.14(c) and (d) .

What is a special docket application for permission to refund or waive freight charges?

See the Commissions's Rules of Practice and Procedure at 46 CFR § 502.271. Under these provisions, a common carrier or a shipper may file a special docket application seeking permission for a common carrier or conference to refund or waive collection of a portion of freight charges if specific criteria is met. Such application must be submitted to the Office of the Secretary, Federal Maritime Commission.

If a tariff is cancelled, who should provide written notice of cancellation to the Commission?

Carriers and conferences shall inform BTA, in writing, whenever a tariff is canceled and the effective date of that cancellation. 46 CFR § 520.7(b) . A carrier or conference may designate its agent to submit, on its behalf, the written cancellation notice to the Commission.

Once a tariff has been canceled, superceded, or withdrawn, how long must its data be maintained in a carrier's publication system?

Carriers and conferences shall maintain the data that appeared i n its their tariff publication system for a period of five (5) years from the date such information is superseded, canceled or withdrawn, and shall provide on-line access to such data for two (2) years. After two (2) years, such data may be retained on-line or in other electronic form, and shall be made available to any person or the Commission upon request in a reasonable period of time. Carriers and conferences may charge a reasonable fee for the provision of historical data, not to exceed the fees for obtaining such data on-line . No fee shall apply to federal agencies. 46 CFR § 520.10(a) .

What if a carrier or conference designates an agent to publish, on its behalf, its tariff in CATS?

It is a carrier's or conference's responsibility for the publication of their tariff in CATS , although they may designate an agent to do so on their behalf. 46 CFR § 520.3(a) and (c) . Also, the Commission will periodically review CATS and may prohibit the use of any system that fails to meet the requirements of rules governing tariffs under 46 C.F.R. Part 520. 46 CFR § 520.10(c) .

What if a carrier or conference fails to pay a designated agent for publishing and maintaining historical tariff data in CATS?

The matter of payment for services between a carrier or conference and its agent involving CATS is a matter between the parties.

When must my tariff be published?

On or before transportation services commence thereunder, or the tariff's effective date - an OTI/NVOCC must also be in compliance with bonding/licensing requirements under 46 CFR part 515 of the Commission's rules.

Does the minimum rate display requirement of 46 CFR § 520.6(e) require a list of assessorial charges that actually apply to the shipment?

For additional analytical, business and investment opportunities information, please contact Global Investment & Business Center, USA at (703) 370-8082. Fax: (703) 370-8083. E-mail: ibpusa3@gmail.com Global Business and Investment Info Databank - www.ibpus.com

Yes. Any assessorial charge that will be added to the basic ocean freight rate must be listed individually. If there are other rules or charges that may otherwise affect the shipment under certain circumstances(e.g., minimum quantity rules, quantity discounts, or demurrage) the tariff should also indicate them.

Does the access date capability required by § 520.10(b) only apply to historical data or does it also apply to future dates?

The requirement that tariffs provide the capability for a retriever to enter an access date to obtain data in effect on that date was primarily intended to apply to historical tariff data. Nonetheless, if carriers know what rates are going to be in effect on some future date, they are certainly free to provide accurate information to retrievers about such rates. Therefore, access data capabilities should apply to objects that will become effective on a future date.

Can carriers use codes other than those in the Standard Terminology Appendix?

As stated in § 520.5(a) , these codes should serve as a standard baseline for tariff publishers. However, the rule makes clear that publishers can use additional codes, if they clearly define them in their tariffs.

Do conferences have to publish a common tariff?

Yes. Section 8(a) (1) of the Shipping Act, requires a conference to keep open for public inspection, in an automated tariff system, a tariff showing all its rates, charges, classifications, rules and practices for the transportation routes served by it. This statutory requirement is carried forward in § 520.3(a) of the tariff rules. In addition, § 520.3(b) requires conferences to publish in their automated tariff systems rates offered pursuant to independent action by their members, and they can only do so if they have a common tariff.

Can a non-binding discussion agreement publish a common tariff?

No. Section 8(a) (1) of the Shipping Act only recognizes tariffs of individual common carriers or conferences. Moreover, the definition of "tariff" in 46 CFR § 520.2 states that it is " . . . a publication containing the actual rates, charges, classifications, rules, regulations and practices of a common carrier or a conference of common carriers." The definition further notes that "practices" in tariffs, " . . . in the case of conferences, must be restricted to activities authorized by the basic conference agreement."

When does the two-year on-line data retention requirement of 46 CFR § 520.10(a) begin?

On May 1, 1999.

Will the blanket special permission for new tariffs with no increases permitting them to go into effect without the 30 days' advance notice requirement also apply to controlled carriers?

Yes, to the extent the rates of the controlled carrier are not decreased also. Any action of a controlled carrier in publishing a new tariff that would deviate from other requirements applicable to controlled carriers would require separate special permission.

For additional analytical, business and investment opportunities information, please contact Global Investment & Business Center, USA at (703) 370-8082. Fax: (703) 370-8083. E-mail: ibpusa3@gmail.com Global Business and Investment Info Databank - www.ibpus.com

If a publisher reissues the same tariff that is now in ATFI, can it carry forward the same effective dates for the ATFI tariff matter rather than changing all effective dates of the tariff items to May 1, 1999?

Tariffs may carry-over ATFI tariff items showing the ATFI effective dates in CATS tariffs. On May 1, 1999, all other CATS' tariff items intended to be effective on May 1, 1999, must show a May 1, 1999 effective date.

What is a correction?

A correction is any change to a service contract which has a retroactive effect. 46 CFR § 530.10(a) (2) .

How does a person correct an error in a service contract?

For electronic errors see question No. 19 (dealing with electronic transmission errors) . For other errors service contract parties may mutually agree to amend the contract, prospectively, or may file an original and duplicate request for a correction with the Commission's Office of the Secretary within (45) forty-five days of the contract's filing with the Commission, accompanied by remittance of a $276/$315 service fee. 46 CFR § 530.10(c) .

How does a person access carrier or agreement essential terms publication?

A person can go to the tariff location address of the ocean common carrier or ocean common carrier agreement or conference to view the ET of a service contract required to be made public.

How are service contract effective dates determined?

Service contract parties determine the effective date of a service contract as long as the date is not before the service contract filing date. The specific beginning and ending dates must be specified in the service contract. The effective date starts at 12:01a.m. eastern standard time on the beginning of the effective date. This rule also applies to effective dates of amendments.

What is Form FMC-83?

Form FMC-83 is a service contract registration form. The Form FMC-83 must be filed in order for a filer to obtain user identification, logon and password, to access the SERVCON system to electronically file service contracts.

How can a copy of Form FMC-83 be obtained? How is Form FMC-83 filed with the Commission?

Go to the Commission's website, www.fmc.gov, click on Forms and Publications, Office of Service Contracts and Tariffs, Service Contract User Registration Form (FMC-83) , print a copy of the form, fill out the form completely with the information requested, and fax a copy of the completed form to the Office of Service Contracts and Tariffs at (202) 523-5867. If there are no problems with the FMC-83, the copy is forwarded to the Office of Information Technology to assign logon and password ID and to send the ID by certified mail to the person named on Line 7 of the form authorized to access SERVCON and file service contracts.

Who is required to file Form FMC-83?

For additional analytical, business and investment opportunities information, please contact Global Investment & Business Center, USA at (703) 370-8082. Fax: (703) 370-8083. E-mail: ibpusa3@gmail.com Global Business and Investment Info Databank - www.ibpus.com

Carriers or conferences that enter into service contracts subject to the Commission's rules governing service contracts must file a FMC-83 Form. 46 CFR § 530.5(c) .

What agreements are required to be filed with the Commission?

Generally, agreements between and among ocean common carriers that provide for the fixing of rates and charges, the pooling of revenues, the fixing of sailing schedules, the sharing of vessel space, the regulating of competition, the discussing service contract matters, or any exclusive, preferential, cooperative working arrangement between carriers or with marine terminal operators are subject to filing. Also, with some exceptions (see 46 CFR §§ 535.308, 309, 310) agreements between and among marine terminal operators or between marine terminal operators and ocean common carriers are required to be filed also.

How do I file an agreement with the Commission?

Agreements subject to filing are to be submitted to the Secretary of the Commission at 800 North Capitol Street, NW, Washington, DC 20573. Along with the original signed copy of the agreement, the parties are to submit seven extra copies of the agreement and the appropriate filing fee (see 46 CFR 535.401(g)) . Certain agreements also require the submission of an Information Form, see 46 CFR 535.501 for applicability.

How do I get a copy of an agreement?

Contact the Bureau by phone 202-523-5796, by fax 202-523-4372, or via email Tradeanalysis@fmc.gov. In the near future, the public will be able to view and download copies of agreements from this website.

Can I get a list of agreements by carrier, type, geographic region?

The Bureau can provide listings of agreements indexed on various keys such as individual carrier name, the type of agreement, for example a list of all conferences, and by a particular region of the world, Asia, North Europe, Indian Subcontinent, and the like. Contact the Bureau as indicated above. There is a nominal fee for this service.

How do I find out if an agreement has been filed?

You may contact the Bureau as indicated above. In the near future, information on weekly agreement filings will be available through this website.

What is FOIA?

FOIA is an abbreviation that stands for the "Freedom of Information Act." You can view the Act at http://www.usdoj.gov/oip/foia_guide07/text_foia.pdf. Pursuant to this Act, the public has the right to request specific documents from the federal government. When requesting information under FOIA, you should provide as much detail as possible describing the documents you seek.

Do I have to file a request under FOIA to obtain any information from the Federal Maritime Commission?

For additional analytical, business and investment opportunities information, please contact Global Investment & Business Center, USA at (703) 370-8082. Fax: (703) 370-8083. E-mail: ibpusa3@gmail.com Global Business and Investment Info Databank - www.ibpus.com

Not necessarily. A great deal of agency information is available without a FOIA request on the Commission's website at www.fmc.gov. For a description of documents available without a FOIA request, see the Commission's regulations at 46 CFR §§ 503.21-24. If you are uncertain whether you need to file a FOIA request to receive information, call the FOIA Requester Hotline at 202523-5707 and our staff will assist you.

Will I receive all the documents I request under FOIA?

While the focus of FOIA is on making government information available to the public, the statute recognizes that certain types of information should not be disclosed. Thus, the FOIA exempts nine categories from the general mandatory disclosure rule. These exemptions are:

1. Classified documents
2. Internal personnel rules and practices
3. Information exempt under other laws
4. Confidential business information
5. Internal government communications
6. Personal privacy
7. Law enforcement
8. Financial institutions
9. Geological information.

The FOIA Officer (FMC Secretary) will determine if any information you requested falls into one of the exempted categories. If so, the entire record may be withheld, or sections of it will be redacted or omitted.

How do I file a FOIA request?

Please submit your FOIA request in writing, reasonably describing the record(s) sought. You may submit a FOIA request by either:

(1) Fax: 202-523-0014 (subject: FOIA Request) ;

(2) Email: secretary@fmc.gov (subject: FOIA Request) ; or

(3) Mail: (clearly mark the envelope exterior "FOIA") .

Address your written request to:

Secretary Federal Maritime Commission 800 North Capitol Street, N.W. Washington, D.C. 20573

What happens if my FOIA request is denied in whole or in part?

The FOIA Officer is required to notify you of the reasons your request has been denied in whole or in part. The FOIA Officer will also include an explanation of the Commission's appeal process. An appeal should be addressed to the Chairman, Federal Maritime Commission. Your appeal letter may contain details of the FOIA request and the FOIA Officer's denial or it may simply refer to the original request and state that the FOIA Officer's decision is being appealed.

Are there any fees or charges in connection with a FOIA request?

For additional analytical, business and investment opportunities information, please contact Global Investment & Business Center, USA at (703) 370-8082. Fax: (703) 370-8083. E-mail: ibpusa3@gmail.com Global Business and Investment Info Databank - www.ibpus.com

There is not an initial fee to file a FOIA request. By law, however, federal agencies are entitled to charge certain fees, which depend on the particular category of FOIA requester you fall into. Thus, you may be charged a fee for search time and document review time, as well as for copying of documents. The Commission's fees for processing FOIA requests are published on our website at 46 CFR §503.43. You may also call the FOIA Requester Hotline to discuss specific fees applicable to your request, at (202) 523-5707.

You may include in your FOIA request a specific statement limiting the amount of money that you are willing to pay in fees. If the total fees for processing your request are likely to exceed that amount, the FMC will contact you and offer you an opportunity to narrow your request in order to reduce your fees.

What if I am unable to pay the fees?

In general, the Commission does not waive or reduce FOIA service and filing fees. In extraordinary situations, the Commission will accept requests for waivers or fee reductions. Such requests are to be made to the Secretary of the Commission at the time of the FOIA request and must demonstrate that the waiver or reduction of a fee is in the best interest of the public, or that payment of a fee would impose an undue hardship. The Secretary will notify the requester of the decision to grant or deny the request for waiver or reduction of fees.

How long does it take to process a FOIA request?

Once the Commission's Secretary receives the request, the FMC has 20 working days (excluding weekends and legal holidays) to make a determination on the request. If expedited processing is sought, you must include the reason for expedited processing in your FOIA request letter.

Where can I go to get more information about FOIA?

The Commission's FOIA information web page is located at: http://www.fmc.gov/reading/FreedomofInformationAct.asp.

The Commission's regulations regarding FOIA requests are located at: http://www.fmc.gov/home/503Publicinformation.asp#503.31%20Records%20available%20upon%20written%20request.

Additional FOIA information from the Department of Justice can be found at: http://www.usdoj.gov/oip/index.html.

Who is a MTO?

A Marine Terminal Operator ("MTO") is a person engaged in the United States in the business of furnishing wharfage, dock, warehouse or other terminal facilities in connection with a common carrier and a water carrier subject to Subchapter II of Chapter 135 of Title 49, United States Code. 49 U.S.C. §13521, or in connection with a common carrier. A marine terminal operator includes, but is not limited to, terminals owned or operated by states and their political subdivisions; railroads who perform port terminal services not covered by their line haul rates; common carriers who perform port terminal services; and warehousemen who operate port terminal facilities. Conferences of marine terminal operators are also considered MTOs. 46 CFR § 525.1(c) (13) .

For additional analytical, business and investment opportunities information, please contact Global Investment & Business Center, USA at (703) 370-8082. Fax: (703) 370-8083. E-mail: ibpusa3@gmail.com Global Business and Investment Info Databank - www.ibpus.com

What are MTOs' obligations for the publication of a schedule?

MTOs are not required to make their schedule(s) of rates, regulations and practices (formerly called "MTO tariffs") available to the public. A MTO that elects to make their schedules available to the public must make them available in electronic form. When an MTO opts to publish its schedule, its name and location address of its schedule(s) provided in its FMC-1. The names of MTOs that opt not to make their schedule(s) available to the public are not posted on the website, but are maintained in the Commission's Form FMC-1 internal database. Should an MTO maintain parallel terminal schedules in paper form for entities in the shipping industry who are unable to access electronic terminal schedules, the electronic version will govern in the event of a conflict with the parallel paper form of terminal schedules since the electronic format is the required method of publication. 46 CFR § 525.2(a) and 46 CFR § 525.3(a) (2) .

How are MTO schedules accessed?

An MTO that elects to make its schedules available to the public will provide a location address in its FMC-1 Form that is submitted to the Commission. 46 CFR § 525.3(f) .

What is Form FMC-1?

Form FMC-1 is an interactive electronic form required under the Commission's rules at to be filed by MTOs notifying the FMC, prior to commencement of marine terminal operations, of its organization name, organization number, home office address, name and telephone number of its representative, the location of its terminal schedule(s) , and the publisher, if any, used to maintain its terminal schedule. 46 CFR 525.3(f)

Where is Form FMC-1 located and how is it filed?

Form FMC-1 is located on the Commission's website, www.fmc.gov. The form is available electronically and filed http://www.fmc.gov,interactively by clicking on Tariff Registration Form (FMC-1) , Click Here to Proceed on the Disclaimer screen, File an Initial FMC-1 Form button and completely filling-in information on the form. When you have finished click Save and Exit to transmit the Form FMC-1 filing to the FMC. If you need assistance completing the form, use the "Help" button in the upper right-hand corner of the form. In addition, if you opt to make your terminal schedule(s) available to the public, before clicking Save and Exit, you must click the "Add Publisher" button at the bottom of the screen, complete all required entries identifying the location and publisher of your electronically published schedule(s) ; when you are finished, click "Save and Return" (this takes you back to the Organization information screen) , next scroll down to the bottom of the Organization information screen and click "Save and Exit" to transmit the FMC-1 Form filing to the FMC.

Are MTOs required to file FMC-1 Form?

Yes. All MTOs subject to Commission jurisdiction must file an FMC-1 form, whether or not they intend to publish their terminal schedules.

If a parent MTO has various subsidiaries that run additional terminals, who needs to file the FMC-1?

For additional analytical, business and investment opportunities information, please contact Global Investment & Business Center, USA at (703) 370-8082. Fax: (703) 370-8083. E-mail: ibpusa3@gmail.com Global Business and Investment Info Databank - www.ibpus.com

The parent must file for itself, and an additional form for a subsidiary need only be filed if the subsidiary intends to publish its terminal schedules at a different electronic location than the parent. Either the parent or the subsidiary may file the additional FMC-1 form.

If an MTO adopts the published terminal schedule of a different MTO, but that schedule does not include a limitation of liability, can the MTO publish its own limitation of liability?

Yes. If an MTO wants to avail itself of the implied contract provision of the rule in relation to a limitation of liability, then it must publish such limitation of liability in the same manner it would publish a terminal schedule.

What are some examples of things that can go wrong on my move?

The Commission receives a number of complaints. Some frequent problems encountered are:

-Late shipments

-The moving company cannot be reached

-The moving company is demanding additional charges such as storage charges, incurred through no fault of the consumer.

-The moving company claims the original estimate as to weight or measure was inaccurate, and demands additional charges.

-The shipment cannot be located, and no one seems to have any idea where it is.

-Goods are damaged and the consumer paid for insurance, but the moving company did not purchase any insurance on behalf of the consumer.

How do I protect myself and find a reputable mover to move my goods overseas?

We strongly urge all individuals undertaking an international move to hire a moving company that is FMC licensed and bonded. It is possible to locate a list of such companies here. We urge individuals to be wary of using online search services as many rogue movers use these services to lure unsuspecting individuals. If you have questions regarding a company you may call FMC's Office of Consumer Affairs & Dispute Resolution Services at 202-523-5807. It is also important to receive several quotes from different companies who have performed an onsite inspection of your goods. Do not rely on a company's telephone quotations as these are often inaccurate. For additional information please visit www.protectyourmove.gov. Although that site provides advice for interstate moves, rather than international, much of its advice is practical advice that could be applied to international moves as well.

What is a rogue mover?

Despite the high number of reputable moving companies, there are some that work to defraud the public. These dishonest companies generally promise good service for a low rate. However, these companies often charge 2-3 times the promised amount and hold the consumer's goods hostage for more money. In some cases, these companies take shipments with no intent to deliver the goods so consumers are left to find their shipment and pay another moving company additional money to ship their goods.

What are signs that I may be dealing with a rogue mover?

There are several red flags associated with rogue movers. For example, any company that does not offer or agree to an onsite inspection of your goods and provides phone estimates can be a sign of trouble to come as these companies offer rates that are too good to be true. Another common sign is that the company refuses credit cards and demands a large cash deposit before the move. Many of these companies also lack a local address and do not have licensing information. For more information on how to spot a rogue mover, please visit www.protectyourmove.gov

Why does my mover need to be FMC licensed and bonded?

Federal law (i.e., the Shipping Act of 1984) requires Ocean Transportation Intermediaries to be licensed and bonded. This provides protection for consumers. In the event that there is a transportation dispute with the company that cannot be resolved, the consumer may submit a claim against that company's bond. In cases where consumers hire unlicensed/ unbonded entities it is much more difficult to seek recovery.

My unlicensed Mover gave me a great rate. Why should I pay more for a licensed mover?

In many situations rogue movers will offer a lower rate and other moving related "perks" such as free insurance to entice consumers into using their services. However, in most cases, after the goods are picked up, such rogue movers may demand a rate that is 2-3 times greater than the initial quote and adds many hidden unexplained charges. The consumer is usually told that unless the extra money is paid the goods will be abandoned. The extra payments do not always guarantee receipt of the goods and the consumer must locate his goods and begin the process again with another mover.

The Company's website states that it is FMC licensed. How can I verify this?

Rogue movers often claim to be FMC licensed when they are not and provide false licensing numbers. The only way to guarantee that your mover is licensed is to confirm that fact with the FMC. The Commission lists licensed ocean transportation intermediaries at its web site, or you may contact the FMC's Bureau of Certification and Licensing (202-523-5843) or the Office of Consumer Affairs & Dispute Resolution Services (202-523-5807) .

My moving company states that all of its agents are FMC licensed. Am I protected?

No. Any company that holds itself out as an international moving company should be licensed by the FMC if it offers international ocean transportation of your goods. In many instances rogue movers have used legitimate companies as intermediaries and failed to pay those companies for services. This leaves the consumer in a position where he must make a double payment, that is, pay the legitimate company in order to receive his goods.

My company states that it is an agent for an FMC licensed company. Am I protected?

Federal law permits companies to act as sales agents for a licensed company. To protect yourself, however, the agent should provide you with a bill of lading or other information identifying which company is taking responsibility for shipment and delivery of your household goods. For your protection, you should ensure that any contract you sign is with the licensed entity and not the agent.

I just gave a deposit to a company that is not licensed. What can I do?

In many situations the best thing to do is to cancel the shipment, cut your losses, and hire a licensed company. While you may lose the deposit you save more time, money, and energy in the long run.

An unlicensed company just picked up my goods and they will not return my calls. What can I do?

Please call the Office of Consumer Affairs & Dispute Resolution Services immediately at 202523-5807, or email to complaints@fmc.gov. Someone will assist you in attempting to locate your goods and ensure delivery.

What is an ocean transportation intermediary (OTI) ?

An OTI may be either an ocean freight forwarder, a non-vessel-operating common carrier (NVOCC) , or both an ocean freight forwarder and an NVOCC.

What is an ocean freight forwarder?

An ocean freight forwarder is an individual or company in the United States that dispatches shipments from the United States via common carriers (defined at 46 U.S.C. app. §1702(6)) and books or otherwise arranges space for those shipments on behalf of shippers (defined at 46

U.S.C. app §1702(21)) .Ocean freight forwarders also prepare and process the documentation and perform related activities pertaining to those shipments.

What is an NVOCC?

An NVOCC is a common carrier that does not operate the vessels by which ocean transportation is provided, and is a shipper in relation to the involved ocean common carrier.

What are OTI services?

Freight Forwarding OTI services refer to the dispatching of shipments on behalf of others to facilitate shipments by common carriers, including ordering cargo to port; preparing or processing export declarations, bills of lading and other export documentation; booking or confirming cargo space; arranging for warehouse space; arranging cargo insurance; clearing shipments in accordance with United States Government export regulations; preparing and/or sending advance notice of shipments to banks, shippers, and consignees; handling freight monies on behalf of shippers; coordinating the movement of shipments from origin to the vessel; and giving expert advice to exporters. NVOCC OTI services refers to the provision of transportation by water of cargo between the United States and a foreign country (whether import or export) for compensation without operating the vessels by which the transportation is provided. NVOCC OTI services may include purchasing transportation services from vessel-operating common carriers for resale; payment of port-to-port or multi-modal transportation charges; entering into affreightment agreements with underlying shippers; issuing bills of lading or equivalent documents; arranging and paying for inland transportation on through transportation movements;

For additional analytical, business and investment opportunities information, please contact Global Investment & Business Center, USA at (703) 370-8082. Fax: (703) 370-8083. E-mail: ibpusa3@gmail.com Global Business and Investment Info Databank - www.ibpus.com

paying lawful compensation to ocean freight forwarders; leasing containers; and entering into arrangements with origin or destination agents.

When is an OTI license required?

An OTI license is required of any individual or entity which is resident in or incorporated in the United States and performs OTI services in the foreign commerce of the United States.

Can I be both an ocean freight forwarder and an NVOCC?

Yes, an entity can operate as a freight forwarder and as an NVOCC, but generally cannot be compensated for serving in both roles on the same transaction. That is, if you issue your own NVOCC bill of lading and collect ocean freight at your published rate for that shipment, you cannot also collect forwarding compensation on that same shipment.

Do I need an OTI license from the FMC to forward shipments by air or modes of ground transportation in foreign or domestic commerce?

No, although other federal agencies may have specific requirements.

Do I need an OTI license to move cargo by ship domestically within the United States or its territories?

No, however, there may be requirements imposed by the Surface Transportation Board ("STB") . You may view the STB website at http://www.stb.dot.gov or call the general information phone number at (202) 565-1500 for further information.

May I share my license to operate as an OTI with an unlicensed person or company?

No, only a licensee may operate pursuant to its license.

May I perform ocean freight forwarding activities without being licensed?

Yes, but only in certain situations. A shipper (a person whose primary business is the sale of merchandise) may perform freight forwarding activities on behalf of its own shipments or the shipments of a parent, subsidiary, affiliate, or associated company. An ocean common carrier, or its agent, may perform freight forwarding activities with respect to cargo carried under the carrier's own bill of lading. Fees for performing these activities must be filed in the carrier's tariff. However, except as provided, unlicensed freight forwarders may not book or arrange vessel space for others, process shipping documentation or collect freight forwarder compensation from the ocean carriers.

How does an ocean freight forwarder OTI get paid?

In providing its various services, an ocean freight forwarder charges fees to its customers (the shippers) and may also collect compensation from the common carrier in accordance with the terms of its tariff.

If I, as a shipper, forward my own shipments, am I entitled to receive ocean freight forwarder compensation from the ocean carrier?

No, only licensed OTI freight forwarders may receive forwarder compensation. Freight forwarders may not receive compensation on shipments in which they have a beneficial interest.

Do I have to renew my license?

No, but if a license is surrendered or revoked by the Commission for cause, you must reapply.

My license as an OTI has an "F" or an "N" on it. What does it mean?

The "F" or "N" identifies a licensee as a freight forwarder ("F") or an NVOCC ("N") .

If I am licensed and decide I no longer want to operate as an OTI or I am a joint NVOCC and freight forwarder OTI and I no longer want to operate one of my services, what must I do?

If you no longer want to operate as an OTI, you must:

-Surrender your license to the Bureau of Certification and Licensing, Federal Maritime Commission, 800 North Capitol Street, N.W., Washington, D.C. 20573.

-Advise your financial responsibility provider, and if you are an NVOCC, your tariff publisher, that you no longer are operating as an OTI. The Commission will issue you a letter of voluntary surrender and the surrender will be effective the date your license was received by the Commission. If you are an NVOCC OTI, your FMC-1 listing will be designated as inactive on the Commission website. A notice of the surrender will be published in the Federal Register. You may no longer offer OTI services once you have surrendered your license. If you are a joint NVOCC/freight forwarder OTI and wish to surrender a portion of your license, you must notify the Commission and your financial responsibility provider of your surrender. A letter of surrender will be issued to you with regard to the surrendered service and a notice published in the Federal Register. You must contact your financial responsibility provider to cancel the coverage of the surrendered service. If you are surrendering the NVOCC portion of your license, you must notify your tariff publisher to cancel your tariff and the Commission will designate your FMC-1 listing as inactive. You will be issued a new license indicating the service you will continue to offer and you must return the joint "NF" license that you held. A reissuance notice will be published in the Federal Register.

Where can I find regulations regarding OTIs?

Regulations governing OTIs can be viewed on the Commission's website at www.fmc.gov. Please click on the "Regulations" heading. Part 515, Licensing, Financial Responsibility Requirements, and General Duties for Ocean Transportation Intermediaries, contains the regulations relating to OTIs. In addition, Part 520, Carrier Automated Tariffs, Part 530, Service contracts, and Part 531, NVOCC Service Arrangements, apply to NVOCC OTIs.

How may I contact the Commission with regard to OTI matters?

The Federal Maritime Commission's Bureau of Certification and Licensing has two offices that deal with OTI issues. (1) . The Office of Transportation Intermediaries reviews OTI applications and issues the licenses. This office may be contacted by telephone at (202) 523-5843, by facsimile at (202) 566-0011 or e-mail at OTI@fmc.gov. (2) . The Office of Passenger Vessels and Information Processing handles the OTI surety bonds and other forms of financial responsibility. This office can be contacted by telephone at (202) 523

For additional analytical, business and investment opportunities information, please contact Global Investment & Business Center, USA at (703) 370-8082. Fax: (703) 370-8083. E-mail: ibpusa3@gmail.com Global Business and Investment Info Databank - www.ibpus.com

5818, by facsimile at (202) 523-5830 or e-mail at OTIbonds@fmc.gov. Normal business working hours are 8:30 a.m. to 5:00 p.m. Street address: Bureau of Certification and Licensing Federal Maritime Commission 800 North Capitol Street, N.W. Washington, D.C. 20573.

How may I contact the Commission for further information about Form FMC-1, tariff, NVOCC service arrangement or service contract requirements?

Issues relating to tariffs, service contracts and NVOCC service arrangements are handled primarily by the Commission's Bureau of Trade Analysis, Office of Service Contracts and Tariffs. This office may be contacted by telephone at (202) 523-5856, by facsimile at (202) 523-5867, or email at form1@fmc.gov.

How do I obtain an OTI license?

Submit a completed Form FMC-18 to the Commission demonstrating that the applicant has the required experience and character to offer OTI services. The applicant must include the appropriate fee and documentation supporting the application and provide evidence of financial responsibility for licensing. Commission staff will review the application, contact references and conduct an investigation of the applicant. If staff determines the applicant has the requisite experience and character, an OTI license will be issued.

How do I submit a license application?

Applicants must file Form FMC-18 in duplicate. This form may be downloaded and printed from the Commission's website at www.fmc.gov (click on "Forms" under "Bureau of Certification and Licensing") or obtained from the Office of Ocean Transportation Intermediaries. The application must be accompanied by a money order, a certified check, cashier's check, or a personal check made payable to the Federal Maritime Commission. The fee for an initial application is $825, and for an amended application, $525. Failure to include the proper fee with your application will cause it to be returned without processing. The completed application may be mailed or sent by courier to: Bureau of Certification and Licensing, Federal Maritime Commission 800 North Capitol Street NW, Washington, D.C. 20573. If you require evidence of delivery, please enclose a stamped, self-addressed envelope and an extra copy of the cover letter or the first page of the application. Commission staff will date stamp the extra copy of the cover letter or the first page of the application and return it to you.

May I apply for an OTI license as both an ocean freight forwarder and an NVOCC on the same Form FMC-18?

Yes. When applying for both NVOCC and ocean freight forwarder authority on the same application, the filing fee is $825. If the applicant is an existing licensed NVOCC OTI and wishes to add freight forwarding service to its license or is an existing licensed freight forwarder and wishes to add NVOCC OTI service to its license, the fee is $525.

Can a lawyer or other third party prepare Form FMC-18?

Yes, but the Form FMC-18 must be signed by the applicant.

What documentation must be submitted with application Form FMC-18?

For additional analytical, business and investment opportunities information, please contact Global Investment & Business Center, USA at (703) 370-8082. Fax: (703) 370-8083. E-mail: ibpusa3@gmail.com Global Business and Investment Info Databank - www.ibpus.com

Documentation that must be submitted with Form FMC-18 includes: Proof of the applicant's name and existence: If sole proprietor: business license and driver's license If corporation: articles of incorporation and certificate of good standing (or its equivalent) If partnership: partnership agreement If a trade name is used: fictitious name statement (or equivalent) issued by the state Proof of the qualifying individual's position: If a corporation:corporate minutes or resolution showing the appointment of the qualifying individual as an officer of the applicant corporation If a partnership: partnership agreement

What fees are required?

As noted above, the fee for an initial application for an OTI license is $825. The fee for applications for changes in operations that require the reissuance of a license is $525. When applying for both NVOCC and ocean freight forwarder authority on the same application, the filing fee is $825. All payments may be made by money order, certified check, cashier's check, or personal check made payable to "Federal Maritime Commission." Please do not send cash. Failure to include the proper fee with your application will cause it to be returned without processing. Fees will not be refunded in any instance where the application has been processed in whole or in part.

How long will it take to process my application?

Applications are normally approved within 45 days from receipt of the application, assuming the application is complete and the Commission's investigation does not reveal any circumstances that would preclude licensing.

What experience must an applicant have?

The applicant must designate a qualifying individual who has a minimum of three (3) years' experience in OTI activities in the United States. A foreign NVOCC seeking to be licensed must also demonstrate that its proposed qualifying individual has a minimum three years experience in OTI activities. However, such experience may be gained outside of the United States. Academic study or course work may not be substituted for this experience. In addition, a potential qualifying individual must possess the necessary character to render OTI services.

Who can be a qualifying individual of an OTI?

A qualifying individual is the person who possesses the OTI experience and necessary character to qualify the OTI applicant for licensing. The qualifying individual must be:

(1) for a sole proprietorship, the applicant sole proprietor.

(2) for a partnership, at least one of the active managing partners, but all partners must execute the application.

(3) for a corporation, at least one of the active corporate officers. Corporate officers include president, vice president, secretary or treasurer. Positions which are largely descriptive of job function, i.e., director of operations or vice president of export, typically are not recognized by state authorities as officers of a corporation.

How is the work experience of the QI verified?

The application must provide the name, address, telephone number, position, and work relationship of at least 3 non-related references who have first hand knowledge of the QI's work experience.

May one person be a qualifying individual for two or more OTI applicants?

A qualifying individual of one active licensee may serve as the qualifying individual of another OTI only if both entities are commonly owned or where one directly controls the other. Separately incorporated branch offices may fit this definition.

What are the financial responsibility requirements?

Every OTI must furnish proof of acceptable financial responsibility in the form of a surety bond, insurance, or guaranty to cover its transportation-related activities while the OTI is acting as an ocean freight forwarder or an NVOCC. An ocean freight forwarder must furnish proof of financial responsibility in the amount of $50,000 plus $10,000 for each unincorporated branch office in the United States.

An NVOCC operating in the United States must furnish proof of financial responsibility in the amount of $75,000 plus $10,000 for each unincorporated branch office in the United States. An unlicensed, foreign-domiciled OTI must furnish proof of financial responsibility in the amount of $150,000. A licensed foreign-domiciled OTI must furnish proof of financial responsibility in the amount of $75,000 plus $10,000 for each additional unincorporated branch office in the United States (not counting the unincorporated presence it has established in the United States to qualify for licensing) . How do I file my proof of financial responsibility? Typically, applicants provide proof of financial responsibility in the form of a surety bond filed on Form FMC-48. This Form may be downloaded from the Commission's website or obtained from the Office of Ocean Transportation Intermediaries or the Office of Passenger Vessels and

Information Processing. The proof of financial responsibility must be signed by both a representative of the OTI and the financial responsibility provider.

When must I provide proof of financial responsibility?

You may file proof of financial responsibility with your application to save time. You must file proof of financial responsibility upon notification by the Commission that your application has been approved. The license will not be issued until the Commission has received acceptable proof of financial responsibility. The applicant's name as principal on the proof of financial responsibility must match exactly the legal name of the applicant, including abbreviations, punctuation, capitalization and assumed or trade names. The address on the proof of financial responsibility must be that of the headquarters office, and the addresses of unincorporated branch offices must be listed and the amount of the proof of financial responsibility increased accordingly. In the case of surety bonds, a power of attorney issued by the surety must be attached to the bond. If more than six (6) months lapse from the time the Commission approves an application and the date it receives the proof of financial responsibility, the Commission may undertake a supplementary investigation to determine the continued qualification of the applicant. The fee for any such supplementary investigation is $225. Should the Commission not receive proof of financial responsibility from the applicant within two (2) years from the date of approval, the Commission will consider the application void.

For additional analytical, business and investment opportunities information, please contact Global Investment & Business Center, USA at (703) 370-8082. Fax: (703) 370-8083. E-mail: ibpusa3@gmail.com Global Business and Investment Info Databank - www.ibpus.com

If I am licensed as both an ocean freight forwarder and an NVOCC, may I provide proof of financial responsibility using one combined instrument?

No. Separate proofs of responsibility must be provided. The NVOCC proof of financial responsibility will only cover claims arising from the NVOCC's transportation-related activities and the freight forwarder proof of financial responsibility will only cover claims arising from its freight forwarder services.

How do I find a surety bonding company?

The Department of Treasury maintains a list of approved surety bonding companies (Circular 570) . It can be viewed at their website: http://www.fms.treas.gov/c570/index.html You also may contact the Department of Treasury in writing at the following address:

U.S. Department of Treasury Financial Management Service (FMS) Surety Bond Branch 3700 East-West Highway Room 6FO7 Hyattsville, MD 20782.

You may also call FMS at (202) 874-6850 or send a facsimile to (202) 874-9978.

I am a licensed OTI and my instrument of financial responsibility is cancelled, what may I expect?

The financial responsibility provider will send notice to the Commission that your coverage will be terminated. Termination becomes effective 30 days after receipt by the Commission of the notice or the date designated by the provider if the cancellation date is greater than 30 days. The Commission will issue you a letter notifying you of the provider's cancellation and the effective date of the cancellation. The provider, and if applicable, your tariff publisher, will receive a copy of this letter. The letter advises you that your license will be revoked by the Commission without hearing or other proceeding after the effective date of the cancellation unless you provide replacement coverage or the provider issues a recission of the cancellation. If you are an NVOCC OTI, you will be directed to cancel all NVOCC tariffs by the cancellation date. If you fail to provide replacement coverage, an Order of Revocation will be issued to you and notice of the revocation will be published in the Federal Register. Revocation is effective on the date of the coverage cancellation. You will be ordered to return your license and will be prohibited from performing OTI services. If you are an NVOCC OTI, the Commission will designate your FMC-1 listing as inactive.

I am an unlicensed foreign NVOCC OTI and my instrument of financial responsibility is cancelled. What may I expect?

The financial responsibility provider will send notice to the Commission that your coverage will be terminated. Termination becomes effective 30 days after receipt by the Commission of the notice or the date designated by the provider if the cancellation date is greater than 30 days. The Commission will issue you a letter notifying you of the provider's cancellation and the effective date of the cancellation. The provider and your tariff publisher will receive a copy of this letter. The letter directs you to cancel your tariffs by the effective date of the cancellation and advises that you may no longer operate as an OTI NVOCC in the foreign trades of the United States. The Commission will designate your FMC-1 filing as inactive.

If my proof of financial responsibility is cancelled and my license is revoked and I obtain new coverage, what must I do?

If the effective date of the new coverage is no later than the effective date of the cancellation of the prior coverage (and license revocation effective date) , you must notify the Office of Passenger Vessels and Information Processing by phone at (202) 523-5818, facsimile at (202) 523-5830 or e-mail at OTIbonds@fmc.gov and submit the replacement coverage. In most cases you will be reissued a license effective the date of the prior coverage cancellation and license revocation. If you are an NVOCC OTI, you will need to have your tariff publisher file a replacement FMC-1 form and publish a replacement tariff. If there is a break in OTI bond coverage, you will need to reapply for licensing by submitting Form FMC-18, a fee of $825 and the replacement coverage.

How do I seek a claim against the bond or insurance of an OTI?

If you seek to pursue a claim against an OTI financial responsibility provider arising from the OTI's transportation-related activities, you may attempt to resolve the claim with the financial responsibility provider prior to seeking payment on any judgment for damages obtained. If you seek payment without a judgment, you must simultaneously notify both the financial responsibility provider and the OTI of the claim by certified mail, return receipt requested. The bond, insurance or other surety may be available to pay your claim if:

(1) the OTI consents to payment, subject to review by the financial responsibility provider; or

(2) the OTI fails to respond within forty-five days from the date of the notice of claim, and the financial responsibility provider deems the claim valid. If the parties fail to reach an agreement within ninety days of the date of the initial notification of the claim, the bond, insurance or other surety shall be available to pay any final judgment for damages obtained from an appropriate court. The financial responsibility provider shall pay such judgment for damages only to the extent they arise from transportation-related activities of the OTI, ordinarily within 30 days, without requiring further evidence related to the validity of the claim. It may, however, inquire into the extent to which the judgment for damages arise from the OTI's transportation-related activities. The financial responsibility provider may be found in the rules section of the NVOCC's tariff. In addition, the name and address of the financial responsibility provider of an OTI may be obtained from the Office of Passenger Vessels and Information Processing Federal Maritime Commission Washington, D.C. 20573.

This office may be contacted by phone at (202) 523-5818, by facsimile at (202) 523-5830 or e-mail at OTIbonds@fmc.gov.

What is the Optional Rider for Additional NVOCC Financial Responsibility ("Optional Rider") ?

The Optional Rider (located on the FMC Forms Page) is a rider that NVOCCs serving the U.S.China Trade may attach to their NVOCC bond to meet the NVOCC licensing requirements of the People's Republic of China ("PRC") . The rider is a convenience offered by the Commission to

U.S. NVOCCs as a result of a bilateral maritime agreement between the United States and the PRC. The agreement's Memorandum of Consultations provides that the PRC will not require U.S. NVOCCs to make a cash deposit in a Chinese bank, as long as the NVOCC:

(1) is a legal person registered by U.S. authorities;

(2) obtains an OTI License from the Commission; and

(3) provides evidence of financial responsibility in the total amount of $96,000. The rider adds an additional $21,000 to the $75,000 bond already maintained by the NVOCC as a condition of licensing.

Can the PRC seek to collect fines and penalties against the entire NVOCC bond?

No. The PRC may only collect fines and penalties for violations of its shipping statutes and regulations from the Optional Rider. It may not collect such fines and penalties from the base $75,000 bond.

Is the Optional Rider available to shippers, carriers or others seeking claims for transportation-related activities under the Shipping Act?

No. The Optional Rider is available only to provide coverage should the PRC seek fines and penalties against the NVOCC for violation of its shipping laws.

Does the Optional Rider affect my ability to seek and collect on a claim for transportation related activities under the Shipping Act?

No. You may file a claim against the base bond. However, the $21,000 Optional Rider is not available for such claims.

Where may I direct questions regarding the shipping regulations of the PRC?

The Commission cannot provide guidance for questions regarding the shipping regulations of the PRC. You should contact the PRC Ministry of Communications to obtain advice.

How may I obtain the Optional Rider?

You may contact the underwriter of your OTI NVOCC bond to determine whether it will be willing to issue an Optional Rider to your bond. If so, it will file the rider to your OTI NVOCC bond. The Optional Rider will be effective on the date shown in 1.c. of the Optional bond.

May I obtain an Optional Rider from a surety other than the surety that underwrites my NVOCC OTI bond?

No. The Optional Rider is a rider to your existing OTI NVOCC bond. It cannot be issued independently of that bond.

Where may I obtain a copy of the Optional Rider?

You may view and copy the Optional Rider forms under the Bureau of Certification and Licensing/Forms heading on the Commission's website at www.fmc.gov. The Optional Rider for the individual OTI bond form, Form FMC-48, is numbered Form FMC-48A and the Optional rider for the OTI group bond, Form FMC-69, is numbered Form FMC- 69-A.

May I terminate the Optional Rider and keep the base bond in effect?

For additional analytical, business and investment opportunities information, please contact Global Investment & Business Center, USA at (703) 370-8082. Fax: (703) 370-8083. E-mail: ibpusa3@gmail.com Global Business and Investment Info Databank - www.ibpus.com

Yes. The Optional Rider may be terminated by either the NVOCC or the surety. Termination will become effective 30 days after receipt of the Notice of Termination by the Commission and proof that the PRC Minister of Communication has been notified.

How may I determine which NVOCCs have filed an Optional Rider?

You may consult the OTI List on the Commission's website and look at the Optional Bond Rider for China Trade column. A date in that field indicates the effective date of the Optional Rider on file with the Commission for the corresponding NVOCC. .

What are the requirements for an unincorporated branch office and one that is separately incorporated?

A branch office is any office in the United States maintained by or under the control of a licensee, performing OTI services, that operates under a common corporate charter. Individual unincorporated branch offices are not required to be licensed provided that they have been reported to the Commission and are covered by increased financial responsibility. A separately incorporated branch office is one operating under a separate corporate charter from its parent or affiliated licensee. Each separately incorporated branch office must provide its own proof of financial responsibility and be separately licensed, but may have the same qualifying individual.

If my headquarters office does not perform OTI services, but my unincorporated branch office performs those services, can I only report the branch office and provide financial responsibility for that office only?

No. Even though the headquarters office does not provide OTI services, its address must appear on the financial responsibility coverage as the headquarters. The branch office must also appear on the coverage and the coverage increased $10,000 for that branch office.

How does an applicant identify its business affiliations or ownership?

Business ownership and all related business affiliations must be explained on the application form by providing the names, addresses, and contact numbers. The percentage of ownership must be indicated and total 100%.

Are OTIs required to publish a tariff?

Freight forwarders are not required to publish tariffs. NVOCCs are required to publish tariffs. However, if a separately incorporated and licensed NVOCC branch office performs OTI services solely for the headquarters office, the branch office does not need to publish its own tariff. The branch office, in this instance, however, must still file an FMC-1 form and indicate the location of the headquarters tariff.

Where do I find the regulations as to publishing a tariff?

Tariff regulations may be found at 46 CFR Part 520. These are accessible at the Commission website at www.fmc.gov. (Click on "Regulations")

How can I find a tariff publisher?

For additional analytical, business and investment opportunities information, please contact Global Investment & Business Center, USA at (703) 370-8082. Fax: (703) 370-8083. E-mail: ibpusa3@gmail.com Global Business and Investment Info Databank - www.ibpus.com

A list of tariff publishers can be obtained from the Commission. You may contact the Bureau of Trade Analysis, Office of Service Contracts and Tariffs by telephone at (202) 523-5856.

What is a NVOCC service arrangement?

NVOCC Service Arrangement ("NSA") means a written contract, other than a bill of lading or receipt, between one or more NSA shippers and an individual NVOCC or two or more affiliated NVOCCs, in which the NSA shipper makes a commitment to provide a certain minimum quantity or portion of its cargo or freight revenue over a fixed time period, and the NVOCC commits to a certain rate or rate schedule and a defined service level. The NSA may also specify provisions in the event of nonperformance on the part of any party.

Where do I find the regulations on NVOCC service arrangements?

NVOCC service arrangement regulations may be found at 46 CFR Part 531. These are accessible at the Commission website under Statutes and Rules.

If I have questions about tariffs, NVOCC service arrangements or service contracts, including filing a FMC-1 form or a FMC-78 form, whom may I contact?

You may contact the Commission's Bureau of Trade Analysis, Office of Service Contracts and Tariffs by telephone at (202) 523-5856 or e-mail at form1@fmc.gov.

I am already licensed as an OTI. What changes in my operations must I report to the Commission?

Generally, all changes in the information contained in a licensee's initial application must be reported to the Commission. A replacement or the addition of a qualifying individual requires Commission approval. In addition, the transfer of a license or change in legal name, including trade name, requires Commission approval. Changes in business structure or address of headquarters or branch offices must be reported. In most instances, changes must be reported within 30 days from their occurrence.

What should I do if a sole-proprietor dies, or if a qualifying individual leaves?

If a licensed sole-proprietor dies, the licensee's executor, administrator, heirs, or assign(s) may continue operating only for those shipments for which the deceased had undertaken to provide OTI services. The death must be reported to the Commission and to all principals and shippers within 30 days. The acceptance or solicitation of any other shipments is prohibited until a new license is issued. If the qualifying individual of a partnership or corporation leaves, the licensee must report the departure to the Commission within 30 days. Within this same 30 days, the licensee must nominate and detail the OTI experience of another managing partner or officer to qualify the licensee. The licensee may continue to operate while the Commission investigates the qualifications of the newly designated qualifying individual.

What must I do if I incorporate my business? Change my name?

Newly incorporated licensees, or licensees that have changed their names, must file an amended FMC-18. A fee of $525 will be charged to reissue the license. A corporate charter or amended corporate charter must accompany the application.

For additional analytical, business and investment opportunities information, please contact Global Investment & Business Center, USA at (703) 370-8082. Fax: (703) 370-8083. E-mail: ibpusa3@gmail.com Global Business and Investment Info Databank - www.ibpus.com

What must I do if I change my headquarters address?

If you move, report your new address by letter or on an amended FMC-18. The Commission does not charge for such notification. You must also notify your financial responsibility provider to amend your coverage to show the new address. If you are an NVOCC OTI, you will need to contact your tariff publisher so that a revised FMC-1 Form is filed and your tariff is updated.

What must I do if I open or close an unincorporated branch office?

If you close an unincorporated branch office which was used to perform OTI services, or open an unincorporated branch office, you will need to report this change to the Commission by letter or amended Form FMC-18. Further, you will need to contact your financial responsibility provider so that your coverage is amended to reflect the change. The Commission charges no fees for changes regarding unincorporated branch offices.

What are the requirements of an unlicensed foreign-based NVOCC OTI?

A foreign-based OTI NVOCC that is not resident in, or incorporated or established under, the laws of the United States and intends on remaining unlicensed, must file proof of financial responsibility in the amount of $150,000. It must also identify an agent for service of process in the United States and use a licensed OTI for any OTI services performed in the United States on its behalf. It must also file Form FMC-1 with the Commission and publish a tariff.

May a foreign-based NVOCC OTI obtain an OTI license?

A foreign-based NVOCC OTI may obtain a license by following the requirements mentioned above for obtaining a license. Its qualifying individual may obtain experience outside the United States. The NVOCC must also establish an unincorporated presence in the United States that meets the requirements of the state in which it is located. If the Commission approves the application, the OTI must provide acceptable proof of financial responsibility in the amount of $75,000 plus $10,000 for each additional unincorporated branch office in the United States (not counting the presence established for licensing purposes) .

I am an unlicensed foreign-based NVOCC OTI and I no longer want to serve the United States trades, what must I do?

You must notify the Office of Passenger Vessels and Information Processing by phone at (202) 523-5818, facsimile at (202) 523-5830 or e-mail at OTIbonds@fmc.gov that you no longer are operating in the United States trades. You must also notify your tariff publisher and your financial responsibility provider. The Commission will designate your FMC-1 listing as inactive. After this is done, you are prohibited from providing OTI NVOCC services in the foreign commerce of the United States.

What are Non-Vessel-Operating Common Carrier Service Arrangements ("NSAs") ?

An exemption recently issued by the Federal Maritime Commission (FMC) , allows non-vesseloperating common carriers (NVOCCs) to now enter into service arrangements with their shipper/customers called NSAs (non-vessel-operating common carrier service arrangements) . 46 CFR Part 531. Under the Commission's rules, an NSA means a written contract, other than a bill of lading or receipt, between one or more NSA shippers and an individual NVOCC or two or more affiliated NVOCCs, in which the NSA shipper makes a commitment to provide a certain minimum quantity or portion of its cargo or freight revenue over a fixed time period, and the NVOCC commits to a certain rate or rate schedule and a defined service level. 46 CFR 531.3(p) . An NSA shipper is a cargo owner, the person for whose account the ocean transportation is provided, the person to whom delivery is to be made, a shippers' association, or a non-vesseloperating common carrier. 46 CFR 531.3(o) .

What activities led to the creation of NSAs?

This FMC action was prompted by petitions that were filed between July 25, 2003 and March 12, 2004 by seven individual NVOCCs and by the National Customs Brokers and Forwarders Association of America, Inc. Although these petitions varied to some extent, they all sought to achieve the result made possible by the FMC's exemption by rulemaking, namely that NVOCCs can contract with their shipper/customers on a confidential basis in much the same manner as can be done by vessel-operating common carriers through service contracts. In August, 2004, several of those petitioners, together with the Transportation Intermediaries Association and the National Industrial Transportation League, urged the FMC to act as quickly as possible to exempt filed NSAs from the tariff publication and adherence requirements of the Shipping Act. This proposal was supported by many individual NVOCCs and NVOCC organizations, as well as associations of vessel-operating common carriers. The FMC issued its Notice of Proposed Rulemaking in late October, 2004 (69 Fed. Reg. 63981) (November 3, 2004) , and received numerous comments in response from several individual NVOCCs and associations of NVOCCs, shippers associations, and the U.S. Department of Justice. The Final Rule became effective on January 19, 2005. 69 Fed. Reg. 75850 (December 20, 2004) .

Is an NVOCC required to negotiate an NSA with its customers?

No. NSAs have been established as a possible alternative for NVOCCs to negotiate confidential shipping arrangements with their shipper customers.

How does the NSA option affect NVOCC/shipper business relationships?

Specifically, the exemption allows individual NVOCCs (including corporately affiliated NVOCCs) , who are compliant with the other requirements of the Shipping Act and the FMC's regulations at 46 CFR Part 515 and 46 CFR Part 520, to enter into an NSA with one or more NSA shippers. 46 CFR 531.2. The FMC's rule allows NVOCCs to enter into service arrangements with their customers in lieu of publishing those arrangements in a publicly-available tariff, as otherwise would be required by sections 8(a) and 10 of the Shipping Act.

Is the use of NSAs restricted in any way?

The FMC limited NVOCC actions through NSAs to ensure shippers and ports are protected in a similar manner to section 10 of the Shipping Act: service rendered under an NSA must be according to rates and charges appearing in a properly filed NSA. 46 CFR 531.6(d) (1) ; and no NVOCC may employ an NSA to unfairly or unjustly discriminate (with respect to rates or charges) , or grant any unreasonable preference or impose any unreasonable prejudice with respect to any port. 46 CFR 531.6(d) (2) , (3) .

Where can a copy of the Commission's rules regarding NSAs be found?

The Commission rules can be found here. See also the Notice of Proposed Rulemaking issued August 8, 2005.

For additional analytical, business and investment opportunities information, please contact Global Investment & Business Center, USA at (703) 370-8082. Fax: (703) 370-8083. E-mail: ibpusa3@gmail.com Global Business and Investment Info Databank - www.ibpus.com

How does an NVOCC become eligible to file NSAs?

To take advantage of the exemption provided for in 46 CFR Part 531, an NVOCC must be in compliance with the Commission's rules located at 46 CFR Part 515, Licensing, Financial Responsibility Requirements and General Duties for Ocean Transportation Intermediaries, and Part 520, Carrier Automated Tariffs, regarding requirements to publish a tariff and file electronic Form FMC-1. An NVOCC in compliance needs to complete Form FMC-78, NVOCC Service Arrangement Registration, with the Commission.

How is a copy of Form FMC-78 obtained and submitted to the Commission?

A printable copy of Form FMC-78 in PDF format can be obtained here. Fill the form out completely, and submit to the Office of Service Contracts ("OSCT") by facsimile at (202) 5235856. If an agent has been designated to file NSAs with the Commission on the NVOCCs behalf, a delegation of authority must accompany the form. A direct link to the pdf version of Form FMC-78 can be found here. It is not an "auto-fill" form, but must be printed, completed, and faxed as mentioned above to the OSCT, or mailed to OSCT, Bureau of Trade Analysis (BTA) , Federal Maritime Commission, 800 North Capitol Street, NW, Washington, DC 20573. This simple form, requesting name & address information, license number and individual to be registered and receive log-on and password user identification ("User ID") for access to the SERVCON electronic filing system, is usually processed in approximately five days. Registrants will be notified by certified mail of their User ID. There are no Commission fees associated either with registering to file or with filing NSA's.

How is an NSA filed with the Commission?

Once an FMC-issued User ID is received, an NVOCC (or its designated publisher or agent) can go to the FMC's website, www.fmc.gov, use the User ID to access electronic SERVCON system, enter minimal information regarding the NSA filing (e.g., organization number, NSA number, amendment number, and effective date) , and upload NSAs into the Commission's automated SERVCON system via the internet. Detailed instructions can be found at the FMC's website (https://www.servcon.fmc.gov) or by contacting OSCT.

Which document formats for NSA texts will the Commission's SERVCON filing system accept?

The internet-based SERVCON filing system will accept original and amendment NSA documents in over 100 off-the-shelf computer software formats, e.g., WordPerfect, Microsoft Word, WordStar, Excel, PDF, ASCII, and many others.

What are confidentiality and content requirements regarding an NSA filing?

The terms of NSAs by the parties are to be kept confidential to the fullest extent permitted by law, and required to be filed with the FMC. Every NSA filed with the Commission is required to include the complete terms of the NSA including, but not limited to, the following: (1) the origin and destination port ranges in the case of port-to-port movements and geographic areas in the case of through intermodal movements; (2) the commodity or commodities involved; (3) minimum volume or portion; (4) service commitments; (5) line haul rate; (6) liquidated damages for nonperformance (if any) ; (7) duration, including the effective date and expiration date; (8) legal names and business addresses of the NSA parties; the legal names of all affiliates of the NSA shipper entitled to access the NSA; the names, titles and addresses of the representatives signing the NSA for the parties; (9) a description of the shipment records which will be maintained

For additional analytical, business and investment opportunities information, please contact Global Investment & Business Center, USA at (703) 370-8082. Fax: (703) 370-8083. E-mail: ibpusa3@gmail.com Global Business and Investment Info Databank - www.ibpus.com

to support the NSA and the address, telephone number, and title of the person who will respond to a request by making shipment records available to the Commission; and various other provisions of the NSA. 46 CFR 531.6. Contemporaneously with the filing of each NSA with the Commission, all authorized persons who choose to file NSAs are also required to make available to the public, in tariff format in the NVOCCs automated tariff system, a concise statement of certain “essential terms” (“ETs”) .

What are the certain essential terms required to be made public?

All authorized persons who choose to file NSAs are also required to make available to the public, contemporaneously with the filing of each NSA with the FMC, in tariff format in the NVOCCs automated tariff system, a concise statement of certain essential terms as follows: (1) origin/destination port ranges; (2) commodity or commodities involved; (3) minimum volume or portion; and (4) the duration of the arrangement. 46 CFR 531.9(a) .

Which FMC office should I call with questions about NSAs?

Bureau of Trade Analysis, Office of Service Contracts and Tariffs 800 N. Capitol Street, NW Washington, DC 20573 Phone: (202) 523-5856 Fax: (202) 523-5867 Email: NSAInquiries@fmc.gov Information related to NSAs is also available on the FMC's website, www.fmc.gov.

Is there any required or preferred standard form for an NSA?

No, the new regulations only require that the "complete terms" of an NSA be reflected in the text filed in SERVCON with the Commission and contain a list at 46 CFR 531.6 of the minimum terms that must be included in an NSA. NSA parties may include additional terms and conditions of the services to be performed by the NVOCC under the agreement and/or additional obligations undertaken by the shipper.

What terms of a service arrangement may cross reference other material? What may that referenced material be, specifically, can it include a published tariff?

The parties may agree to make their NSAs refer to any widely available published material which is well known in the industry. An example of such cross-referencing would be to the currency exchange rates as published in the Wall Street Journal. Such cross-referencing may also include reference to an NVOCC's general rules tariff. Filers should particularly note that the terms of NSAs may not be "uncertain, vague or ambiguous." 46 CFR 531.9(b) (1) . Reference may not be made to a tariff of a common carrier other than that of the NVOCC offering the NSA.

Where must service arrangement "boiler plate" be filed?

"Boiler plate" may either be published as a general rules tariff and cross-referenced in the NSA or kept confidential by filing the terms in the text of each NSA filed in SERVCON.

Must the public ETs appear in any particular format?

The regulations require ETs to be in "tariff format". 46 CFR 531.9. The Commission regulation allow ETs to be published in a separate part of an NVOCC's existing tariff publication. ETs may be organized in any manner the publisher or NVOCC sees fit: organized by trade, as a separate tariff type, etc..

For additional analytical, business and investment opportunities information, please contact Global Investment & Business Center, USA at (703) 370-8082. Fax: (703) 370-8083. E-mail: ibpusa3@gmail.com Global Business and Investment Info Databank - www.ibpus.com

What is the Federal Maritime Commission's Passenger Vessel Operator Certification Program ("PVO Program") ?

The Office of Passenger Vessels and Information Processing at The Federal Maritime Commission ("Commission") issues Certificates (Performance) and Certificates (Casualty) to cruise lines which have provided proof of financial responsibility in an amount sufficient to reimburse passengers for claims against the cruise line for failure to perform cruises, and claims to cover death or injury to passengers and other persons.

What is meant by "proof of financial responsibility?"

Proof of financial responsibility is the coverage provided by the cruise line to demonstrate that it can reimburse passengers for the water portion of fares paid by passengers should the cruise line fail to perform, or provide coverage for death or injury of passengers or other persons in the amounts required by law. In most instances, coverage is shown through the filing of a surety bond, guaranty or similar financial instrument. Separate coverage is filed for non-performance and casualty.

What statute and rules govern this program?

Public Law 89-777, Financial Responsibility for Death and Injury to Passengers and Nonperformance of Voyages (46 App. USC 817d and e) , and 46 CFR Part 540, Passenger Vessel Financial Responsibility

When is a vessel subject to the PVO program?

A vessel is subject to the PVO program when:

(1)

the vessel has berth or stateroom accommodations for 50 or more passengers, and

(2)

the vessel embarks passengers at U.S. ports.

To be considered a passenger, the individual must have embarked at a U.S. port and purchased a ticket entitling him to water transportation aboard that vessel.

Does the PVO program cover all vessels serving U.S. ports and cruises on those vessels?

No. The program only covers those vessels that are subject to the PVO program, i.e., those that have berth or stateroom accommodations for 50 or more passengers and embark passengers at

U.S. ports.

Does the PVO program provide coverage for all the vessels in a cruise line's fleet when some vessels have coverage and have been issued Certificates and others do not?

No. Coverage is available only for those vessels for which Certificates have been issued.

For additional analytical, business and investment opportunities information, please contact Global Investment & Business Center, USA at (703) 370-8082. Fax: (703) 370-8083. E-mail: ibpusa3@gmail.com Global Business and Investment Info Databank - www.ibpus.com

Does the vessel need to be a U.S. flagged vessel?

No. The regulations do not make a distinction as to flag of vessel.

Does the program cover non-U.S. citizens?

Yes. The regulations do not make a distinction as to citizenship of the passenger.

Does the program cover voyages originating from a foreign port and ending at a U.S. port?

No. The passenger must embark in the U.S.

Does the program cover passengers who first travel by air from the U.S. to a foreign destination to embark on a vessel?

No. The passenger must board the vessel at a U.S. port.

Does the program cover U.S. citizens who embark a foreign port?

No. The program covers only those passengers who embark at a U.S. port, regardless of citizenship.

What is a U.S. port?

A U.S. port is any port in the United States, the Commonwealth of Puerto Rico, the U.S. Virgin Islands, Guam, and any other territory or possession of the United States.

How may I contact the Commission should I have questions about this program?

You may contact the Office of Passenger Vessels and Information Processing with questions regarding the application process, coverage and how to make a claim: Office of Passenger Vessels and Information Processing Federal Maritime Commission 800 North Capitol Street, N.W. Washington, D.C. 20573

Phone: (202) 523-5818 Fax: (202) 523-5830 E-mail: pvo@fmc.gov

Whom should I contact if I have a complaint or consumer concern about a cruise line?

You may contact the Office of Consumer Affairs and Dispute Resolution Services at:

Office of Consumer Affairs and Dispute Resolution Services Federal Maritime Commission 800 North Capitol Street, N.W. Washington, D.C. 20573

Phone: (202) 523-5807 Fax: (202) 275-0059 E-mail: complaints@fmc.gov You may also wish to consult the Office of Consumer Affairs and Dispute Resolution Services web page. The office posts cruise line consumer information at that site.

What is a Certificate (Performance) ?

For additional analytical, business and investment opportunities information, please contact Global Investment & Business Center, USA at (703) 370-8082. Fax: (703) 370-8083. E-mail: ibpusa3@gmail.com Global Business and Investment Info Databank - www.ibpus.com

A Certificate (Performance) is a certificate issued by the Commission to a vessel which indicates that the cruise line has filed acceptable proof of financial responsibility, i.e., coverage, which is available to pay passenger claims should the cruise line fail to perform contracted cruises.

When is a Certificate (Performance) required?

A Certificate (Performance) is required prior to any person in the United States arranging, offering, advertising or providing passage on a vessel subject to the PVO program.

To whom is a Certificate (Performance) issued?

The Certificate is generally issued in the name of the vessel operator and/or ticket issuer and specifies the name of the vessel covered. A separate Certificate is issued for each vessel in the cruise line fleet subject to the PVO program.

What constitutes “non-performance?”

In general, non-performance is the failure to commence or complete cruises upon which payment has been made. To date, the instances of non-performance which resulted in a payout from the coverage filed as proof of financial responsibility have been caused by the bankruptcy of a cruise line.

How is the amount of non-performance coverage calculated?

Cruise lines are required to provide coverage in the amount calculated by the Commission. The amount, in most cases, is 110% of the highest unearned passenger revenue collected by the cruise line in the prior two fiscal years. Non-performance coverage is capped at $15 million.

What is unearned passenger revenue?

Unearned passenger revenue consists of the deposits and/or advance payments for voyages that have not yet been performed. The unearned passenger revenue will fluctuate from week to week as the cruise line’s season proceeds and bookings are made and cruises are completed.

When does a cruise line earn monies paid by passengers for water transportation?

Revenue is earned upon completion of the water transportation for which the passenger paid.

What type of coverage is provided as proof of financial responsibility for nonperformance?

In most instance, the coverage is provided by guaranty issued by an acceptable Protection and Indemnity Association or a surety bond issued by an acceptable surety, e.g., on the Department of Treasury list of acceptable sureties. In lieu of these financial instruments, the cruise line may establish an escrow account administered by a neutral financial institution in which these unearned passenger revenues are deposited, to be withdrawn by the cruise line as voyages are completed and the revenue earned.

Where may a passenger make a claim against a cruise line for failure to perform?

Claims may be filed against the coverage provider. The cruise line, coverage provider and/or the Commission generally provide guidance on how to make such claims. The coverage only covers the water portion of the fare. If the fare includes hotel or air fare charges, reimbursement from the coverage provider will not include those charges. If the passenger fares were paid by credit card, in most cases the credit card processor can credit the passenger's account for the total amount of the charge. Therefore, charge backs may cover air fare, hotel and other non-water transportation not included under non-performance coverage. In these instances, the passenger may be able to obtain a full refund for all amounts charged to the credit card. Passengers who have purchased third party insurance should contact the underwriter to determine if their claim will be honored and what documentation will be required to file a claim.

For what sums can a passenger seek reimbursement?

Passengers may make a claim for any monies paid for water transportation and all other accommodations, services, and facilities not yet performed when those services cannot be separated from the water transportation costs. A Certificate (Performance) does not cover air transportation to the port even if arranged through the cruise line. It also does not cover any sums paid for hotels, shore excursions or tours unless they were required with the water passage.

In the event of the bankruptcy of the cruise line, will passenger coverage be reduced in order to satisfy claims other than for non-performance?

No. The coverage remains outside the reach of the bankruptcy court and is only available for the reimbursement of fares and deposits paid by passengers. Credit card companies and other such parties may not seek reimbursement from the coverage. Travel agents may not seek to obtain commissions from the coverage

What is a Certificate (Casualty) ?

A Certificate (Casualty) is a certificate issued by the Commission to a vessel which indicates that the cruise line has filed acceptable proof of financial responsibility which is available to pay passenger claims for death or injury or such claims filed on behalf of other persons such as crew or staff aboard the vessel.

When is a Certificate (Casualty) required?

A Certificate (Casualty) is required prior to the embarkation of passengers aboard a vessel subject to the PVO program.

To whom is the Certificate (Casualty) issued?

The Certificate is generally issued in the name of the vessel owner and operator and specifies the name of the vessel covered. A separate Certificate is issued for each vessel in the cruise line fleet subject to the PVO program.

How is the amount of non-performance coverage calculated?

The amount of coverage is based on the number of berths on the cruise line's largest vessel and the formula contained in the statute. The formula is as follows:

(a)

$20,000 for each passenger accommodation up to and including 500, plus

(b)

$15,000 for each passenger accommodation between 501 and 1,000, plus

(c)

$10,000 for each passenger accommodation between 1,001 and 1,500, plus

(d)

$5,000 for each passenger accommodation in excess of 1,500. For example, if we apply the formula to a vessel of 1,200 berths, coverage is calculated as follows:

First 500 berths @ $20,000 = $10,000,000 Next 500 berths @ $15,000 = 7,500,000 Next 200 berths @ $10,000 = 2,000,000 Total required coverage = $19,500,000

Regulations regarding coverage for casualty liability refer to passengers and other persons. Who are "other persons."

Other persons include, but are not limited to, visitors, crew, and temporary workers aboard ship.

What type of coverage is provided as proof of financial responsibility to meet liability for death or injury?

In most instances, the coverage is provided by guaranty issued by an acceptable Protection and Indemnity Association or insurance provided by an acceptable insurance company.

Where may passengers make a claim against the cruise line for death or injury?

The passenger or his representative may contact the coverage provider. The contact information may be obtained by contacting the Office of Passenger Vessels and Information Processing by phone at (202) 523-5818 or e-mail at pvo@fmc.gov.

Is there a separate application form to apply for Certificate (Performance) and a Certificate (Casualty) ?

No. The same form (Form FMC-131) is used to apply for either Certificate. The applicant needs to indicate on the form which type of certificate is requested.

Where may I obtain a copy of the Form FMC-131 - Application for Certificate of Financial Responsibility?

Form FMC-131 may be printed from the Commission's website at the Forms link at www.fmc.gov. You may also call the Office of Passenger Vessels and Information Processing at (202) 523-5818 and request a copy of the form be mailed or faxed to you.

How does a cruise line apply for a Certificate (Performance) ?

For additional analytical, business and investment opportunities information, please contact Global Investment & Business Center, USA at (703) 370-8082. Fax: (703) 370-8083. E-mail: ibpusa3@gmail.com Global Business and Investment Info Databank - www.ibpus.com

The cruise line completes and submits Form FMC-131 and indicates the application is for a Certificate (Perfomance) . It is advisable that the applicant contact the Office of Passenger Vessels and Information Processing prior to submitting Form FMC-131 to discuss what is needed to complete the application and determine the amount of coverage that will be required.

The application should be submitted to: Office of Passenger Vessels and Information Processing Federal Maritime Commission 800 North Capitol Street, N.W. Washington, DC 20573 You may contact the Office of Passengers Vessels and Information Processing at the following: Phone: (202) 523-5818 Fax: (202) 523-5830 E-mail: pvo@fmc.gov

What is the application fee for a Certificate (Performance) ?

The fee for a Certificate (Performance) excluding one filed for the addition or substitution of a vessel, is $2,767.00. The fee for a Certificate (Performance) for a vessel addition or substitution to the cruise line's fleet is $1,382.00. Payment is made by check and the check is to be made payable to the Federal Maritime Commission. The check must accompany the Form FMC-131 application form.

When should the Form FMC-131 application form be filed for a Certificate (Performance) ?

The Form FMC-131 should be filed at least 60 days in advance of the arranging, offering, advertising, or providing of any water transportation or tickets. In addition, an amended application or written description is required to be filed within 5 days should a change in service result in a decrease or increase in the amount of coverage filed as proof of financial responsibility.

When should the non-performance coverage be filed with the Commission?

The coverage needs to be filed as soon as possible after the coverage amount is set. The original executed instrument is required.

What factors determine the amount of coverage for non-performance?

The coverage is typically set at 110% of the cruise line's unearned passenger revenue experienced in the two fiscal years prior to application. If this information is not available, e.g., the cruise line is initiating a new service, then an estimate is made based upon the fare structure, itinerary, pre-payment policy and other factors to determine a coverage amount. Commission staff will monitor the unearned passenger revenue reports filed with the Commission to ensure that the coverage amount is appropriate and request adjustment as necessary. Commission rules cap the coverage amount for non-performance at $15 million.

What types of coverage may be filed to establish proof of responsibility for nonperformance?

Cruise lines file a surety bond, guaranty or an escrow account as coverage. The surety must be on the Department of the Treasury's Listing of Approved Sureties (Department Circular 570) available at http://fms.treas.gov/c570. The guarantor must be acceptable to the Commission, i.e., a protection and indemnity association with sufficient assets in the U.S. Please contact the Office of Passenger Vessels and Information Processing to determine acceptability. The surety and guaranty forms are available by clicking on the Forms link at the Bureau of Certification and Licensing home page. The escrow agreement must be approved by the Commission. Please contact the Office of Passenger Vessels and Information Processing to discuss escrow agreement and escrow agent requirements.

For additional analytical, business and investment opportunities information, please contact Global Investment & Business Center, USA at (703) 370-8082. Fax: (703) 370-8083. E-mail: ibpusa3@gmail.com Global Business and Investment Info Databank - www.ibpus.com

How does a cruise line apply for a Certificate (Casualty) ?

The cruise line completes and submits Form FMC-131 and indicates the application is for a Certificate (Casualty) . It is advisable that the applicant contact the Office of Passenger Vessels and Information Processing prior to submitting the Form FMC-131 to be sure the coverage provider is acceptable. The application should be submitted to:

Office of Passenger Vessels and Information Processing Federal Maritime Commission 800 North Capitol Street, N.W. Washington, D.C. 20573

You may contact the Office of Passenger Vessels and Information Processing at the following: Phone: (202) 523-5818 Fax: (202) 523-5830 E-mail: pvo@fmc.gov.

What is the application fee for a Certificate (Casualty) ?

The fee for a Certificate (Casualty) excluding one filed for the addition or substitution of a vessel is $1,206.00. The fee for a Certificate (Casualty) for the addition or substitution of a vessel is $605.00 Payment is made by check and the check is to be made payable to the Federal Maritime Commission. The check must accompany the Form FMC-131 application form.

When should the Form FMC-131 application form be filed for a Certificate (Casualty) ?

An application for Certificate (Casualty) should be filed with the Office of Passenger Vessels and Information Processing at least 60 days in advance of the first sailing. In addition, an amended application or written description is required to be filed within 5 days should a change in service occur which results in a decrease or increase in the amount of coverage required.

Must I apply for the Certificate (Casualty) at the same time as I apply for the Certificate (Performance) ?

No. You may apply at different times. In most cases, the cruise line will apply for the Certificate (Performance) on a new vessel, much earlier than the Certificate (Casualty) , since the Certificate (Performance) is required before advertising may begin but the Certificate (Casualty) is required before embarkation.

When should the casualty coverage be filed with the Commission?

Casualty coverage should be filed with the Form FMC-131 application for Certificate (Casualty) or shortly thereafter.

What types of coverage may be filed to establish proof of financial responsibility for casualty?

Cruise lines file acceptable guaranties or insurance. The guarantor must be acceptable to the Commission, i.e., a protection and indemnity association with sufficient assets in the U.S. The insurance company must have an acceptable financial rating. The guaranty form is available by clicking on the Forms link at the Bureau of Certification and Licensing home page. Please contact the Office of Passenger Vessels and Information Processing to ensure the coverage to be provided is acceptable.

What must I do with the Certificate(s) when I receive it?

For additional analytical, business and investment opportunities information, please contact Global Investment & Business Center, USA at (703) 370-8082. Fax: (703) 370-8083. E-mail: ibpusa3@gmail.com Global Business and Investment Info Databank - www.ibpus.com

The Certificate(s) will be needed when the vessel clears Customs from any U.S. port of embarkation. It should be physically available onboard the vessel for that purpose.

What reports are required after Certification?

For all cruise lines holding a Certificate (Performance) :

a.A semiannual report which indicates the highest unearned passenger revenue for each month in the six month period and due 30 days after the close of every such six -month period.

b.A semiannual statement of any changes that have occurred during the six month period; a negative statement is necessary should there be no change. Reports are due 30 days after the close of every such six-month period.

For those cruise lines evidencing financial responsibility by means of escrow account:

a.Weekly recomputation schedule indicating the balance, receipts, refunds and withdrawal of earned funds from escrow. These are to be provided to the escrow agent and the Commision.

b.A monthly report prepared by the escrow agent which lists investment assets of the account. The reports are due 15 days after the end of the each month and must be provided to the cruise line and directly to the Commission

c.Quarterly reports prepared by the cruise line's independent auditors and to be provided directly to the Commission and the escrow agent

d.Any other reports the Commission deems necessary to monitor the escrow account.

What can happen if the Certificates are required but not obtained?

U.S. Customs is required to refuse clearance to any vessel that is required to have a Certificate (Performance) and a Certificate (Casualty) but has failed to secure such certificates from the Commission. In addition, the Commission may impose civil penalties of $220 per passage sold against any cruise line it finds to be in violation of the PVO Certification Program.

Does the Federal Maritime Commission have information about training, educational requirements, and job opportunities with the U.S. Merchant Marine?

No. The Federal Maritime Commission has no records or information regarding requirements or opportunities with the United States Merchant Marine. The websites of the United States Coast Guard, Department of Homeland Security, and the Maritime Administration, Department of Transportation, provide a variety of information about the Merchant Marine.

Does the Federal Maritime Commission have information about Veterans' benefits for people who served in the Merchant Marine during World War II?

No. If you served in the United States Merchant Marine (including the Army Transport Service and the Naval Transport Service) during World War II and would like to know if you qualify for Veterans' benefits, information on the United States Coast Guard website may be helpful.

Does the Federal Maritime Commission have information about U.S. Cabotage Laws?

No. Information concerning Cabotage laws, including the Jones Act, is available from the Maritime Administration.

Does the FMC provide certified copies of documents in its files?

Yes. Requests for certification of documents should be made in writing and should be addressed to: Commission's Secretary Office of the Secretary 800 N. Capitol Street, NW Washington, DC 20573

Phone: (202) 523-5725; Fax: (202) 523-0014; Email: Secretary@fmc.gov.

Your written request should thoroughly identify the specific documents you need certified, and indicate specific dates or information you need included in the certification language. The charges associated with certifications and duplication of documents are located at 46 CFR Part 503 of the Commission's rules.

How do I make a Freedom of Information Act (FOIA) Request?

Freedom of Information Act Requests must be directed in writing to: Secretary Federal Maritime Commission Washington, D.C. 20573 and must reasonably describe the record or records sought. E-mail requests may be directed to the Secretary at secretary@fmc.gov. More information about how to make FOIA requests and the associated charges may be found at 46 CFR Part 503 of the Commission's rules or on the Commission's FOIA site.

Is the Commission's Docket Activity Library available to the public for research?

Yes. The Docket Activity Library is the Commission's repository for legal pleadings filed in various types of proceedings such as, formal and informal dockets (private complaints or Commission instituted investigations) and rulemakings. Docket files can be viewed at: 800 North Capitol Street, N.W. Room 1049, Washington, DC.

Docket logs (a chronological listing of all filings/issuances in each docket) also are available through the Commission's website. For assistance in locating or requesting copies of documents in the Docket Library please contact our Docket Activity Library at (202) 523-5760 or send email to secretary@fmc.gov.

Is the Commission's Reference/Law Library available to the public for research?

Yes. The Commission's Public Reference/Law Library is available to the public. Its holdings consist of specialized material primarily covering the various segments of the international shipping industry, as well as historical and current regulatory materials covering all phases of shipping in the U.S. foreign trades. Members of the public are welcome to visit the Library and use the materials; however, all collection materials must be used in the Library during Library hours. The Librarian can be reached at (202) 523-5762, or by email at LibraryInquires@fmc.gov.

What is a service contract?

For additional analytical, business and investment opportunities information, please contact Global Investment & Business Center, USA at (703) 370-8082. Fax: (703) 370-8083. E-mail: ibpusa3@gmail.com Global Business and Investment Info Databank - www.ibpus.com

A service contract is a contract, other than a bill of lading, between a shipper and an ocean common carrier or an ocean common carrier agreement in which the shipper commits to provide a certain minimum quantity of cargo over a fixed period of time and the ocean common carrier or the ocean common carrier agreement commits to a certain rate or rate schedule and a defined level of service. 46 C.F.R. § 530.3(q) .

Must all service contracts be filed with the Commission?

Generally, yes, although there are exceptions for service contracts for certain commodities: bulk cargo, forest products, recycled metal scrap, new assembled motor vehicles and waste paper or paper waste. 46 C.F.R. § 530.13.

Who must file service contracts?

Carrier parties, i.e. ocean common carriers, agreements among ocean common carriers or conferences, are responsible for filing service contracts with the Commission. 46 C.F.R. § 530.5

How are service contracts filed?

All service contracts must be filed electronically in SERVCON, the Commission's internet-based filing system. See 46 C.F.R. Part 530.

What is SERVCON?

SERVCON is the Federal Maritime Commission's internet-based filing system for ocean common carrier service contracts and non-vessel-operating common carrier service arrangements ("NSAs") . It is located on the Commission's website, www.fmc.gov, under SERVCON. For more information on NSAs, see NSA FAQs on this website.

Which document formats will the Commission's SERVCON internet-based filing system accept?

SERVCON accepts service contracts and amendments written in more than 90 off-the-shelf software formats, including e.g., WordPerfect, Microsoft Word, WordStar and ASCII.

Are there user fees associated with SERVCON?

There is no user fee required at this time for SERVCON filings.

How do I register to file service contracts?

Anyone wishing to file service contracts on their own behalf or as an agent for an ocean common carrier must register to access the SERVCON system by filing Form FMC-83.

What is Form FMC-83?

Form FMC-83 is a service contract registration form. Form FMC-83 must be filed in order for a filer to obtain user identification, logon and password, to access the SERVCON system to file service contracts.

Who is required to file Form FMC-83?

For additional analytical, business and investment opportunities information, please contact Global Investment & Business Center, USA at (703) 370-8082. Fax: (703) 370-8083. E-mail: ibpusa3@gmail.com Global Business and Investment Info Databank - www.ibpus.com

Carriers or conferences that enter into service contracts subject to the Commission's rules governing service contracts must file a FMC-83 Form. 46 C.F.R. § 530.5(c) .

How can a copy of Form FMC-83 be obtained and filed with the Commission?

Go to the Commission's website, www.fmc.gov, click on Forms and Applications, scroll down to For Service Contracts, click on Service Contract Registration (FMC-83) , print a copy of the form, fill out the form completely with the information requested, and fax a copy of the completed form to the Office of Service Contracts and Tariffs at (202) 523-5867. If there are no problems with the FMC-83, a request is forwarded to the Commission's Office of Information Technology (OIT) to assign a logon and password ID. OIT will send the ID by certified mail to the person named on Line 7 of the form authorized to access SERVCON and file service contracts.

Are SERVCON filings confidential?

Yes. Except for the public essential terms, discussed below in these FAQs, the Commission keeps all service contracts and amendments to service contracts confidential. Shipping Act of 1984, as amended. The parties may elect to disclose the terms of their service contracts, if they so agree.

Are there any publishing requirements related to service contracts?

Yes. All authorized persons who have a duty to file service contracts under 46 C.F.R. § 530.5 (i.e. carrier parties) must also make available to the public, contemporaneously with the filing of each service contract with the Commission, and in tariff format, a concise statement of the following essential terms ("public ETs") : (1) origin and destination port ranges; (2) the commodity or commodities; (3) cargo minimum quantity or portion; and (4) the duration. 46 C.F.R. § 530.12.

What is an Essential Terms Publication?

An Essential Terms Publication (ETP) is a quasi-tariff formatted publication that contains the public ETs only of a carrier or conference in a single publication made available to the public at the location of the carrier's or conference's tariff(s) .

Must the public Essential Terms ETs) appear in any particular format?

Federal law requires that public ETs be made public in "tariff format." Shipping Act of 1984, as amended. The Commission's rules require that public ETs be published in a separate part of the carrier party's tariff publication. 46 C.F.R. § 530.12(c) . Carrier parties may publish public ETs in a separate service contract essential terms publication tariff. Public ETs may be organized in any manner, e.g., by trade, as a separate tariff type, etc. All public ETs must include a reference to a carrier-assigned service contract ("SC") number.

Where can I find a common carrier's or conference's public ETs?

The public ETs are available at the common carrier's or conference's tariff location. A list of tariff locations associated with a particular common carrier or conference is available on the FMC's website Links to Tariffs.

When must public ETs be published?

For additional analytical, business and investment opportunities information, please contact Global Investment & Business Center, USA at (703) 370-8082. Fax: (703) 370-8083. E-mail: ibpusa3@gmail.com Global Business and Investment Info Databank - www.ibpus.com

Public ETs must be made available to the public contemporaneously with the filing of each service contract with the Commission. 46 C.F.R. § 530.12(a) .

How and where must the public ETs of a non-conference agreement be published?

Where a service contract is entered into by an agreement among ocean common carriers that is not a conference, each individual carrier party to such a service contract must publish the ETs in its individual tariff publication and clearly indicate the relevant FMC-assigned agreement number. 46 C.F.R. § 530.12(c) (2) .

May service contracts cross reference other material, specifically a published tariff?

Service contracts may refer to any widely available published material which is well known in the industry. 46 C.F.R. Part 530. An example of such cross-referencing would be to the currency exchange rates as published in the Wall Street Journal. Such cross-referencing may also include reference to the carrier party's general rules tariff. Filers should particularly note that the terms of service contracts may not be "uncertain, vague or ambiguous." 46 C.F.R. § 530.8(c) (1) .

Must common service contract standard terms ("boiler plate") be filed in every service contract?

Standard, repetitive or common contract terms ("boiler plate") may either be published as a general rules tariff and cross-referenced to the carrier's tariff or kept confidential by incorporating the terms into the filed service contract.

Must service contracts for inland movements in Europe be filed with the Commission?

Unlike U.S. federal law, the European Union views inland movements as separate and distinct from the ocean movement and does not allow common pricing by carriers offering such through movements. U.S. law, on the other hand, views the entire movement as ocean shipping. As such, contracts for through movements are service contracts and should be filed in their entirety. Accordingly, if an ocean common carrier provides continuous transportation involving more than one mode of service (e.g., ship, rail, motor, air) for pickup or delivery at a point beyond the port at which the vessel calls, the service contracts covering the entire intermodal movement must be filed. If the rate for an intermodal movement between the United States and Europe is computed by adding an ocean contract rate and an inland contract rate, both contracts must be filed with the Commission.

Must ocean common carriers enter into service contracts?

No. Ocean common carriers may either offer service pursuant to a tariff or a service contract. However agreements among ocean common carries must not prohibit or restrict its individual members from offering or negotiating service contracts. Shipping Act of 1984, as amended.

Who may offer a service contract?

An individual ocean common carrier, conference or an agreement between or among ocean common carriers may enter into a service contract. 46 C.F.R. § 530.2. NVOCCs may offer NVOCC service arrangements ("NSAs") . See FAQs on NSAs.

For purposes of service contracts, what is a "shipper"?

For additional analytical, business and investment opportunities information, please contact Global Investment & Business Center, USA at (703) 370-8082. Fax: (703) 370-8083. E-mail: ibpusa3@gmail.com Global Business and Investment Info Databank - www.ibpus.com

A shipper means cargo owner, person for whose account the ocean transportation is provided, the person to whom delivery is to be made, a shippers' association, or NVOCCs that accept responsibility for payment of all applicable charges under the service contract. 46 C.F.R. § 530.3(r) .

Can a freight forwarder act as a shipper party to a service contract?

Generally, no. See discussion at FMC Order Denying Petition No. P5-98.

Can a freight forwarder sign a service contract as an agent for a shipper?

In general, one party may sign a service contract "as agent for" or "on behalf of" a second party so long as both parties are clearly identified. However, it should be clear that it is the second party which is the contract party and it is that party's cargo, not the agent's cargo, that is entitled to service contract rates.

Can an NVOCC act as a shipper party to a service contract?

Generally, yes. To sign service contracts as shipper, an NVOCC must be in compliance with Commission tariff, licensing and financial responsibility regulations, as shown on the shipper status certification. 46 C.F.R. § 530.8(b) (10) .

Must a shipper provide certification of its status under a service contract?

Yes. The shipper party must certify its shipper status (e.g., owner of the cargo, shippers' association, NVOCC) as well as the status of any affiliates with access to service under the service contract, and sign on the signature page of a service contract or amendment. 46 C.F.R. § 530.8(b) (10) .

Who is responsible for verifying that an NVOCC shipper signing a service contract has tariff and financial responsibility related to a service contract?

An NVOCC must provide proof that it has a published tariff and financial responsibility when signing a service contract. 46 C.F.R. § 530.6(c) ; 46 C.F.R. § 515.27. It is the responsibility of the ocean common carrier, conference, or ocean common carrier agreement to obtain the proof.

Such information can be obtained from the Commission's website at its NVOCC List and its NVOCC Tariff List.

What is a shipper affiliate?

Although "affiliate" is not defined by the Commission's rules governing service contracts, the Commission is guided by this commonly-accepted definition, such as that included in its licensing and NSA regulations: associated with, under common control with, or otherwise related through stock ownership or common directors or officers. 46 C.F.R. § 515.11(c) ; 46 C.F.R. 531.3(b) .

What is a correction?

A correction is any change to a service contract which has retroactive effect. 46 C.F.R. § 530.10(a) (2) .

How does a person correct an error in a filed service contract?

For clerical or administrative errors in a filed service contract, either of the service contract parties may file an original and duplicate request for a correction with the Commission's Office of the Secretary within (45) forty-five days of the contract's filing with the Commission, accompanied by remittance of a $315 service fee. 46 C.F.R. § 530.10(c) .

How do I file a correction to an electronic transmission error?

Commission rules permit VOCCs to correct an original filing that is defective due to an electronic transmission clerical error. The time to correct such SERVCON filing errors is limited to two business days after the initial, defective, electronic transmission. 46 C.F.R. § 530.10(d) .

How are service contract effective dates determined?

A service contract must be filed with the Commission on or before cargo may move under it. The specific beginning and ending dates must be specified in the service contract. The effective date starts at 12:01 a.m. eastern standard time on the beginning of the effective date, which cannot take place until the service contract is filed. This rule also applies to effective dates of amendments to service contracts. 46 C.F.R. § 530.3(i) .

What is a common carrier tariff?

A tariff is a publication containing the actual rates, charges, classifications, rules, regulations and practices of a common carrier or a conference of common carriers.

Who must publish a common carrier tariff?

Each vessel operating common carrier, non-vessel-operating common carrier, and conference, except with regard to bulk cargo, forest products, recycled metal scrap, new assembled motor vehicles, waste paper, and paper waste. 46 C.F.R. § 520.3(a) .

Must ocean common carriers publish a common tariff?

Yes. The Shipping Act of 1984, as amended requires a conference to keep open for public inspection, in an automated tariff system, a tariff showing all its rates, charges, classifications, rules and practices for the transportation routes served by the conference. This statutory requirement is carried forward in 46 C.F.R. § 520.3(a) of the tariff rules. In addition, 46 C.F.R. § 520.3(b) requires conferences to publish in their automated tariff systems rates offered pursuant to independent action by their members.

May other types of ocean common carrier agreements publish a common tariff?

No. The Shipping Act of 1984, as amended only recognizes tariffs of individual common carriers or conferences. Moreover, the definition of "tariff" in 46 C.F.R. § 520.2 states that it is "a publication containing the actual rates, charges, classifications, rules, regulations and practices of a common carrier or a conference of common carriers." The definition further notes that "practices" in tariffs, "in the case of conferences, must be restricted to activities authorized by the basic conference agreement."

For additional analytical, business and investment opportunities information, please contact Global Investment & Business Center, USA at (703) 370-8082. Fax: (703) 370-8083. E-mail: ibpusa3@gmail.com Global Business and Investment Info Databank - www.ibpus.com

Must marine terminal operators publish tariffs?

No. See MTO FAQs.

What must be included in a tariff?

Rates, charges, classifications, rules, and practices between all points or ports on a carrier's or conference's own route and on any through transportation route that has been established must be included in the published tariff. Content requirements for tariff provisions include: places between which cargo will be carried; level of ocean transportation intermediary compensation; each terminal or other charge; sample copies of bills of lading; any tariff rules; organization record; commodity descriptions; commodity index; and tariff rate items. 46 C.F.R. § 520.4.

What types of services are exempt from tariff publication requirements?

Tariff publication exemptions extend to equipment interchange agreements between common carriers subject to 46 C.F.R. Part 520 and inland carriers where such agreements are not referred to in carriers' tariffs and do not affect the tariff rates, charges or practices of the carriers as well as terminal barge operators in Pacific Slope states transporting containers and containerized cargo by barge between points in the U.S. in certain instances. 46 C.F.R. § 520.13(b) (1) , (2) , and (3) . Also tanker services and non-regularly scheduled liner services, such as with tramp vessel operations are exempt from tariff publication requirements.

Does the exemption from tariff publication for certain cargo types such as bulk cargo, forest products, etc., apply equally to both ocean common carriers (VOCC) and non-vessel-operating common carriers (NVOCC) ?

Yes.

When did the requirement that a tariff could be published rather than filed with the Commission take effect?

The requirement took effect on May 1, 1999, but it could be published earlier.

Does the minimum rate display requirement of 46 C.F.R. § 520.6(e) require a list of assessorial charges that actually apply to the shipment?

Yes. Any assessorial charge that will be added to the basic ocean freight rate must be listed individually. If there are other rules or charges that may otherwise affect the shipment under certain circumstances (e.g., minimum quantity rules, quantity discounts, or demurrage) the tariff should also indicate them.

Does the access date capability required by 46 C.F.R. § 520.10(b) only apply to historical data or does it also apply to future dates?

The requirement that tariffs provide the capability for a retriever to enter an access date to obtain data in effect on that date was primarily intended to apply to historical tariff data. Nonetheless, if carriers know what rates are going to be in effect on some future date, they are free to provide accurate information about such rates in their tariff publication. In these circumstances, access data capabilities should apply to "objects" that will become effective on a future date.

For additional analytical, business and investment opportunities information, please contact Global Investment & Business Center, USA at (703) 370-8082. Fax: (703) 370-8083. E-mail: ibpusa3@gmail.com Global Business and Investment Info Databank - www.ibpus.com

Can carriers use codes other than those in the Standard Terminology Appendix?

As stated in 46 C.F.R. § 520.5(a) , the Standard Terminology Appendix serves as a standard baseline for tariff publishers. However, the rule makes clear that publishers can use additional codes, if they clearly define them in their tariffs.

What is Form FMC-1?

Form FMC-1 is an internet-based electronic form to collect tariff location addresses and other specific organizational information of conferences, ocean common carriers, OTIs and MTOs. The information is entered directly into the FMC-1 Form on-line via the internet.

The Commission's Rules governing Form FMC-1 are located under 46 C.F.R. § 520.3(d) and (e) for common carriers/conferences and 46 C.F.R. § 525.3(f) for marine terminal operators. Electronic submission of the Form FMC-1 data is mandatory under Commission Rules. The system processes the information collected in the electronic form and posts the carriers, ocean transportation intermediaries, conferences, and marine terminal operators' tariff location addresses on the FMC-1 List at Links to Tariffs located on the Commission's homepage. The Commission uses the information collected to access the actual tariff publication and review for compliance with Commission rules and regulations. The public uses the FMC-1 List to locate carriers' tariff location addresses to access tariff publications, and to verify OTI/NVOCC status as set forth under 46 C.F.R. § 515.27(d) . Click Here To File a Form FMC-1. For assistance completing the form, please click the HELP button in the upper right-hand corner of the form or contact the Commission at (202) 523-5856.

Is Form FMC-1 required in order to offer service pursuant to a tariff(s) ?

Yes. Each common carrier (including NVOCCs) and conferences shall notify the Bureau of Trade Analysis , prior to the commencement of common carrier service pursuant to a published tariff, of its organization number, home office address, name and telephone number of the firm's representative, the location of its tariffs, and the publisher, if any, used to maintain its tariffs, by electronically submitting Form FMC-1 via the Commission's website at www.fmc.gov. 46 C.F.R. § 520.3(d) .

How are changes submitted to Form FMC-1?

Any changes to the FMC-1 information shall be immediately transmitted to the Bureau of Trade Analysis . 46 C.F.R. § 520.3(d) . The filer's changes can be entered electronically from the Tariff Registration Form (FMC-1) main menu, by selecting "Edit an Existing FMC-1 Form" via the Commission's website, www.fmc.gov.

How do I obtain an Organization Number?

The Commission's staff will provide a unique organization number to a new entity operating as a common carrier or conference in the foreign commerce. 46 C.F.R. § 520.3(d) . When an organization changes its name, a new organization number is assigned. The filer completes an "Initial" FMC-1 Form submission and may leave the organization number field blank. A number will be assigned by FMC staff.

How do I access a carrier or conference automated tariff system?

For additional analytical, business and investment opportunities information, please contact Global Investment & Business Center, USA at (703) 370-8082. Fax: (703) 370-8083. E-mail: ibpusa3@gmail.com Global Business and Investment Info Databank - www.ibpus.com

Go to the Commission's website, www.fmc.gov, Click on Links to Tariffs, Click on tab for FMC 1 VOCC, or FMC-1 OTI/NVOCC for "accepted filings," scroll down the list alphabetically to the desired carrier, obtain from the Location of Tariff(s) column the carrier's tariff location address, then logon to the internet using the tariff location address to find the carrier's tariff publication in the carrier's automated tariff system ("CATS") . Some CATS may require that you register to obtain a logon and password to access the system. In addition, a reasonable charge may be assessed to access a CATS system.

When do I file a special permission application?

Where there may be good cause shown to permit a common carrier to deviate from the provisions of rules governing tariffs under part 520, e.g., for issuance of effective dates on less than the statutory notice under the Commission's rules; or typographical or clerical errors in tariff publication that cause defective tariff material. 46 C.F.R. § 520.14(a) and (b) .

How do I correct a clerical error in a tariff?

An application for special permission ("SP") may be submitted, in letter form in duplicate, to the Bureau of Trade Analysis , accompanied with a filing fee of $195. The application must contain: organization name, number and trade name of the conference or carrier; tariff number and title; and the rate, commodity, or rules related to the application, and the special circumstances which the applicant believes constitutes good cause to depart from the requirements of the Commission's rules under 46 C.F.R. Part 520, Carrier Automated Tariffs. Should the authority sought under the SP application be granted and assigned a Special Case number, implementation of the authority granted by the Commission must be used in its entirety, including the prompt publishing of the material for which permission was requested. The Applicants shall use the special case number assigned by the Commission. 46 C.F.R. § 520.14(c) and (d) .

What is a special docket application for permission to refund or waive freight charges?

A common carrier or a shipper may file a special docket application seeking permission for a common carrier or conference to refund or waive collection of a portion of freight charges if there is: an error in the tariff; an error in failing to publish a new tariff; or, an error in quoting a new tariff. Such application must be submitted to the Office of the Secretary, Federal Maritime Commission. See the Commission's Rules of Practice and Procedure at 46 C.F.R. § 502.271 for further information.

If a tariff is canceled, who should provide written notice of cancellation to the Commission?

Carriers and conferences shall inform BTA, in writing, whenever a tariff is canceled and the effective date of that cancellation. 46 C.F.R. § 520.7(b) . A carrier or conference may designate its agent to submit, on its behalf, the written cancellation notice to the Commission.

Once a tariff has been canceled, superceded, or withdrawn, how long must its data be maintained in a carrier's publication system?

Carriers and conferences shall maintain the data that appeared in its their tariff publication system for a period of five (5) years from the date such information is superseded, canceled or withdrawn, and shall provide on-line access to such data for two (2) years. After two (2) years, such data may be retained on-line or in other electronic form, and shall be made available to any person or the Commission upon request in a reasonable period of time. Carriers and conferences may charge a reasonable fee for the provision of historical data, not to exceed the fees for obtaining such data on-line. No fee shall apply to federal agencies. 46 C.F.R. § 520.10(a) .

What if a carrier or conference designates an agent to publish, on its behalf, its tariff in CATS?

It is a carrier's or conference's responsibility to publish tariffs in CATS, although they may designate an agent to do so on their behalf. 46 C.F.R. § 520.3(a) and (c) . The Commission periodically reviews CATS and may prohibit the use of any system that fails to meet the requirements of rules governing tariffs under 46 C.F.R. Part 520. 46 C.F.R. § 520.10(c) .

What if a carrier or conference fails to pay a designated agent for publishing and maintaining historical tariff data in CATS?

The matter of payment for services between a carrier or conference and its agent involving CATS is a matter between the parties.

When must my tariff be published?

The tariff must be published on or before transportation services commence thereunder, or on the tariff's effective date. 46 C.F.R. Part 515.

Can a non-binding discussion agreement publish a common tariff?

No. The Shipping Act of 1984, as amended only recognizes tariffs of individual common carriers or conferences. Moreover, the definition of "tariff" in 46 C.F.R. § 520.2 states that it is "a publication containing the actual rates, charges, classifications, rules, regulations and practices of a common carrier or a conference of common carriers." The definition further notes that "practices" in tariffs, "in the case of conferences, must be restricted to activities authorized by the basic conference agreement."

When did the two-year on-line data retention requirement of 46 C.F.R. § 520.10(a) begin?

On May 1, 1999. Prior to this date tariffs were filed with the Commission and historical tariff data was maintained by the Commission.

Will the blanket special permission for new tariffs with no increases permitting them to go into effect without the 30 days' advance notice requirement also apply to controlled carriers?

Yes, to the extent the rates of the controlled carrier are not decreased also. Any action of a controlled carrier in publishing a new tariff that would deviate from other requirements applicable to controlled carriers would require separate special permission.

If a publisher reissued the same tariff that was in AFTI, would it carry forward the same effective dates for the ATFI tariff matter rather than change all effective dates of the tariff items to May 1, 1999?

Tariffs were allowed to carry-over ATFI tariff items showing the ATFI effective dates in CATS tariffs. On May 1, 1999, all other CATS tariff items intended to be effective on May 1, 1999, were required to show a May 1, 1999 effective date.

For additional analytical, business and investment opportunities information, please contact Global Investment & Business Center, USA at (703) 370-8082. Fax: (703) 370-8083. E-mail: ibpusa3@gmail.com Global Business and Investment Info Databank - www.ibpus.com

How will a new carrier instituting a new service be treated after May 1, 1999? Will they be required to provide 30-days' notice for their new tariffs?

There is no 30-day notice requirement that applies to new service tariffs. Consequently, there is no need for special permission to advance the effective date of such new tariffs. They may go into effect immediately.

For additional analytical, business and investment opportunities information, please contact Global Investment & Business Center, USA at (703) 370-8082. Fax: (703) 370-8083. E-mail: ibpusa3@gmail.com Global Business and Investment Info Databank - www.ibpus.com

BASIC COMMISSION RULES

46 CFR 500 CHAPTER IV FEDERAL MARITIME COMMISSION

SUBCHAPTER A - GENERAL AND ADMINISTRATIVE PROVISIONS

501 The Federal Maritime Commission - General

502 Rules of practice and procedure

503 Public information

504 Procedures for environmental policy analysis

505 Administrative offset

506 Civil monetary penalty inflation adjustment

507 Enforcement of nondiscrimination on the basis of handicap

in programs or activities conducted by the Federal Maritime

Commission

508 Employee ethical conduct standards and financial disclosure regulations

SUBCHAPTER B - REGULATIONS AFFECTING OCEAN SHIPPING IN FOREIGN COMMERCE

515 Licensing and surety requirements for ocean transportation intermediaries 520 Carrier automated tariffs 525 Marine terminal operator schedules

530 Service contracts 535 Agreements by ocean common carriers and other persons subject to the Shipping Act of 1984

540 Passenger vessel financial responsibility 545 Interpretations and statements of policy

SUBCHAPTER C - REGULATIONS AND ACTIONS TO ADDRESS RESTRICTIVE FOREIGN MARITIME PRACTICES

550 Regulations to adjust or meet conditions unfavorable to shipping in the foreign trade of the United States

551 Actions to adjust or meet conditions unfavorable to shipping in the U.S. foreign trade

555 Actions to address adverse conditions affecting U.S.-flag carriers that do not exist for foreign carriers in the United States

560 Actions to address conditions unduly impairing access of U.S.-flag vessels to ocean trade between foreign ports

565 Controlled carriers

SELECTED RULES AND REGUALTIONS[1]

NEW COMISSION RULES

Service Contracts Subject to the Shipping Act of 1984 (Interim Final Rule) - Docket #98-30
Service Contracts Subject to the Shipping Act of 1984 (Confirmation of interim final rule with changes - Docket #98-30
Carrier Automated Tariff Systems - Docket #98-29
Carrier Automated Tariff Systems (Adoption of Final Rule) - Docket #98-29
Licensing, Financial Responsibility Requirements, and General Duties for Ocean Transportation Intermediaries (Final Rule and Interim Final Rule) - Docket #98-28
Licensing, Financial Responsibility Requirements, and General Duties for Ocean Transportation Intermediaries (Confirmation of Final Rule and Correction) - Docket #98-28
Marine Terminal Operator Schedule - Docket #98-27
Ocean Common Carriers and Marine Terminal Operator Agreement Subject to the Shipping Act of 1984 - Docket #98-26
Amendments to Regulations Governing Restrictive Foreign Shipping Practices, and New Regulations Governing Controlled Carriers - Docket #98-25
Miscellaneous Amendments to Rules of Practice and Procedure - Docket #98-21

PART 501 -- THE FEDERAL MARITIME COMMISSION - GENERAL

SUBPART A -- ORGANIZATION AND FUNCTIONS

Sec.

501.1 Purpose.

501.2 General.

For additional analytical, business and investment opportunities information, please contact Global Investment & Business Center, USA at (703) 370-8082. Fax: (703) 370-8083. E-mail: ibpusa3@gmail.com
Global Business and Investment Info Databank - www.ibpus.com

501.3 Organizational components of the Federal Maritime Commission.

[1] For a complete set of rules and regulations please contact Global Investment and Business Center, USA at 202-546-3275 (Fax) or E-mail: rusric@erols.com

501.4 Lines of responsibility.

501.5 Functions of the organizational components of the Federal Maritime Commission.

SUBPART B -- OFFICIAL SEAL

501.11 Official seal.

SUBPART C -- DELEGATION AND REDELEGATION OF AUTHORITIES

501.21 Delegation of authorities.

501.22 [Reserved]

501.23 Delegation to the General Counsel.

501.24 Delegation to the Secretary.

501.25 Delegation to the Managing Director.

501.26 Delegation to the Director, Bureau of Economics and Agreement Analysis.

501.27 Delegation to and redelegation by the Director, Bureau of Tariffs, Certification and Licensing.

501.28 Delegation to the Director, Bureau of Enforcement.

501.29 [Reserved]

501.30 Delegation to and redelegation by the Director, Bureau of Administration.

SUBPART D -- PUBLIC REQUESTS FOR INFORMATION

501.41 Public requests for information and decisions.

SUBPART A -- ORGANIZATION AND FUNCTIONS

§ 501.1 Purpose. This part describes the organization, functions and Official Seal of, and the delegation of authority within, the Federal Maritime Commission (``Commission'') .

§ 501.2 General.

(a) *Statutory functions*. The Commission regulates common carriers by water and other persons involved in the foreign and domestic offshore commerce of the U.S. under provisions of the

For additional analytical, business and investment opportunities information, please contact Global Investment & Business Center, USA at (703) 370-8082. Fax: (703) 370-8083. E-mail: ibpusa3@gmail.com Global Business and Investment Info Databank - www.ibpus.com

Shipping Act, 1916, [46 U.S.C. app. 801-842]; the Intercoastal Shipping Act, 1933 [46 U.S.C. app. 843-848]; the Shipping Act of 1984 [46 U.S.C. app. 1701-1720]; section 19 of the Merchant Marine Act, 1920 [46 U.S.C. app. 876]; the Foreign Shipping Practices Act of 1988 [46 U.S.C.

app. 1710a]; sections 2 and 3, Pub. L. 89-777, Financial Responsibility for Death or Injury to Passengers and for Non-Performance of Voyages [46 U.S.C. app. 817d and 817e]; and other applicable statutes.

(b) *Establishment and composition of the Commission*. The Commission was established as an independent agency by Reorganization Plan No. 7 of 1961, effective August 12, 1961, and is composed of five Commissioners (``Commissioners'' or ``members'') , appointed by the President, by and with the advice and consent of the Senate. Not more than three Commissioners may be appointed from the same political party. The President designates one of the Commissioners to be the Chairman of the Commission (``Chairman'') .

(c) *Terms and vacancies*. The term of each member of the Commission is 5 years and begins when the term of the predecessor of that member ends (i.e., on June 30 of each successive year) , except that, when the term of office of a member ends, the member may continue to serve until a successor is appointed and qualified. A vacancy in the office of any Commissioner shall be filled in the same manner as the original appointment, except that any person chosen to fill a vacancy shall be appointed only for the unexpired term of the Commissioner whom he or she succeeds. Each Commissioner shall be removable by the President for inefficiency, neglect of duty, or malfeasance in office.

(d) A vacancy or vacancies in the Commission shall not impair the power of the Commission to execute its functions. The affirmative vote of a majority of the members of the Commission is required to dispose of any matter before the Commission. For purposes of holding a formal meeting for the transaction of the business of the Commission, the actual presence of two Commissioners shall be sufficient. Proxy votes of absent members shall be permitted.

(e) *Meetings; records; rules and regulations*. The Commission shall, through its Secretary, keep a true record of all its meetings and the yea-and-nay votes taken therein on every action and order approved or disapproved by the Commission. In addition to or in aid of its functions, the Commission adopts rules and regulations in regard to its powers, duties and functions under the shipping statutes it administers.

[64 FR 23545, May 3, 1999]

§ 501.3 ORGANIZATIONAL COMPONENTS OF THE FEDERAL MARITIME COMMISSION.

The major organizational components of the Commission are set forth in the Organization Chart attached as Appendix A to this part. An outline table of the components/functions follows:

(a) Office of the Chairman of the Federal Maritime Commission.

(Chief Executive and Administrative Officer, and *FOIA and Privacy Act Appeals Officer.*)

(1) Information Security Officer.

(2) Designated Agency Ethics Official.

For additional analytical, business and investment opportunities information, please contact Global Investment & Business Center, USA at (703) 370-8082. Fax: (703) 370-8083. E-mail: ibpusa3@gmail.com Global Business and Investment Info Databank - www.ibpus.com

(b) Offices of the Members of the Federal Maritime Commission.

(include the *Chairman, ADP Committee.*)

(c) Office of the Secretary.

(*FOIA and Privacy Act Officer, Federal Register Liaison; Alternative Disputes Resolution Coordinator.*)

(1) Office of Informal Inquiries, Complaints and Informal Dockets.

(d) Office of the General Counsel. (*Ethics Official.*)

(e) Office of Administrative Law Judges.

(f) Office of Equal Employment Opportunity.

(g) Office of the Inspector General.

(h) Office of the Managing Director.

(*Chief Operating Officer; Designated Senior IRM Official; Senior Procurement Executive* and *ATFI Contracting Officer, Audit Followup* and *Management Controls.*)

(1) Office of Information Resources Management. *(Senior IRM Manager; Computer Security; Forms Control; Records Management.)*

(2) [Reserved].

(i) Bureau of Economics and Agreement Analysis.

(1) Office of Agreements and Information Management.

(2) Office of Monitoring I.

(3) Office of Monitoring II.

(j) Bureau of Tariffs, Certification and Licensing.

(1) Office of Tariffs.

(2) Tariff Control Center.

(3) Office of Service Contracts and Passenger Vessel Operations.

(4) Office of Freight Forwarders.

(k) [Reserved].

For additional analytical, business and investment opportunities information, please contact Global Investment & Business Center, USA at (703) 370-8082. Fax: (703) 370-8083. E-mail: ibpusa3@gmail.com Global Business and Investment Info Databank - www.ibpus.com

(l) Bureau of Enforcement.

(m) Bureau of Administration. (*Competition Advocate*; *Information Security*; *Principal Management Official* on *Small Agency Council*.)

(1) Office of Administrative Services. (*Physical Security; FMC Contracting Officer*.)

(2) Office of Budget and Financial Management. (*Chief Financial Officer*.)

(3) Office of Personnel.

(n) Boards and Committees.

(1) Executive Resources Board.

(2) Committee on Automated Data Processing.

(3) Performance Review Board.

(4) Incentive Awards Committee.

[59 FR 62329, Dec. 5, 1994; 59 FR 67227, Dec. 29, 1994; 60 FR 57940, Nov. 24, 1995; 61 FR 51230, Oct. 1, 1996]

§ 501.4 LINES OF RESPONSIBILITY.

(a) *Chairman*. The Office of the Secretary, the Office of the General Counsel, the Office of Administrative Law Judges, the Office of Equal Employment Opportunity, the Office of the Inspector General, the Office of the Managing Director, and officials performing the functions of Information Security Officer and Designated Agency Ethics Official, report to the Chairman of the Commission.

(b) *Office of the Managing Director*. The Bureau of Economics and Agreement Analysis; Bureau of Tariffs, Certification and Licensing; Bureau of Enforcement; and Bureau of Administration report to the Office of the Managing Director. The Offices of Equal Employment Opportunity and of the Inspector General receive administrative assistance from the Managing Director. All other units of the Commission receive administrative guidance from the Managing Director.

(c) *Bureau of Enforcement and Area Representatives*. The Area Representatives report to the Director, Bureau of Enforcement.

[59 FR 67227, Dec. 29, 1994; 60 FR 57940, Nov. 24, 1995; 61 FR 51230, Oct. 1, 1996]

§ 501.5 FUNCTIONS OF THE ORGANIZATIONAL COMPONENTS OF THE FEDERAL MARITIME COMMISSION.

As further provided in subpart C of this part, the functions, including the delegated authority of the Commission's organizational components and/or officials to exercise their functions and to take all actions necessary to direct and carry out their assigned duties and responsibilities under the lines of responsibility set forth in § 501.4, are briefly set forth as follows:

For additional analytical, business and investment opportunities information, please contact Global Investment & Business Center, USA at (703) 370-8082. Fax: (703) 370-8083. E-mail: ibpusa3@gmail.com Global Business and Investment Info Databank - www.ibpus.com

(a) *Chairman*. As the chief executive and administrative officer of the Commission, the Chairman presides at meetings of the Commission, administers the policies of the Commission to its responsible officials, and assures the efficient discharge of their responsibilities. The Chairman provides management direction to the Offices of Equal Employment Opportunity, Inspector General, Secretary, General Counsel, Administrative Law Judges, and Managing Director with respect to all matters concerning overall Commission workflow, resource allocation (both staff and budgetary) , work priorities and similar managerial matters; and establishes, as necessary, various committees and boards to address overall operations of the agency. The Chairman serves as appeals officer under both the Freedom of Information Act and the Privacy Act. The Chairman appoints the heads of major administrative units after consultation with other Commissioners. In addition, the Chairman, as ``head of the agency,'' has certain responsibilities under Federal Laws and directives not specifically related to shipping. For example, the special offices or officers within the Commission, listed under paragraphs (a) (1) through (a) (4) of this section, are appointed or designated by the Chairman, are under his or her direct supervision and report directly to the Chairman:

(1) Under the direction and management of the Office Director, the *Office of Equal Employment Opportunity* (``EEO'') ensures that statutory and regulatory prohibitions against discrimination in employment and the requirements for related programs are fully implemented. As such, the Office administers and implements comprehensive programs on discrimination complaints processing, affirmative action and special emphasis. The Director, EEO, advises the Chairman regarding EEO's plans, procedures, regulations, reports and other matters pertaining to policy and the agency programs. Additionally, the Director provides leadership and advice to managers and supervisors in carrying out their respective responsibilities in equal employment opportunity. The Office administers and implements these program responsibilities in accordance with Equal Employment Commission (``EEOC'') Regulations at 29 CFR Part 1614 and other relevant EEOC Directives and Bulletins.

(2) Under the direction and management of the Inspector General, the *Office of Inspector General* conducts, supervises and coordinates audits and investigations relating to the programs and operations of the Commission; reviews existing and proposed legislation and regulations pertaining to such programs and operations; provides leadership and coordination and recommends policies for activities designed to promote economy, efficiency, and effectiveness in the administration of, and to prevent and detect waste, fraud and abuse in, such programs and operations; and advises the Chairman and the Congress fully and currently about problems and deficiencies relating to the administration of such programs and operations and the necessity for and progress of corrective action.

(3) The *Information Security Officer* is a senior agency official designated under § 503.52 of this chapter to direct and administer the Commission's information security program, which includes an active oversight and security education program to ensure effective implementation of Executive Order 12356.

(4) The *Designated Agency Ethics Official and Alternate* are appropriate agency employees formally designated under 5 CFR 2638.202 and § 500.105 of this chapter to coordinate and manage the ethics program as set forth in 5 CFR 2638.203, which includes the functions of advising on matters of employee responsibilities and conduct under Part 500 of this chapter, and serving as the Commission's designee(s) to the Office of Personnel Management on such matters. They provide counseling and guidance to employees on conflicts of interest and other ethical matters.

For additional analytical, business and investment opportunities information, please contact Global Investment & Business Center, USA at (703) 370-8082. Fax: (703) 370-8083. E-mail: ibpusa3@gmail.com Global Business and Investment Info Databank - www.ibpus.com

(b) *Commissioners*. The members of the Commission, including the Chairman, implement various shipping statutes and related directives by rendering decisions, issuing orders, and adopting and

enforcing rules and regulations governing persons subject to the shipping statutes; and perform other duties and functions as may be appropriate under reorganization plans, statutes, executive orders, and regulations.

(c) *Secretary*. Under the direction and management of the Secretary, the Office of the Secretary:

(1) Is responsible for the preparation, maintenance and disposition of the official files and records documenting the business of the Commission. In this regard, the Office:

(i) Prepares and, as appropriate, publishes agenda of matters for action by the Commission, prepares and maintains the minutes with respect to such actions; signs, serves and issues, on behalf of the Commission, documents implementing such actions, and coordinates follow-up thereon.

(ii) Receives and processes formal and informal complaints involving alleged statutory violations, petitions for relief, special dockets applications (including the issuance of decisions therein) , applications to correct clerical or administrative errors in service contracts, requests for conciliation service, staff recommendations for investigation and rulemaking proceedings, and motions and filings relating thereto.

(iii) Disseminates information regarding the proceedings, activities, functions, and responsibilities of the Commission to the maritime industry, news media, general public, and other government agencies. In this capacity the Office also:

(A) Administers the Commission's Freedom of Information Act, Privacy Act and Government in the Sunshine Act responsibilities; the Secretary serves as the Freedom of Information Act and Privacy Act Officer.

(B) Authenticates records of the Commission.

(C) Receives and responds to subpoenas directed to Commission personnel and/or records.

(D) Compiles and publishes the bound volumes of Commission decisions.

(E) Coordinates publication of documents, including rules and modifications thereto with the Office of the Federal Register; the Secretary serves as the Federal Register Liaison Officer and Certifying Officer.

(2) Through the Secretary and, in the absence or preoccupation of the Secretary, through the Assistant Secretary, administers oaths pursuant to 5 U.S.C. 2903(b) .

(3) Coordinates Alternative Dispute Resolution activities within the Commission.

(4) Through the Office of Informal Inquiries, Complaints and Informal Dockets:

(i) Advises the Commission on significant public interest issues in current and proposed policies, programs, and decisions;

For additional analytical, business and investment opportunities information, please contact Global Investment & Business Center, USA at (703) 370-8082. Fax: (703) 370-8083. E-mail: ibpusa3@gmail.com Global Business and Investment Info Databank - www.ibpus.com

(ii) Receives, coordinates, and responds to informal inquiries, complaints, suggestions, and expressions of concern from the public and contacts carriers, conferences, and other persons to effect solutions;

(iii) Publicizes Commission policies, programs, and activities of interest to the Commission's shipping public; and

(iv) Adjudicates small claims ($10,000 or less) arising from alleged violations of the shipping statutes.

(d) *General Counsel.* Under the direction and management of the General Counsel, the Office of the General Counsel:

(1) Reviews for legal sufficiency all staff memoranda and recommendations that are presented for Commission action and staff actions acted upon pursuant to delegated authority under §§ 501.26(i) and 501.26(k) .

(2) Provides written or oral legal opinions to the Commission, to the staff, and to the general public in appropriate cases.

(3) Prepares and/or reviews for legal sufficiency, before service, all final Commission decisions, orders, and regulations.

(4) Monitors, reviews and, as requested by the Committees of the Congress, the Office of Management and Budget, or the Chairman, prepares comments on all legislation introduced in the Congress affecting the Commission's programs or activities, and prepares draft legislation or amendments to legislation; coordinates such matters with the appropriate Bureau, Office or official and advises appropriate Commission officials of legislation which may impact the programs and activities of the Commission. Also prepares testimony for Congressional hearings and responses to requests from Congressional offices.

(5) Serves as the legal representative of the Commission in courts and in administrative proceedings before other Government agencies.

(6) Monitors and reports on international maritime developments, including laws and practices of foreign governments which affect ocean shipping; and identifies potential state-controlled carriers within the meaning of section 3(8) of the Shipping Act of 1984, researches their status, and makes recommendations to the Commission concerning their classification.

(7) Represents the Commission in U.S. Government interagency groups dealing with international maritime issues; serves as a technical advisor on regulatory matters in bilateral and multilateral maritime discussions; and coordinates Commission activities through liaison with other Government agencies and programs and international organizations.

(8) Screens, routes, and maintains custody of U.S. Government and international organization documents, subject to the classification and safekeeping controls administered by the Commission's Information Security Officer.

(9) Reviews for legal sufficiency all adverse personnel actions, procurement activities, Freedom of Information Act and Privacy Act matters and other administrative actions.

For additional analytical, business and investment opportunities information, please contact Global Investment & Business Center, USA at (703) 370-8082. Fax: (703) 370-8083. E-mail: ibpusa3@gmail.com Global Business and Investment Info Databank - www.ibpus.com

(10) Manages the Commission's library and related services.

(e) *Administrative Law Judges.* Under the direction and management of the Chief Administrative Law Judge, the Office of Administrative Law Judges holds hearings and renders initial or

recommended decisions in formal rulemaking and adjudicatory proceedings as provided in the Shipping Act of 1984, and other applicable laws and other matters assigned by the Commission, in accordance with the Administrative Procedure Act and the Commission's Rules of Practice and Procedure.

(f) The *Office of the Managing Director.*

(1) The Managing Director:

(i) As senior staff official, is responsible to the Chairman for the management and coordination of Commission programs managed by the operating Bureaus of Enforcement; Administration; Economics and Agreement Analysis; and Tariffs, Certification and Licensing, as more fully described in paragraphs (g) through (k) of this section, and thereby implements the regulatory policies of the Commission and the administrative policies and directives of the Chairman;

(ii) Provides administrative guidance to all units of the Commission other than the operating bureaus listed in paragraph (f) (1) of this section, except the Offices of Equal Employment Opportunity and the Inspector General, which are provided administrative assistance;

(iii) Is the agency's Senior Procurement Executive under 41 U.S.C. 414(3) and Commission Order No. 112;

(iv) As the Designated Senior Information Resources Management Official under 44 U.S.C. 501520 and 3501-3520 and Commission Order No. 117, reviews recommendations of the Commission's Committee on Automated Data Processing and submits them to the Chairman under Commission Orders Nos. 98 and 117;

(v) Is the Audit Follow-up and Management (Internal) Controls Official for the Commission under Commission Orders Nos. 103 and 106; and

(vi) Is the agency's Chief Operating Officer, as appointed by the Chairman in response to the President's October 1, 1993, memorandum on management reform.

(2) The Office of Managing Director ensures the periodic review and updating of Commission orders.

(3) A Deputy Managing Director, reporting directly to the Managing Director, supervises the development of, and serves as Contracting Officer for, the Commission's Automated Tariff Filing and Information (``ATFI'') System.

(4) Is responsible for the administration and coordination of the Office of Information Resources Management. The *Office of Information Resources Management*, under the direction and management of the Office Director, provides administrative support with respect to information resources management to the program operations of the Commission. The Office interprets governmental policies and programs for information management and administers these in a manner consistent with Federal guidelines. The Office initiates recommendations, collaborating

with other elements of the Commission as warranted, for long-range plans, new or revised policies and standards, and rules and regulations, with respect to its program activities. The Office's major functions include: administration of the information resources management program under the Paperwork Reduction Act; management studies and surveys; data telecommunications/database management and application development; records management; IRM contract administration; development of Paperwork Reduction Act clearances for submission

to the Office of Management and Budget; computer security; and forms management. The Director of the Office serves as Senior IRM Manager, Forms Control Officer, Computer Security Officer, Records Management Officer, and ADP Coordinator for the Committee on Automated Data Processing.

(g) Under the direction and management of the Bureau Director, the *Bureau of Economics and Agreement Analysis* develops and administers programs in connection with the anticompetitive and cooperative arrangements and practices of common carriers by water, freight forwarders and terminal operators in the foreign commerce of the U.S., including the filing of ocean common carrier agreements under section 5 of the Shipping Act of 1984, and the filing of agreements by marine terminal operators under section 5 of the Shipping Act of 1984. The Bureau provides expert economic testimony and support in formal proceedings, particularly regarding unfair foreign shipping practices under section 19 of the Merchant Marine Act, 1920, and the Foreign Shipping Practices Act of 1988.

(h) Under the direction and management of the Bureau Director, the *Bureau of Tariffs, Certification and Licensing* plans, develops and administers programs in connection with tariffs filed by common carriers and marine terminal operators; ocean common carrier service contracts; financial responsibility of non-vessel operating common carriers; licensing ocean freight forwarders; and certifying the financial responsibility of passenger vessel owners and operators. These programs carry out provisions of the Shipping Act of 1984; and Pub. L. 89-777, as implemented under Parts 510, 514, 540, 582 and 583 of this chapter. The Bureau maintains tariff data filed in electronic form on the Commission's Automated Tariff Filing and Information System (``ATFI'') . The Bureau develops long-range plans, new or revised policies and standards, and rules and regulations with respect to these programs. It also cooperates with other Commission components with regard to the enforcement of the Commission's regulatory requirements, and provides expert testimony and support in formal proceedings. The Bureau's program activities are carried out by the Office of Tariffs, the Office of Service Contracts and Passenger Vessel Operations and the Office of Freight Forwarders.

(i) *Bureau of Enforcement; Area Representatives.* Under the direction and management of the Bureau Director, the Bureau of Enforcement.

(1) Participates as trial counsel in formal Commission proceedings when designated by Commission order, or when intervention is granted;

(2) Initiates, processes and negotiates the informal compromise of civil penalties under § 501.28 of this part and § 502.604 of this chapter, and represents the Commission in proceedings and circumstances as designated;

(3) Acts as staff counsel to the Managing Director and other bureaus and offices;

(4) Coordinates with other bureaus and offices to provide legal advice, attorney liaison, and prosecution, as warranted, in connection with enforcement matters; and

For additional analytical, business and investment opportunities information, please contact Global Investment & Business Center, USA at (703) 370-8082. Fax: (703) 370-8083. E-mail: ibpusa3@gmail.com Global Business and Investment Info Databank - www.ibpus.com

(5) Conducts investigations leading to enforcement action, advises the Federal Maritime Commission of evolving competitive practices in international and domestic offshore commerce, assesses the practical repercussions of Commission regulations, educates the industry regarding policy and statutory requirements, assists in the resolution of disputes within the industry, and provides liaison, cooperation, and other coordination between the Commission and the maritime industry, shippers, and other government agencies.

(6) Maintains a presence in locations other than Washington, D.C. through Area Representatives whose activities include the following:

(i) Representing the Commission within their respective geographic areas;

(ii) Providing liaison between the Commission and the shipping industry and interested public; conveying pertinent information regarding regulatory activities and problems; and recommending courses of action and solutions to problems as they relate to the shipping public, the affected industry, and the Commission;

(iii) Furnishing to interested persons information, advice, and access to Commission public documents;

(iv) Receiving and resolving informal complaints, in coordination with the Director, Office of Informal Inquiries, Complaints and Informal Dockets;

(v) Investigating potential violations of the shipping statutes and the Commission's regulations;

(vi) Conducting shipping industry surveillance programs to ensure compliance with the shipping statutes and Commission regulations. Such programs include common carrier audits, service contract audits and compliance checks of ocean freight forwarders;

(vii) Upon request of the Bureau of Tariffs, Certification and Licensing, auditing passenger vessel operators to determine the adequacy of performance bonds and the availability of funds to pay liability claims for death or injury, and assisting in the background surveys of ocean freight forwarder applicants;

(viii) Conducting special surveys and studies, and recommending policies to strengthen enforcement of the shipping laws;

(ix) Maintaining liaison with Federal and State agencies with respect to areas of mutual concern; and

(x) Providing assistance to the various bureaus and offices of the Commission as appropriate and when requested.

(j) [Reserved].

(k) Under the direction and management of the Bureau Director, the *Bureau of Administration* is responsible for the administration and coordination of the Offices of: Administrative Services; Budget and Financial Management; and Personnel. The Bureau provides administrative support to the program operations of the Commission. The Bureau interprets governmental policies and programs and administers these in a manner consistent with Federal guidelines, including those involving procurement, financial management and personnel. The Bureau initiates recommendations, collaborating with other elements of the Commission as warranted, for long-range plans, new or revised policies and standards, and rules and regulations, with respect to its program activities. The Office of the Bureau Director is responsible for directing and administering the Commission's training and development function. The Bureau Director is the Commission's Competition Advocate under 41 U.S.C. 418(a) and Commission Order No. 112, as well as the Commission's representative, as Principal Management Official, to the Small Agency Council. Other Bureau programs are carried out by its Offices, as follows:

(1) The *Office of Administrative Services*, under the direction and management of the Office Director, directs and administers a variety of management support service functions of the Commission. The Director of the Office is the Commission's principal Contracting Officer under Commission Order No. 112. Programs include communications; audio and voice telecommunications; procurement of and contracting for administrative goods and services, including the utilization of small and disadvantaged businesses; management of property, space, printing and copying; mail and records services; forms and graphic designs; facilities and equipment maintenance; and transportation.

(2) The *Office of Budget and Financial Management*, under the direction and management of the Office Director, administers the Commission's financial management program, including fiscal accounting activities, fee and forfeiture collections, and payments, and ensures that Commission obligations and expenditures of appropriated funds are proper; develops annual budget justifications for submission to the Congress and the Office of Management and Budget; develops and administers internal controls systems that provide accountability for agency funds; administers the Commission's travel and cash management programs, as well as the Commission's Imprest Funds; ensures accountability for official passports; and assists in the development of proper levels of user fees. The Director of the Office is the Commission's Chief Financial Officer.

(3) The *Office of Personnel*, under the direction and management of the Office Director, plans and administers a complete personnel management program including: recruitment and placement; position classification and pay administration; occupational safety and health; employee counseling services; employee relations; workforce discipline; performance appraisal; incentive awards; retirement; and personnel security. The Director of the Office is the Chairman of the Incentive Awards Committee.

(l) *Boards and Committees.*

The following boards and committees are established by separate Commission orders (``C.O.'') to address matters relating to the overall operations of the Commission:

(1) The *Executive Resources Board* is comprised of three voting members, chosen from the ranks of those above the grade 15 level, with the majority being career members of the Senior Executive Service. The members serve staggered terms of three years, beginning October 1 of each year; the member serving in the last year of his/her term serves as Chairman. The board meets on an ad hoc basis to discuss, develop and submit recommendations to the Chairman on matters related to the merit staffing process for career appointments in the Senior Executive Service, including the executive qualifications of candidates for career appointment. The board also plans and manages the Commission's executive development programs. Serving the board in a non-voting advisory capacity are the Director, Office of Equal Employment Opportunity, the Training Officer, and the Director, Office of Personnel, who also serves as the board's secretary.

C.O. No. 95.

For additional analytical, business and investment opportunities information, please contact Global Investment & Business Center, USA at (703) 370-8082. Fax: (703) 370-8083. E-mail: ibpusa3@gmail.com Global Business and Investment Info Databank - www.ibpus.com

(2) The *Committee on Automated Data Processing* is chaired by a Commissioner designated by the Chairman, and is comprised of the Directors of the Bureaus of Economics and Agreement Analysis; Tariffs, Certification and Licensing; Administration; and Enforcement; the General Counsel; the Secretary; the Inspector General; the Director, Office of Equal Employment Opportunity; the Chief Administrative Law Judge; a representative of the Chairman's office; the Deputy Managing Director in charge of the Commission's Automated Tariff Filing and Information System; and the Director, Office of Information Resources Management, who serves as Committee Coordinator for the Committee Chairperson. The Committee meets on an ad hoc basis to review, evaluate and recommend to the Chairman, through the Managing Director, policies and actions on the acquisition, management and use of ADP equipment and services.

C.O. No. 98.

(3) The *Performance Review Board* is chaired by a Commissioner designated by the Chairman, and is composed of a standing register of members which is published in the *Federal Register*. Once a year, the PRB Chairman appoints performance review panels from the membership to review individual performance appraisals and other relevant information pertaining to Senior Executives at the Commission, and to recommend final performance ratings to the Chairman.

C.O. No. 115.

(4) The *Incentive Awards Committee* is composed of two permanent voting members: the Director of Personnel, who serves as Chairman; and the Director of Equal Employment Opportunity; and two other voting members approved by the Chairman upon the recommendation of the Managing Director. The committee meets on an ad hoc basis to determine if incentive award nominations meet established criteria, and to review suggestions. C.O. No. 62.

[59 FR 54396, Oct. 31, 1994; 59 FR 62329, Dec. 5, 1994; 59 FR 67227, Dec. 29, 1994; 60 FR 5322, Jan. 27, 1995; 60 FR 27228, May 23, 1995; 60 FR 57940, Nov. 24, 1995; 61 FR 51230, Oct. 1, 1996; 61 FR 66616, Dec. 18, 1996]

SUBPART C -- DELEGATION AND REDELEGATION OF AUTHORITIES

§ 501.21 Delegation of authorities.

(a) *Authority and delegation.* Section 105 of Reorganization Plan No. 7 of 1961, August 12, 1961, authorizes the Commission to delegate, by published order or rule, any of its functions to a division of the Commission, an individual Commissioner, an administrative law judge, or an employee or employee board, including functions with respect to hearing, determining, ordering, certifying, reporting or otherwise acting as to any work, business or matter. In subpart A of this part, the Commission has delegated general functions, and in this subpart C, it is delegating miscellaneous, specific authorities set forth in §§ 501.23, et seq., to the delegatees designated therein, subject to the limitations prescribed in subsequent subsections of this section.

(b) *Deputies.* Where bureau or office deputies are officially appointed, they are hereby delegated all necessary authority to act in the absence or incapacity of the director or chief.

(c) *Redelegation.* Subject to the limitations in this section, the delegatees may redelegate their authorities to subordinate personnel under their supervision and direction; but only if this subpart is amended to reflect such redelegation and notice thereof is published in the *Federal Register*.

For additional analytical, business and investment opportunities information, please contact Global Investment & Business Center, USA at (703) 370-8082. Fax: (703) 370-8083. E-mail: ibpusa3@gmail.com Global Business and Investment Info Databank - www.ibpus.com

Under any redelegated authority, the redelegator assumes full responsibility for actions taken by subordinate redelegatees.

(d) *Exercise of authority; policy and procedure.* The delegatees and redelegatees shall exercise the authorities delegated or redelegated in a manner consistent with applicable laws and the established policies of the Commission, and shall consult with the General Counsel where appropriate.

(e) *Exercise of delegated authority by delegator.* Under any authority delegated or redelegated, the delegator (Commission) , or the redelegator, respectively, shall retain full rights to exercise the authority in the first instance.

(f) *Review of delegatee's action.* The delegator (Commission) or redelegator of authority shall retain a discretionary right to review an action taken under delegated authority by a subordinate delegatee, either upon the filing of a written petition of a party to, or an intervenor in, such action; or upon the delegator's or redelegator's own initiative.

(1) Petitions for review of actions taken under delegated authority shall be filed within ten (10) calendar days of the action taken:

(i) If the action for which review is sought is taken by a delegatee, the petition shall be addressed to the Commission pursuant to § 502.69 of this chapter.

(ii) If the action for which review is sought is taken by a redelegatee, the petition shall be addressed to the redelegator whose decision can be further reviewed by the Commission under paragraph (f) (1) (i) of this section, unless the Commission decides to review the matter directly, such as, for example, in the incapacity of the redelegator.

(2) The vote of a majority of the Commission less one member thereof shall be sufficient to bring any delegated action before the Commission for review under this paragraph.

(g) *Action - when final.* Should the right to exercise discretionary review be declined or should no such review be sought under paragraph (f) of this section, then the action taken under delegated authority shall, for all purposes, including appeal or review thereof, be deemed to be the action of the Commission.

(h) *Conflicts.* Where the procedures set forth in this section conflict with law or any regulation of this chapter, the conflict shall be resolved in favor of the law or other regulation.

§ 501.22 [Reserved]

§ 501.23 Delegation to the General Counsel.

The authority listed in this section is delegated to the General Counsel: authority to classify carriers as state-controlled carriers within the meaning of section 3(8) of the Shipping Act of 1984, except where a carrier submits a rebuttal statement pursuant to § 514.4(c) (2) (ii) of this chapter.

[60 FR 27228, May 23, 1995]

§ 501.24 Delegation to the Secretary.

For additional analytical, business and investment opportunities information, please contact Global Investment & Business Center, USA at (703) 370-8082. Fax: (703) 370-8083. E-mail: ibpusa3@gmail.com Global Business and Investment Info Databank - www.ibpus.com

The authorities listed in this section are delegated to the Secretary (and, in the absence or preoccupation of the Secretary, to the Assistant Secretary) .

(a) Authority to approve applications for permission to practice before the Commission and to issue admission certificates to approved applicants.

(b) Authority to extend the time to file exceptions or replies to exceptions, and the time for Commission review, relative to initial decisions of administrative law judges and decisions of Special Dockets Officers.

(c) Authority to extend the time to file appeals or replies to appeals, and the time for Commission review, relative to dismissals of proceedings, in whole or in part, issued by administrative law judges.

(d) Authority to establish and extend or reduce the time:

(1) To file documents either in docketed proceedings or relative to petitions filed under Part 502 of this chapter, which are pending before the Commission itself; and

(2) To issue initial and final decisions under § 502.61 of this chapter.

(e) Authority to prescribe a time limit for the submission of written comments with reference to agreements filed pursuant to section 5 of the Shipping Act of 1984.

(g) Authority to prescribe a time limit less than ten days from date published in the *Federal Register* for filing comments on notices of intent to prepare an environmental assessment and notice of finding of no significant impact and authority to prepare environmental assessments of No Significant Impact.

(h) [Removed and Reserved]

(i) Authority, in the absence or preoccupation of the Managing Director and Deputy Managing Directors, to sign travel orders, nondocketed recommendations to the Commission, and other routine documents for the Managing Director, consistent with the programs, policies, and precedents established by the Commission or the Managing Director.

[59 FR 67227, Dec. 29, 1994; 61 FR 66616, Dec. 18, 1996]

§ 501.25 Delegation to and redelegation by the Managing Director.

Except where specifically redelegated in this section, the authorities listed in this section are delegated to the Managing Director.

(a) Authority to adjudicate, with the concurrence of the General Counsel, and authorize payment of, employee claims for not more than $1,000.00, arising under the Military and Civilian Personnel Property Act of 1964, 31 U.S.C. 3721.

(b) Authority to determine that an exigency of the public business is of such importance that annual leave may not be used by employees to avoid forfeiture before annual leave may be restored under 5 U.S.C. 6304.

(c) (1) Authority under Part 514 of this chapter, after consultation with the Bureau of Tariffs, Certification and Licensing, to issue letters notifying applicants for certification of ATFI batch filing capability that their applications have or have not been granted.

(2) The authority under this paragraph is redelegated to the Director, Office of Information Resources Management.

(d) (1) Authority under §514.21(m) (2) of this chapter, after consultation with the Bureau of Tariffs, Certification and Licensing, to evaluate and approve or disapprove by letter the accounting or charging system the applicant intends to use for charging users and remitting to the Commission indirect (subsequent) access user fees under 46 U.S.C. app. 1107a(d) (1) (B) (ii) , and by letter to deny access to ATFI data tapes for failure to operate under an approved accounting or charging system or for failure to remit user fees to the Commission.

(2) The authority under this paragraph is redelegated to the Director, Office of Information Resources Management.

[59 FR 62329, Dec. 5, 1994]

SUBPART D -- PUBLIC REQUESTS FOR INFORMATION

§ 501.41 Public requests for information and decisions.

(a) *General.* Pursuant to 5 U.S.C. 552(a) (1) (A) , there is hereby stated and published for the guidance of the public the established places at which, the officers from whom, and the methods whereby, the public may secure information, make submittals or requests, or obtain decisions, principally by contacting by telephone, in writing, or in person, either the Secretary of the Commission at the Federal Maritime Commission, 800 North Capitol Street, N.W., Washington,

D.C. 20573, or the Area Representatives listed in paragraph (d) of this section. See also Part 503 of this chapter.

(b) The *Secretary* will provide information and decisions, and will accept and respond to requests, relating to the program activities of the Office of the Secretary and of the Commission, generally. Unless otherwise provided in this chapter, any document, report, or other submission required to be filed with the Commission by statute or the Commission's rules and regulations relating to the functions of the Commission or of the Office of the Secretary shall be filed with or submitted to the Secretary.

(c) The *Directors of the following bureaus and offices* will provide information and decisions, and will accept and respond to requests, relating to the specific functions or program activities of their respective bureaus and offices as set forth in this chapter; but only if the dissemination of such information or decisions is not prohibited by statute or the Commission's Rules of Practice and Procedure:

(1) Office of the General Counsel

(2) Office of the Administrative Law Judges

(3) Office of the Managing Director

For additional analytical, business and investment opportunities information, please contact Global Investment & Business Center, USA at (703) 370-8082. Fax: (703) 370-8083. E-mail: ibpusa3@gmail.com Global Business and Investment Info Databank - www.ibpus.com

(4) Office of the Inspector General

(5) Office of Equal Employment Opportunity

(6) Bureau of Enforcement

(7) Bureau of Economics and Agreement Analysis

(8) Bureau of Tariffs, Certification and Licensing

(9) [Reserved]

(10) Bureau of Administration

(11) Office of Personnel

(12) Office of Budget and Financial Management

(13) Office of Information Resources Management

(14) Office of Administrative Services

(15) Office of Informal Inquiries, Complaints and Informal Dockets

(d) The Area Representatives will provide information and decisions to the public within their geographic areas, or will expedite the obtaining of information and decisions from headquarters. The addresses of these Area Representatives are as follows. Further information on Area Representatives, including Internet-E mail addresses, can be obtained on the Commission's home page on the World Wide Web at "www.fmc.gov."

Los Angeles
Los Angeles Area Representative
U.S. Customs House Building
P.O. Box 3164 300 S. Ferry Street, Room 1018 Terminal Island Station San Pedro, CA 90731

Miami
Miami Area Representative Customs Management Center 909 SE, 1st Ave., Room 736 Miami, FL 33131

New Orleans
New Orleans Area Representative
U.S. Customs House 423 Canal Street, Room 303 New Orleans, LA 70130

Seattle
Seattle Area Representative
U.S. Customs 3236 16th Ave., SW Seattle, WA 98134

North Atlantic

For additional analytical, business and investment opportunities information, please contact Global Investment & Business Center, USA at (703) 370-8082. Fax: (703) 370-8083. E-mail: ibpusa3@gmail.com Global Business and Investment Info Databank - www.ibpus.com

North Atlantic Area Representative Federal Maritime Commission 800 North Capitol Street, NW, Suite 928 Washington, DC 20573

(e) Any document, report or other submission required to be filed with the Commission by statute or the Commission's rules and regulations relating to the specific functions of the bureaus and offices shall be filed with or submitted to the Director of such Bureau or Office.

[59 FR 67227, Dec. 29, 1994; 60 FR 57940, Nov. 24, 1995; 61 FR 51230, Oct. 1, 1996]

PART 502 --RULES OF PRACTICE AND PROCEDURE: BASIC LIST

SUBPART A -- GENERAL INFORMATION

Sec.

502.1 Scope of rules in this part.
502.2 Filing of documents; hours; mailing address.
502.3 Compliance with rules or orders of Commission.
502.4 Authentication of rules or orders of Commission.
502.5 -- 502.6 [Reserved]
502.7 Documents in foreign languages.
502.8 Denial of applications and notice thereof.
502.9 Suspension, amendment, etc., of rules in this part.
502.10 Waiver of rules in this part.
502.11 Ex parte communications.
502.12 Applicability of Federal Rules of Civil Procedures.

SUBPART B -- APPEARANCE AND PRACTICE BEFORE THE COMMISSION

502.21 Appearance.
502.22 Authority for representation.
502.23 Notice of appearance; written appearance; substitutions.
502.24 Practice before the Commission defined.
502.25 Presiding officer defined.
502.26 Attorneys at law.
502.27 Persons not attorneys at law.
502.28 [Reserved]
502.29 Hearings.
502.30 Suspension or disbarment.
502.31 Statement of interest.
502.32 Former employees. Exhibit No. 1 to Subpart B [§§ 502.23, 502.26, 502.27] -- Notice of Appearance

SUBPART C -- PARTIES

502.41 Parties; how designated.

502.42 Bureau of Enforcement.

502.43 Substitution of parties.

502.44 Necessary and proper parties in certain complaint proceedings.

For additional analytical, business and investment opportunities information, please contact Global Investment & Business Center, USA at (703) 370-8082. Fax: (703) 370-8083. E-mail: ibpusa3@gmail.com Global Business and Investment Info Databank - www.ibpus.com

SUBPART D -- RULEMAKING

SUBPART E -- PROCEEDINGS; PLEADINGS; MOTIONS; REPLIES

SUBPART F -- SETTLEMENT; PREHEARING PROCEDURE

For additional analytical, business and investment opportunities information, please contact Global Investment & Business Center, USA at (703) 370-8082. Fax: (703) 370-8083. E-mail: ibpusa3@gmail.com Global Business and Investment Info Databank - www.ibpus.com

SUBPART G -- TIME

SUBPART H -- FORM, EXECUTION, AND SERVICE OF DOCUMENTS

SUBPART I -- SUBPENAS

SUBPART J -- HEARINGS; PRESIDING OFFICERS; EVIDENCE

For additional analytical, business and investment opportunities information, please contact Global Investment & Business Center, USA at (703) 370-8082. Fax: (703) 370-8083. E-mail: ibpusa3@gmail.com Global Business and Investment Info Databank - www.ibpus.com

502.160 Records in other proceedings.
502.161 Commission's files.
502.162 Stipulations.
502.163 Receipt of documents after hearing.
502.164 Oral argument at hearings.
502.165 Official transcript.
502.166 Corrections of transcript.
502.167 Objection to public disclosure of information.
502.168 Copies of data or evidence.
502.169 Record of decision.

SUBPART K -- SHORTENED PROCEDURE

502.181 Selection of cases for shortened procedure; consent required.

502.182 Complaint and memorandum of facts and arguments and filing fee.

502.183 Respondent's answering memorandum.

502.184 Complainant's memorandum in reply.

502.185 Service of memoranda upon and by interveners.

502.186 Contents of memoranda.

502.187 Procedure after filing of memoranda.

SUBPART L -- DEPOSITIONS, WRITTEN INTERROGATORIES, AND DISCOVERY

502.201 General provisions governing discovery.

502.202 Persons before whom depositions may be taken.

502.203 Depositions upon oral examination.

502.204 Depositions upon written interrogatories.

502.205 Interrogatories to parties.

502.206 Production of documents and things and entry upon land for inspection and other purposes.

502.207 Requests for admission.

502.208 Use of discovery procedures directed to Commission staff personnel.

502.209 Use of depositions at hearings.

502.210 Refusal to comply with orders to answer or produce documents; sanctions; enforcement.

**For additional analytical, business and investment opportunities information, please contact Global Investment & Business Center, USA at (703) 370-8082. Fax: (703) 370-8083. E-mail: ibpusa3@gmail.com
Global Business and Investment Info Databank - www.ibpus.com**

SUBPART M -- BRIEFS; REQUESTS FOR FINDINGS; DECISIONS; EXCEPTIONS

502.221 Briefs; requests for findings.

502.222 Requests for enlargement of time for filing briefs.

502.223 Decisions -- administrative law judges.

502.224 Separation of functions.

502.225 Decisions -- Commission.

502.226 Decision based on official notice; public documents.

502.227 Exceptions to decisions or orders of dismissal of administrative law judge; replies thereto; review of decisions or orders of dismissal by Commission; and judicial review.

502.228 Request for enlargement of time for filing exceptions and replies thereto.

502.229 Certification of record by presiding or other officer.

502.230 Reopening by presiding officer or Commission.

SUBPART N -- ORAL ARGUMENT; SUBMISSION FOR FINAL DECISION

502.241 Oral argument.

502.242 Submission to Commission for final decision.

502.243 Participation of absent Commissioner.

SUBPART O -- REPARATION

502.251 Proof on award of reparation.

502.252 Reparation statements.

502.253 Interest in reparation proceedings.

502.254 Attorney's fees in reparation proceedings. Exhibit No. 1 to Subpart O [§ 502.252] -- Reparation Statement to be Filed Pursuant to Rule 252

SUBPART P -- RECONSIDERATION OF PROCEEDINGS

502.261 Petitions for reconsideration and stay.

502.262 Reply to petition for reconsideration or stay.

For additional analytical, business and investment opportunities information, please contact Global Investment & Business Center, USA at (703) 370-8082. Fax: (703) 370-8083. E-mail: ibpusa3@gmail.com Global Business and Investment Info Databank - www.ibpus.com

Subpart Q -- Refund or Waiver of Freight Charges

502.271 Special docket application for permission to refund or waive freight charges.

Exhibit No. 1 to Subpart Q [§ 502.271] - Application for Refund or Waiver of Freight Charges Due to Tariff or Quoting Error

Subpart R -- Nonadjudicatory Investigations

502.281 Investigational policy.
502.282 Initiation of investigations.
502.283 Order of investigation.
502.284 By whom conducted.
502.285 Investigational hearings.
502.286 Compulsory process.
502.287 Depositions.
502.288 Reports.
502.289 Noncompliance with investigational process.
502.290 Rights of witness.
502.291 Nonpublic proceedings.

Subpart S -- Informal Procedure for Adjudication of Small Claims

502.301 Statement of policy.

502.302 Limitations of actions.

502.303 [Reserved]

502.304 Procedure and filing fee.

502.305 Applicability of other rules of this part.

Exhibit No. 1 to Subpart S [§ 502.304(a)] -- Small Claim Form for Informal Adjudication and Information Checklist Exhibit No. 2 to Subpart S [§ 502.304(e)] -- Respondent's Consent Form for Informal Adjudication

Subpart T -- Formal Procedure for Adjudication of Small Claims

502.311 Applicability.
502.312 Answer to complaint.
502.313 Reply of complainant.
502.314 Additional information.
502.315 Request for oral hearing.
502.316 Intervention.
502.317 Oral argument.
502.318 Decision.
502.319 Date of service and computation of time.
502.320 Service.
502.321 Applicability of other rules of this part.

For additional analytical, business and investment opportunities information, please contact Global Investment & Business Center, USA at (703) 370-8082. Fax: (703) 370-8083. E-mail: ibpusa3@gmail.com Global Business and Investment Info Databank - www.ibpus.com

SUBPART U -- ALTERNATIVE DISPUTE RESOLUTION

SUBPART V -- IMPLEMENTATION OF THE EQUAL ACCESS TO JUSTICE ACT IN COMMISSION PROCEEDINGS

SUBPART W -- COMPROMISE, ASSESSMENT, SETTLEMENT AND COLLECTION OF CIVIL PENALTIES

SUBPART W -- COMPROMISE, ASSESSMENT, MITIGATION, SETTLEMENT, AND COLLECTION OF CIVIL PENALTIES

Source: 49 FR 44418, Nov. 6, 1984, unless otherwise noted. Redesignated at 58 FR 27211, May 7, 1993.

§ 502.601 Purpose and scope.

The purpose of this subpart is to implement the statutory provisions of section 19 of the Merchant Marine Act, 1920, section 13 of the Shipping Act of 1984, and sections 2(c) and 3(c) of Public Law 89-777 by establishing rules and regulations governing the compromise, assessment, settlement and collection of civil penalties arising under certain designated provisions of the Merchant Marine Act , 1920, the Shipping Act of 1984, Public Law 89-777, and/or any order, rule, or regulation (except for procedural rules and regulations contained in this part) issued or made

For additional analytical, business and investment opportunities information, please contact Global Investment & Business Center, USA at (703) 370-8082. Fax: (703) 370-8083. E-mail: ibpusa3@gmail.com Global Business and Investment Info Databank - www.ibpus.com

by the Commission in the exercise of its powers, duties and functions under those statutes. [Rule 601.]

[64 FR 7804, Feb. 17, 1999]

§ 502.602 Definitions.

For the purposes of this subpart:

(a) ``*Assessment*'' means the imposition of a civil penalty by order of the Commission after a formal docketed proceeding.

(b) ``*Commission*'' means the Federal Maritime Commission.

(c) ``*Compromise*'' means the process whereby a civil penalty for a violation is agreed upon by the respondent and the Commission outside of a formal, docketed proceeding.

(d) ``*Mitigation*'' means the reduction, in whole or in part, of the amount of a civil penalty.

(e) ``*Person*'' includes individuals, corporations, partnerships, and associations existing under or authorized by the laws of the United States or of a foreign country.

(f) ``*Respondent*'' means any person charged with a violation.

(g) ``*Settlement*'' means the process whereby a civil penalty or other disposition of the case for a violation is agreed to in a formal, docketed proceeding instituted by order of the Commission.

(h) *"Violation"* includes any violation of sections 19(6) (d) , 19(7) (d) and 19(11) of the Merchant Marine Act, 1920; any provision of the Shipping Act of 1984; sections 2 and 3 of Public Law 89777; and/or any order, rule or regulation (except for procedural rules and regulations contained in this part) issued or made by the Commission in the exercise of its powers, duties and functions under the Merchant Marine Act, 1920, the Shipping Act of 1984, or Public Law 89-777.

(i) Words in the plural form shall include the singular and vice versa; and words importing the masculine gender shall include the feminine and vice versa. The terms ``includes'' and ``including'' do not exclude matters not listed but which are in the same general class. The word ``and'' includes ``or'', except where specifically stated or where the context requires otherwise. [Rule 602.]

[64 FR 7804, Feb. 17, 1999]

§ 502.603 Assessment of civil penalties: Procedure; criteria for determining amount; limitations; relation to compromise.

(a) *Procedure for assessment of penalty.* The Commission may assess a civil penalty only after notice and opportunity for hearing. Civil penalty assessment proceedings, including settlement negotiations, shall be governed by the Commission's Rules of Practice and Procedure in this part. All settlements must be approved by the Presiding Officer. The full text of any settlement must be included in the final order of the Commission.

For additional analytical, business and investment opportunities information, please contact Global Investment & Business Center, USA at (703) 370-8082. Fax: (703) 370-8083. E-mail: ibpusa3@gmail.com Global Business and Investment Info Databank - www.ibpus.com

(b) *Criteria for determining amount of penalty.* In determining the amount of any penalties assessed, the Commission shall take into account the nature, circumstances, extent and gravity of the violation committed and the policies for deterrence and future compliance with the Commission's rules and regulations and the applicable statutes. The Commission shall also consider the respondent's degree of culpability, history of prior offenses, ability to pay and such other matters as justice requires.

(c) *Limitations; relation to compromise.* When the Commission, in its discretion, determines that policy, justice or other circumstances warrant, a civil penalty assessment proceeding may be instituted at any time for any violation which occurred within five years prior to the issuance of the order of investigation. Such proceeding may also be instituted at any time after the initiation of informal compromise procedures, except where a compromise agreement for the same violations under the compromise procedures has become effective under § 502.604(e) . [Rule 603.]

§ 502.604 Compromise of penalties: Relation to assessment proceedings.

(a) *Scope.* Except in pending civil penalty assessment proceedings provided for in § 502.603, the Commission, when it has reason to believe a violation has occurred, may invoke the informal compromise procedures of this section.

(b) *Notice.* When the Commission considers it appropriate to afford an opportunity for the compromise of a civil penalty, it will, except when otherwise authorized by the Commission, or where circumstances render it unnecessary, send a Notice and Demand Letter ("NDL") to the respondent, by registered or certified mail, or by other means reasonably calculated to give notice. The NDL will describe specific violation(s) on which the claim is based, including the particular facts, dates and other elements necessary for the respondent to identify the specific

conduct constituting the alleged violation; the amount of the penalty demanded; and the names of Commission personnel with whom the demand may be discussed, if the person desires to compromise the penalty. The NDL also will state the deadlines for the institution and completion of compromise negotiations and the consequences of failure to compromise.

(c) *Request for compromise.* Any person receiving a NDL provided for in paragraph (b) of this section may, within the time specified, deny the violation, or submit matters explaining, mitigating or showing extenuating circumstances, as well as make voluntary disclosures of information and documents.

(d) *Criteria for compromise.* In addition to the factors set forth in § 502.603(b) , in compromising a penalty claim, the Commission may consider litigative probabilities, the cost of collecting the claim and enforcement policy.

(e) *Disposition of claims in compromise procedures.* (1) When a penalty is compromised and the respondent agrees to settle for that amount, a compromise agreement shall be executed. (One example of such compromise agreement is set forth as Appendix A to this subpart.) This agreement, after reciting the nature of the claim, will include a statement evidencing the respondent's agreement to the compromise of the Commission's penalty claim for the amount set forth in the agreement and will also embody an approval and acceptance provision which is to be signed by the appropriate Commission official. Upon compromise of the penalty in the agreed amount, a duplicate original of the executed agreement shall be furnished to the respondent.

For additional analytical, business and investment opportunities information, please contact Global Investment & Business Center, USA at (703) 370-8082. Fax: (703) 370-8083. E-mail: ibpusa3@gmail.com Global Business and Investment Info Databank - www.ibpus.com

(2) Upon completion of the compromise, the Commission may issue a public notice thereof, the terms and language of which are not subject to negotiation.

(f) *Relation to assessment proceedings.* Except by order of the Commission, no compromise procedure shall be initiated or continued after institution of a Commission assessment proceeding directed to the same violations. Any offer of compromise submitted by the respondent pursuant to this section shall be deemed to have been furnished by the respondent without prejudice and shall not be used against the respondent in any proceeding.

(g) *Delegation of compromise authority.* The compromise authority set forth in this subpart is delegated to the Director, Bureau of Enforcement. [Rule 604.]

[61 FR 51230, Oct. 1, 1996; 64 FR 7804, Feb. 17, 1999]

§ 502.605 Payment of penalty: Method; default.

(a) *Method.* Payment of penalties by the respondent is to be made by bank cashier's check or other instrument acceptable to the Commission.

(1) By bank cashier's check or other instrument acceptable to the Commission;

(2) Upon execution of a promissory note containing a confess-judgment agreement, by periodic regular installments, with interest where appropriate, by bank cashier's check or other instrument acceptable to the Commission; or

(3) By combination of the above alternatives.

(b) All checks or other instruments submitted in payment of claims shall be made payable to the Federal Maritime Commission.

(c) *Default in payment.* Where a respondent fails or refuses to pay a penalty properly assessed under § 502.603, or compromised and agreed to under § 502.604, appropriate collection efforts will be made by the Commission, including, but not limited to referral to the Department of Justice for collection. Where such defaulting respondent is a licensed freight forwarder, such default also may be grounds for revocation or suspension of the respondent's license, after notice and opportunity for hearing, unless such notice and hearing have been waived by the respondent in writing. [Rule 605.]

[64 FR 7804, Feb. 17, 1999]

APPENDIX A TO SUBPART W - EXAMPLE OF COMPROMISE AGREEMENT

COMPROMISE AGREEMENT

FMC File No. ___________

This Agreement is entered into between:

(1) the Federal Maritime Commission, hereinafter referred to as Commission, and

For additional analytical, business and investment opportunities information, please contact Global Investment & Business Center, USA at (703) 370-8082. Fax: (703) 370-8083. E-mail: ibpusa3@gmail.com Global Business and Investment Info Databank - www.ibpus.com

(2) ______________ , hereinafter referred to as Respondent.

Whereas, the Commission is considering the institution of an assessment proceeding against Respondent for the recovery of civil penalties provided under the [appropriate statute] , for alleged violations of section ________________;

Whereas, this course of action is the result of practices believed by the Commission to have been engaged in by Respondent, to wit:

[General description of practices and dates or time period involved]

Whereas, the Commission has authority under the Shipping Act of 1984 to compromise and collect civil penalties; and,

Whereas, Respondent has terminated the practices which are the basis for the allegations of violation set forth herein, and has instituted and indicated its willingness to maintain measures designed to eliminate these practices by Respondent, its officers, directors or employees.

Now Therefore, in consideration of the premises herein, and in compromise of all civil penalties arising from the alleged violations, Respondent and the Commission hereby agree upon the following terms and conditions of compromise and settlement:

1. Respondent shall make a monetary payment to the Commission herewith, by bank cashier's check, in the total amount of $ ______.
    1. Upon acceptance in writing of this Agreement by the Director of the Bureau of Enforcement of the Commission, this instrument shall forever bar the commencement or institution of any
    2. assessment proceeding or other claim for recovery of civil penalties from the Respondent arising from the alleged violations set forth above.
2. It is expressly understood and agreed that this Agreement is not, and is not to be construed as, an admission by Respondent to the alleged violations set forth above. (Respondent's Name) By: ________________

Title: ______________ Date: ______________

APPROVAL AND ACCEPTANCE The above terms, conditions and consideration are hereby approved and accepted: By the Federal Maritime Commission:

Director, Bureau of Enforcement Date: [65 FR 81748, Dec. 27, 2000]

Subpart X -- Paperwork Reduction Act § 502.991 OMB control numbers assigned pursuant to the Paperwork Reduction Act. This section displays the control numbers assigned to information collection requirements of the Commission in this part by the Office of Management and Budget (OMB) pursuant to the Paperwork Reduction Act of 1980, Pub. L. 96 - 511. The Commission intends that this section comply with the Act, which requires that agencies display a current control number assigned by the Director of OMB for each agency information collection requirement:

Section	Current OMB Control No.
502.27..........(Form FMC 12)	3072-0001

For additional analytical, business and investment opportunities information, please contact Global Investment & Business Center, USA at (703) 370-8082. Fax: (703) 370-8083. E-mail: ibpusa3@gmail.com Global Business and Investment Info Databank - www.ibpus.com

Last Update: June 11, 2002

46 CFR PART 530 DOCKET NO. 98-30 SERVICE CONTRACTS SUBJECT TO THE SHIPPING ACT OF 1984

AGENCY: Federal Maritime Commission.

ACTION: Interim final rule.

SUMMARY: The Federal Maritime Commission has revised its regulations governing service contracts between shippers and ocean common carriers to implement changes made to the Shipping Act of 1984 ("Act") by P.L. 105-258 (the Ocean Shipping Reform Act of 1998) and section 424 of P.L. 105-383 (the Coast Guard Authorization Act of 1998) . Specifically, the Commission has revised its regulations implementing section 8(c) of the Act and has created a new 46 CFR part 530 to govern service contract filing. The interim nature of this rule is due to a major revision of the proposed regulation, which did not include the internet-based filing system of the interim final rule. The proposed regulations have been revised to accommodate the alternative system. Portions of the proposed rule have been redrafted for clarity, repetitive sections have been deleted and the remaining sections are accordingly renumbered.

DATES: Effective date May 1, 1999. Submit comments on this interim final rule on or before April 1, 1999.

ADDRESSES: Address all comments to:

Bryant L. VanBrakle Secretary Federal Maritime Commission 800 North Capitol Street, N.W., Room 1046 Washington, D.C. 20573-0001

FOR FURTHER INFORMATION CONTACT:

Thomas Panebianco General Counsel Federal Maritime Commission 800 North Capitol Street, N.W. Washington, D.C. 20573-0001 (202) 523-5740

Austin L. Schmitt Director Bureau of Tariffs, Certification and Licensing Federal Maritime Commission 800 North Capitol Street, N.W. Washington, D.C. 20573-0001 (202) 523-5796

SUPPLEMENTARY INFORMATION:

On December 23, 1998, the Federal Maritime Commission ("Commission") issued proposed regulations to implement changes to the Shipping Act of 1984 ("Act") mandated by the Ocean Shipping Reform Act of 1998, Pub. L. No. 105-258, 112 Stat. 1902 ("OSRA") , enacted on October 14, 1998. 63 Fed. Reg. 71062-71076. OSRA made several changes to the existing system by which the Federal Maritime Commission regulates ocean shipping in the foreign commerce of the United States, particularly to the provisions governing service contracts under the Act.

As noted in the Notice of Proposed Rulemaking ("NPR") , the Commission sought to balance the general deregulatory intent of OSRA with the important oversight role that Congress has assigned to it, through the proposed rules. The difficulty in achieving that balance is apparent in the reactions the proposal received from members of the industry. Further, while the Commission recognized that the filing requirements must be crafted with an appreciation for regulated entities'

For additional analytical, business and investment opportunities information, please contact Global Investment & Business Center, USA at (703) 370-8082. Fax: (703) 370-8083. E-mail: ibpusa3@gmail.com Global Business and Investment Info Databank - www.ibpus.com

interests in simple, speedy and straightforward filing procedures, the Commission also noted in the NPR that the procedures must enable the Commission to fulfill its statutory duty to guard against section 10 violations and perform its section 6 functions. As several of the comments urge, this responsibility on the part of the Commission is especially important as service contracts will be confidential and potentially aggrieved parties will have to rely on the Commission for oversight. This will be complicated by the predicted increase in the sheer number of service contracts filed. It was with these goals in mind that the Commission originally proposed the draft regulations, designed to enable the Commission to fulfill its regulatory mandate while imposing a minimal burden on regulated parties.

§ 530.3 - DEFINITIONS

One commenter takes issue with the proposed definition of "conference," being different from the statute, and not referring to the requirement of a common tariff. APL, 1. The comment suggests that the definition track the statute. The change to the definition of "conference" in this rule conforms with the changes made in the Commission's rulemaking on agreements, Docket No. 98-26, and tariffs, Docket No. 98-29.

Similarly, the Commission in this proceeding had proposed a new definition of "ocean common carrier" to match that proposed in the agreements rulemaking. However, upon receipt of opposition to that proposal from one commenter and little input from other industry interests, the Commission has determined to carry over its former definition of "ocean common carrier" and take the matter up in a later, separate rulemaking. See, Docket No. 98-26.

APL also questioned the proposed definition of "service contract." APL, 1-2. The comment urges the Commission to adopt a definition of "service contract" which would correct a "persisting drafting error in OSRA" as a contract between one or more shippers and an ocean common carrier or an agreement between or among carriers. APL, 1-2. APL complains that this definition literally contemplates an agreement that is a party to an agreement, a circular and legally impossible definition. APL, 2. The comment suggests either redefining or interpreting OSRA so that wherever the statute refers to "an agreement," that the meaning will be two or more ocean common carriers acting pursuant to an agreement on file with the Commission or exempt from such filing. APL, 2.

Prior to revisions made by OSRA, the Act provided that only a certain type of agreement between ocean common carriers, namely a conference agreement, could enter into service contracts. OSRA changed the definition of service contract from "a contract between a shipper and an ocean common carrier or conference" to "a written contract, other than a bill of lading or a receipt, between one or more shippers and an individual ocean common carrier or an agreement between or among ocean common carriers." This had two effects. First, it allows a group of two or more unrelated (i.e. not a shippers' association) shippers to jointly enter into a service contract. Second, it allows any ocean common carrier agreement (not just a conference agreement) to enter into service contracts. Therefore, the definition of service contract in the regulation is revised to appear as it does in the Act. APL's observation appears correct. The authority to enter into service contracts extends to carriers acting collectively pursuant to a filed agreement, even if the agreement does not provide for any central administrative entity.

For the sake of clarity, the definitions of "effective date" and "expiration date" are moved from the Appendix to the definitions section, § 530.3. Finally, a definition of "motor vehicle" is added, comporting with the definition of that term in the Commission's tariff regulation, Docket No. 98-29. See also infra, discussion of exempt commodities.

For additional analytical, business and investment opportunities information, please contact Global Investment & Business Center, USA at (703) 370-8082. Fax: (703) 370-8083. E-mail: ibpusa3@gmail.com Global Business and Investment Info Databank - www.ibpus.com

§ 530.4 -- CONFIDENTIALITY

Carriers, shippers and one filing service commented on § 530.4 of the proposed rule. While most agree that the Commission has the authority to share service contract information with other federal agencies, they also request clarification on how the Commission intends to ensure that other agencies maintain confidentiality. CMA, 3; DuPont, 5. One suggests the following addition to the section:

any information from or access to service contracts to another agency of the Federal government shall, to the full extent permitted by law, also will be [sic] held in confidence by such other agency or notice of the confidentiality of such information will be provided by the Commission to such other agency.

ETM, 1.

Another suggests,

The Commission shall seek to ensure, prior to providing access to confidential service contract information to another Government agency, that such other agency will protect the confidentiality of the service contract information.

NITL, 23.

Two comments suggest that the regulations should ensure that information shared not be inadvertently publicized through the Freedom of Information Act ("FOIA") or other means, and that the same level of protection afforded within the Commission should follow the information when it is shared with another federal agency. DuPont, 5; NITL, 23.

Exemption 4 of FOIA would presumably protect service contract information confidentially filed with the Commission from requests for public disclosure. 5 U.S.C. § 552(b) (4) (1994) . Exemption 4 of FOIA protects "commercial or financial information obtained from a person [that is] privileged or confidential." The exemption affords protection to those submiters who are required to furnish commercial or financial information to the government by safeguarding them from the competitive disadvantages that could result from disclosure. See U.S. Department of Justice, Office of Information and Privacy, Freedom of Information Act Guide and Privacy Act Overview, at 123.

Another comment suggests this provision should be amended to provide that all confidential information will be provided to other government agencies which have a Memorandum of Understanding ("MOU") agreeing that they will maintain confidentiality of the information in accordance with the letter and spirit of OSRA. Conagra, 4. The Commission has concluded that it will provide confidential service contract information only to federal government agencies with which it has an MOU ensuring that the recipient agency will accordingly protect the information from public disclosure. This should adequately address the reasonable concerns expressed in the comments.

One commenter asserts that the confidentiality requirement of the Act applies to the Commission only, and does not give the Commission any authority to review the parties' complaints for breach of a confidentiality clause in the contract itself. Such a breach, they argue is purely a contract matter and as such, for a court to decide. APL, 2. The comment suggests that in order to clarify this point, the phrase "by the Commission" should be added at the end of the first sentence. APL,

For additional analytical, business and investment opportunities information, please contact Global Investment & Business Center, USA at (703) 370-8082. Fax: (703) 370-8083. E-mail: ibpusa3@gmail.com Global Business and Investment Info Databank - www.ibpus.com

2. The statute appears to be adequately clear on this matter, and there is no need for further clarification at this time.

Wal-Mart is concerned that disclosure of the actual international freight rate required by U.S. Customs Service ("USCS") (form CF 7501) will provide an opportunity for unscrupulous customs brokers to obtain confidential rate information and disclose it. Wal-Mart, 1. Wal-Mart is concerned that, even with a confidentiality agreement with the broker, the monitoring and enforcement of such confidentiality agreements may prove difficult, or impossible. Wal-Mart, 2. Wal-Mart therefore requests the Commission coordinate with other federal government agencies, especially USCS, in its final implementation of the regulations to ensure that the confidentiality of service contracts be preserved by those other agencies, and suggests that one approach may be to declare average or estimated freight rates on the CF 7501 form supplemented by actual data directly to USCS without using the broker. Wal-Mart, 2.

The commenter's request is outside the Commission's jurisdiction. While it understands WalMart's concerns, the Commission has no authority to dictate to other agencies what information they may or may not require from the entities they regulate. Therefore, the comment is more appropriately directed towards USCS.

In contrast, one commenter argues that the proposed regulations do not acknowledge limitations on the Commission's authority to release service contract information, recognize the complexity of the associated issues, or provide procedures for making a determination to release information. Carriers, 2. First, the Carriers argue, the Commission's authority to disclose confidential service contract information to other federal government agencies at all is questionable. Carriers, 2. These comments argue that the colloquy between Senators McCain and Hutchison is of limited value for the purpose of legislative history because it followed, rather than preceded, the adoption of the bill which became OSRA. Carriers, 2 n.1. This argument is unconvincing, however, as we note that Senator Hutchison, with specific reference to section 8(c) (2) of S. 414 (which remained unchanged in the final passage of OSRA) , remarked on April 21, 1998, that the Commission "is encouraged to work with affected Federal agencies to address" their concerns about how they are to ensure rate compliance with U.S. cargo preference law in an era of service contract rate confidentiality. Cong. Rec S3320 (daily ed., April 21, 1998) (statement of Sen. Hutchison) . While the statute itself reads only, "each contract entered into under this subsection . . . shall be filed confidentially with the Commission" (section 8(c) (2) of OSRA) , and "[w]hen a service contract is filed confidentially with the Commission, a concise statement of the essential terms . . . shall be published and made available to the general public in tariff format" (section 8(c) (3)) , taken with the remarks made on the same day the Senate passed S. 414, the legislative history indicates that it was the intent of the drafters that the confidentiality provision not hamper other federal government agencies which have legitimate need to access the confidentially filed information in order to carry out their respective duties.

There is further indication that the drafters intended that the confidentiality provision would apply to preclude Commission disclosure to the public. As Senator Hutchison remarked in the aforementioned floor colloquy, "[o]f course. . .confidential service contract information would remain protected from disclosure to the public consistent with the Shipping Act of 1984, as amended by the Ocean Shipping Reform Act and other applicable Federal laws." Cong. Rec. S11302 (daily ed. Oct. 1, 1998) (Statement of Sen. Hutchison) (emphasis added) . This emphasized the importance of the Commission protecting information filed confidentially with it from disclosure to the public, but does not limit the Commission's right to disclose such information to other federal agencies where clearly warranted and justified. Finally, the Commission noted in the NPR that it would only "allow access to filed contracts to Federal government agencies where appropriate; any such disclosure will not jeopardize the statutory aim

For additional analytical, business and investment opportunities information, please contact Global Investment & Business Center, USA at (703) 370-8082. Fax: (703) 370-8083. E-mail: ibpusa3@gmail.com Global Business and Investment Info Databank - www.ibpus.com

of non-disclosure of confidential service contract information to non-governmental entities." 63 Fed. Reg. 71065. This continues to correctly express Commission policy on the subject.

The Carriers argue further that even if the authority of the colloquy is accepted, the only exception to the statutory requirement that the Commission keep service contract information confidential is "to ensure compliance of U.S.-flag ocean common carriers with cargo preference law shipping rate requirements." Carriers, 3. Therefore, they contend that this does not authorize the Commission to disclose such information when a government agency is acting in a proprietary capacity as shipper. Carriers, 2. This implies that the following language of the second sentence of proposed § 530.4 is at least over broad: "Nothing contained in this part shall preclude the Commission from providing certain information from or access to service contracts to another agency of the Federal government of the United States." The Carriers are concerned that there is too large a potential for procurement officials to use such information to drive down rates. Carriers, 4.

The Carriers question whether any statutory requirements, including the cargo preference laws, actually exist which would require information from confidentially filed service contracts and further question the relevancy of the information, as procurement is typically based on "competitively bid, lowest landed cost awards." Carriers, 4. We are not persuaded that service contract information should be withheld from agencies that ship cargo with ocean carriers. The Commission, however, is not attempting in these regulations to predict every situation in which the requested information may or may not be relevant to the purposes of the requesting agency. This would be another matter most appropriately addressed by an MOU.

The Carriers' reference to the pending litigation against the Department of Defense ("DoD") serves to further illustrate this point. Carriers, 5. The Commission simply does not have the ability to predict in what situations confidential service contract information may or may not be relevant to the execution of the requesting agency's statutory duties, but can require that the agency support its request with a good faith argument for relevancy, in an accordingly drafted MOU.

Furthermore, because Congress did not indicate that it wished to limit the agencies with which the Commission should cooperate, but instead used the term "other federal agencies," the Commission interprets this admonition to include agencies other than DoD and laws other than the Cargo Preference Act of 1904. Again, as the Commission cannot presently predict which statutory requirements other agencies may have for confidential service contract information, the Commission declines to add to its regulations at this time any such limitation on its future action. Rather, the Commission asserts that disclosure of confidentially filed service contract information will only be made to other federal government agencies with which it has negotiated an MOU which will protect the information from disclosure to the public.

The Carriers complain that the proposed regulations do not provide for procedures for informed comment on and consideration of the conflicting interests, but rather appear to envision an approach to such interagency requests on a unilateral and ad hoc basis. Carriers, 2. The Carriers assert that they are entitled to a "careful and open appraisal" based on an informed record before the Commission, rather than the approach contemplated by the proposed rule. Carriers at 6. The Carriers' comments appear to request that the Commission create a formal review proceeding for each request before any service contract information is released to a requesting Federal government agency. Again, the MOU should adequately address the Carriers' concerns without requiring that the Commission initiate an adversary proceeding which would require the Commission to implement new procedures, and undertake the time and expense which would accompany each evaluation.

For additional analytical, business and investment opportunities information, please contact Global Investment & Business Center, USA at (703) 370-8082. Fax: (703) 370-8083. E-mail: ibpusa3@gmail.com Global Business and Investment Info Databank - www.ibpus.com

Finally, the Carriers comment that if the Commission does not delete the provision in question, that a separate proceeding should be initiated to "permit full ventilation of the issues by concerned parties." Carriers at 6. On the contrary, it appears that the notice and comment period in this rulemaking proceeding has given the Carriers an opportunity, of which they have availed themselves, to address such issues.

For the foregoing reasons, therefore, the Commission shall require a requesting federal agency to enter into a Memorandum of Understanding that it will protect the confidentiality of any information it receives from the Commission and that such information is necessary to its statutory functions, and adopts as final the language in § 530.4 of the proposed regulations.

§ 530.5 -- DUTY TO FILE

As stated in the NPR, the Commission's past regulations generally imposed on a conference the duty to file and publish service contract material on behalf of its members. 46 CFR § 514.4(d) (duty and authority to file) . Specifically, the Commission's former regulation placed the duty to file service contracts and publish their essential terms on either: a service contract signatory carrier which is not a member of a conference for the service covered by the contract; or the conference which is signatory or has one or more members for service otherwise covered by the conference agreement. Conferences could file for and on behalf of one or more of its member lines for service outside the scope of the conference agreement. § 514.4(d) (5) (B) (ii) . In such case, the statement of essential terms was to be filed simultaneously in both the essential terms publication of the conference and the carriers involved.[(1)]

The Commission's past approach distinguished duty to file based on the subject matter of the contract itself. In this respect, for contracts entered into by a member of a conference but which fell outside the scope of that conference, the duty to file and publish fell on the signatory carrier. For contracts which concerned subject matter within the scope of a conference agreement, the duty to file and publish fell upon the conference which was the signatory to the contract or whose member or members were signatories. Conferences, under the Commission's prior regulations, were authorized to file and publish for their member lines for services outside the scope of the conference. § 514.4(d) (5) (ii) . For such filing, essential terms were required to be published by both individual carrier and conference. Id. OCWG suggests that the Commission continue this approach, and merely revise the previous regulations by changing the term "conference" to "agreement."

In the proposed rule, the Commission recognized that agreement service contracts would pose somewhat different problems for filing and publishing than did conferences, which unlike some other agreements, maintain a central authority or secretariat. The proposed regulation sought to anticipate situations in which members of an agreement without a central authority enter a service contract. The proposal would have allowed members of such an agreement to delegate the filing duty to one member, but also indicated that such delegation would not relieve the other carrier parties from any liability should there be a failure to comply with the filing requirements of the regulations.

OCWG objects to the proposed rules' provisions placing filing requirements generally on individual carriers. OCWG asserts that a carrier breach of contract confidentiality[(2)] is not a violation of the Act, citing Senator Hutchison's April 21, 1998 floor remarks. OCWG further asserts that a carrier could publish confidential service contract information in the New York Times and not violate the Act. OCWG at 16. We note, however, that some disclosures could raise issues under Section 10(b) (13) of the Act which prohibits any common carrier, either alone or in conjunction with any other person, indirectly or directly, from knowingly disclosing, offering,

For additional analytical, business and investment opportunities information, please contact Global Investment & Business Center, USA at (703) 370-8082. Fax: (703) 370-8083. E-mail: ibpusa3@gmail.com Global Business and Investment Info Databank - www.ibpus.com

soliciting, or receiving any information concerning the nature, kind, quantity, destination, consignee or routing of any property tendered or delivered to a common carrier without the consent of the shipper or consignee if that information may be used to the detriment or prejudice of the shipper or consignee, may improperly disclose its business transaction to a competitor, or may be used to the detriment or prejudice of any common carrier.

Carriers and conferences urge they should have the ability to take advantage of the efficiencies membership in an agreement provides for the accomplishment of such ministerial acts as filing. OCWG, 13; CENSA, 2; COSCO, 2; JUSEFC, 2-5. The comments of BSA reveal serious concerns shippers rightfully may have about filing done by agents closely controlled by agreement authorities. The comments of COSCO and JUSEFC also recognize this legitimate shipper concern.

The Commission has determined to revise section 530.5 and simplify the filing duties in accordance with the comments. Section 530.5, as revised, places the duty to file on the individual carrier party to a service contract, as Commission regulations always have. For multi-party service contracts, the duty to file falls equally upon all the carrier parties participating or eligible to participate in the contract. Multi-party service contracts must indicate the agreement (conference or otherwise) under whose authority the contract is entered. Carrier parties may designate any agent they choose for filing, including an agreement secretariat. The Commission shall closely monitor filing or other ministerial tasks undertaken by central authorities for violations of section 10(b) (13) and other activities which may have implications for the Commission's section 6(g) oversight.

Contrary to the assertion of OCWG, simply adopting the former regulation language and substituting the term "agreement" for "conference" will not account for the individual member of an agreement which wishes to take independent action within the scope of the agreement, but which does not wish to disclose the service contract information to the agreement. The regulation, therefore, makes clear provision for the contract parties' election on who shall be authorized as filer. Furthermore, the regulation would allow shippers to negotiate a requirement, for filing done by a conference or agreement secretariat, for example, that provisions for confidentiality be undertaken, e.g., through the use of "firewalls." Finally, the use of an agent for filing does not relieve the carrier parties in any way for a failure to duly file or publish. They are unquestionably responsible for ensuring their agents comply with these regulatory requirements.

§ 530.6 -- CERTIFICATION OF SHIPPER STATUS

Proposed § 530.6(a) requires each shipper party to a service contract to sign and certify on the signature page of the service contract its shipper status and the status of all its affiliates which have access to the service contract. NITL, AIFA, and DuPont oppose the proposed regulation, and particularly complain that the rationale for the requirement is unclear and the certification itself is burdensome. NITL, 21; AIFA, 3; DuPont, 3. They recommend that this requirement should only apply when the shipper is an NVOCC. DuPont, 3; AIFA, 3, NITL, 21.

NITL, APL and DuPont assert that contracting parties should be able to resolve on their own the capacity in which a particular shipper is acting with respect to the service contract as a matter of negotiation between the parties, not one mandated by the Commission. NITL, 21; APL, 3; DuPont, 3.

The regulation as proposed, however, does not appear to impose any limitations on the commercial negotiations of service contracts. The parties are free to contract with any individual or entity entitled to enter into service contracts under the Act, and in certain capacities (e.g., no

For additional analytical, business and investment opportunities information, please contact Global Investment & Business Center, USA at (703) 370-8082. Fax: (703) 370-8083. E-mail: ibpusa3@gmail.com Global Business and Investment Info Databank - www.ibpus.com

NVOCCs as carrier parties) .[3] This was one of the compromises made by OSRA: in return for confidentiality, the parties would report their operations to the Commission, in order that it would continue to be able to monitor the industry for prohibited acts.

DuPont is concerned that the requirement would unnecessarily increase the Commission's workload. DuPont, 3. NITL comments that there are less burdensome ways for the Commission to obtain information about the status of a shipper party. For instance, they suggest that the Commission could request the information informally after the service contract has been executed. Further, AIFA comments that the proposed regulation would require the parties to make fine legal judgments. AIFA, 3.

Contrary to several comments, it appears that the certification does not create an unreasonable burden for shippers. Proposed § 530.7 (here renumbered § 530.6) was adopted nearly verbatim from the Commission's current regulation, 46 CFR § 514.7(e) (1) , which requires the shipper party to certify its status. Original § 514.7(e) (1) had the same intent, namely to enable the Commission to monitor service contract arrangements for discrimination. Rather than increasing any burden on the parties to service contracts, or creating additional workload for the Commission, § 530.6(a) continues to enable the Commission to monitor service contracts for trends in practices and to guard against OSRA's prohibition on refusals to deal and on concerted unjust discrimination based on shipper status. The burden on the shipper signatory is also minimal. Contrary to the comments of AIFA, determining the shipper's status should be relatively simple and shippers have been doing this since the rules were first implemented.

While NITL is correct that there are other ways for the Commission to obtain this information, the method promulgated herein is not unreasonable because the burden it places on service contract parties is light, and it is of high utility to the Commission, not only because of its intrinsic nature, but also because of the early point at which it is provided. Finally, contrary to the concerns of DuPont, the maintenance of this provision will not create an additional burden on the Commission.

Some commenters suggest that the certification provision should be deleted altogether or redrafted. APL, 3; AIFA, 3; NITL, 22. NITL suggests the proposed regulation be revised to read as follows:

If the shipper contract party or any affiliate or member of a shippers' association entitled to access a service contract is an NVOCC, it shall sign and certify on the signature page of the service contract that its status under the service contract is that of an NVOCC. NITL, 22.

With respect to the first purpose of the proposed regulation, NITL and DuPont incorrectly assert that OSRA prohibits discriminatory treatment and refusal to deal towards NVOCCs only. As the shippers' comments correctly point out, smaller shippers which negotiate for service contracts through their shippers' associations are also entitled to such protection, as are all shippers, regardless of whether they are beneficial cargo interests, their representatives, or unaffiliated groups of shippers. OSRA prohibits discrimination and refusals to deal based on anything other than valid transportation factors (such as volumes) and the regulation as proposed intends to guard against such discrimination, prohibited by section 10(b) (10) of the Act.

The comments of several shippers' organizations point to the competing congressional mandates with which the Commission must craft these regulations: to allow parties to negotiate their commercial arrangements with as little interference as possible while maintaining its ability to monitor for discrimination and refusals to deal in violation of section 10. AISA, 5. AISA's comments remind the Commission that with confidential contracts, smaller shippers will be

For additional analytical, business and investment opportunities information, please contact Global Investment & Business Center, USA at (703) 370-8082. Fax: (703) 370-8083. E-mail: ibpusa3@gmail.com Global Business and Investment Info Databank - www.ibpus.com

disadvantaged and will, therefore, rely more on the Commission's oversight. AISA, 3. AISA asserts that the Act places an affirmative obligation upon carriers to negotiate and deal in good faith with shippers' associations and to offer them competitively equivalent contracts to those offered to beneficial shippers for the same volumes and goods between the same ports. AISA, 5.

AISA asserts that OSRA requires the Commission to establish mechanisms by which it and the public can discover such discrimination, and point out that filing and publishing essential terms of confidential contracts, as well as establishing a listing on the Commission's website is only a first step in the right direction. AISA, 3-6. AISA is disappointed with the proposed regulations because they fail to be strong enough to enforce section 10 anti-discrimination prohibitions. Further, they allege that the Commission is wrong in saying the law does not continue to prohibit carrier actions which unreasonably discriminate against small- and medium-sized shippers and shippers' associations. AISA, 3-6.

One commenter urges the Commission to acknowledge Congress' intent that anti-discrimination protections be strengthened and expanded as they apply to shippers' associations and OTIs. BSA, 13-15. NCBFAA believes OSRA directs the Commission to concentrate on discrimination based on a shipper's status as an OTI. NCBFAA, 1. For AImpSA, OSRA's direction to the Commission is to concentrate on status-based discrimination against shippers' associations or OTIs. AImpSA, 2-3. While NCBFAA is concerned about the possibility of collusive, discriminatory and anti-competitive behavior by carrier agreements, it recognizes that Congress intended to allow parties to service contracts to behave like private contract parties in a deregulated environment. NCBFAA, 1. NCBFAA, also, however, recognizes a need for the service contract regulations to be sufficient for Commission oversight in order to combat discriminatory practices such as those which have been carried out by the carriers in the past. NCBFAA, 1.

The opposition of some shipper parties, especially NVOCCs, to this provision is puzzling. Shippers should be willing to assist the Commission in its enforcement of the Act's prohibition on discrimination against them due to their status and refusals to deal because of shipper status. Indeed, the comments of shippers' associations (BSA, AISA, AImpSA) and OTIs (NCBFAA) urge the Commission to adopt strong regulations to protect against shipper status-based discrimination by carriers. This provision serves the simultaneous functions of giving shipper parties to contracts an additional reminder of the capacity in which they may act (e.g., not as an "agent," "broker" or "freight forwarder") while also decreasing the need for investigations which may unnecessarily burden shippers.

One commenter urges the Commission to establish a separate docket to address regulations to specifically guard against section 10 violations. AImpSA, 2-3. We decline, and point out that the regulations in all the areas that the Commission regulates were drafted with an eye toward our responsibilities in this regard. There is no need for another, separate rulemaking to address this issue at this point. The certification requirement has served the Commission well in the past and appears to continue to be a useful tool for monitoring without being an intrusion into commercial contract negotiations or an overly burdensome reporting requirement. Whether other regulations will be necessary will be a question better answered after the Commission has had some experience with and insight into the way the industry will develop in the new era of confidential service contracting.

BSA requests that the Commission give notice to the shipping public of the extent to which shippers' associations can rely on DOJ safe harbor guidelines for unaffiliated shippers entering joint contracts. BSA, 2-5. The Commission, in Docket 92-31, revised its definition of "shippers' association" and found that "such associations between or among shippers will remain subject to anti-trust laws." 57 Fed. Reg. 49665, 49666 (Nov. 3, 1992) . Presumably, therefore, shippers

For additional analytical, business and investment opportunities information, please contact Global Investment & Business Center, USA at (703) 370-8082. Fax: (703) 370-8083. E-mail: ibpusa3@gmail.com Global Business and Investment Info Databank - www.ibpus.com

operating in informal groups would be similarly subject to the antitrust laws, and could rely on DOJ guidelines for their behavior.

APL complains that the proposed regulation's requirement that carriers identify NVOCC parties and determine that they are compliant is "overkill." APL, 3. The provision, they complain, unreasonably delegates the policing of NVOCCs to ocean common carriers. APL, 3. APL offers that there are other effective and less burdensome ways of ensuring that NVOCC members of shippers' associations are compliant: for instance, requiring an association in the contract to warrant that any of its NVOCC members are compliant and providing evidence of such compliance. APL recommends that § 530.6(b) be deleted or redrafted by changing the word "signing" to "implementing" and deleting "or an affiliate or member of a shippers' association". APL, 3.

Section 530.6(b) as proposed was intended to ensure that carriers do not violate section 10(b) (11) of the Act, which forbids the knowing or willful acceptance of cargo for the account of unbonded or unlicensed NVOCCs. Similar to the benefit to shippers provided by § 530.6(a) , § 530.6(b) also inures to the benefit of the carrier party, as certification of its belief that the NVOCC with whom it contracts is in compliance with Commission regulation may assist in establishing it did not act knowingly and/or willfully if later the Commission finds the NVOCC was not properly licensed or bonded.

Furthermore, the burden on the carrier signatory has been significantly reduced, as carriers will now have the ability to confirm an NVOCC's bond status by checking the Commission's website (see, 46 CFR § 515.27(d)) and its license by reference to an NVOCC's letterhead, as required by 46 CFR § 515.31(b) . Finally, this provision does not appear to intrude into the negotiations between contract parties, as parties generally would already have a desire to either assert their status, or have good commercial reasons for avoiding entering into business arrangements with a non-compliant entity. Proposed § 530.6, entitled "service contracts with NVOCCs" was seen to be repetitive of the certification language of final § 530.6(b) . That section is therefore deleted, and the remaining sections are renumbered. For the foregoing reasons, the provision is adopted as it appeared in the notice of proposed rulemaking, except that it is renumbered as § 530.6.

§ 530.7 -- DUTY TO LABOR ORGANIZATIONS

The proposed regulation included a definition of "reasonable period of time" by which a carrier must respond to a labor organization's request. § 530.7(a) (2) . This definition was crafted with sensitivity toward labor organizations' interests in knowing about cargo that is due to arrive in port before it arrives, so that the movement of that cargo may be "claimed" as labor work.

However, labor interests contend that the definition is inadequate as it will not ensure a timely response, which they claim should be within 24 hours of receipt of request. ILA, 4. If the carrier is unable to respond, labor argues, the regulation should specify that it shall so state and explain. ILA, 4.

Carrier interests, on the other hand, object to any definition of the term, and assert that it should be determined on a case-by-case basis. OCWG, 21-22. Several argue that the Commission contravenes OSRA by defining the term at all. One maintains that implicit in the concept of "reasonable" is the phrase "under the circumstances." APL, 3. If Congress had intended the term to be defined on anything other than a case-by-case basis, it would have defined the term itself in OSRA. APL, 3. It is arbitrary, they argue, for the Commission to fix a reasonable time for reporting. Furthermore, consideration should be given to the carrier's situation and reasonable ability to respond to the request. APL, 3; Sea-Land, 6. Sea-Land asserts that because the

For additional analytical, business and investment opportunities information, please contact Global Investment & Business Center, USA at (703) 370-8082. Fax: (703) 370-8083. E-mail: ibpusa3@gmail.com Global Business and Investment Info Databank - www.ibpus.com

Commission determines what is reasonable for other matters (e.g., Sections 6(g) ; 10(b) (8) ,(9) ,(10) ; 10(c) (8) ; and 10(d) (1)) on a case-by-case basis, it should do the same in this context. Sea-Land, 7.

The carriers argue that fixing a reasonable period of time is unfair because it gives the labor organization the exclusive control of the timetable in that it is labor who starts the clock with the request. APL, 3; Sea-Land, 6. Also, the comments urge, the requests might be repetitious or unclear, or the labor organization could inundate the carrier with hundreds of requests at a time in which it could not possibly respond in the time allotted by this definition. Sea-Land, 6.

One carrier comments that because service contracts run for terms of many months, no significant union work will be irrevocably lost if the information is not acted on within a matter of hours or days. APL, 3. This assertion is in direct contradiction to the emphatic comments by the ILWU and the ILA that time is most certainly of the essence in these matters. Another carrier is concerned that imposing a specific time limit may be inconsistent with obligations under collective bargaining agreements or labor laws. Sea-Land, 7.

It appears that the approach taken by the Commission in the proposed rule will achieve a workable compromise and protect both carrier and labor interests. But we note the objections of the carriers that the definition of "reasonable period of time" as two or four days would not appear to recognize that the reasonableness of any response may depend on the circumstances. Requests may, for example, be made in large batches, or at a time when a two or four day response is not reasonably achievable. It is also unknown at this time how often labor organizations will invoke these provisions, and how simple or burdensome it will be for the carriers to supply the appropriate response. To this end, the Commission amends the definition to include the word "ordinarily." The definition provides the sense, at this pre-implementation stage, of what should normally constitute a reasonable, good faith response to a legitimate request. Any complaints of deviations from these standards resulting in harm to labor organizations would be adjudged in the context of the particular circumstances and the Commission's overall experience with this new provision of the statute.

The Commission is not persuaded by the arguments of the carriers that no definition of reasonable time is appropriate. OSRA is replete with general guidelines and standards for which the Commission is expected to supply more detailed qualifications of elements such as time and dollar amounts. Here, the amended rule provides only general guidelines of what the Commission expects will meet the general standard, in hopes that such guidance will help obviate the need for more formal complaints and procedures. As to the carrier concern that the time limit contravenes collective bargaining agreements or labor laws, it is impossible for the Commission to respond in a meaningful way, as it has no direct involvement in administering either.

Labor organizations criticize other provisions of this section as falling short of the mark. ILA, 1; ILWU, 1-2. They recommend that the Commission add a requirement that a response be adequate as well as timely. The required response, they argue, should include supporting documentation, such as bills of lading, delivery orders, and other non-privileged documents. This is a determination that the Commission must make on a case-by-case basis, as the text of the statute requires only that the response state "whether" the carrier is responsible. While one floor remark by Senator Hutchison alludes to the requirement that further documentation be produced,[(4)] it is unclear what the Commission's role in the disclosure of this information may be and therefore, the Commission declines to assume the authority to impose a requirement that particular documents be produced.

For additional analytical, business and investment opportunities information, please contact Global Investment & Business Center, USA at (703) 370-8082. Fax: (703) 370-8083. E-mail: ibpusa3@gmail.com Global Business and Investment Info Databank - www.ibpus.com

ILWU and ILA comments recommend that a particular Commission investigator be assigned in advance to all of the investigations which might arise out of complaints of non-compliance with this section. The ILWU suggests that the regulations include a requirement that requests for information be concurrently filed with the Commission to help avoid disputes over whether a given response was made within a reasonable period of time. ILWU, 5-6. Then, the ILWU suggests, the regulation should require that the Commission shall promptly solicit the carrier's written position on the complaint and conduct an administrative investigation on the merits of the complaint. The recommended procedure further includes the requirement that the Commission's investigator issue a report within thirty days, including findings to recommend a formal proceeding or dismissal and penalties. ILA, 5; ILWU, 1,2.

There is no requirement that such a procedure be contained in the regulations, and no indication from the legislative history of OSRA that it was the intent of Congress for the Commission to use any procedures other than its current complaint procedures to address violations of this section of the Act. An early version of the bill, which was to become OSRA, did include specific procedures which the Commission would undertake to enforce the responsiveness of ocean common carriers to labor requests for information. The April 3, 1998 version of S. 414 included a different version of section 8(c) (4) and included a section 8(c) (5) , which read:

(4) Disclosure of Certain Unpublished Terms. -- A party to a collective-bargaining agreement may petition the Commission for the disclosure of any service contract terms not required to be published by paragraph (3) which that party considers to be in violation of that agreement. The petition shall include evidence demonstrating that

(A) a specific ocean common carrier is a party to a collective-bargaining agreement with the petitioner;

(B) the ocean common carrier may be violating the terms and conditions of that agreement; and

(C) the alleged violation involves the moment [sic] of cargo subject to this Act.

(5) Action By Commission. -- The Commission, after reviewing a petition under paragraph (4) , the evidence provided with the petition, and the filed service contracts of the carrier named in the petition, may disclose to the petitioner only such unpublished terms of that carrier's service contracts that the Commission reasonably believes may constitute a violation of the collective-bargaining agreement. The Commission may not disclose any unpublished service contract terms with respect to a collective-bargaining agreement term or condition determined by the Commission to be in violation of this Act.

Cong. Rec. S3194 (daily ed., April 3, 1998) .

Between the version of April 3, 1998 and the bill as finally adopted by the Senate on April 21, 1998, this section underwent significant change. It is clear, therefore, that Congress specifically considered requiring the Commission's involvement in disclosing confidential carrier information to labor organizations. In the final analysis, Congress rejected such Commission involvement, and chose instead to minimize the role of the Commission in implementing the objectives of this section of the statute. The Commission indicated in the NPR that it "expects that aggrieved labor organizations will use existing Commission processes in the event of noncompliance by a carrier. The Commission would entertain proposals for more specific and stringent rules if the existing standards and procedures prove inadequate in practice." 63 Fed. Reg. 71064. We are hopeful that labor organizations and carriers will operate diligently and in good faith in exercising their rights and responsibilities in implementing this section of the Act. The Commission expects not to

For additional analytical, business and investment opportunities information, please contact Global Investment & Business Center, USA at (703) 370-8082. Fax: (703) 370-8083. E-mail: ibpusa3@gmail.com Global Business and Investment Info Databank - www.ibpus.com

have to initiate programs or promulgate particularized procedures to ensure what should be the routine and noncontentious transmittal of information. We reiterate, however, that the Commission will revisit these issues if experience under the provision suggests such a need. Therefore, the proposed rule in § 530.7 will be finalized, except that the term "ordinarily" is added to the definition of "reasonable period of time" in § 530.7 (a) (2) , and the placement of the provisions defining relevant terms have been re-organized for clarity.

§ 530.8 -- FILING PROVISIONS

The proposed regulation requires service contracts to be filed in their entirety (except for signatures) in a system which would be modified from the current ATFI essential terms publication system. The proposed regulations make no provision for waiver, transition, or other filing options. As stated in the supplemental information to the proposed rule, the Commission proposed that, "due to the volume of service contract filings . . . expect[ed] after May 1, 1999, adoption of an electronic, as opposed to paper-based, system appears to be the most practical approach." 63 Fed. Reg. at 71063. Further, the Commission noted that while the "only viable approach to implementing an electronic system at this juncture would be to create a system adapted from the Commission's currently used filing system for Essential Terms of service contracts," it also sought comment on other "approaches to establishing a new system . . . treating the proposed system as a transitional solution." Id. Furthermore, comment on continuing the paper filing of service contracts was specifically requested. Id.

The comments generally oppose the use of any modified ATFI system for filing, even as an optional system. Seaboard; CENSA; USCIB; NITL; AIFA; OCWG; P&O; Conagra; and Sea-Land. Several commenters assert that using ATFI (as modified) is inconsistent with the deregulatory thrust of OSRA, and the regulations should allow for filing by any electronic means which "meet the OSRA objective." CENSA, 1-2; Sea-Land, 3; NITL, 5-8. Two comments assert that because Congress expressly rejected continuing ATFI for tariffs, it could not have intended to continue its use for service contract filing. NITL, 5-6; Sea-Land, 3.

NITL urges that the Commission, rather than "clinging to an outmoded electronic system" for filing common carrier tariffs, and imposing that system on a very different contracting environment, give up its reliance on ATFI in the face of systems for communication that are changing for the better on a daily basis. NITL 5-8. Sea-Land contends that the Commission's assertion that ATFI is the "only viable approach" is incorrect and that there are other viable approaches, as evidenced by other agencies which have adopted electronic filing systems using "off the shelf" software. Sea-Land, 3.

Generally, CMA and other commenters are concerned that the Appendix requirements are too detailed and would restrict the freedom of parties to negotiate terms. CMA, 2; NITL, 14-15; DuPont, 4. NITL urges the Commission to delete the Appendix entirely because it is completely unworkable, unnecessarily burdensome, very costly and because there is no statutory basis for its requirements. NITL, 14. Further, NITL is concerned that the risks of contract rejection, and its associated costs and penalties, are heightened by the inclusion of so many technical details. NITL, 14.

Two comments object to the regulation as proposed because it appears that it was designed for the administrative ease of the agency without regard to the convenience to the parties. NITL, 5-8; OCWG. 3-4. While electronic filing is the preferred long-term approach, OCWG comments that the proposal to use ATFI would impose substantial burdens on carriers. OCWG, 3-4. OCWG objects to using ATFI because, like CENSA, it believes that the proposal would require filers to create two documents: one for the commercial transaction, and another for FMC filing. CENSA, 1.

For additional analytical, business and investment opportunities information, please contact Global Investment & Business Center, USA at (703) 370-8082. Fax: (703) 370-8083. E-mail: ibpusa3@gmail.com Global Business and Investment Info Databank - www.ibpus.com

These concerns appear somewhat justified. While in the past filers have been required to file an "essential terms publication" in ATFI format, the Commission concludes that applying ATFI-like restrictions on the entirety of a filed service contract may not fully benefit both filers and the Commission. In the ATFI-based system, filers may be required to either re-format their commercial agreement or draft it in ATFI format in the first place, or the system may make it difficult for filers to provide the Commission with the true and complete terms of the contract.

On the other hand, several commenters support the draft regulation's proposal to modify and utilize ATFI. ETM; PTCB; AISA; and NCBFAA. Others accept the modification of ATFI provided that there is at least one alternative means of filing. JUSEFC; COSCO. JUSEFC finds the Commission's proposal to use ATFI "logical." JUSEFC, 6. NCBFAA comments that the detailed filing requirements of the proposed regulation (and Appendix A) are required if the Commission is to be able to police prohibited conduct. NCBFAA, 1. NCBFAA asserts that the industry will not be able to monitor for prohibited conduct because public essential terms will be limited. NCBFAA, 2. Furthermore, NCBFAA presents, as indication that this was the intent of Congress, that while OSRA specifically eliminates tariff filing, it also retains the requirement that service contracts be filed with the Commission. NCBFAA, 2.

Other commenters oppose any justification of the filing requirements based on section 10(b) (2) monitoring. NITL, 5-8. They suggest rather than imposing strict filing requirements, that the Commission determine whether carriers are providing service in accordance with the rates in their service contracts in the same way that shippers and carriers themselves will monitor each other's contract compliance, namely by consulting the terms of the contracts, and comparing those terms to the actual billed amounts. NITL, 5-8. Similarly, Sea-Land comments that the Commission's interest in oversight for unjust discrimination is limited to protecting ports, shippers' associations and OTIs due to their status and that carriers are relieved by the Act of any affirmative obligations towards shippers. Sea-Land, 5-6. It asserts that the Commission's enforcement of section 10 does not require continuation of ATFI in any form. Sea-Land, 5.

P&O complains that continuing the use of ATFI is not a secure option because it will require third party compilers and filers who will have access to confidential information. P&O, 3-4. BSA also worries that the proposal to "grandfather" previously approved software might not ensure confidentiality. BSA, 6. It requests clarification from the Commission on the ability of the proposed system to ensure rate confidentiality, and urges the use of new software and systems which would provide total assurance of confidentiality. BSA, 6-7. BSA recommends that the Commission draft specific regulations to address technical qualifications which software must meet to ensure and guarantee to shippers that service contract information will be confidential during filing, and that the Commission also draft regulations which include penalties for violating the security of the websites and computer systems which contain service contract information ("hacking") . BSA, 8.

Similar to the preceding comments expressing concern for modernity and the ability to upgrade any system based on ATFI, BSA suggests that the Commission require that all common carrier websites are "Y2K" compliant. BSA, 6-7. As the internet is a communication line, and digital, this is not a concern for filing.

With regard to the registration requirements in the proposed regulation, PTCB urges the Commission to allow current ATFI registrants to maintain their current registrations and organization records without having to re-register. PTCB, 3. PTCB agrees that requiring batch filers to re-register for new log-ons and passwords is acceptable, but requests clarification that the organization number will remain the same, thus avoiding a requirement that filing services' clients amend their organizational records in order to re-authorize. PTCB, 4.

For additional analytical, business and investment opportunities information, please contact Global Investment & Business Center, USA at (703) 370-8082. Fax: (703) 370-8083. E-mail: ibpusa3@gmail.com Global Business and Investment Info Databank - www.ibpus.com

The Commission has directed its Office of Information Management ("OIRM") to allow filers who intend to use either the internet-based system (discussed infra) or the dial-ups system to apply for registration and obtain log-on IDs and passwords prior to May 1, 1999 in order that they may be ready on May 1 for filing on that date. Organization numbers will remain the same in the service contract database. OIRM will notify via U.S. mail all presently- registered organization record holders to ensure that the individual will remain the same. If the "org. holder" will not be the same individual, a registration form will be included in the letter for the recipient to respond regarding who would "own" the organizational I.D. Any other log-ons will have to re-register.

Also, PTCB requests that the Commission continue, as is currently the case in ATFI, the method by which delegation of authority to file is done, namely by revising the organizational record. PTCB, 4. PTCB points out a deficiency in proposed Form FMC-83: it does not have a place to indicate delegation. PTCB, 4. Finally, PTCB requests that the Commission delete the requirement that individuals only (as opposed to organizations) are registered for filing because this unnecessary limitation is time-consuming and expensive. PTCB, 4.

The Commission must deny PTCB's request to allow log-on IDs and passwords to be granted to organizations, not individuals, due to security concerns and the requirements of the Computer Security Act. Therefore, the requirement that individuals, rather than organizations will be the registered filers will continue. Filing authority and delegation will be indicated on the Registration Form, FMC-83.

Four of the comments opposing the proposed regulation's adaptation of the ATFI system for service contract filings offer alternatives. Seaboard; OCWG; NITL; and P&O. Seaboard, OCWG, and P&O propose that the Commission allow filing in a generic word processing format as an attachment via electronic mail ("e-mail") . Seaboard, 1. OCWG suggests the Commission adopt a system based on commercially available software already in common use in the industry, but does not suggest precisely what that may be. OCWG, 4. NITL and OCWG offer generally that there are electronic alternatives to the proposed regulation which include filing via e-mail, internet, and diskettes. NITL, 7; OCWG, 8. OCWG proposes that the only technical requirements which would arise from using "off-the-shelf" software would be the assignment of user identification codes and security. OCWG, 4. Sea-Land recommends that filers be allowed to file their service contracts via the internet on a confidential site established by the Commission or via diskette, which apparently would be mailed to the Commission. Sea-Land, 4. They assert that this would be simple, flexible, inexpensive, complete, accessible and accurate and would fulfill all statutory requirements. Sea-Land, 4. Finally, while DuPont praises the Commission's desire to use modern electronic means, it recommends that the Commission approach the U.S. Customs Service to ascertain whether a joint system, or at least a compatible system, could be created to serve both agencies and their "customers." DuPont, 5.

NITL recommends that the Commission revise proposed § 530.8(a) to read:

Authorized persons pursuant to section 530.5 of this part shall file with the Commission electronically or in paper format a true and complete copy of every service contract before any cargo moves pursuant to that service contract. Service contracts filed electronically may be submitted via electronic mail, the internet, or on diskettes using software that is compatible with the Commission's computer systems.

NITL, 14-15.

P&O offers the most detailed suggestion. P&O suggests the Commission adopt an electronic filing system which allows the carrier/filer to send the entire text of the service contract via e-mail

For additional analytical, business and investment opportunities information, please contact Global Investment & Business Center, USA at (703) 370-8082. Fax: (703) 370-8083. E-mail: ibpusa3@gmail.com Global Business and Investment Info Databank - www.ibpus.com

as an attachment to a Commission-designated e-mail address, which would be based on the filer's current organizational record. P&O, 2-3. Upon receipt of the service contract, P&O suggests, the Commission then open a directory for each carrier into which it downloads the service contract and therefore would be able to organize the information according to its own needs. P&O, 3. This information could be easily organized because all word-processing programs are searchable. P&O, 3. P&O analogizes the management of this system to the Commission's current maintenance of a list of filed agreements, which is done on a WordPerfect file. P&O, 3. Finally, P&O recommends that the Commission use passwords for confidentiality. P&O, 3.

Other federal agencies' approaches

Several comments urge the Commission to follow the examples of other Federal government agencies in crafting its approach to electronic service contracts filing, namely the Federal Communication Commission ("FCC") and the Surface Transportation Board ("STB") . NITL, 7; OCWG, 8. It appears that, after review of the approaches of these agencies, as well as that of the Federal Energy Regulatory Commission ("FERC") , the Commission is still faced with limitations of time and resources which might make the adoption of one of these systems inappropriate for the FMC.

1. Federal Communications Commission
2. Under the Telecommunications Act of 1996, the FCC receives tariff filings for its common carrier tariffs via its website. This process was developed over two years. The FCC requires that tariff publications be filed in both paper copy and on diskette, subject to various format requirements.[(5)] Filers must submit a cover letter on paper with the diskette and changes (amendments) to the tariff must be made by re-filing the entire tariff on a new diskette, with the changed material, and indicating the changes. The FCC also receives filing via its internet homepage. This filing system was designed and is managed by a private contractor.

2. Surface Transportation Board

One commenter suggested that because the STB "requires the filing of pleadings and reports in electronic form, which permits those agencies to analyze filings electronically," that modifying ATFI is not the only feasible approach available to the Commission. NITL, 7. A review of the STB regulations on filing methods, however, indicates that the STB has not reached an electronic panacea for filing. For the filing of summaries of railroad contracts for the transportation of agricultural products, the STB requires that "two copies of each contract summary" be filed. 49 CFR § 1313.4(a) (1) . There does not appear to be an electronic option for this type of filing. For the filing of tariffs for the transportation of cargo by or with a water carrier in a noncontiguous domestic trade, the STB requires that "tariffs shall be printed on paper not larger than 8 ½ x 11 inches." 49 CFR § 1312.4(b) . Filers for these tariffs do have the option of electronic filing; however, that option is accomplished through the FMC's ATFI system. 49 CFR § 1312.17. Obviously, this option will be eliminated with the removal of the ATFI system, and there appears to be no contemplation by the STB for the implementation of a new method for receiving these filings electronically after ATFI is discarded.

The notice requirements, on the other hand, under STB regulations may be achieved electronically, but only where there is agreement between the parties. See, e.g., 49 CFR §§ 1300.2(b) ; 1300.4(b) ; 1305.2(b) ,(c) ; 1305.3; and 1305.4(a) ,(b) . These notice requirements are between carrier and shipper and are not official filings.

3. Federal Energy Regulatory Commission

For additional analytical, business and investment opportunities information, please contact Global Investment & Business Center, USA at (703) 370-8082. Fax: (703) 370-8083. E-mail: ibpusa3@gmail.com Global Business and Investment Info Databank - www.ibpus.com

While none of the comments referred to the approach of FERC, the Commission has investigated FERC's approach to the crafting of a viable electronic filing system. FERC issued a Notice of Inquiry on May 19, 1998 (Docket No. PL98-1-000, 63 Fed. Reg. 27529-27533) requesting comments on various issues which arise with the implementation of electronic filing, including formats, citations, signatures, methods of transmission, confidentiality, security, attestation and service. FERC held a conference on electronic filing on October 22, 1998. FERC has since taken a broader, agency-wide approach for completely re-engineering its methods for accepting filings and managing documents. For the present, the official copies of filed documents are still in paper form. FERC staff manually scans those documents which are not filed electronically (about 120,000 pages per month) but hopes to achieve a system which would provide for hyper-linking all public filings in a particular docket to the docket sheet so the user has the ability to select a document on the docket sheet list and go to the full text of the document immediately.

Due to the general response in opposition to adapting the ATFI filing system for service contract filings, the Commission will make available an option which will address most of the commenters' concerns that the proposed regulations would be too rigid, cumbersome and costly. Interactive internet filing of service contracts with the Commission will be provided, and while the dial-up system will be available, the Commission expects to phase it out as soon as possible, but certainly no later than the end of Fiscal Year 1999.

Specific details on internet-based filing will be made available on the Commission's website (http://www.fmc.gov) when final development and testing is complete. This option will provide for interactive internet filing of service contracts via the Commission's homepage. Individuals filing service contracts will presumably already have filed Form FMC-1, registering them as tariff publishers, and will have been assigned an organization number. Upon review, the Commission will provide prospective service contract filers with a user ID and password. A service contract filer will sign on to the Commission's website and provide its user ID and password. A screen will then indicate several options (e.g., filing a single contract, amendment or batches of contracts or amendments) in addition to detailed filing instructions. A single initial service contract will be filed by providing certain basic information such as a carrier contract number (which will enable linking of amendments to the initial contract) , effective date, organization number, and the location of the service contract file which will be uploaded to the Commission upon activating the screen's "submit" button. Amendment filings will be done in the same manner, with the addition of a filer-provided service contract amendment number. Batch filings will require similar information for each contract, but will enable the filer to submit more than one contract per session. Finally, the Commission foresees assessing user fees at a later date, as the Commission gains experience and the details of the system are completed.

Therefore, § 530.8 and Appendix A to this part, in which the options for filing are detailed, are accordingly revised to reflect the addition of internet-based filing.

§ 530.8 and APPENDIX A -- TRANSITION ISSUES

Several commenters request that the Commission accept paper filings of service contracts as well as electronic filings for a transitional period. COSCO, 1-2; CMA, 3; JUSEFC, 5-7; OCWG, 6 ; P&O, 4; NITL,7; DuPont, 5. OCWG recommends that such a transition period be at least one year. OCWG, 6 n.1. OCWG also asserts that there is no need to have a system in place on May 1, 1999. OCWG, 5. P&O also suggests that if the Commission needs more time to put an electronic system into place, it can receive paper filings. P&O, 4. Only BSA and the filing services (PTCB and ETM) support the immediate adoption of electronic-only filing. BSA, 5.

For additional analytical, business and investment opportunities information, please contact Global Investment & Business Center, USA at (703) 370-8082. Fax: (703) 370-8083. E-mail: ibpusa3@gmail.com Global Business and Investment Info Databank - www.ibpus.com

A satisfactory response to the commenters' general opposition to the modification of the Automated Tariff Filing Information ("ATFI") system and their general support for electronic filing is achieved by the Commission's determination to offer an alternative filing method to the modified ATFI filing which is internet filing (herein referred to as "internet-based" or "option 1") . This option offers filers great ease and flexibility, while allowing the Commission to receive the entirety of the contract information and to organize those filings for the Commission's monitoring and enforcement duties. Furthermore, most of the commenters' concerns about the rigidity and the cumbersome nature of the dial-up filing system are removed with the implementation of this filing method.

While most comments oppose any transitional system which does not include a paper option, the flexibility of the new system will make it extremely easy to file. Filers need only have created their contract on one of several word-processing systems and have access to the internet. It is not unreasonable to expect that carriers have access to this equipment, or that if they do not, they may choose to out source the filing. Removal of the requirement that they use a dial-up system appears to enable all carriers to do their own filing, if they wish to do so, thus removing any confidentiality concerns they expressed in the comments regarding the use of third party filing services.

The Commission intends to allow the filing of service contracts which have an effective date of May 1, 1999 or later in advance of May 1, 1999, as soon as filing systems are ready. The Commission contemplates that the systems could be ready in the week prior to May 1, 1999. The Commission will issue further advisory notices of the status of the availability of the revised filing systems as information becomes available.

Again, due to the expense of maintaining the dial-up service, the Commission expects to phase it out as soon as possible, but certainly by the end of FY 1999. Finally, the Commission will request further industry input, if necessary, as it refines the internet-based system.

§ 530.8(c) and 530.12 -- CROSS REFERENCING

Two comments generally voice support for the regulation allowing for the cross-referencing to tariffs and general rules filing as part of service contract register. BSA, 16; JUSEFC, 7. BSA recommends that the Commission make available on its FMC website the general rules tariff of any carrier or conference and periodically inspect that tariff to determine that changes made by amendments have been made, and thereby ensure that the shipping public will be able to obtain necessary information regarding applicable items (e.g. rules for hazardous cargo) . BSA, 16.

P&O comments that the proposed regulation's prohibition against cross-referencing has no support in OSRA and no reasonable regulatory purpose, and that as such it should be withdrawn and the regulations should allow cross-referencing to a carrier's own tariff as well as its conference tariffs. P&O, 8. NITL and OCWG, as a means to allow greater commercial flexibility, both support revision of § 530.8(c) (2) to allow cross-referencing not only to tariffs but also to "widely available public information." OCWG, 19; NITL, 13. OCWG recommends that the Commission add to § 530.8(c) (2) the phrase, "or unless those terms are available in a regularly published and readily available public source commonly known in the industry." OCWG, 18-19. NITL also believes that this change will ensure that the Commission could obtain all of the contract's terms. NITL, 13.

The Commission, in an effort to make filing less burdensome for carriers, but while ensuring that it had the entire contents of, or access to, the service contract terms, proposed that carriers may "cross-reference" their own tariff publications or their conference tariff publications in their filed service contracts. This provision was intended to allow carriers to refer to rules of general applicability (free time and demurrage, bunkering rates, currency matters, etc.) for the "boilerplate" or terms which appear in all their contracts. Further, the Commission recognized that it was Congress' intent, by lifting the requirement that tariffs be filed with the Commission, to allow parties to service contracts more freedom and flexibility in their commercial arrangements. For those reasons, the proposed rule, originally numbered § 530.9(c) (2) , was drafted to permit filed service contracts to refer to terms outside the four corners of the filed service contract, but only if they are contained in the carrier's or conference's tariff publication. P&O appears to have misread the proposed rules as not allowing any cross-referencing whatsoever. This was not the intent of the proposed rules. Rather, the regulation would have allowed cross-referencing, but only to matter contained in a published tariff of the carrier or conference of which it was a member.

However, in response to comments that allowing cross-referencing only to published tariff matter would unduly stifle the parties' contract terms, the Commission has decided to allow cross-reference to a "publication widely available to the public and well known within the industry." § 530.8(c) (2) . The Commission wishes to stress, however, that exact terms of the contract must be determinable and certain, in keeping with the requirements of the Act. In response to a comment by COSCO that this approach would undermine the confidentiality of the contract terms, we point out that any term, except of course published essential terms, can be kept confidential by inclusion in a general rules filing or by filing in the text of the contract itself. The Commission is confident that this approach will satisfy both the concerns of filers for confidentiality, and the requirement that the complete contract be filed.

§ 530.8(b) (9) -- NAMING AFFILIATES

AISA believes that proposed § 530.8(b) (9) should be amended to remove the requirement that shippers' associations name all of their members. They assert that this requirement is not mandated by any change made by OSRA and is contrary to current Commission regulation and policy which requires only such naming if the contract specifically excludes or includes specific members. AISA, 7. AISA is concerned that such disclosure would give carriers blackmail potential, as was found in Fact Finding 15, and Docket 91-1. AISA, 8.

AISA suggests the provision be revised to read as follows:

(9) The legal names and business addresses of the contract parties; the legal names of affiliates entitled to access the contract, except that in the case of a contract entered into by a shippers' association, individual members need not be named unless the contract includes or excludes specific members; the names, titles and addresses of the representatives signing the contract for the parties; and the date upon which the service contract was signed. An agreement service contract must identify the FMC Agreement Number(s) under which the service contract is filed. Carriers, conferences, and/or agreements which enter into contracts that include affiliates must in each instance either:[further unchanged].

AISA, 10.

CMA and NITL agree that reporting all names and addresses of shippers would be unnecessarily burdensome. CMA, 2; NITL, 12-13. NITL questions the purpose of this requirement. NITL, 12. If the Commission has a question about identity or location of a particular affiliate, NITL suggests that it obtain the information informally, on a case-by-case basis. Therefore, NITL argues, this requirement should be either deleted or the production period of 10 days should be increased. NITL, 12.

For additional analytical, business and investment opportunities information, please contact Global Investment & Business Center, USA at (703) 370-8082. Fax: (703) 370-8083. E-mail: ibpusa3@gmail.com Global Business and Investment Info Databank - www.ibpus.com

The deletion of the exception for shippers' associations being required to list all members in a service contract was a drafting oversight. We therefore re-insert the exception. However, the production period of 10 days was fully explored when the currently effective rule was put into place and this will be unchanged. OSRA makes no changes which would have an impact on this requirement.

APL complains that proposed § 530.8(b) (9) (ii) (identifying affiliates) is unintelligible, as it is unclear to whom the certification information must be provided. APL, 4. Further, it asserts that the last two sentences of the paragraph seem to be unrelated to clause 9(ii) , and requests clarification of the regulation. APL, 4.

Section 530.8(b) (9) as proposed reads, [the filed contract or amendment shall include]

(9) the legal names and business addresses of the contract parties; the legal names of affiliates entitled to access the contract; the names, titles and addresses of the representatives signing the contract for the parties; and the date upon which the service contract was signed. An agreement service contract must identify the FMC Agreement Number(s) under which the service contract is filed. Carriers, conferences and/or agreements which enter into contracts that include affiliates must in each instance either:

(i) list the affiliates' business addresses; or

(ii) certify that this information will be provided to the Commission upon request within ten (10) business days of such request. However, the requirements of this section do not apply to amendments to contracts that have been filed in accordance with the requirements of this section unless the amendment adds new parties or affiliates. Subsequent references in the contract to the contract parties shall be consistent with the first reference (e.g., (exact name) , "carrier," "shipper," or "association," etc.) ;

The Commission has re-drafted this provision for clarity, and these alterations should sufficiently address the reasonable concerns of the commenters.

GENERAL RULES FILINGS

COSCO and JUSEFC comment that allowing filers to make general rules filings or register filings is beneficial and will allow carriers to avoid repetitious filing. COSCO, 1; JUSEFC, 7. COSCO urges that publishing general rules in a tariff would be unacceptable because of the confidentiality issues and, further are concerned that such publication would require a thirty-day delay for the implementation of such rules. COSCO, 1.

ETM is concerned that the proposed regulations are unclear as to whether the Commission would allow for multiple service contract registers, and whether the registers are to be based on strict location group application or if overlapping scopes are allowed. ETM 2-3. Both ETM and PTCB foresee future problems if the Commission intends for the registers to be unique, such as by location group, without conflicting scopes or overlapping of scopes and does not allow different and overlapping scopes between registers. These problems may include amendment numbering, effective dates and contract terms. ETM 2-3; PTCB, 9.

Other comments disfavor allowing service contract registers as being unnecessary, burdensome and without meaningful regulatory purpose. P&O, 7. P&O further comments that using a service contract register for general rules filing seems contrary to the continued requirement to publish

For additional analytical, business and investment opportunities information, please contact Global Investment & Business Center, USA at (703) 370-8082. Fax: (703) 370-8083. E-mail: ibpusa3@gmail.com Global Business and Investment Info Databank - www.ibpus.com

essential terms where carriers have traditionally published, and they assume would continue to publish, their "boilerplate." P&O, 7.

The provision for a "general rules" filing is somewhat complicated by the fact that there may be two electronic filing systems in place. However, the Commission allowance of more liberal cross-referencing as well as a filing system which would accept the full text of the document in a word processing format (i.e., the same as the document signed by the parties) , this should relieve any burden on filers to file with the Commission anything other than the commercially agreed upon service contract, and should be adequate for the Commission to determine the terms of the contract with precision.

Other Term Requirements

Many of the system requirements and restrictions opposed in the comments diminish, if not completely disappear, with the addition of the option for a web-based filing system. First, PTCB's concern that ATFI will not accept port ranges disappears when filers file the full and original text of their contract on-line. PTCB, 5. The Commission has revised the regulations relating to the ATFI-based system to allow the filed matter+ to reflect the true agreement of the parties, to the maximum extent possible, given some inherent technical limitations of that system. The same is true for location and commodity descriptions: there would be no need to require NIMA or WPI locations, or to use the Harmonized Schedule for commodity descriptions in a "free text" system. OCWG, 21; P&O,8; NITL, 11; Conagra, 4. The Commission agrees that this unduly limited the parties in contracting and might cause confusion, and so has removed references to the US HTS, NIMA and WPI in the interim final rule.

For duration requirements, however, the Commission will continue to require service contracts to have specific effective and expiration dates. P&O, 7; NITL, 12. This is required by the statutory definition, that a service contract be "a commitment . . . over a fixed time period." Section 2(19) of the Act. See below, discussion on amendments for renewal of service contracts.

System requirements may also dictate the Commission's ability to allow filers to have access to their filed contracts for reviewing and auditing. PTCB, 3. At first blush, this may create confidentiality/security issues which are, at present, unforeseen. While the new system may give the filer the ability to review (on a read-only basis) its filings, the contents of a filed service contract may only be changed through a subsequent filed amendment or correction.

Finally, the Commission will make the addition of a provision which requires agreement-authorized service contracts to include the filed agreement number, § 530.8(d) (3) , and a provision for filers to inform the Commission where the statement of essential terms will be filed, § 530.8(d) (4) . For the reasons described above, the proposed regulation is revised to add the alternative system, remove unnecessary requirements and further simplify the filing procedures.

§ 530.9 -- NOTICES

Proposed § 530.9 (as renumbered) requires the carrier party to a service contract to notify the Commission within 10 days of the occurrence of certain events which affect the service contract. Those events include: correction ((a) (1)) ; cancellation ((a) (2)) ; termination not covered by the contract ((a) (3)) ; adjustment of accounts (by re-rating, liquidated damages, or otherwise under § 530.16) ((a) (4)) ; final settlement of any account adjusted as described in § 530.16 ((a) (5)) ; and any changes to the name of a basic contract party or the list of affiliates, including changes to legal names and business addresses, of any contract party entitled to receive or authorized to offer services under the contract ((a) (6)) .

For additional analytical, business and investment opportunities information, please contact Global Investment & Business Center, USA at (703) 370-8082. Fax: (703) 370-8083. E-mail: ibpusa3@gmail.com Global Business and Investment Info Databank - www.ibpus.com

Commenters suggest that there is no need for the Commission to receive notice of matters which are affected by amendment of the service contract because such amendments are filed with the Commission. NITL, 15. They suggest that the events which are enumerated in the proposed regulation are events that would require such amendment.

CMA and NITL believe that requiring changes to be reported within ten days is overly burdensome. CMA, 2. NITL suggests that if the proposal is not completely deleted, the time period should be lengthened to ninety days. NITL, 15-17. In the original regulation, found at § 514.7(g) (2) , notices were required to inform the Commission within thirty days of such events, and that period of time was based on the commercial practice for settlements of accounts.

The proposed rules reduced the time in which notification must be made from thirty to ten days based on an understanding that this would be in line with the speed at which these transactions now occur and that, therefore, no additional burden would be created for regulated entities. However, due to the commentary to the contrary, the Commission has decided to simply revert to the former requirement of thirty days.

NITL and DuPont comment that the requirements cover too many events, and are overly broad. DuPont asserts that such notices should only be required to be reported when events occur which affect the essential terms of the service contract. DuPont, 2. The proposed regulation would give the Commission power to limit, restrict and dictate the content of changes to service contracts. DuPont, 2.

Contrary to these assertions, the Commission will continue to require that all changes to a filed service contract must be filed with the Commission, not only those which effect the essential terms. The Commission must monitor the operation of service contracts for acts prohibited by the statute and simply cannot fulfill this duty if it is not guaranteed of having all the terms of service contracts within its jurisdiction.

The comments suggest the proposed regulation be altered to permit periodic reporting, perhaps on a semi-annual basis in a prescribed format (but not one which would restrict the parties right to mutually alter, modify or terminate) of routine changes which effect essential terms. DuPont, 2,3. CMA suggests this approach for changes to shipper affiliates only. CMA, 2.

Proposed § 530.9 (as renumbered) was adapted from original § 581.5(b) (52 Fed. Reg. at 23939, 23999) , which the Commission asserted was

necessary to enable the Commission to perform its contract surveillance role and ensure the terms of contracts are met. The notice requirements should not be burdensome since such information is exchanged in the normal course of business by the contract parties. Compliance with the notice requirement can be met merely by providing the Commission with a copy of whatever documents are exchanged between the parties under such circumstances.

The Commission continues to have such a surveillance role, which is made more important by the fact that service contracts will not be publicly available. Furthermore, the Commission particularly reminds filers that any changes to the public essential terms must be updated in the essential terms publication, regardless of such notification to the Commission. See § 530.12 (publication) .

NITL is correct not only that the Commission "would like" to receive notice, but that it must receive notice of changes in service contracts in order that it have the complete terms of the

For additional analytical, business and investment opportunities information, please contact Global Investment & Business Center, USA at (703) 370-8082. Fax: (703) 370-8083. E-mail: ibpusa3@gmail.com Global Business and Investment Info Databank - www.ibpus.com

contract which are in effect, and to be aware that a certain filed contract is no longer in effect. NITL, 15. Also, NITL argues that corrections should be handled through amendments. NITL, 15

17. If the filer uses the modified ATFI, the filer will receive a special case number with which it will make its own corrections. As the Commission itself does not enter the corrections into the system, the Commission must know when that is done. The introduction of an alternate system filing may or may not have the capability of alerting the Commission when a correction is made, so while there may be no need for notice, the Commission will continue to require it at this point. See, discussion regarding correction, § 530.10.

As cancellations (§ 530.10(a) (2)) are necessarily only those not anticipated by the terms of the contract, there is a clear need for the Commission to have notice of that event. If the termination has occurred as anticipated by the service contract, we agree, in accordance with the rationale above, that there is no need for additional notice to the Commission. If, however, an event has occurred which was not contemplated by the parties in the service contract but which affects its operation, the Commission must be so notified in order to assess whether the parties are employing an unjust device to obtain rates otherwise not applicable. Similarly, for terminations not covered by the contract (§ 530.10(a) (3)) , the parties will no longer have the right to use the rates in the service contract and there are section 10(a) (1) concerns.

Several commenters assert that the notification requirements of §§ 530.10 (a) (4) ,(a) (5) and (b) for account adjustments are unnecessary and arbitrary, intrude into the commercial relationship, create needless burdens and are outside the Commission's oversight functions. OCWG, 20; Conagra, 4-5; NITL, 15-17. Notice of account adjustments and final settlement which are made pursuant to the terms of the service contract filed with the Commission appear to have no legitimate basis. NITL, 16. They appear to stem from prior "me-too" requirements. NITL, 16.

Again, and contrary to the comments, however, the Commission must know what the adjustments or final settlements of an account may be, not to impose the rate differential on the carrier or shipper, but to ensure that no section 10 violations are being carried out. There is little burden on the filers in providing this information, as they may simply copy the information to the Commission as they send it to the shipper.

Similarly, for final settlement of any account adjusted, the Commission requires notice. Both of these notice requirements were "intended to apply to only those service contracts where there has been a change to the basic compensation required by the terms of the service contract." 52 Fed. Reg. at 23999. The applicable rate must be determinable at any given time, to ensure compliance with the Act and section 10(a) (1) . Therefore, while parties are free to provide for liquidated damages, contingencies, etc., in their service contracts, using a rate from a service contract which is not lawful under the Act would create section 10(a) (1) and possibly other violations.

NITL comments that changes to names of parties (requirement of which is discussed supra) should be handled through amendments, and that additional notice of these should therefore not be required. NITL 15-17. NCBFAA and CMA suggest that there is no need to notify the Commission of changes to lists of shipper affiliates as required in § 530.9(a) (6) (ii) . NCBFAA, 2; CMA, 2. Furthermore, this is too burdensome to shippers. NCBFAA, 2; CMA, 2. DuPont recommends that § 530.9(a) (6) (ii) be altered to eliminate the requirement to report all names and addresses of shippers (except NVOCC) because identity of shippers is not an essential term, is not reported to the public and could be required to be maintained in the records of the carrier, records which can be obtained by the FMC through subpoena power. DuPont, 2-3.

For additional analytical, business and investment opportunities information, please contact Global Investment & Business Center, USA at (703) 370-8082. Fax: (703) 370-8083. E-mail: ibpusa3@gmail.com Global Business and Investment Info Databank - www.ibpus.com

Notice to the Commission of changes to shipper parties arises from the same concerns the Commission has when any other term of the filed service contract changes. The Commission must have the ability at any time to examine the filed service contract and assess whether or not parties (or non-parties) are operating in conformity to the service contract, or whether they may be employing an unjust means or device to elude the requirements of the Act. The Commission must be able to ascertain at any given moment who has the right to access a service contract.

Furthermore, there appears to be no reason at this juncture for the Commission to consider whether periodic reporting of changes to who may have access to a service contract (affiliates) would be adequate to meet its responsibilities. No change to OSRA mandates such a change, and the regulation was carried over from prior Commission regulation found at 46 CFR § 514.7(g) (2) .

OCWG complains that proposed § 530.9(b) (notice to contract party) fails to acknowledge commercial realities, including the sometimes protracted negotiations and communications delays relating to the covered subject matter and, further, that carriers and shippers have both regulatory and commercial incentives to promptly pursue their contract rights. Thus, they argue, there is no reason to graft further deadlines onto the commercial relationship. OCWG, 20-21.

Originally, this provision was crafted with respect to the general commercial practice of settling accounts in thirty days; additional time was provided, and the regulation as adopted required notice to the shipper party of the final settlement of account within 60 days of the termination of the contract. 52 Fed. Reg. 23999.

OSRA shifts parties' remedies to their common law contract rights, and as such, this provision appears to be no longer necessary, as it was originally intended to protect the shipper party. With the deregulatory goals of OSRA, parties are expected to protect their own contract rights and as such the Commission's role as mediator between the parties for contract disputes is removed. Accordingly, § 530.10(b) (as originally numbered) is deleted completely.

§ 530.10 -- AMENDMENT, CORRECTION AND CANCELLATION

The proposed regulation provides that either party to a filed service contract may request permission to correct clerical or administrative errors in a filed service contract by filing a request with the Commission's Office of the Secretary within 45 days of the contract's filing with the Commission, for a fee of $233 pursuant to § 530.11(c) (4) . Any notices in connection with the filing of such corrections would be filed with the Commission under § 530.9 within 10 days. Amendments are intended by the rule as proposed to be filed in the same manner as initial service contracts. Finally, cancellation of the service contract is provided for by this section.

COSCO requests clarification about what rules, and specifically whether confidentiality, will apply to service contract amendments filed after May 1, 1999, where the original service contract was filed before May 1, 1999. COSCO, 2.

Amendments filed on or after May 1, 1999 to service contracts filed before May 1, 1999 must comply with the regulations in effect as of May 1, 1999. The Commission expects that many parties to service contracts entered into before May 1, 1999 may wish to obtain confidentiality for more of their service contract terms under OSRA, and therefore will terminate the contracts, write new ones and file them in their entirety rather than simply making amendments. As we previously indicated, the Commission will strive to have the filing systems ready to accept service contracts in the week prior to May 1, 1999 and thereby allow the filing of service contracts which have an effective date of May 1, 1999 or later as soon as possible.

For additional analytical, business and investment opportunities information, please contact Global Investment & Business Center, USA at (703) 370-8082. Fax: (703) 370-8083. E-mail: ibpusa3@gmail.com Global Business and Investment Info Databank - www.ibpus.com

Two commenters believe that requiring a formal correction proceeding and justification for correcting clerical errors of proposed § 530.10(b) incorrectly carries over provisions from the previous regulations on "me-too," which has been eliminated by OSRA. CMA, 2; DuPont, 3. It appears that confusion has arisen among the commenters regarding the differences between the terms "correction" and "amendment" to a service contract filed with the Commission under the Act. Parties to a filed service contract are free to amend its terms prospectively at any time, by filing their amendments pursuant to § 530.8. Meanwhile, the ability to correct clerical or administrative errors retroactively helps contract parties avoid undue hardships in instances where the parties discover, subsequent to filing a contract with the Commission, that a clerical or an administrative error had been made.

There is utility to having in place a procedure by which the parties may correct inadvertent errors through the correction procedure. However, this procedure must be structured so as to enable the Commission to distinguish between legitimate requests and requests crafted to avoid the statutory requirements of the Act, regardless of the fact that me-too rights have been eliminated by OSRA. The ability to change provisions retroactively without Commission scrutiny would undermine the clear intent of section 10(b) (2) (A) which provides that no common carrier, either alone or in conjunction with any other person, directly or indirectly may provide service in the liner trade that is not in accordance with the rates, charges, classifications, rules, and practices contained in a tariff published or a service contract entered into under section 8 of OSRA.

Furthermore, allowing parties to "correct" retroactively terms of the filed service contract would make any such agreement illusory and thereby bring it outside the requirements contained in section 2(19) of the Act that a service contract be certain and contain commitments on the parts of both parties. It appears that allowing for corrections (retroactive) and amendments (prospective) to filed service contracts provides more than adequate flexibility for parties to take advantage of their commercially negotiated arrangements while ensuring adherence to the Act's requirements.

CMA asserts that the Commission has no authority to accept or reject a contract change, as it is a matter for the parties. CMA, 2; DuPont, 3. NITL believes it is nonsensical to require permission to correct a clerical error. NITL, 17. We disagree. The authority for the Commission to scrutinize a retroactive change to a service contract is based on the requirement of section 8(c) of the Act that service contracts be filed with the Commission and that they reflect certain, meaningful commitments. Thus, allowing parties to make retroactive corrections devoid of any review or oversight would render that statutory requirement meaningless. CMA argues that there should be no distinction between changes that are made prospectively (amendments) and changes that are made retrospectively (corrections) . CMA, 2. Again, we disagree, and point out that the Commission has made such a distinction: the terms of corrections, but not those of amendments, are subject to Commission review before they may be made.

Two commenters complain that the correction procedure is excessively burdensome. NITL, 15; NCBFAA, 2. Further, NITL argues, the fee for corrections is too high. NITL, 17. The service fee associated with such requests became effective November 2, 1998, and reflects the costs incurred by the Commission in providing this service to the parties which elect to use it. Correction requires a significant amount of work by Commission staff, because the request must be scrutinized to ensure it is not an attempt to circumvent the requirements of the Act. Again, the need for notice of correction (see § 530.9(a)) will depend on the capabilities of the filing system.

PTCB comments that filers should have access to their filings to check them for errors and to audit them. PTCB, 1. The read-only access to filings may be possible, but certainly filers will have

For additional analytical, business and investment opportunities information, please contact Global Investment & Business Center, USA at (703) 370-8082. Fax: (703) 370-8083. E-mail: ibpusa3@gmail.com Global Business and Investment Info Databank - www.ibpus.com

no ability to change their filings (except by amendment) once submitted to the Commission's database for the reasons set forth above.

NITL comments that the 45-day period by which filers must report clerical and administrative errors is too short. NITL, 17. This deadline, however, has been a longstanding requirement of the regulations and the Commission is unaware of complaints of hardship in the past. Furthermore, given the recent advances in communication technologies, 45 days would be more than adequate time for parties to detect clerical errors in their service contracts. Also, the requirement that such request be filed within a 45-day period for a service fee encourages contract parties to carefully review contracts before submitting them to the Commission and to take corrective action without undue delay. Finally, the Commission has previously fully assessed the time period required for requesting a correction, and it is not apparent why this analysis would have changed. Docket No. 88-61, 54 Fed. Reg. 1363 (Jan. 13, 1989) .

The correction procedure set forth under § 530.10 will serve a useful purpose and will be maintained. Experience has shown that there will likely be only a minimal need to file such requests: during FY 1998, only four such requests were filed with the Commission and this number is not anticipated to increase significantly in the future, particularly given the Commission's determination to encourage contract parties to file their actual arrangements rather than arrangements "translated" into FMC formats.

Commenters complain that § 530.10(c) (2) (cancellation) is anachronistic and urge the Commission to delete the provision. One commenter complains that these provisions are inconsistent with general principles of contract law and would penalize shippers in situations where both the shipper and the carrier believe the termination is in their self-interest, and as such is not appropriate in a marketplace oriented system, such as the one OSRA contemplates. AImpSA, 1-2. NCBFAA complains that the proposed rule is burdensome and inappropriately harms shippers when the carrier may not have suffered any damages due to unilateral cancellation of a service contract. NCBFAA 3,4. NCBFAA also complains that it is unfairly punitive to re-rate at tariff rates when a shipper cancels a service contract. NCBFAA, 3,4.

The Commission has concluded to redraft this section to reflect the very limited situations in which re-rating will be required. First, we point out that the rejection provision has been eliminated. Second, re-rating, as discussed below, will only be required in situations where a filed service contract has not contemplated and which the parties have not determined to amend the contract. If there is a liquidated damages, or another fall-back rate provision, there will be no need to re-rate cargo which has already been carried. Therefore, most of the shippers' concerns that they may be held unreasonably accountable for a carrier-filer's filing mistakes are removed.

The Commission first added the allowance that parties prospectively may amend their filed service contracts in Docket 92-21, 57 Fed. Reg. 46318 (Oct. 8, 1992) . There, the Commission noted that the parties may make retroactive corrections of clerical or administrative errors through the corrections procedure. Id. at 46318. Second, the Commission noted, the parties can similarly provide for substantive modifications through contingency clauses. As pointed out below, examples of such contingency clauses had been listed in § 514.17 (d) (7) (viii) .[(6)] As further discussed in the supplemental information to this regulation, any of the terms of the service contract may be amended with prospective effect. 57 Fed. Reg. at 46322.

The terms amendment, correction and cancellation are clarified by the revised section. It is apparent that commenters are confused about the reasoning behind the distinction the Commission has made in the past. Further, we point out that the Commission's Bureau of Tariffs, Certification and Licensing ("BTCL") received only four petitions for correction last year. This is

For additional analytical, business and investment opportunities information, please contact Global Investment & Business Center, USA at (703) 370-8082. Fax: (703) 370-8083. E-mail: ibpusa3@gmail.com Global Business and Investment Info Databank - www.ibpus.com

simply an issue which has not been a problem in the past, but which the Commission will continue to monitor against the abuse of procedures such as correction to evade the prescriptions and prohibitions of the Act.

Therefore, due to the apparent confusion of the comments over the distinction between the terms correction, amendment, and cancellation the proposed regulations are revised to include definitions of these terms.

§ 530.12 -- PUBLICATION OF ESSENTIAL TERMS

OSRA continues to require the publication of certain essential terms of service contracts and instructs carrier parties to service contracts to make these essential terms available to the public "in tariff format." Section 530.12 of the proposed regulation suggested that carriers and conferences should be able to satisfy this obligation in the same way they publish their tariff information under proposed 46 CFR part 520. Further, in an effort to assist the shipping public to find statements of essential terms published according to this part, the Commission proposed making a list of the locations of all such publications available on the FMC website. 46 CFR § 530.12(f) .

OCWG comments that the proposed regulation's requirement that essential terms be published with the tariffs is misplaced because that is just format, not location. OCWG, 18. The proposed rule cross-referenced many of the technical requirements of the newly proposed tariff publication regulations to effectuate the essential terms publication required under this part, in an effort to ease the burden on carriers, and to allow them to take advantage of means by which they would already publish their tariff information. The Carrier Automated Tariff regulation, Commission Docket No. 98-29, gives carriers a wide array of options regarding the location at and method by which they publish. Therefore, requiring carriers to publish statements of essential terms alongside their tariffs would not create any new burdens. Indeed, requiring that a different location be used would appear to be much more burdensome, as it would not allow carriers to take advantage of publications they must already make in accordance with the tariff regulations.

However, the Commission is again faced with issues which arise when a service contract is entered by members of a non-conference agreement which does not publish a common tariff with which its service contract essential terms may be published. One commenter supports the proposal that individual service contracts are published by the individual, and that multiparty service contracts are filed by one party, but published by all the parties. P&O, 8. However, the comments request that the Commission clarify that for individual service contracts, essential terms would be published on the carrier's own essential terms publication and not on a conference's essential terms publication. P&O, 8. We agree that this remains the simplest approach.

Individual carrier service contracts are to be published alongside that carrier's tariff matter, in a separate document, as outlined in § 530.12. Multi-party service contracts entered into under the authority of a conference must be published alongside the conference tariff, and not in the individual member's tariff. For service contracts jointly entered into by multiple parties of a non-conference agreement, the publication of the statement of essential terms will be published as for individual service contracts, but note must be made of the relevant FMC-designated Agreement number. Commenters assert that, by requiring a list of fellow carrier participants, the proposed regulation was adding a non-statutory public essential term: the names of the carrier parties. With that in mind, together with the limitations which exist as to tariff-associated statements of essential terms publication, reference to the agreement number will allow the public to ascertain whether certain activity is joint or independent. This approach, while it does not provide the public

For additional analytical, business and investment opportunities information, please contact Global Investment & Business Center, USA at (703) 370-8082. Fax: (703) 370-8083. E-mail: ibpusa3@gmail.com Global Business and Investment Info Databank - www.ibpus.com

with a list of which member is or is not participating in an agreement-authorized multi-party service contract, will indicate that the service contract is not an independent, sole-carrier service contract.

One commenter suggested that rather than require all individual carriers to publish the full text of their non-conference agreement contract statements of essential terms, simply a reference to where the published essential terms may be found would be adequate and less burdensome to carriers. COSCO, 2. Due to the automated nature and the limited terms which are required to be published in a statement of essential terms under OSRA, the burden appears to be rather light on carriers, in comparison to the benefits it provides the shipping public.

P&O further requests that the Commission clarify the different publication requirements for non-conference agreement multi-party service contracts, conference agreement multi-party service contracts where the conference is the signatory but not all members are participants, and conference agreement multi-party service contracts where the carriers themselves are the signatories. P&O, 8. We agree that for statements of essential terms, because the terms are public in contrast to the balance of the filed matters, there is no corresponding issue of confidentiality. The clarification in § 530.12 will indicate that service contracts which are entered jointly by members of conferences, regardless of signatory, must be published with the conference's tariff and not in the individual carrier's publication. For an independent service contract, the statement of essential terms will be published with the individual carrier's tariff publication, but not with the conference's tariff. Allowing such would lead to public confusion.

ETM requests that the Commission provide further clarification regarding the failure to make published essential terms contemporaneously available. ETM, 1. We reiterate that such liability would rest on the carrier parties to a service contract under the Commission's jurisdiction, regardless of the appointed agent for publishing.

§ 530.13 -- EXCEPTIONS

One commenter asks the Commission to clarify in supplementary statements that service contracts which are limited to the carriage of used military household goods and personal effects, or shipments of used household goods and personal effects of civilian executive agencies tendered to OTIs under the International Household goods program, administered by GSA, or both, are required to be filed with the Commission. HGFAA, 3. The exemption for used military household goods, granted by the Commission under section 16 of the Act, exempts those services from the tariff filing requirement only. The language in the rule as revised should remove any confusion.

The inclusion of the phrase, "as those terms are defined in section 3 of the Act" appears to adequately address any concerns regarding the definitions for exempted commodities. The one exception to this is for the term "motor vehicle" which is not defined by the Act. Therefore, the addition of that term to the definitions, § 530.3, which mirrors the terms definition in the Commission's regulation on Carrier Automated Tariffs Systems (Docket 98-29) will adequately address such concern. It does not appear necessary to further repeat other definitions here.

The proposed regulations also provided for "non-acceptance," a new term reflecting the congressional mandate that the Commission not accept for filing service contracts which cover only excepted commodities. It appears now that this was a confusing new term. The term "nonacceptance" has been removed from the regulation, and the provisions in this section should otherwise adequately address "mixed" contracts.

The Commission will retain the provision requiring any service contracts which are filed to relate to commodities or services for which a tariff rate can be established. This is because the situation may arise in which the Commission would require re-rating, and for such re-rating, an "otherwise applicable rate" would be required. While such need may be very rare, those concerns remain for replacement applicable rates for such situations.

Finally, issues arise similar to those discussed under the sections on rejection and re-rating. For the reasons discussed, mixed commodity contracts may only be filed if a replacement rate is available. We therefore revise the proposed regulations to clarify this approach. Finally, as it was repetitious, § 530.15, as originally numbered in the proposed regulation, entitled "nonacceptance" is deleted entirely, and the following sections have been accordingly renumbered.

PROPOSED § 530.15 -- REJECTION

Several comments remark on the Commission's authority and criteria it would use for rejection of service contracts as presented in proposed § 530.15. Commenters generally argue that the Commission may only reject service contracts submitted for filing if they do not meet the requirements of the Act, but that the Commission does not have the authority to reject them on the basis that they do not meet the requirements of the Commission's regulations. OCWG, 19-20; CENSA, 3; P&O, 6; NITL, 19. IBP urges the Commission to revise the regulation, and to provide more guidance on when a service contract could be rejected and suggests that rather than a general reference to the Act, this section refer to the requirements in § 530.8 (as renumbered) . IBP, 1. Finally, P&O complains that the Commission is wrongfully attempting to intrude on the commercial nature of service contracts through rejection. P&O, 6.

Commission regulations currently outline the procedures for rejection of service contracts and essential terms filed with the Commission. 46 CFR § 514.7(j) . The Commission rejects service contract essential terms publications filed into the ATFI system which do not conform to the requirements of the Act or Commission regulation, including timeliness of filing and adequacy and accuracy of the publication of the statement of essential terms. The proposed regulation attempted to adapt the current rejection rules as necessary to meet the changes to the Act made by OSRA.

JUSEFC recommends the re-insertion of § 514.7(j) (2) which specifies that rejection is limited to those instances where parties fail to file a corrected copy. JUSEFC, 8-9. The filer, they comment, should be given a chance to cure even if the deficiencies are major, and a notice of intent to reject be sent to the shipper party, because the sanction of re-rating is too harsh on the shipper who relies on the carrier party to do the filing. IBP, 2. This argument is considerably diminished, as the Commission under section 13(f) (1) of the Act as revised by OSRA no longer has the ability to order shippers to pay the undercharge if there is an enforceable agreement in writing.[(7)] See infra, discussion of re-rating at § 530.14, originally numbered §530.16 in the proposed regulation.

Several commenters request that the Commission decrease the "review period" and increase the "cure period" proposed in the regulations. COSCO requests that the Commission shorten the review period from 20 days to 1 day. COSCO, 2. OCWG also recommends a no-penalty cure period of 20 days. OCWG, 20.

NITL suggests amending § 530.15(b) as proposed to read:

Within 20 days after the initial filing of an initial or amended service contract, the Commission may reject a service contract that does not conform to the requirements of section 8(c) of the

1984 Act. Prior to rejection, the Commission shall provide notice to the filing party of the deficiencies in the contract and shall provide such party 20 days to cure the deficiencies. A failure to cure the deficiencies within the stated time period will result in rejection of the contract.

The filer of the contract shall notify the shipper of any contract rejection within 10 days of its receipt of notice of rejection. Until the cause for potential rejection is cured, no cargo may be transported under the contract following the receipt of notice of the rejection by the shipper.

NITL, 21

JUSEFC suggests a two-tier approach to review. First, they suggest, a short period (3 days) in which the Commission would determine whether there is a serious enough breach as to require rejection ab initio, notify the filer and give it the opportunity to make corrections. Then, a second period (10 days) (if the deficiency is not corrected) for continuing review, after which (again if not corrected) , rejection would be effective as of the close of the correction period, but not as of the date the contract was originally filed. JUSEFC, 8-9. JUSEFC's proposal would appear to allow the contract rates to be effective for a period of up to 13 days, even if the deficiencies are never cured, and to allow the contract rates to be lawful. JUSEFC, 8-9. This procedure, JUSEFC claims, would comply with the Commission's practice with respect to tariff rates rejected after they have become effective as well as the Filed Rate Doctrine as affirmed in Maislin Industries, Inc. v. Primary Steel, Inc., 497 U.S. 116 (1990) .(8)

With the changes the Commission has made to the filing system, and the relief from many of the technical requirements which accompany those changes, the Commission will completely remove the rejection procedure in the proposed regulation. There will therefore be no requirement that the Commission conduct a review of service contract filings according to any deadline. Of course, this would have no effect on the Commission's ability to review service contract filings for statutory and regulatory compliance and pursue investigatory or enforcement action as it deems necessary.

JUSEFC's concern that the Commission has compromised the right of filing parties to amend their contracts to meet the Commission's objections and preserve the original effective dates of their contracts is misplaced. The assertion that parties have a right to "correct" or "cure" their deficient service contracts and preserve the filing date is unsupported by any statutory requirement. Commenters who argue for the Commission to give filers time to correct deficiencies appear to suggest that the Commission must review filings for facial defects as they are filed, and further, that if the Commission does not notify the filer of a deficiency, that the service contract is compliant with the Act and regulations. While it has been the past policy and practice of the Commission in the past to review essential terms documents as they were filed with the ATFI system and its ability to conduct associative checks, there is no statutory requirement that the Commission give parties time to "cure" their defective filings during which they may operate under the defective service contract.

The rejection procedure was originally intended to, first, be a service to filers and, second, to preserve the system integrity of the data in the ATFI-based statements of essential terms. When transmission to ATFI failed, BTCL, through the rejection procedure outlined in the proposed regulations, would notify filers that the essential terms publication they had attempted to file was defective. The automated nature of conformity checks made this possible.

Acceptance by the Commission of a document, including an electronically-filed statement of essential terms does not and never did, indicate the Commission's "approval" of a service contract. The Commission expects that BTCL, as it detects minor deficiencies in filed service

For additional analytical, business and investment opportunities information, please contact Global Investment & Business Center, USA at (703) 370-8082. Fax: (703) 370-8083. E-mail: ibpusa3@gmail.com Global Business and Investment Info Databank - www.ibpus.com

contracts, may notify the filers and allow for re-filing within a reasonable period of time, at their discretion, but will not be required to do so. Therefore, the rejection procedures are deleted entirely.

Carrying cargo under a service contract before it has been filed with the Commission is prohibited by proposed Commission regulation § 530.8(a) . Carrying cargo under a defective service contract (for example, one which does not contain one of the eight essential terms or which fails to state them with adequate certainty; or does not contain the shipper certification; or does not conform to the filing requirements of § 530.8; or does not concurrently publish the four public essential terms) would be a violation of the Act, and subject to penalties of section 13 of the Act. The comments reveal confusion on this point which the Commission wishes to dispel. The filing of a service contract does not, nor did it ever, imbue the service contract with any type of Commission approval or imprimatur, any more than would the filing of a tax return with the Internal Revenue Service.

It has, however, been the past practice of BTCL to informally notify filers of deficiencies in their service contract filings. BTCL would provide filers of essential terms statements an opportunity to cure the defects by re-transmitting the electronic data to the ATFI system. Furthermore, it appears that BTCL has rarely, if ever, invoked the predecessor section of this regulation. However, the reception of the entirety of service contracts in electronic form will significantly change the method by which the Commission may review the filings. Therefore, with that, and the following discussion in mind, the Commission has concluded that the rejection provision of the proposed rule will be removed.

A service contract is defined by section 2(19) of the Act, as revised by OSRA, as

a written contract, other than a bill of lading or a receipt, between one or more shipper and an individual ocean common carrier or an agreement between or among ocean common carriers in which the shipper or shippers makes a commitment to provide a certain volume or portion of cargo over a fixed period of time, and the ocean common carrier or the agreement commits to a certain rate or rate schedule and a defined service level, such as assured space, transit time, port rotation, or similar service features. The contract may also specify provisions in the event of nonperformance on the part of any party.

Two specific requirements for service contracts are found in section 8(c) (2) : first, that the service contract be filed with the Commission; and second, that it contain seven specific terms. Section (8) (c) (2) (A) -(G) . If the service contract either (1) does not meet the definition in the Act; (2) is not filed with the Commission; or (3) does not contain one of the terms required by the Act, it is not a service contract as defined by the Act.

Finally, the comments agree that the Commission should accept for filing mixed contracts, but recommend that the requirement that exempt commodities in such filed service contracts have a tariff rate be deleted, as there is no need for the Commission to regulate exempt commodity rates, charges and conditions of service in a mixed exempt and non-exempt commodity service contract any more than the Commission has a need to regulate contracts that are exclusively exempt commodities. P&O, 5. The exempt commodities to which P&O refers are those exempted from tariff publication and from service contract filing by the Act in section 8. A service contract of mixed exempt and non-exempt commodities therefore may not have corresponding tariff rates. Therefore, in the unlikely event that the service contract is canceled as described in § 530.10 (as renumbered) , and there is no provision for such cancellation in the terms of the contract itself, there would be no corresponding tariff rate at which the exempt cargo would be re-rated. Therefore, some "general rate" must be available if an exempt commodity is to be filed in a

For additional analytical, business and investment opportunities information, please contact Global Investment & Business Center, USA at (703) 370-8082. Fax: (703) 370-8083. E-mail: ibpusa3@gmail.com Global Business and Investment Info Databank - www.ibpus.com

service contract, and the proposed rule will not be amended in this regard. As this is adequately provided for in § 530.13 as revised, and with regard to the foregoing discussion of rejection, §

530.15 is deleted entirely and the following sections are accordingly renumbered.

PROPOSED REGULATION § 530.16 -- IMPLEMENTATION, PROHIBITION AND RE-RATING

The proposed regulations in § 530.16 (as originally numbered) had carried over some of the provisions of current § 514.7(l) (ii) which read,

In the event of a contract which is not provided for in the contract itself and which results from mutual agreement of the parties or because the shipper . . . has failed to tender the minimum quantity required by the contract: . . . (B) The cargo previously carried under the contract shall be re-rated according to the otherwise applicable tariff provisions of the carrier or conference in effect at the time of each shipment.

The proposed regulations anticipated re-rating(9) for service contracts with non-conference agreements, but did not address how the regulations should be changed in recognition of the new limitations to penalties added by section 13(f) (1) of OSRA. Re-rating under the proposed rules would take place only if the contract did not contemplate mutual termination or if the shipper failed to meet minimum cargo requirements. Many comments generally appear to misconstrue the congressional intent of the prohibition of 13(f) (1) , and the Commission seeks to clarify the matter in this supplemental information and in the revised text of the regulations.

Commenters have three basic objections to proposed regulation § 530.16, namely that re-rating by the Commission is: (1) contrary to section 13(f) (1) of the Act as amended by OSRA; (2) contrary to the deregulatory spirit of OSRA; and (3) unfair to the shipper parties to service contracts.

Several comments point to section 13(f) (1) of OSRA as expressly forbidding the re-rating provision in the proposed rules. Conagra, 5; P&O, 6. Other commenters express the belief that re-rating for rejection based on failure to meet regulatory, as opposed to statutory requirements. BSA, 11; CMA, 2; Dupont, 4; NITL, 19-20. NITL asserts that re-rating either for termination by the parties or for rejection by the Commission would be contrary to OSRA. NITL, 18. NITL comments that section 13(f) (1) of the revised Act "expressly prohibits the Commission or a court from ordering a shipper to pay the difference between rates that the shipper and carrier agree upon in writing and that are billed by the carrier, and the rates that are set forth in a tariff or service contract that would otherwise cover the transportation movements." NITL, 18-19.

BSA remarks that re-rating during the period between initial filing and rejection by the Commission under § 530.16 is counter to the deregulatory spirit of OSRA. BSA, 11. Commenters also point to this deregulatory spirit to support their assertion that Congress intended parties resolve the question of re-rating due to FMC rejection as a private contractual matter. BSA, 11. Further, P&O comments, re-rating is not consistent with the ability of service contract terms to include liquidated damages or amendments to reduce minimum volume requirements. P&O, 6. NITL also complains that proposed § 530.10(c) (2) (as renumbered) appears to be mandating liquidated damages terms (i.e., the tariff rate) even though parties did not do so. NITL, 19-20.

Comments also cite OSRA's permission to parties to resolve undercharge matters with a written agreement. Dupont, 4. The proposed provisions for re-rating, Dupont complains, would deprive parties of their right to mutually determine settlement of outstanding charges. Dupont, 3-4.

For additional analytical, business and investment opportunities information, please contact Global Investment & Business Center, USA at (703) 370-8082. Fax: (703) 370-8083. E-mail: ibpusa3@gmail.com Global Business and Investment Info Databank - www.ibpus.com

Therefore, if there is any Commission rejection at all, the regulations should require the Commission to also notify the shipper of the rejection, and either limit re-rating to shipments made after receipt of such notice or impose penalty on the carrier alone. Dupont, 4.

Shippers complain that re-rating for rejection penalizes the shipper, when it is the carrier who has the responsibility of complying with the filing requirements. Conagra, 4; Dupont, 4; NITL, 19-20; IBP, 2. Several comments suggest that a solution to this injustice would be for the regulations to require the filing of corrections within a specific period of time and to impose a monetary penalty on the filing carrier for significant filing errors. Conagra, 6; Dupont, 4.

NCBFAA complains that proposed § 530.10(c) (2) (ii) (as renumbered) , which requires all cargo to be re-rated in the event the service contract is canceled, is arbitrary and punitive. NCBFAA, 20. Furthermore, proposed § 530.16(b) (2) (as originally numbered) would unfairly impose the higher tariff rates on the shipper when it is the carrier who is at fault, especially in a situation, for instance, in which the Commission rejects a service contract six months after filing. NCBFAA 4,5. Our response to rejection arguments is outlined in the previous discussion of proposed § 530.15 (as originally numbered) which has been deleted from this interim final rule.

As the comments correctly indicate, OSRA adds a new limitation to the remedies the Commission may impose on parties with an added sentence to section 13(f) (1) of the Act, which as revised reads

[n]either the Commission nor any court shall order any person to pay the difference between the amount billed and agreed upon in writing with a common carrier or its agent and the amount set forth in any tariff or service contract by that common carrier for the transportation service provided.

As explained by Senator Hutchison as she introduced the amendment to S. 414 which added the above language, the drafters intended to

[r]evise section 13(f) of the 1984 Act to make clear that, while a common carrier may be penalized for charging shippers less than its tariff or service contract rates, a carrier should not be able to collect from the shipper the difference between the tariff or contract rate and the rate actually charged and agreed upon in writing. The collection of these so-called "undercharges" was a major problem for shippers when the trucking industry was deregulated. We want to avoid any recurrence of that problem in connection with ocean shipping reform.

144 Cong. Rec. S1068 (March 4, 1998) (Statement of Sen. Hutchison) .

The intent of the provision was not, contrary to the assertion of some comments, that parties to a meaningless service contract may circumvent the prohibitions of sections 10(a) and (b) of the Act. Nor was it Congress' intent that parties which wrongfully terminate a service contract have the ability to impose higher rates on an innocent party for cargo that has already moved. The redrafted regulations at §§ 530.10 (as renumbered) and 530.14 (as renumbered) therefore make it clear that if a service contract does not contemplate termination, neither can the parties have illegal access to contract rates, nor can the carrier which wrongfully terminates bill the shipper at the higher tariff rates. Section 530.14 (as renumbered) indicates re-rating is only applicable to such cancellation, and prohibition or suspension of service contracts pursuant to the Commission's authority under Sections 9 and 11 of the Act. See, Docket No. 98-25; 46 CFR § 560.7.

For additional analytical, business and investment opportunities information, please contact Global Investment & Business Center, USA at (703) 370-8082. Fax: (703) 370-8083. E-mail: ibpusa3@gmail.com Global Business and Investment Info Databank - www.ibpus.com

In regard to comments on the unfairness of re-rating after rejection, the concerns of the commenters generally become moot with the elimination of the rejection provisions. The regulations have been redrafted with these particular shipper concerns in mind. First, the Commission points out that it is in the best interests of both parties that a service contract make provision for mutual termination, unilateral termination, and termination for failure to meet minimum cargo commitments. It is only in the absence of such provisions in the terms of the contract itself that the re-rating provisions will apply. The regulations are intended to ensure that parties conform to sections 10(a) (1) [(10)] (illusory contract or failure to meet minimum quantity commitment) ; 10(b) (1) [(11)] (carrier billing contract rate when shipper fails to meet minimum quantity commitment) ; and 10(b) (2) [(12)] (failing to charge rate other than that in a filed and valid service contract) of the Act.

If a carrier has entered into a contract with a shipper, that contract would appear to satisfy the requirements of section 13(f) ("an amount agreed upon in writing") which would in turn protect the shipper from having the cargo re-rated; the charged rates would be those in the service contract. The carrier would likely be hard-pressed to seek to enforce contract obligations upon a shipper where the carrier has unilaterally terminated. Finally, depending on the circumstances, the carrier may be in violation of various proscriptions of section 10, or the shipper may have a cause of action in court for breach of contract.

The Commission finds that section 13(f) (1) was particularly intended to avoid the type of requirement ordered by the Supreme Court in Maislin. In Maislin, the trustee in bankruptcy of a carrier sought to recover the difference between amount billed (negotiated rate) and the tariff rate. Maislin at 135. In response to the deregulatory spirit of the Motor Carrier Act, the Interstate Commerce Commission ("ICC") had instituted a "Negotiated Rates Policy," namely, that the ICC would not order the shipper to pay the shortfall between a negotiated rate and a tariff rate. The Court found that the ICC was required by the Interstate Commerce Act ("ICA") to review for reasonableness the rates charged to shippers. Because "secret" (negotiated) rates were unreasonable under the ICA, in the event that those rates were not in conformity to the tariff rates, the ICC was required by the Interstate Commerce Act to order the shippers to pay the difference between the filed rate and the negotiated rate (the "filed rate" doctrine) . Maislin at 129. The Court further found that "if strict adherence to . . . the filed rate doctrine has become an anachronism in the wake of the MCA, it is the responsibility of Congress to modify or eliminate these sections." Maislin at 135. With this background squarely in mind, taken together with the balance of the Act and the remarks of the sponsors of the bill as finally adopted, it is clear that section 13(f) (1) , as added by OSRA, only limits the Commission from ordering a shipper to pay the undercharge in a Maislin-type situation. The limitation of section 13(f) (1) was not intended to allow shippers and carriers to use service contracts as an "unfair or unjust means or device" to avoid the application of the "otherwise applicable rate" contrary to other provisions in the Act. If there are no provisions which anticipate the shipper's failure to meet the minimum cargo requirements of the service contract and the cargo is not subject to re-rating, the contract would appear to be illusory. Allowing the parties to take advantage of an illusory contract would be contrary to the prohibitions of section 10 and the intent of the Act.

Proposed regulations §§ 530.10 and 530.14 (as renumbered) are revised to reflect OSRA's intent that parties to a service contract may not use that agreement as an unfair means or device to avoid the otherwise applicable rate.[(13)] Thus, the regulations require re-rating for cargo which has already moved under a service contract which is nullified due to a shipper shortfall (unless due to carrier misconduct) and which is not contemplated by the contract's terms.

Finally, subpart D is re-titled, "Exceptions and Implementation," proposed regulation § 530.15 is deleted, and proposed regulation § 530.16 is retitled "Implementation" and correspondingly renumbered § 530.14.

§ 530.15 (as renumbered) -- RECORDKEEPING AND AUDIT

P&O comments that the notice of proposed rulemaking did not adequately explain why this rule is necessary or appropriate. P&O, 7. Further, it complains, there is no statutory authority for the requirement, and it is pointless because the service contract is already subject to a filing requirement. P&O, 7. Also it questions why there is no provision for confidentiality for records obtained by the Commission under this provision of the proposed regulations. P&O, 7.

Section 530.15 (as renumbered) was carried over nearly verbatim from the current §§ 514.7(m) (1) and 514.7(m) (3) , which read:

(1) Every common carrier or conference shall maintain service contract records in an organized, readily accessible or retrievable manner for a period of five years from the termination of each contract.

* * *

(3) Every common carrier or conference shall, upon written request from the FMC's Director, Bureau of Enforcement or any Area Representative, submit requested service contract records within 30 days from the date of the request.

The purpose and statutory authority for these provisions has been examined previously by the Commission and its regulated entities when §§ 514.7(m) (1) and (m) (3) were added to the Commission's regulation.

The electronic filing options that the Commission has chosen to offer, in an effort to reduce burdens on ocean common carrier filers and at their urging, both fall short in one significant respect: the electronic versions of the documents will not have the ability to capture the signature of the parties. Because the Commission will still need to examine the originally executed service contracts, the shortcoming of the electronic filing system continues to make the language in the proposed regulation necessary. While it is true that the Commission has the authority to obtain the information in any event under section 12 of the Act, the Commission has found it useful to reiterate that authority here in order to impress upon carriers that their executed service contracts and related records must be retained and ready for inspection.

It is difficult to imagine how this provision would create any additional burden on filers, as they would presumably retain the originally executed service contract to protect their rights under that contract. With respect to P&O's concerns about confidentiality, the statute already provides for the confidentiality of service contracts and there appears to be no need for further clarification of the issue through rulemaking. For the foregoing reasons, the regulation in this section will be adopted as proposed.

GLOBAL SERVICE CONTRACTS

The Commission, in an effort to minimize burden on filers, and encourage them to structure their commercial negotiations based on market forces rather than to conform them to regulatory requirements, requested comment on the filing of global service contracts. Comments generally commend the Commission for recognizing the commercial desirablility of global service contracting. Dupont, Conagra, NITL, CENSA, P&O. P&O and CENSA request confirmation from the Commission that the voluntary inclusion of extrajurisidictional matter in a filed service contract would not expand the Commission's jurisdiction over those matters.

For additional analytical, business and investment opportunities information, please contact Global Investment & Business Center, USA at (703) 370-8082. Fax: (703) 370-8083. E-mail: ibpusa3@gmail.com Global Business and Investment Info Databank - www.ibpus.com

The Commission's intent was to allow parties to enter into service contracts which fit their commercial needs, and relieve them of the burden of negotiating contracts which "carve out" the U.S. trades simply because of U.S. filing requirements. Again we confirm that Commission will not assert jurisdiction over foreign-to-foreign matters due solely to the fact that they are included in a service contract filed with the Commission. We also note, however, that the extent to which the U.S. trade matters are affected by, contingent on or reliant on foreign-to-foreign movements, the Commission will have the statutory duty and jurisdiction to obtain the relevant records.

While voluntary filing of global contracts will not subject the non-U.S. matters to FMC jurisdiction, as discussed above, there is a difficulty with how the statement of essential terms shall be made. There is too great a danger that the public will be misled if only the "U.S. trade" volumes, for instance, are published, when those volumes are affected by foreign-to-foreign volumes. Therefore, the interim final rules require that the statement of essential terms for filed contracts which include both U.S. trade and non-U.S. trade matters which affect those terms must indicate that the contract includes matter outside the Commission's jurisdiction. Failing to require this disclaimer has too great a potential for confusion by the public reviewing those essential terms. See, § 530.12 (publication section regarding exempt and global service contracts) .

INLAND EUROPEAN MOVEMENTS IN CONFERENCE CONTRACTS

In the NPR, the Commission noted the difference in the approaches by the United States and the European Commission ("E.C.") to the question of inland rate setting by conferences. The NPR requested comment on how the Commission may treat carriers which participate in a conference service contract covering U.S.-Europe ocean movements but sign an individual service contract covering European inland transport for the same shipper customer. The Commission noted in the NPR that it would appear that filing would be consistent with statutory requirements to the extent the contracts establish the European inland portion of a through rate charged by a carrier in a U.S.-Europe intermodal movement. However, the Commission wished to make an effort to minimize the regulatory burdens occasioned by these differences in regulatory regimes, to the extent it may do so given its own statutory responsibility.

The comments make three basic arguments with respect to inland rates in Europe. First, to the extent that service contracts for inland movements in Europe are within the Commission's jurisdiction, they should be exempt from filing because the EU regulates them adequately. BSA and TACA. Second, that they are completely outside the Commission's jurisdiction. BSA. Finally, P&O comments that European charges, if included in a service contract, must be filed with the Commission and are part of the filed essential terms, but not the public essential terms.

P&O's approach appears to be sound. As rate information is not one of the essential terms required to be published by the Act, any regulatory requirement would not order rate information to be published, although it would be filed. As discussed in the filing of "mixed contracts" it would appear that the allowance of such filing is for the ease of the filer.

TACA suggests that sections of a service contract relating to inland movements of cargo in Europe should not be required to be filed with the Commission. TACA, 8. TACA proposes that sections of service contracts stating the terms and conditions of European inland transport of shipments covered by the service contract be available from the individual carrier upon request from the Commission (in electronic or paper format at the option of the carrier) within ten days of the request. TACA, 8-9. This would ease the burden on the Commission, completely harmonize with E.C. law, ensure no breach of confidentiality that might take place due to filing via third parties, and ensure public access to the information. TACA, 9.

For additional analytical, business and investment opportunities information, please contact Global Investment & Business Center, USA at (703) 370-8082. Fax: (703) 370-8083. E-mail: ibpusa3@gmail.com Global Business and Investment Info Databank - www.ibpus.com

The disparity between Commission and E.C. requirements generally only becomes problematic when a conference or members of an agreement enter into a service contract in which the rate calculation for port-to-port rates are included, but for which the inland movements in Europe are not included because of the E.C. prohibition on joint rate setting for inland rates. The conference contract filed with the Commission would presumably include a "multi-factor through rate" which would be the ocean transport rate as laid out in the contract, plus an unspecified rate arising from the inland portion of the transportation. If the conference is required by the Commission to file the independent inland rate so that the Commission can calculate the total through rate, the conference may be in violation of the E.C.'s prohibition on confidentiality.

P&O argues that it is clear that inland European charges, if included in a service contract, would have to be filed with the FMC. P&O points out that carriers and shippers may choose to construct multi-factor through rates to and from Europe by using a confidential port/port rate, or a point/port and then adding a published European inland tariff rate to construct a "multi-factor through rate."

TACA's suggestion that the Commission exempt these inland movements from filing is a substantial deviation from the filing requirements under the Act. Such an exemption is more properly adopted after a full examination of the matter under Section 16 of the Act. For these reasons and because the change is not mandated by OSRA, the Commission will continue to require that the service contracts in question be filed.

INTERIM FINAL RULE STATUS

As the Commission is introducing substantial matters which were not explored in the NPR, this shall be an interim final rule, under the Commission's authority granted by section 17(b) of the Act.

REGULATORY FLEXIBILITY ACT ANALYSIS

In accordance with the Regulatory Flexibility Act, 5 U.S.C. 601 et seq., the Chairman of the Commission has certified to the Chief Counsel for Advocacy, Small Business Administration, that the rule will not have a significant impact on a substantial number of small entities. In its NPR, the Commission stated that it intended to certify the rulemaking since the affected universe of parties is limited to vessel-operating common carriers. The Commission has determined that such entities do not typically qualify as small under the Small Business Administration guidelines. No comments disputed the Commission's intention to certify. The certification is, therefore, continued.

The Commission has received Office of Management and Budget (OMB) approval for the collection of this information required in this part. Section 530.91 displays the control numbers assigned by OMB to information collection requirements of the Commission in this part by the pursuant to the Paperwork Reduction Act of 1995, as amended. In accordance with that Act, agencies are required to display a currently valid control number. In this regard, the valid control number for this collection of information is 3072-0065.

This regulatory action is not a "major rule" under 5 U.S.C. § 804(2) .

List of subjects for 46 CFR part 530

Freight, Maritime carriers, Reporting and recordkeeping requirements

For additional analytical, business and investment opportunities information, please contact Global Investment & Business Center, USA at (703) 370-8082. Fax: (703) 370-8083. E-mail: ibpusa3@gmail.com Global Business and Investment Info Databank - www.ibpus.com

For the reasons set out in the preamble, the Commission will remove 46 CFR part 514 and add new 46 CFR part 530, as set forth below:

1. Remove 46 CFR part 514.
2. Add 46 CFR part 530 to subchapter B - REGULATIONS AFFECTING MARITIME CARRIERS AND RELATED ACTIVITIES IN FOREIGN COMMERCE.
3. Add 46 CFR part 530 -- Service Contracts, to read as set forth below:

PART 530 -- SERVICE CONTRACTS

Subpart A -- General ProvisionsSec.

530.1 Purpose.
530.2 Scope and applicability.
530.3 Definitions.
530.4 Confidentiality.
530.5 Duty to file.
530.6 Certification of shipper status.
530.7 Duty to labor organizations.

Subpart B - Filing Requirements530.8 Service contracts.

530.9 Notices.

530.10 Amendment, correction, and cancellation.

530.11 Filing fees and other costs.

Subpart C - Publication of Essential Terms

530.12 Publication.

Subpart D - Exceptions and Implementation

530.13 Exceptions.

530.14 Implementation.

Subpart E - Recordkeeping and Audit

530.15 Recordkeeping and audit.

530.91 OMB control numbers assigned pursuant to the Paperwork Reduction Act.

APPENDIX A TO PART 530 -- INSTRUCTIONS FOR THE FILING OF SERVICE CONTRACTS

Exhibit 1 to Part 530 -- FILER REGISTRATION FORM AND INSTRUCTIONS

For additional analytical, business and investment opportunities information, please contact Global Investment & Business Center, USA at (703) 370-8082. Fax: (703) 370-8083. E-mail: ibpusa3@gmail.com Global Business and Investment Info Databank - www.ibpus.com

Authority: 5 U.S.C. 553; 46 U.S.C. App. 1704, 1705, 1707, 1716; Pub. L. No. 105-258, 112 Stat. 1902; and sec. 424 of Pub. L. No. 105-383.

SUBPART A - GENERAL PROVISIONS

§ 530.1 Purpose.

The purpose of this part is to facilitate the filing of service contracts and the publication of certain essential terms of those service contracts as required by section 8(c) of the Shipping Act of 1984 ("Act") . This part enables the Commission to review service contracts to ensure that these contracts and the parties to them comport with the requirements of the Act. This part also implements electronic filing provisions for service contracts to facilitate compliance and minimize the filing burdens on the oceanborne commerce of the United States.

§ 530.2 Scope and applicability.

An individual ocean common carrier or an agreement between or among ocean common carriers may enter into a service contract with one or more shippers subject to the requirements of the Act.

§ 530.3 Definitions.

When used in this part:

(a) Act means the Shipping Act of 1984 as amended by the Ocean Shipping Reform Act of 1998.

(b) Agreement means an understanding, arrangement, or association (written or oral) and any modification or cancellation thereof which has been filed and effective under part 535 of this chapter with the Commission. The term does not include a maritime labor agreement.

(c) Authorized person means a carrier or a duly appointed agent who is authorized to file service contracts on behalf of the carrier party to a service contract and to publish the corresponding statement of essential terms and is registered by the Commission to file under §530.5(d) and Appendix A of this part.

(d) BTCL means the Commission's Bureau of Tariffs, Certification and Licensing or its successor bureau.

(e) Commission means the Federal Maritime Commission.

(f) Common carrier means a person holding itself out to the general public to provide transportation by water of passengers or cargo between the United States and a foreign country for compensation that:

(1) assumes responsibility for the transportation from the port or point of receipt to the port or point of destination; and

(2) utilizes, for all or part of that transportation, a vessel operating on the high seas or the Great Lakes between a port in the United States and a port in a foreign country, except that the term does not include a common carrier engaged in ocean transportation by ferry boat, ocean tramp,

For additional analytical, business and investment opportunities information,
please contact Global Investment & Business Center, USA
at (703) 370-8082. Fax: (703) 370-8083. E-mail: ibpusa3@gmail.com
Global Business and Investment Info Databank - www.ibpus.com

or chemical parcel tanker, or by a vessel when primarily engaged in the carriage of perishable agricultural commodities:

(i) if the common carrier and the owner of those commodities are wholly owned, directly or indirectly, by a person primarily engaged in the marketing and distribution of those commodities and

(ii) only with respect to those commodities.

(g) Conference means an agreement between or among two or more ocean common carriers which provides for the fixing of and adherence to uniform rates, charges, practices and conditions of service relating to the receipt, carriage, handling and/or delivery of passengers or cargo for all members. The term does not include joint service, pooling, sailing, space charter, or transshipment agreements.

(h)

Controlled carrier means an ocean common carrier that is, or whose operating assets are, directly or indirectly owned or controlled by a government. Ownership or control by a government shall be deemed to exist with respect to any ocean common carrier if:

(1) a majority portion of the interest in the carrier is owned or controlled in any manner by that government, by any agency thereof, or by any public or private person controlled by that government; or

(2) that government has the right to appoint or disapprove the appointment of a majority of the directors, the chief operating officer or the chief executive officer of the carrier.

(i)

Effective date means the date upon which a service contract or amendment is scheduled to go into effect by the parties to the contract. A service contract or amendment becomes effective at

12:01 a.m. Eastern Standard Time on the beginning of the effective date. The effective date cannot be prior to the filing date of the service contract or amendment with the Commission.

(j) Expiration date means the last day after which the entire service contract is no longer in effect.

(k) File or filing (of service contracts or amendments thereto) means use of the Commission's electronic filing system for receipt of a service contract or an amendment thereto by the Commission, consistent with one of the methods set forth in Appendix A of this part, and the recording of its receipt by the Commission.

(l) Labor agreement means a collective-bargaining agreement between an employer subject to the Act, or group of such employers, and a labor organization or an agreement preparatory to such a collective-bargaining agreement among members of a multi-employer bargaining group, or an agreement specifically implementing provisions of such a collective-bargaining agreement or providing for the formation, financing, or administration of a multi-employer bargaining group, but the term does not include an assessment agreement.

(m) Motor vehicle means an automobile, truck, van or other motor vehicle used for the transportation of passengers and cargo; but does not include equipment such as farm or road equipment which has wheels, but whose primary purpose is other than transportation.

(n) Ocean common carrier means a vessel-operating common carrier.

(o) OIRM means the Commission's Office of Information and Resources Management.

(p) Non-vessel-operating common carrier ("NVOCC") means an ocean transportation intermediary as defined by section 3(17) (B) of the Act.

(q) Service contract means a written contract, other than a bill of lading or receipt, between one or more shippers and an individual ocean common carrier or an agreement between or among ocean common carriers in which the shipper makes a commitment to provide a certain minimum quantity or portion of its cargo or freight revenue over a fixed time period, and the individual ocean common carrier or the agreement commits to a certain rate or rate schedule and a defined service level, such as, assured space, transit time, port rotation, or similar service features. The contract may also specify provisions in the event of nonperformance on the part of any party.

(r) Shipper means a cargo owner; the person for whose account the ocean transportation is provided; the person to whom delivery is to be made; a shippers' association; or an NVOCC that accepts responsibility for payment of all applicable charges under the service contract.

(s) Statement of essential terms means a concise statement of the essential terms of a service contract required to be published under §530.12 of this part.

§ 530.4 Confidentiality.

All service contracts and amendments to service contracts filed with the Commission shall, to the full extent permitted by law, be held in confidence. Nothing contained in this part shall preclude the Commission from providing certain information from or access to service contracts to another agency of the Federal government of the United States.

§ 530.5 Duty to file.

(a) The duty under this part to file service contracts, amendments and notices, and to publish statements of essential terms shall be upon the individual carrier party or parties participating or eligible to participate in the service contract.

(b) Filing may be accomplished by any duly agreed-upon agent, as the parties to the service contract may designate, and subject to conditions as the parties may agree.

(c) Registration. (1) Application. For filing pursuant to dial-up filing (option 2 as outlined in Appendix A of this part) , authority to file or delegate the authority to file must be requested by a responsible official of the service contract carrier party in writing, by submitting to BTCL the Registration Form in Exhibit 1 to this part and the appropriate fee as defined under §530.11.

(2) Approved registrations. OIRM shall provide approved Registrants a log-on ID and password for filing and amending service contracts and so notify Registrants via U.S. mail.

For additional analytical, business and investment opportunities information, please contact Global Investment & Business Center, USA at (703) 370-8082. Fax: (703) 370-8083. E-mail: ibpusa3@gmail.com Global Business and Investment Info Databank - www.ibpus.com

(3) Software certification. For filing pursuant to dial-up filing (option 2 as outlined in Appendix A of this part) , certification of software may be requested by appointment through OIRM and payment of the appropriate fee as set forth in §530.11. OIRM will test the software as set out in Appendix A to this part. Organizations certified prior to May 1, 1999 for the batch filing of "Essential Terms Publications" ("ETs") in the Commission's former "Automated Tariff Filing Information System" ("ATFI") are not required to re-certify their software but may if they so choose using the same procedure as for initial certification.

(4) Emergencies. In an emergency, a person, already authorized to maintain and edit its firm's organization record under Appendix A of this part, may change its designated "publisher" under Appendix A of this part, verbally notify BTCL, and promptly submit the proper documents.

(5) Prior registration and certification. Each organization registered to file essential terms publications in the Commission's dial-up system before May 1, 1999 will be issued a log-on ID and password for access to file service contracts under the Commission's electronic filing system pursuant to option 2 as set forth in Appendix A of this part.

§ 530.6 Certification of shipper status.

(a) Certification. The shipper contract party shall sign and certify on the signature page of the service contract its shipper status (e.g., owner of the cargo, shippers' association, NVOCC, or specified other designation) , and the status of every affiliate of such contract party or member of a shippers' association entitled to receive service under the contract.

(b) Proof of tariff and financial responsibility. If the certification completed by the contract party under paragraph (a) of this section identifies the contract party or an affiliate or member of a shippers' association as an NVOCC, the ocean common carrier, conference or agreement shall obtain proof that such NVOCC has a published tariff and proof of financial responsibility as required under sections 8 and 19 of the Act before signing the service contract. An ocean common carrier, conference or agreement can obtain such proof by the same methods prescribed in §515.27 of this chapter.

(c) Joining shippers' association during term of contract. If an NVOCC joins a shippers' association during the term of a service contract and is thereby entitled to receive service under the contract, the NVOCC shall provide to the ocean common carrier, agreement or conference the proof of compliance required by paragraph (b) of this section prior to making any shipments under the contract.

(d) Reliance on NVOCC proof; independent knowledge. An ocean common carrier, agreement or conference executing a service contract shall be deemed to have complied with section 10(b) (12) of the Act upon meeting the requirements of paragraphs (a) and (b) of this section, unless the carrier party had reason to know such certification or documentation of NVOCC tariff and bonding was false.

§ 530.7 Duty to labor organizations.

(a) Terms. When used in this section, the following terms will have these meanings:

(1) Dock area and within the port area shall have the same meaning and scope as defined in the applicable collective bargaining agreement.

For additional analytical, business and investment opportunities information, please contact Global Investment & Business Center, USA at (703) 370-8082. Fax: (703) 370-8083. E-mail: ibpusa3@gmail.com Global Business and Investment Info Databank - www.ibpus.com

(2) Reasonable period of time ordinarily means:

(i) if the cargo in question is due to arrive in less than five (5) days from the date of receipt of the request as defined in paragraph (b) of this section, two (2) days from the date of receipt of the request; but

(ii) if cargo in question is due to arrive in more than five (5) days from the date of receipt of the request as defined in paragraph (b) of this section, four (4) days from the date of receipt of the request.

(3) Movement includes, but is not necessarily limited to, the normal and usual aspects of the loading and discharging of cargo in containers; placement, positioning and re-positioning of cargo or of containers; the insertion and removal of cargo into and from containers; and the storage and warehousing of cargo.

(4) Assignment includes, but is not limited to, the carrier's direct or indirect control over the parties which, the manner by which, or the means by which the shipper's cargo is moved, regardless of whether such movement is completed within or outside of containers.

(5) Transmit means communication by first-class mail, facsimile, telegram, hand-delivery, or electronic mail ("e-mail") .

(b) Procedure. In response to a written request transmitted from a labor organization with which it is a party or is subject to the provisions of a collective bargaining agreement with a labor organization, an ocean common carrier shall state, within a reasonable period of time, whether it is responsible for the following work at dock areas and within port areas in the United States with respect to cargo transported under a service contract:

(1) the movement of the shipper's cargo on a dock area or within the port area or to or from railroad cars on a dock area or within a port area;

(2) the assignment of intraport carriage of the shipper's cargo between areas on a dock or within the port area;

(3) the assignment of the carriage of the shipper's cargo between a container yard on a dock area or within the port area and a rail yard adjacent to such container yard; or

(4) the assignment of container freight station work and maintenance and repair work performed at a dock area or within the port area.

(c) Applicability. This section requires the disclosure of information by an ocean common carrier only if there exists an applicable and otherwise lawful collective bargaining agreement which pertains to that carrier.

(d) Disclosure not deemed admission or agreement. No disclosure made by an ocean common carrier shall be deemed to be an admission or agreement that any work is covered by a collective bargaining agreement.

(e) Dispute resolution. Any dispute regarding whether any work is covered by a collective bargaining agreement and the responsibility of the ocean common carrier under such agreement shall be resolved solely in accordance with the dispute resolution procedures contained in the

For additional analytical, business and investment opportunities information, please contact Global Investment & Business Center, USA at (703) 370-8082. Fax: (703) 370-8083. E-mail: ibpusa3@gmail.com Global Business and Investment Info Databank - www.ibpus.com

collective bargaining agreement and the National Labor Relations Act, and without reference to this section.

(f) Jurisdiction and lawfulness. Nothing in this section has any effect on the lawfulness or unlawfulness under the Shipping Act of 1984, the National Labor Relations Act, the Taft-Hartley Act, the Federal Trade Commission Act, the antitrust laws, or any other federal or state law, or any revisions or amendments thereto, of any collective bargaining agreement or element thereof, including any element that constitutes an essential term of a service contract under section 8(c) of the Act.

SUBPART B -- FILING REQUIREMENTS

§ 530.8 Service Contracts.

(a) Authorized persons shall file with BTCL, in one of the manners set forth in Appendix A of this part, a true and complete copy of every service contract or amendment to a filed service contract before any cargo moves pursuant to that service contract or amendment.

(b) Every service contract filed with the Commission shall include the complete terms of the service contract including, but not limited to, the following:

(1) the origin port ranges in the case of port-to-port movements and geographic areas in the case of through intermodal movements;

(2) the destination port ranges in the case of port-to-port movements and geographic areas in the case of through intermodal movements;

(3) the commodity or commodities involved;

(4) the minimum volume or portion;

(5) the service commitments;

(6) the line-haul rate;

(7) liquidated damages for non-performance (if any) ;

(8) duration, including the

(i) effective date; and

(ii) expiration date;

(9) the legal names and business addresses of the contract parties; the legal names of affiliates entitled to access the contract; the names, titles and addresses of the representatives signing the contract for the parties; and the date upon which the service contract was signed, except that in the case of a contract entered under the authority of an agreement or by a shippers' association, individual members need not be named unless the contract includes or excludes specific members. Subsequent references in the contract to the contract parties shall be consistent with

the first reference (e.g., (exact name) , "carrier," "shipper," or "association," etc.) . Carrier parties which enter into contracts that include affiliates must either:

(i) list the affiliates' business addresses; or

(ii) certify that this information will be provided to the Commission upon request within ten (10) business days of such request. However, the requirements of this section do not apply to amendments to contracts that have been filed in accordance with the requirements of this section unless the amendment adds new parties or affiliates;

(10) a certification of shipper status;

(11) a description of the shipment records which will be maintained to support the service contract and the address, telephone number, and title of the person who will respond to a request by making shipment records available to the Commission for inspection under §530.15 of this part; and

(12) all other provisions of the contract.

(c) Certainty of terms. The terms described in paragraph (b) of this section may not:

(1) be uncertain, vague or ambiguous; or

(2) make reference to terms not explicitly contained in the service contract filing itself, unless those terms are contained in a publication widely available to the public and well known within the industry.

(d) Other requirements. Every service contract filed with BTCL shall include, as set forth in Appendix A of this part by:

(1) A unique service contract number of more than one (1) but less than ten (10) alphanumeric characters in length ("SC Number") ; and

(2) A consecutively numbered amendment number no more than three digits in length, with initial service contracts using "0"("Amendment number") ;

(3) The filed FMC Agreement Number(s) assigned by the Commission under 46 CFR part 535(if applicable) ; and

(4) An indication of the method by which the statement of essential terms will be published.

§ 530.9 Notices.

Within thirty (30) days of the occurrence of any event listed below, there shall be filed with the Commission, pursuant to the same procedures as those followed for the filing of an amendment pursuant to §530.10 and Appendix A of this part, a detailed notice of:

(a) correction (clerical or administrative errors) ;

(b) cancellation (as defined in §530.10(a) (3)) ;

For additional analytical, business and investment opportunities information, please contact Global Investment & Business Center, USA at (703) 370-8082. Fax: (703) 370-8083. E-mail: ibpusa3@gmail.com Global Business and Investment Info Databank - www.ibpus.com

(c) adjustment of accounts, by re-rating, liquidated damages, or otherwise;

(d) final settlement of any account adjusted as described in paragraph (c) of this section; and

(e) any change to:

(1) the name of a basic contract party; or

(2) the list of affiliates under §530.8(b) (9) , including changes to legal names and business addresses, of any contract party entitled to receive or authorized to offer services under the contract.

§ 530.10 Amendment, correction, and cancellation.

(a) Terms. When used in this section, the following terms will have these meanings:

(1) Amendment means any change to a service contract which has prospective effect and which is mutually agreed upon by the service contract parties.

(2) Correction means any change to a service contract which has retroactive effect.

(3) Cancellation means an event which is unanticipated by the service contract, in liquidated damages or otherwise, and is due to the failure of the shipper party to tender minimum cargo as set forth in the contract, unless such tender was made impossible by an action of the carrier party.

(b) Amendment. Service contracts may be amended by mutual agreement of the parties to the contract. Amendments shall be filed electronically with the Commission in the manner set forth in §530.8 and Appendix A of this part.

(1) Where feasible, service contracts should be amended by amending only the affected specific term(s) or subterms.

(2) Each time any part of a service contract is amended, the filer shall assign a consecutive amendment number (up to three digits) , beginning with the number "1."

(3) Each time any part of the service contract is amended, the "Filing Date" will be the date of filing of the amendment.

(c) Corrections. Either party to a filed service contract may request permission to correct clerical or administrative errors in the terms of a filed contract. Requests shall be filed, in duplicate, with the Commission's Office of the Secretary within forty-five (45) days of the contract's filing with the Commission, and shall include:

(1) a letter of transmittal explaining the purpose of the submission, and providing specific information to identify the initial or amended service contract to be corrected;

(2) a paper copy of the proposed correct terms. Corrections shall be indicated as follows:

(i) matter being deleted shall be struck through; and

For additional analytical, business and investment opportunities information, please contact Global Investment & Business Center, USA at (703) 370-8082. Fax: (703) 370-8083. E-mail: ibpusa3@gmail.com Global Business and Investment Info Databank - www.ibpus.com

(ii) matter to be added shall immediately follow the language being deleted and be underscored;

(3) an affidavit from the filing party attesting with specificity to the factual circumstances surrounding the clerical or administrative error, with reference to any supporting documentation;

(4) documents supporting the clerical or administrative error; and

(5) a brief statement from the other party to the contract concurring in the request for correction.

(6) If the request for correction is granted, the carrier, agreement or conference shall file the corrected contract provisions using a special case number as described in Appendix A of this part.

(d) Cancellation. (1) An account may be adjusted for events and damages covered by the service contract. This shall include adjustment necessitated by either liability for liquidated damages under §530.8(b) (8) , or the occurrence of an event described in paragraph (2) .

(2) In the event of cancellation as defined in §530.10(a) (3) :

(i) Further or continued implementation of the service contract is prohibited; and

(ii) The cargo previously carried under the contract shall be re-rated according to the otherwise applicable tariff provisions.

(e) If the amendment, correction or cancellation affects an essential term required to be published under §530.12 of this part, the statement of essential terms shall be changed as soon as possible after the filing of the amendment to accurately reflect the change to the contract terms.

§ 530.11 Filing Fees and other costs.

(a) Under the authority of the Independent Offices Appropriation Act, 31 U.S.C 9701, the Commission assesses a filing fee for the filing of service contracts, modifications and corrections thereto. Unless otherwise provided in this part, checks, drafts or money orders shall be remitted and made payable to "Federal Maritime Commission," 800 N. Capitol Street, N.W., Washington, DC 20573.

(b) Unless otherwise specified, overdue payments will be charged interest in accordance with the rate established by the Department of the Treasury for each 30-day period or portion thereof that the payment is overdue. In addition to any other remedy and penalty provided by law and regulation, if payment is overdue for ninety (90) days the Commission may suspend or terminate electronic filing access.

(c) Fees. (1) Service contracts and amendments. For filing pursuant to option 2, as set forth in Appendix A of this part ("dial-up filing") , the filing fee shall be $1.63 per filing for all initial and amended service contract filings.

(2) Filer registration. For filing pursuant to option 2, filer registration fee shall be $91 for initial registration for one firm and one individual; and $91 for additions and changes. No fee will be assessed to continue filer registration for organizations registered for batch filing with the Commission prior to May 1, 1999.

For additional analytical, business and investment opportunities information, please contact Global Investment & Business Center, USA at (703) 370-8082. Fax: (703) 370-8083. E-mail: ibpusa3@gmail.com Global Business and Investment Info Databank - www.ibpus.com

(3) Filing Guide. For filing pursuant to option 2, filing guides shall cost $25 for diskette; $49 for paper format. Requests for filing guides should be made in writing and addressed to: "BTCL Manuals," Federal Maritime Commission, 800 N. Capitol Street, NW, Washington, DC 20753.

(4) Corrections. The fee for corrections to service contracts under §530.10(c) shall be $233.

(5) Software certification. For filing pursuant to option 2, the fee for software certification shall be $496 per test submission.

SUBPART C -- PUBLICATION OF ESSENTIAL TERMS

§ 530.12 Publication.

(a) Contents. All authorized persons who have a duty to file service contracts under §530.5 are also required to make available to the public, contemporaneously with the filing of each service contract with the Commission, and in tariff format, a concise statement of the following essential terms:

(1) the port ranges:

(i) origin; and

(ii) destination;

(2) the commodity or commodities involved;

(3) the minimum volume or portion; and

(4) the duration.

(b) Certainty of terms. The terms described in paragraph (a) of this section may not:

(1) be uncertain, vague or ambiguous; or

(2) make reference to terms not explicitly detailed in the statement of essential terms, unless those terms are contained in a publication widely available to the public and well known within the industry.

(c) Location. (1) The statement of essential terms shall be published as a separate part in the filer's automated tariff publication, conforming to the format requirements set forth in part 520 of this chapter.

(2) Multi-party service contracts. For contracts in which more than one carrier party participates or is eligible to participate, the statement of essential terms may be published:

(1) as a separate part of the parties' relevant conference tariff; or

(2) by each of the parties as a separate part of their individual tariff publication pursuant to part 520, clearly indicating the relevant FMC-assigned agreement number.

For additional analytical, business and investment opportunities information, please contact Global Investment & Business Center, USA at (703) 370-8082. Fax: (703) 370-8083. E-mail: ibpusa3@gmail.com Global Business and Investment Info Databank - www.ibpus.com

(c) References. The statement of essential terms shall contain a reference to the same number as that for the confidentially filed service contract ("SC Number" as described in §530.8(d) (1)) .

(d) Terms. (1) The publication of the statement of essential terms shall accurately reflect the terms as filed confidentially with the Commission.

(2) If any of the published essential terms include information not required to be filed with the Commission but filed voluntarily, the statement of essential terms shall so note.

(e) Agents. Common carriers, conferences, or agreements may use agents to meet their publication requirements under this part.

(f) Commission listing. The Commission will publish on its website, www.fmc.gov, a listing of the locations of all service contract essential terms publications.

(g) Updating statements of essential terms. To ensure that the information contained in a published statement of essential terms is current and accurate, the statement of essential terms publication shall include a prominent notice indicating the date of its most recent publication or revision. When the published statement of essential terms is affected by filed amendments, corrections, or cancellations, the current terms shall be changed and published as soon as possible in the relevant statement of essential terms.

SUBPART D - EXCEPTIONS AND IMPLEMENTATION

§ 530.13 Exceptions.

(a) Generally. The Commission will not accept for filing service contracts which exclusively concern bulk cargo, forest products, recycled metal scrap, new assembled motor vehicles, waste paper or paper waste, as those terms are defined in Section 3 of the Act or § 530.3 of this part, or service contracts which relate solely to commodities or services exempted from service contract filing by the Commission under Section 16 of the Act.

(b) Inclusion in service contracts. An excepted commodity or exempted service, as listed in paragraph (a) of this section, may be included in a service contract filed with the Commission, but only if:

(1) there is a tariff of general applicability for the transportation, which contains a specific commodity rate for the excepted commodity; or

(2) the contract itself sets forth a rate or charge which will be applied if the contract is canceled, as defined in §530.10(a) (3) .

(c) Waiver of exemption. Upon filing under this section, the service contract shall be subject to the same requirements as those for service contracts generally.

§ 530.14 Implementation

(a) Generally. Performance under a service contract or amendment thereto may not begin before the day it is effective and filed with the Commission.

For additional analytical, business and investment opportunities information, please contact Global Investment & Business Center, USA at (703) 370-8082. Fax: (703) 370-8083. E-mail: ibpusa3@gmail.com Global Business and Investment Info Databank - www.ibpus.com

(b) Prohibition or suspension. When the filing parties receive notice that an initial or amended service contract has been prohibited under Section 9(d) or suspended under Section 11a(e) (1) (B) of the Act:

(1) further or continued implementation of the service contract is prohibited;

(2) all services performed under the contract shall be re-rated in accordance with the otherwise applicable tariff provisions for such services with notice to the shipper within five (5) days of the date of prohibition or suspension; and

(3) detailed notice shall be given to the Commission under §530.9 within thirty (30) days of:

(i) the re-rating or other account adjustment resulting from prohibition or suspension under paragraph (b) (2) of this section; or

(ii) final settlement of the account adjusted under §530.10. (c) Agreements. If the prohibited or suspended service contract was that of an agreement with no common tariff, the re-rating shall be in accordance with the published tariff rates of the carrier which transported the cargo in effect at the time.

SUBPART E - RECORDKEEPING AND AUDIT

§ 530.15 Recordkeeping and audit.

(a) Records retention for five years. Every common carrier, conference or agreement shall maintain original signed service contracts, amendments, and their associated records in an organized, readily accessible or retrievable manner for a period of five (5) years from the termination of each contract.

(b) [paragraph (b) is stayed until further notice.] Where maintained. (1) Service contract records shall be maintained in the United States, except that service contract records may be maintained outside the United States if the Chairman or Secretary of an agreement or President or Chief Executive Officer of the carrier certifies annually by January 1, on a form to be supplied by the Commission, that service contract records will be made available as provided in paragraph (c) of this section.

(2) Penalty. If service contract records are not made available to the Commission as provided in paragraph (c) of this section, the Commission may cancel any carrier's or agreement's right to maintain records outside the United States pursuant to the certification procedure of paragraph

(b) of this section.

(c) Production for audit within 30 days of request. Every carrier or agreement shall, upon written request of the FMC's Director, Bureau of Enforcement, any Area Representative or the Director, Bureau of Economics and Agreements Analysis, submit copies of requested original service contracts or their associated records within thirty (30) days of the date of the request.

(d) Agreement service contracts. In the case of service contracts made by agreements, the penalties for a failure to maintain records pursuant to this section shall attach jointly and severally on all of the agreement members participating in the service contract in question.

For additional analytical, business and investment opportunities information, please contact Global Investment & Business Center, USA at (703) 370-8082. Fax: (703) 370-8083. E-mail: ibpusa3@gmail.com Global Business and Investment Info Databank - www.ibpus.com

§ 530.91 OMB control numbers assigned pursuant to the Paperwork Reduction Act.

The Commission has received OMB approval for this collection of information pursuant to the Paperwork Reduction Act of 1995, as amended. In accordance with that Act, agencies are required to display a currently valid control number. The valid control number for this collection of information is 3072-0065.

**For additional analytical, business and investment opportunities information,
please contact Global Investment & Business Center, USA
at (703) 370-8082. Fax: (703) 370-8083. E-mail: ibpusa3@gmail.com
Global Business and Investment Info Databank - www.ibpus.com**

BASIC AGREEMENTS AND OFFICIAL DOCUMENTS

CARRIER AGREEMENTS IN THE U.S. OCEANBORNE TRADES

Carrier Agreements in the U.S. Oceanborne Trades is published electronically by the Bureau of Trade Analysis, and is updated quarterly. The publication provides essential information about all carrier agreements filed with the Federal Maritime Commission and in effect as of the most recent update. Agreements are listed in order of the number assigned by the Commission at the time of filing.

In addition to the agreement number, each page lists the full legal name of the agreement, as well as its type, followed by several items of relevant information:

x Scope describes the geographic extension of the agreement in general terms. Particular

U.S. or foreign coasts or ports are listed only when the agreement does not include the entire country. The designation *intermodal authority* indicates whether U.S. or foreign inland points are served. In some instances, Canada is shown as part of the U.S. scope. This reflects only the current wording of the agreement, and does not imply that the Commission exercises jurisdiction over that portion of the scope.

x Authority lists the principal kinds of authority set forth in the agreement.

Binding rate-making authority is that which typically characterizes conference agreements, while *non-binding rate-making authority* is ordinarily found in cooperative working agreements and discussion agreements.

Neutral body self-policing is shown in the listing whenever an agreement contains language beyond what is required by statute, whether or not such self-policing has actually been implemented.

Service contract authority may apply to an agreement as a whole, or to individual member carriers. The designation *member (I/A) service contract authority* means that individual carriers may choose not to participate in a service contract entered into by the conference of which they are members.

Pooling authority specifies whether the agreement includes revenue or cargo pooling among the member lines.

Other less common types of authority listed include *alternate port service*, *loyalty contracts* and *discussion of intermodal issues*.

x Members are listed alphabetically, as of the most recent update.

x Filing Counsel indicates the person and, in most instances, the name and address of the law firm responsible for filing the agreement and any amendments to it. Where applicable, the same information is furnished for the Administrative Official of an agreement.

There are four appendices immediately following the primary agreement listing. These provide cross-references to the agreements by name, participant, geographic area and type.

For additional analytical, business and investment opportunities information, please contact Global Investment & Business Center, USA at (703) 370-8082. Fax: (703) 370-8083. E-mail: ibpusa3@gmail.com Global Business and Investment Info Databank - www.ibpus.com

GRAND ALLIANCE AGREEMENT

Type: COOPERATIVE WORKING AGREEMENT Scope: BETWEEN U.S. ATLANTIC, GULF AND PACIFIC COAST PORTS AND POINTS AND POINTS AND PORTS IN THE FAR EAST, SOUTH EAST AND WEST ASIA, ARABIAN GULF, RED SEA, GULF OF OMAN, EUROPE, CANADA AND MEXICO

Authority: RATE AUTHORITY (NON-BINDING) SPACE CHARTERING SAILING

U.S. INTERMODAL AUTHORITY FOREIGN INTERMODAL AUTHORITY Members: HAPAG-LLOYD, A.G.

NEPTUNE ORIENT LINES, LTD. NIPPON YUSEN KAISHA P&O CONTAINERS LIMITED

Filing Counsel: NEAL M. MAYER HOPPEL, MAYER & COLEMAN SUITE 400 1000 CONNECTICUT AVENUE, N.W. WASHINGTON, DC 20036

For additional analytical, business and investment opportunities information, please contact Global Investment & Business Center, USA at (703) 370-8082. Fax: (703) 370-8083. E-mail: ibpusa3@gmail.com Global Business and Investment Info Databank - www.ibpus.com

SUPPLEMENTS

IMPORTANT CONTACTS

Assistance with household goods, cargo shipment disputes, and passenger vessel complaints:

Contact the Consumer Affairs & Dispute Resolution Services:
Phone: 202-523-5807
Email: complaints@fmc.gov

Questions regarding Service Contracts, Tariffs and Carrier/MTO Agreements:

Contact the Bureau of Trade Analysis:
Phone: 202-523-5796
Email: tradeanalysis@fmc.gov

For Information about OTI Regulatory Requirements:

Visit our Ocean Transportation Intermediaries resource page

For Information on how to apply for an OTI License:

Visit our How to Become FMC Licensed page

General Help or Information

If you are not sure where to send your question or request, please submit general information, comments, & inquiries to:Inquiries@fmc.gov

Freedom of Information Act (FOIA) requests: foia@fmc.gov

Questions or filings in Docketed Proceedings, Commission Sunshine Act Meetings, or Press Inquiries, please contact the FMC's Secretary:secretary@fmc.gov

Docket Activity Library
Phone: 202-523-5760
E-mail: Magdalene Grant

Law & Reference Library
Phone: 202-523-5762

Additional Points of Contact:

Visit the Commissioners' Pages for individual contact information

Visit the Bureaus & Offices Page and click on the office you'd like to contact

By Mail

Federal Maritime Commission
800 North Capitol Street, N.W
Washington, D.C. 20573

AREA REPRESENTATIVES

HOUSTON
Houston Area Representative
Adam Sinko
Phone: 281-386-8211
Email: ASinko@fmc.gov

LOS ANGELES
Los Angeles Area Representatives
Oliver E. Clark
Phone: 310-514-4905
Fax: 310-514-3931
Email: oclark@fmc.gov

Nash D. Asandas
Phone: 310-514-8618
Fax: 310-514-3931
E-mail: nasandas@fmc.gov

NEW ORLEANS
Please contact Michael Carley at the Washington D.C. office until further notice.
Phone: 202-523-5800
Fax: 202-523-3646
Email: mcarley@fmc.gov
New Orleans Area Representative
(VACANT)
Phone: 504-466-6380
Fax: 504-466-6379

NEW YORK
New York Area Representative
Ronald Podlaskowich

Phone: 732-283-2496
Fax: 732-283-2498
E-Mail: RPodlaskowich@fmc.gov
Matthew D. Forst, Assistant Area Representative
732-283-2497 (VMS)
E-Mail: MForst@fmc.gov

SEATTLE
Seattle Area Representative
Michael A. Moneck

Phone: 253-922-7622
Fax: 253-922-7859
E-mail: mmoneck@fmc.gov

SOUTH FLORIDA
South Florida Area Representatives
Andrew Margolis
Phone: 954-963-5362
Fax: 954-963-5630
E-mail: amargolis@fmc.gov

Eric O. Mintz
Phone: 954-963-5284
Fax: 954-963-5630
E-mail: emintz@fmc.gov

OCEAN FREIGHT FORWARDERS

#	Business	Phone	Distance (mi)
1	"A" PACIFIC EXPRESS, ENTERPRISES SOUTH EL MONTE, CA 91733	(626) 618-3888	2296.2
2	"K" LINE LOGISTICS (U.S.A.) INC. SPRINGFIELD GARDENS, NY 11413	(718) 807-3200	214.6
3	1 JML CORPORATION INC DORAL, FL 33166	(786) 331-9406	928.5
4	1 TRADE FWDNG INC GRAPEVINE, TX 76051	(817) 310-0222	1198.5
5	1-800 SHIPPING, INC. TAYLORS, SC 29687	(800) 480-5158	880.6
6	20CUBE LOGISTICS WORLDWIDE, LLC FOREST PARK, GA 30297	(678) 884-8300	550.1

#	Business	Phone	Distance (mi)
7	311 LLC SUNRISE, FL 33322	(305) 343-8727	905.7
8	3PLUS LOGISTICS CO. RANCHO DOMINGUEZ, CA 90221	(310) 667-5160	2311.0
9	4 SEAS INTERNATIONAL SHIPPING, INC. WEST PALM BEACH, FL 33410	(561) 775-6621	858.4
10	7 CARGO CORP. WEST NEW YORK, NJ 07093	(201) 422-9795	207.7
11	721 LOGISTICS LLC LESTER, PA 19113	(610) 994-5060	116.1
12	A & A LTD. NEW BEDFORD, MA 02740	(508) 999-1383	375.7
13	A & E LOGISTICS, INC. CHICAGO, IL 60608	(312) 375-1668	597.4
14	A & K FORWARDING, INC. HOUSTON, TX 77027	(713) 961-9042	228.9
15	A & S SHIPPING COMPANY, INC. MIAMI, FL 33126	(305) 884-1268	930.1
16	A 1 WORLDWIDE LOGISTICS, INC. MIAMI LAKES, FL 33016	(305) 821-8995	924.7
17	A A EQUIPMENT AND SALES, LLC KATY, TX 77493	(713) 489-8911	1239.2
18	A C WILSON COMPANY L.L.C. PORTLAND, OR 97205	(503) 223-7762	2361.6
19	A CUSTOM BROKERAGE, INC. DORAL, FL 33172	(305) 805-6797	928.6
20	A G WORLD TRANSPORT, INC. SOUTH SAN FRANCISCO, CA 94080	(650) 246-3737	2450.6

#	Business	Phone	Distance (mi)
21	A PLUS INTERNATIONAL (U.S.A.) INC. VALLEY STREAM, NY 11581	(516) 887-3664	215.1
22	A R O CARGO SERVICES, INC. WOODSIDE, NY 11377	(718) 779-5711	210.5
23	A&A CONTRACT CUSTOMS BROKERS, USA, INC. BLAINE, WA 98230	(888) 332-2202	2352.2
24	A&C IMPORT EXPORT SERVICES, INC. BROOKLYN, NY 11219	(718) 259-0162	202.1
25	A. HARTRODT (U.S.A.) , INC. LYNBROOK, NY 11563		217.0
26	A. J. ARANGO, INC. TAMPA, FL 33605	(813) 248-9220	821.5
27	A. N. DERINGER, INC. ST. ALBANS, VT 05478	(802) 524-8108	459.2
28	A. NAIMOLI FREIGHT FORWARDING, INC. OZONE PARK, NY 11417	(718) 848-3050	210.7
29	A. R. SAVAGE & SON, INC. TAMPA, FL 33606	(813) 247-4550	823.1

30	A.C. GLOBAL LLC LINDEN, NJ 07036	(732) 680-1998	190.8
31	A.E. & N. CARGO, INC. MIAMI, FL 33166	(305) 599-0204	927.7
32	A.G. CARGO IMPORT, INC. HOUSTON, TX 77060	(713) 933-9300	1219.6
33	A.I.B INTERNACIONAL, LLC. DORAL, FL 33126	(305) 629-9710	928.8
34	A.J. KEELER U.S.A. INCORPORATED IRVINE, CA 92604-3717	(949) 216-7808	2292.2
35	A.J. WORLDWIDE SERVICES INC. SECAUCUS, NJ 07094	(201) 348-1800	205.3
36	A.J.B. INTERNATIONAL TRANSPORT, INC. DORAL, FL 33178	(305) 477-9960	929.4
37	A.L'S FREIGHT FORWARDING, INC. MIAMI, FL 33122	(305) 592-0057	929.9
38	A.M. CARGO SERVICES, INC. MIAMI, FL 33166	(305) 640-9857	928.5
39	A.ROYAL SHIPPING LINE INC. HOUSTON, TX 77067	(281) 931-8877	1223.2
40	A.V. REILLY INTERNATIONAL LTD. WOOD DALE, IL 60191	(630) 238-4900	617.1

#	Business	Phone	Distance (mi)
41	A.W.L.I. GROUP OF FLORIDA INC. MIAMI, FL 33166	(305) 716-1119	931.0
42	A.W.L.I. GROUP, INC. JAMAICA, NY 11434	(718) 244-8923	213.2
43	A+ AIRFREIGHT, INC. SPRING, TX 77391	(281) 655-9955	1222.7
44	A-1 FARGO VAN AND STORAGE, INC. MIAMI, FL 33156	(305) 670-9501	938.3
45	A2B CARGO LLC KENNESAW, GA 30144	(678) 934-1335	541.2
46	AAA COOPER TRANSPORTATION DOTHAN, AL 36303	(334) 793-2284	711.9
47	AAA DISPATCH INTERNATIONAL, INC. SONOMA, CA 95476	(707) 996-7960	2442.0
48	AAA INTERCONTINENTAL CARGO, INC. WEBSTER, TX 77598	(281) 772-7785	1222.5
49	AAA INTERNATIONAL SHIPPING, LLC OAKLAND, FL 32819	(407) 347-0702	766.5
50	AAPKO FORWARDERS, INC. POINT PLEASANT BEACH, NJ 08742	(908) 688-1050	180.3
51	AAWI LOGISTICAL SERVICES, LLC FARMERSVILLE, TX 75442	(972) 744-0205	1153.9
52	AB GLOBAL LOGISTICS CONSULTING INC. SANTA MONICA, CA 90403	(310) 404-9075	2321.0

For additional analytical, business and investment opportunities information, please contact Global Investment & Business Center, USA at (703) 370-8082. Fax: (703) 370-8083. E-mail: ibpusa3@gmail.com Global Business and Investment Info Databank - www.ibpus.com

#	Business	Phone	Distance (mi)
53	AB GROUP SHIPPING CORP MIAMI, FL 33166	(305) 635-2525	927.9
54	AB INTERNATIONAL BROKERS INC. MIAMI, FL 33186	(305) 416-3255	940.0
55	AB PLANT SHIPPING USA, L.L.C. HOUSTON, TX 77068	(832) 300-5925	1221.6
56	ABBA TRANS, LLC ELK GROVE VILLAGE, IL 60007	(847) 338-7757	616.8
57	ABIS FORWARDING, INC. MIAMI, FL 33178	(305) 463-7625	924.9
58	ABLE FREIGHT SERVICES, INC. LOS ANGELES, CA 90045	(310) 568-8883	2317.1
59	ABLE MOVING AND STORAGE, INC. MANASSAS, VA 20109	(703) 330-3772	27.4
60	ABOARD CARGO SERVICE, INC. MIAMI, FL 33172	(305) 593-7072	930.7
61	ABSLOGIX IRVINE, CA 92604	(949) 294-1142	2291.8
62	ABSOLUTE GLOBAL SHIPPING INCORPORATED BRANDON, FL 33511	(813) 731-3959	821.0
63	ABSOLUTE SHIPPING LLC ELIZABETH, NJ 07208	(908) 354-8980	194.5
64	AC EXPORT, LLC MIAMI, FL 33166	(305) 597-3945	928.5
65	AC INTERNATIONAL HOLDINGS, INC. MIAMI, FL 33172	(305) 593-1750	930.8
66	ACAE LOGISTICS COMPANY, INC. PASADENA, TX 77506	(713) 472-3013	1219.4
67	ACC SHIPPING U.S.A., LTD. STATEN ISLAND, NY 10306	(718) 980-6871	195.2
68	ACCELERATED GLOBAL LOGISTICS LLC SEATTLE, WA 98158	(206) 418-6713	2335.2
69	ACCELERATED INTERNATIONAL FORWARDERS, LLC FT. WAYNE, IN 46805	(260) 490-7473	454.9
70	ACCESS FREIGHT FORWARDERS, LLC NORTH CHARLESTON, SC 29418	(843) 724-3434	451.1
71	ACCESS INTERNATIONAL SERVICES, CORP. MIAMI, FL 33166	(305) 639-6762	927.7
72	ACCO FOREIGN SHIPPING, INC. DORAL, FL 33172	(305) 591-8380	930.8
73	ACD CARGO, INC. DORAL, FL 33172	(305) 463-0818	930.7
74	ACE GLOBAL DISTRIBUTION LLC OAK BROOK, IL 60523	(630) 990-6600	612.6
75	ACI CARGO, INC. DORAL, FL 33166	(305) 418-4104	928.6

#	Business	Phone	Distance (mi)
76	ACM LOGISTICS & CONSULTING, INC. THE WOODLANDS, TX 77385	(832) 932-2930	1212.4
77	ACROCARGO EXPRESS INC. WEST HILLS, CA 91304	(818) 224-7258	2324.4
78	ACS LOGISTICS USA INC. MANALAPAN, NJ 07726	(732) 536-5000	176.1
79	ACTION CUSTOMS EXPEDITERS, INC. JERSEY CITY, NJ 07302	(201) 333-8888	203.9
80	ACTION ONE LOGISTICS, INC. WHITEFORD, MD 21160	(410) 877-1501	58.0
81	ACTION WORLDWIDE CARGO SERVICES, INC. HOUSTON, TX 77060	(281) 447-5552	1218.8
82	ADM LOGISTICS, INC. DECATUR, IL 62526	(317) 451-5200	639.4
83	ADMIRAL AIR EXPRESS, INC. BENSENVILLE, IL 60106	(630) 350-7000	615.3
84	ADMIRAL GLOBAL LINES INC. SECAUCUS, NJ 07094	(201) 319-6647	206.2
85	ADMIRAL INTERNATIONAL FREIGHT FORWARDERS, INC MEDLEY, FL 33178-1047	(305) 885-4636	927.1
86	ADP GLOBAL LOGISTICS LLC ELMHURST, IL 60126	(630) 279-6630	613.0
87	ADP GLOBAL LOGISTICS, INC. (USA) CITY OF INDUSTRY, CA 91789	(310) 381-9599	2288.8
88	ADUAMERICA USA CORP. MIAMI, FL 33186	(786) 260-0160	940.0
89	ADVANCE CARGO CORPORATION MIAMI, FL 33166	(786) 837-1833	927.7
90	ADVANCE SHIPPING COMPANY, INC. NEW YORK, NY 10007	(212) 964-1050	205.0
91	ADVANTEX EXPRESS INC. HUMBLE, TX 77338	(281) 645-4143	1214.0
92	ADVECTUS TRANSPORTATION SERVICES LLC LINDEN, NJ 07036	(973) 271-9690	191.5
93	AE EAGLE LOGISTICS INC. BENSENVILLE, IL 60106	(630) 238-8833	615.6
94	AEROMUNDO EXPRESS, INC. MIAMI, FL 33176	(305) 463-8335	927.9
95	AERONET, INC. IRVINE, CA 92606-3103	(949) 474-3000	2293.9
96	AEROSTAR GLOBAL LOGISTICS, INC. LOMBARD, IL 60148	(630) 458-8854	616.8
97	AEROTYME, INC. KENNER, LA 70062	(504) 466-2176	975.9
98	AES LOGISTICS, INC. BURIEN, WA 98166	(206) 214-0341	2335.9

For additional analytical, business and investment opportunities information, please contact Global Investment & Business Center, USA at (703) 370-8082. Fax: (703) 370-8083. E-mail: ibpusa3@gmail.com Global Business and Investment Info Databank - www.ibpus.com

#	Business	Phone	Distance (mi)
99	AETNA FORWARDING, INC. VALLEY STREAM, NY 11580	(516) 825-5885	216.6
100	AETNA LOGISTICS GROUP, INC. WESTCHESTER, IL 60154	(773) 312-3862	609.4

#	Business	Phone	Distance (mi)
101	AFC LS, LLC KENNESAW, GA 30144	(877) 837-3178	541.1
102	AFC WORLDWIDE EXPRESS, INC. ATLANTA, GA 30331	(800) 543-5589	734.4
103	AFRICA 2000, INCORPORATED HOUSTON, TX 77032	(281) 445-0400	1215.1
104	AFS ADVANTAGE, L.L.C. SHREVEPORT, LA 71101	(318) 798-2111	1040.1
105	AG INTERNATIONAL CARGO CORP MIAMI, FL 33166	(305) 396-6093	928.5
106	AG INTERNATIONAL, INC. SEATTLE, WA 98144	(206) 281-7617	2334.7
107	AG TECHNICAL GROUP, LLC DALLAS, TX 75217	(214) 881-4003	1182.8
108	AGENCY INTERNATIONAL FORWARDING, INC. MIAMI, FL 33122	(305) 513-4142	930.0
109	AGILITY INTERNATIONAL INC. ALEXANDRIA, VA 22312	703-440-7150	9.2
110	AGILITY LOGISTICS CORP. IRVINE, CA 92602	(714) 617-6300	2291.1
111	AGILITY PROJECT LOGISTICS, INC. HOUSTON, TX 77032	(713) 452-3500	1216.4
112	AGILOC INTERNATIONAL, INC. BRISBANE, CA 94005	(650) 588-7108	2450.0
113	AGLI MARITIME, LTD. BENSENVILLE, IL 60106-1509	(224) 260-0010	615.1
114	AGLO, INC. MIAMI, FL 33166	(305) 418-9020	928.8
115	AGMARK LOGISTICS, LLC NASHVILLE, TN 37201	(615) 313-6585	569.0
116	AGRI OCEAN SERVICE, INC. NAPERVILLE, IL 60563	(630) 364-7703	624.3
117	AGS INTERNATIONAL FORWARDERS INC. NEW LONDON, PA 19360	(610) 255-5400	87.1
118	AHC LOGISTICS CARGO CONSULTANT, INC. DORAL, FL 33172	(786) 536-4054	929.5
119	AHMED M. MOHAMMED HOUSTON, TX 77057	(713) 783-7888	1232.7
120	AIECA INTERNATIONAL LOGISTICS CORP MIAMI, FL 33166	(305) 885-4195	928.3

#	Business	Phone	Distance (mi)

121	AIR & SEA INTERNATIONAL, INC. MURRAY, UT 84121	(801) 264-9130	1852.2
122	AIR 7 SEAS TRANSPORT LOGISTICS, INC. MILPITAS, CA 95305	(408) 957-8787	2428.8
123	AIR AND CARGO SERVICES, INC. ATLANTA, GA 30349	(770) 775-3330	555.7
124	AIR CARGO TRANSPORT SERVICES, INC. HANOVER, MD 21076	(410) 766-7470	26.3
125	AIR MARINE FORWARDING CO. MIAMI, FL 33182	(305) 477-3496	931.1
126	AIR OCEAN INTERNATIONAL FORWARDERS, INC. MIAMI, FL 33126	(305) 463-0470	931.0
127	AIR PARCEL EXPRESS, INC. MIAMI, FL 33172	(305) 597-0258	928.3
128	AIR SEA AMERICA, INC. KENT, WA 98032	(253) 395-9551	2333.8
129	AIR SEA EXPRESS, INC. SOUTH SAN FRANCISCO, CA 94080	650-871-2883	2450.5
130	AIR SEA INTERNATIONAL FORWARDING, INC. LINDEN, NJ 07036	(908) 583-5086	177.8
131	AIR SEA LAND SHIPPING & MOVING INC. NEW YORK, NY 10017	(212) 983-8886	208.2
132	AIR SEA SHIPPING, INC. MIAMI, FL 33126	(305) 592-5176	930.4
133	AIR SEA TRANSPORT (CHICAGO) INC. ELK GROVE VILLAGE, IL 60007	(847) 298-8080	616.4
134	AIR TIGER EXPRESS (USA) , INC. SPRINGFIELD GARDENS, NY 11413	(718) 917-6700	213.4
135	AIR TRANS MARINE, INC. SUNRISE, FL 33326	(305) 513-8589	909.3
136	AIRBRIDGE USA CORP. JAMAICA, NY 11413	(718) 949-5644	214.6
137	AIR-CITY INC. JAMAICA, NY 11434	(718) 949-2900	213.0
138	AIRCONEX, INC. REVERE, MA 02151	(781) 284-8550	401.2
139	AIRLIFT (U.S.A.) , INC. LOS ANGELES, CA 90045 Organization No. : 016162 License No. : 016162 Trade Name(s) : AIRLIFT CONTAINER LINE Full Address : 11099 S. LA CIENEGA BLVD. SUITE 151 LOS ANGELES, CA 90045 UNITED STATES	(310) 337-0700	2317.1
140	AIRLINE CARGO SERVICES INC INWOOD, NY 11096	(516) 371-1545	212.8

For additional analytical, business and investment opportunities information, please contact Global Investment & Business Center, USA at (703) 370-8082. Fax: (703) 370-8083. E-mail: ibpusa3@gmail.com Global Business and Investment Info Databank - www.ibpus.com

#	Business	Phone	Distance (mi)
141	AIRPORT CLEARANCE SERVICE, INC. ROCHELLE PARK, NJ 07662	(201) 270-4600	210.1
142	AIRSCHOTT, INC. HANOVER, MD 21076-1662	(410) 863-4777	26.4
143	AIR-SEA CONTAINER LINE INC. JAMAICA, NY 11434	(718) 978-3888	213.2
144	AIR-SEA FORWARDERS, INC. INGLEWOOD, CA 90301	(310) 216-1616	2316.6
145	AIRTRUK/SEATRUK INC. JAMAICA, NY 11434	(718) 244-8923	213.2
146	AIRWAVES GLOBAL LOGISTICS LLC JAMAICA, NY 11434	(718) 977-3159	213.1
147	AIRWAYS FREIGHT CORPORATION FAYETTEVILLE, AR 72704	(800) 643-3525	965.7
148	AJ FREIGHT SERVICES INC. MIAMI, FL 33166	(305) 599-6802	929.4
149	AJC LOGISTICS, LLC ATLANTA, GA 30328	(404) 252-6750	537.7
150	AKINS INTERNATIONAL, INC. BLOOMINGDALE, IL 60108	(630) 694-0800	616.3
151	ALADDIN SHIPPING INC. HOUSTON, TX 77076	(281) 650-4849	1221.0
152	A-LAS FREIGHT & CARGO GROUP, LLC DORAL, FL 33172	(305) 888-5566	932.2
153	ALASKA SEAVAN, INC. SEATTLE, WA 98188	(206) 575-6800	2332.6
154	ALBA WHEELS UP INTERNATIONAL INC. VALLEY STREAM, NY 11580	(718) 276-3000	213.0
155	ALBARQ SHIPPING SERVICES INC. ORANGE, CA 92867	(714) 484-7866	2299.8
156	ALBATRANS, INC. JAMAICA, NY 11413	(718) 917-6795	213.4
157	ALBERT L. TOKIN, JR. GIG HARBOR, WA 98335	(206) 851-5773	2351.4
158	ALCAR INTERNATIONAL, INC. MIAMI, FL 33166	(305) 756-0080	927.7
159	ALEXIM TRADING CORPORATION DORAL, FL 33166	(305) 513-0888	929.0
160	ALFA CARGO FORWARDERS CORP. MIAMI, FL 33122	(305) 715-9000	929.5

#	Business	Phone	Distance (mi)
161	ALISON TRANSPORT, INC. INWOOD, NY 11096	(516) 563-6500	217.4
162	ALL AMERICA FREIGHT SERVICES CORP. MIAMI, FL 33172	(305) 591-2572	930.8
163	ALL AMERICAN CARGO-SERVICIOS NICARAGUENSES,	(305) 324-4675	929.1

For additional analytical, business and investment opportunities information, please contact Global Investment & Business Center, USA at (703) 370-8082. Fax: (703) 370-8083. E-mail: ibpusa3@gmail.com Global Business and Investment Info Databank - www.ibpus.com

	CORP. MIAMI, FL 33142		
164	ALL CITY AIR AND OCEAN, INC. MAYWOOD, NJ 07607	(201) 346-1119	211.0
165	ALL EXPRESS CARGO INC. SOUTH OZONE PARK, NY 11420	(718) 738-3400	211.5
166	ALL EXPRESS CARGO, LLC. DORAL, FL 33122	(305) 669-2146	935.0
167	ALL FREIGHT INTERNATIONAL, INC. SEATTLE, WA 98166	(206) 244-2646	2335.9
168	ALL IN ONE CUSTOM BROKERS INC. ELIZABETH, NJ 07206	(908) 820-9443	195.5
169	ALL LOGISTICS CARGO, INC. COMPTON, CA 90222	(310) 609-0144	2309.6
170	ALL MY SERVICES, CORP. MIAMI, FL 33166	(305) 798-0181	928.8
171	ALL OVER EXPORT, INC. MIAMI, FL 33144	(305) 266-9006	932.9
172	ALL POINTS EXPORT INCORPORATED BELLEVUE, WA 98008	(425) 502-8570	2327.3
173	ALL POINTS GLOBAL LOGISTICS, INC. JACKSONVILLE, FL 32225-3267	(904) 329-1187	646.2
174	ALL SHORE FORWARDERS, LTD. RED BANK, NJ 07701	(732) 212-1515	187.9
175	ALL STATES TRANSPORT, INC. SPRINGFIELD, MA 01105	(413) 737-1402	323.7
176	ALL TRANS CARGO, CORP. MIAMI, FL 33178	(786) 399-8580	929.7
177	ALL TRANSPORT EXPORT INC NORCROSS, GA 30093	(770) 837-2569	525.7
178	ALL TRANSPORT, INC. MIAMI, FL 33166	(305) 591-2762	927.9
179	ALL-CARGO EXPRESS INC. CORAL SPRINGS, FL 33071 Organization No. : 013596 License No. : 003981 Trade Name(s) : N/A Full Address : 12558 WEST ATLANTIC BLVD. LAKEVIEW PROFESSIONAL VILLAGE CORAL SPRINGS, FL 33071 UNITED STATES	(954) 753-0600	899.0
180	ALLEGHENY BROKERAGE COMPANY, INC. DUBLIN, VA 24084	(540) 674-0900	234.8

#	Business	Phone	Distance (mi)
181	ALLEN LUND COMPANY, LLC	(800) 644-5863	2301.3

For additional analytical, business and investment opportunities information, please contact Global Investment & Business Center, USA at (703) 370-8082. Fax: (703) 370-8083. E-mail: ibpusa3@gmail.com Global Business and Investment Info Databank - www.ibpus.com

	LA CANADA, CA 91011		
182	ALLGREEN WORLDWIDE EXPRESS CORPORATION SCHAUMBURG, IL 60173	(847) 885-9900	622.6
183	ALLIANCE INTERNATIONAL SHIPPING LLC MIAMI, FL 33176	(305) 629-9898	940.2
184	ALLIANCE MOVING SOLUTIONS, INC. BROOKLYN, NY 11235	(347) 654-5295	202.2
185	ALLIANCE PACIFIC CORPORATION, INC. SMYRNA, GA 30082	(770) 434-3516	545.9
186	ALLIANCE SHIPPERS, INC. LONG BEACH, CA 90803	(562) 437-5702	2307.3
187	ALLIED INTERNATIONAL N.A., INC. OAKBROOK TERRACE, IL 60181	(630) 717-3000	612.5
188	ALLMIA INTERNATIONAL CORPORATION MEDLEY, FL 33178	(786) 354-4900	926.0
189	ALLPOINTS SHIPPING LTD. FOX LAKE, IL 60020	(847) 587-4639	635.2
190	ALLPOINTS UNLIMITED, INC. BALDWIN, NY 11510	(917) 612-7332	220.1
191	ALLPORTS FORWARDING, INC. PORTLAND, OR 97220	(503) 242-1201	2354.0
192	ALLROUND FORWARDING CO., INC. NEW YORK, NY 10001	(212) 255-8444	207.1
193	ALLROUND FORWARDING MIDWEST INC. NORTH OLMSTED, OH 44070	(216) 650-7674	312.8
194	ALLROUND LOGISTICS INC. JOPPA, MD 21085	(410) 612-5881	54.2
195	ALLROUND LOGISTICS INC. FOREST HILLS, NY 11375	(718) 544-8945	212.1
196	ALLSTATE INT'L FREIGHT USA, INC. GARDENA, CA 90248	(310) 635-0700	2313.5
197	ALLSTATES LOGISTICS, INC. BAYVILLE, NJ 08721	(305) 594-2026	169.9
198	ALL-WAYS FORWARDING INT'L INC. ELIZABETH, NJ 07208	(908) 353-4000	195.4
199	ALLY GLOBAL LOGISTICS LLC NORWELL, MA 02061	(781) 544-3970	402.7
200	ALLYN INTERNATIONAL SERVICES, INC. FT. MYERS, FL 33919	(239) 489-9900	903.8

For additional analytical, business and investment opportunities information, please contact Global Investment & Business Center, USA at (703) 370-8082. Fax: (703) 370-8083. E-mail: ibpusa3@gmail.com Global Business and Investment Info Databank - www.ibpus.com

GOVERNMENT CONTACTS RELATED TO EXPORT-IMPORT ACTIVITY

U.S. DEPARTMENT OF AGRICULTURE

Agricultural Marketing Service
Washington, DC 20250
Tel. 202.720.8998
www.ams.usda.gov

Animal and Plant Health Inspection Service (APHIS)

Animals:
USDA-APHIS-VS
Riverdale, MD 20737–1231
Tel. 301.734.7885
Plants:
USDA-APHIS-PPQ
Riverdale, MD 20737–1231
Tel. 301.734.8896
www.aphis.usda.gov

Food Safety and Inspection Service
Import Inspection Division
Landmark Center
1299 Farnam, Suite 300
Omaha, NE 68102
Tel. 402.221.7400

Foreign Agricultural Service
Room 5531-S
Washington, D.C. 20250-1000
Tel. 202.720.2916
Fax 202.720.8076
www.usda.gov

U.S. DEPARTMENT OF COMMERCE

Exporter Counseling Division
14th Street & Pennsylvania Ave., N.W.
Washington, DC 20230
Tel. 202.482.4811
www.bxa.doc.gov

National Marine Fisheries Service Headquarters
National Oceanic and Atmospheric Administration
1315 East-West Highway
Silver Spring, MD 20910
Tel. 301.713.2289

NMFS Southwest Region

For additional analytical, business and investment opportunities information, please contact Global Investment & Business Center, USA at (703) 370-8082. Fax: (703) 370-8083. E-mail: ibpusa3@gmail.com Global Business and Investment Info Databank - www.ibpus.com

Protected Species Management Division
501 West Ocean Blvd.
Long Beach, CA 90802-4213
Tel. 562.980.4019
www.kingfish.ssp.nms.gov

FEDERAL COMMUNICATIONS COMMISSION

Laboratory Division
7435 Oakland Mills Road
Columbia, MD 21046
Tel. 301.362.3000
www.fcc.gov

U.S. CONSUMER PRODUCT SAFETY COMMISSION

Office of Compliance
4330 East West Highway
Bethesda, MD 20814
Tel. 301.504.0608
Fax 301.504.0359
www.cpsc.gov

ENVIRONMENTAL PROTECTION AGENCY

Hazardous Materials Hotline
1.800.424.9346

TSCA Assistance Information Service
Tel. 202.554.1404

Motor Vehicles Investigation/Imports Section (6405-J) Washington, D.C. 20460
Tel. 202.564.9660

U.S. DEPARTMENT OF HEALTH AND HUMAN SERVICES

Food and Drug Administration

Center for Biologics Evaluation and Research
1401 Rockville Pike
Suite 200 North
Rockville, MD 20852
Tel. 301.827.6201
www.fda.gov/cber

Center for Drug Evaluation and Research
7520 Standish Place
Rockville, MD 20855
Tel. 301.594.3150
www.fda.gov/cber

Center for Devices and Radiological Health
Rockville, MD 20850
Tel. 301.594.4692
www.fda.gov/cber

For additional analytical, business and investment opportunities information, please contact Global Investment & Business Center, USA at (703) 370-8082. Fax: (703) 370-8083. E-mail: ibpusa3@gmail.com Global Business and Investment Info Databank - www.ibpus.com

Division of Import Operations and Policy (HFC–170)
5600 Fishers Lane
Rockville, MD 20857
Tel. 301.443.6553
Fax 301.594.0413
www.fda.gov/ora/import

CENTER FOR FOOD SAFETY AND APPLIED NUTRITION

Office of Food Labeling (HFS–156)
200 "C" St., NW
Washington, DC 20204
Tel. 202.205.4606
http//vm.cfsan.fda.gov

Office of Seafood
Washington, DC 20005
Tel. 202.418.3150

U.S. Public Health Service

Centers for Disease Control and Prevention
Office of Health and Safety
1600 Clifton Road
Atlanta, Georgia 30333
Tel. 404.639.3235
www.cdc.gov

U.S. DEPARTMENT OF ENERGY

Office of Codes and Standards
Washington, DC 20585
Tel. 202.586.9127
www.eren.doe.gov

U.S. DEPARTMENT OF THE INTERIOR

Fish and Wildlife Service
Office of Management Authority
4401 N. Fairfax Drive
Arlington, VA 22203
Tel. 703.358.2093
www.fws.gov

U.S. DEPARTMENT OF JUSTICE

Drug Enforcement Administration
700 Army-Navy Drive
Arlington VA 22202
Tel. 202.307.7977
Fax 202.307.7965
www.usdoj.gov/dea

For additional analytical, business and investment opportunities information, please contact Global Investment & Business Center, USA at (703) 370-8082. Fax: (703) 370-8083. E-mail: ibpusa3@gmail.com Global Business and Investment Info Databank - www.ibpus.com

NUCLEAR REGULATORY COMMISSION

Office of International Programs
One White Flint North
11555 Rockville Pike
Rockville, MD 20852
Tel. 301.415.7000

FEDERAL TRADE COMMISSION

Bureau of Consumer Protection
Washington, DC 20580
Tel. 202.326.2996
Division of Enforcement
Washington, DC 20580
Tel. 202.326.2996
www.ftc.gov

INTERNATIONAL TRADE COMMISSION

500 "E" Street, SW
Washington, DC 20436
Tel. 202.205.2000
www.usitc.gov

U.S. DEPARTMENT OF STATE

Office of Defense Trade Controls
Bureau of Political/Military Affairs
2401 "E" Street, NW
Washington, DC 20037
Tel. 202.663.2700
www.pmdtc.org

U.S. DEPARTMENT OF TRANSPORTATION

National Highway Traffic Safety Administration
Office of Vehicle Safety Compliance (NEF-32)
400 7th Street SW
Washington, DC 20590
Tel. 1-800-424-9393
Fax 202.366.1024
www.nhtsa.dot.gov

U.S. Coast Guard
Office of Boating Safety
2100 Second Street, SW
Washington, DC 20593-0001
Tel. 202.267.1077

National Vessel Documentation Center
792 T.J. Jackson Drive
Falling Waters, W.Va. 25419-9502
Tel. 304.271.2400
Fax 304.271.2405

For additional analytical, business and investment opportunities information, please contact Global Investment & Business Center, USA at (703) 370-8082. Fax: (703) 370-8083. E-mail: ibpusa3@gmail.com Global Business and Investment Info Databank - www.ibpus.com

Office of Hazardous Materials
400 7th Street SW
Washington, DC 20590-0001
Tel. 202.366.4488

U.S. DEPARTMENT OF THE TREASURY

Bureau of Alcohol, Tobacco, and Firearms
Washington, DC 20226
Tel. 202.927.7920 (arms and ammunition)
202.927.8110 (alcoholic beverages)
www.atf.treas.gov

U.S. CUSTOMS SERVICE

Office of Regulations and Rulings
1300 Pennsylvania Avenue NW
Washington, DC 20229
Tel. 202.927.0760

National Commodity Specialist Division
One Penn Plaza
11th Floor
New York, NY 10119
Tel. 201.443.0367
Fax 201.443.0595

Office of Field Operations
Trade Programs Division
1300 Pennsylvania Ave. NW
Washington, DC 20229
Tel. 202.927.0300
www.customs.gov

Office of Foreign Assets Control
1500 Pennsylvania Avenue NW
Washington, DC 20220
Tel. 202.622.2500
Fax 202.622.1657
www.treas.gov/treasury/services/fac

MAJOR US PORTS OF ENTRY

Anchorage
605 W. Fourth Ave., Anchorage, AK 99501

Atlanta
700 Doug Davis Dr., Atlanta, GA 30354

Baltimore
200 St. Paul Place, Baltimore, MD 21202

Baton Rouge
5353 Essen Lane, Baton Rouge, LA 70809

Blaine
9901 Pacific Highway, Blaine, WA 98230

Boston
10 Causeway St., Boston, MA 02222-1059

Buffalo
111 W. Huron St., Buffalo, NY 14202-2378

Calais
1 Main Street, Calais, ME 04619

Calexico
P.O. Box 632, Calexico, CA 02231

Champlain
198 W. Service Road, Champlain, NY 12919

Charleston
200 E. Bay Street, Charleston, SC 29401

Charlotte
1901-K Cross Beam Dr., Charlotte, NC 28217

Charlotte Amalie
Main Post Ofc-Sugar Est., St. Thomas, VI 00801

Chicago
610 S. Canal Street, Chicago, IL 60607

Christiansted
Church St. PO Box 249, St Croix, VI 00820

Cleveland
6747 Engle Rd., Middleburg Hgts, OH 44130

Dallas/Ft. Worth
PO Box 619050, DFW Airport, TX 75621

Denver
4735 Oakland St., Denver, CO 80239

Derby Line
Interstate 91, Derby Line, VT 05830

Detroit
477 Michigan Ave., Detroit, MI 48226

Douglas
1st St. & Pan American Ave., Douglas AZ 85607

Duluth
515 W. 1st St., Duluth, MN 55820-1390

El Paso
9400 Viscount, Suite 104, El Paso, TX 79925

Grand Rapids
Kent City Airport, Grand Rapids, MI 49512

Great Falls
300 2nd Ave South, Great Falls, MT 59404

Greenville/Spartanburg
150-A W. Phillips Rd., Greer, SC 29650

Harrisburg
Harrisburg Airport #135, Middletown, PA 17507

Hartford
135 High St., Hartford, CT 06103

Highgate Springs
RR #2 Box 170, Swanton, VT 05488

Honolulu
335 Merchant St., Honolulu, HI 96813

Houlton
RR #3 Box 5300, Houlton, ME 04730

For additional analytical, business and investment opportunities information, please contact Global Investment & Business Center, USA at (703) 370-8082. Fax: (703) 370-8083. E-mail: ibpusa3@gmail.com Global Business and Investment Info Databank - www.ibpus.com

Houston/Galveston
2350 N. Sam Houston East, Houston, TX 77032

Jacksonville
2831 Talleyrand Ave., Jacksonville, FL 32206

Kansas City
2701 Rockcreek Pkwy, N. Kansas City, MO 64116

Laredo/Colombia
PO Box 3130, Laredo, TX 78044

Los Angeles
300 S. Ferry St., Terminal Island, CA 90731

Los Angeles Airport Area
300 S. Ferry St., Terminal Island, CA 90731

LA/Long Beach Seaport Area
300 S. Ferry St., Terminal Island, CA 90731

Louisville
601 W. Broadway, Louisville, KY 40202

Miami Airport
PO Box 523215, Miami, FL 35152

Milwaukee
PO Box 37260, Milwaukee, WI 53237-0260

Minneapolis
110 S. 4th St., Minneapolis, MN 55401

Mobile
150 N. Royal St., Mobile, AL 36602

Nashville
939 Airport Service Rd., Nashville, TN 37277

New Orleans
423 Canal St., Ste 245, New Orleans, LA 70130

New York
6 World Trade Ctr., New York, NY 10048

New York-JFK Area
Building #77, Jamaica, NY 11430

New York - NY/Newark Area
Rt 1&9 S., Hemisphere Ctr., Newark, NJ 07114

Nogales
9 N. Grand Ave., Nogales, AZ 85621

Norfolk
200 Granby St., Norfolk, VA 23510

Ogdensburg
127 N. Water St., Ogdensburg, NY 13669

Orlando
5390 Bear Road, Orlando, FL 32827

Oroville
Route 1, Box 130, Oroville, WA 98844

Pembina
112 W. Stutsman, #102, Pembina, ND 58271

Philadelphia
2nd & Chestnut St., Philadelphia, PA 19106

Phoenix
1315 S. 27th St., Phoenix, AZ 85034

Port Huron
526 Water St., Port Huron, MI 48060

Portland, ME
312 Fore St., Portland, ME 04101

Portland, OR
511 NW Broadway, Ste 198, Portland, OR 97209

Providence
49 Pavilion Ave., Providence, RI 02905

Raleigh/Durham
120 Southcenter Ct., Morrisville, NC 27560

Richmond
4501 Williamsburg Rd., Richmond, VA 23231

San Antonio
9800 Airport Blvd., San Antonio, TX 78216

San Diego
610 W. Ash St., San Diego, CA 92101

San Francisco
33 New Montgomery St.
San Francisco, CA 94126

San Juan
#1 La Puntilla, San Juan, PR 00901

San Luis
PO Box H, San Luis, AZ 85349

Sault Ste Marie
Intl Bridge Plaza, Sault Ste Marie, MI 49783

Savannah
1 East Bay St., Savannah, GA 31401

Seattle
1000 2nd Ave., Seattle, WA 98104-1049

Seattle Airport
Sea-Tac Intl Airport, Seattle, WA 98158

Seattle Waterfront
3236 16th Ave., SW, Rm 2100, Seattle, WA 98134

St. Albans
PO Box 1490, St. Albans, VT 05478

St. Louis
4477 Woodson Rd., St. Louis, MO 63134

Syracuse
4034 S. Service Rd., Syracuse, NY 13212

Tacoma
2202 Port of Tacoma Rd., Tacoma, WA 98421

Tampa
1624 E. 7th Ave., #101, Tampa, FL 33605

Tucson
7150 S. Tucson Blvd., Tucson AZ 85706

Washington, DC
PO Box 17423, Washington, DC 20041

Wilmington
1 Virginia Ave., Wilmington, NC 28401

Nogales
9 N. Grand Ave., Nogales, AZ 85621

Norfolk
200 Granby St., Norfolk, VA 23510

Ogdensburg
127 N. Water St., Ogdensburg, NY 13669

Orlando
5390 Bear Road, Orlando, FL 32827

Oroville
Route 1, Box 130, Oroville, WA 98844

Pembina
112 W. Stutsman, #102, Pembina, ND 58271

Philadelphia
2nd & Chestnut St., Philadelphia, PA 19106

Phoenix
1315 S. 27th St., Phoenix, AZ 85034

Port Huron
526 Water St., Port Huron, MI 48060

Portland, ME
312 Fore St., Portland, ME 04101

Portland, OR
511 NW Broadway, Ste 198, Portland, OR 97209

Providence
49 Pavilion Ave., Providence, RI 02905

Raleigh/Durham
120 Southcenter Ct., Morrisville, NC 27560

Richmond
4501 Williamsburg Rd., Richmond, VA 23231

San Antonio
9800 Airport Blvd., San Antonio, TX 78216

San Diego
610 W. Ash St., San Diego, CA 92101

San Francisco
33 New Montgomery St.
San Francisco, CA 94126

San Juan
#1 La Puntilla, San Juan, PR 00901

San Luis
PO Box H, San Luis, AZ 85349

Sault Ste Marie
Intl Bridge Plaza, Sault Ste Marie, MI 49783

Savannah
1 East Bay St., Savannah, GA 31401

Seattle
1000 2nd Ave., Seattle, WA 98104-1049

Seattle Airport
Sea-Tac Intl Airport, Seattle, WA 98158

Seattle Waterfront
3236 16th Ave., SW, Rm 2100, Seattle, WA 98134

St. Albans
PO Box 1490, St. Albans, VT 05478

St. Louis
4477 Woodson Rd., St. Louis, MO 63134

Syracuse
4034 S. Service Rd., Syracuse, NY 13212

Tacoma
2202 Port of Tacoma Rd., Tacoma, WA 98421

Tampa
1624 E. 7th Ave., #101, Tampa, FL 33605

Tucson
7150 S. Tucson Blvd., Tucson AZ 85706

Washington, DC
PO Box 17423, Washington, DC 20041

Wilmington
1 Virginia Ave., Wilmington, NC 28401

BASIC TITLES ON THE UNITES STATES

IMPORTANT!
All publications are updated annually!
Please contact IBP, Inc. at ibpusa3@gmail.com for the latest ISBNs and additional information

Title
United States Banking & Financial Market Handbook
United States Business and Investment Opportunities Yearbook Volume 1 Strategic Information and Opportunities
United States Business Law Handbook - Strategic Information and Basic Laws
United States Business Law Handbook - Strategic Information and Basic Laws
United States Chambers of Commerce Directory, Vol.1 Alaska, Arkansas, Arizona
United States Clothing & Textile Industry Handbook
United States Congress Guide
United States Country Study Guide - Strategic Information and Developments Volume 1 Strategic Information and Developments
United States Ecology & Nature Protection Handbook
United States Energy Policy, Laws and Regulations Handbook
United States Healthcare Sector Organization, Management and Payment Systems Handbook - Strategic Information, Programs and Regulations
United States Industrial and Business Directory
United States Internet and E-Commerce Investment and Business Guide - Strategic and Practical Information: Regulations and Opportunities
United States Investment and Business Guide - Strategic and Practical Information

Title
United States Investment and Business Guide - Strategic and Practical Information
United States Justice System and National Police Handbook
United States Medical & Pharmaceutical Industry Handbook
United States Mineral & Mining Sector Investment and Business Guide - Strategic and Practical Information
United States Oil & Gas Sector Business & Investment Opportunities Yearbook
United States Privatization Programs and Regulations Handbook
United States Recent Economic and Political Developments Yearbook
United States Research & Development Policy Handbook
United States Telecommunication Industry Business Opportunities Handbook
United States: How to Invest, Start and Run Profitable Business in United States Guide - Practical Information, Opportunities, Contacts
United States: Importacion a los Estados Unidos
United States: Starting Small Business In the US Handbook
US - Korea North: Political and Economic Cooperation Handbook
US - Utah Investment & Business Guide
US - Utah Small Business Assistance and Programs Handbook
US "Green Card" How to Become US Permanent Resident Handbook
US "War on Terror" Handbook
US "War on Terror" Handbook
US "War on Terror" Handbook
US "War on Terror" Military Strategy Handbook
US & Canada Literary Agents and Publishers
US & International Economic Assistance to Palestine Handbook
US & International Economic Assistance to Palestine Handbook
US A "Spy" Guide - Strategic Information and Developments
US A Spy" Guide"
US Aerospace and Space Doctrine Handbook
US Affordable Healthcare Act Handbook - Strategic Information and Implementation
US African Development Fund Handbook
US African Development Fund Handbook
US AGENCY FOR INTERNATIONAL DEVELOPMENT BUSINESS OPPORTUNITIES HANDBOOK
US AGENCY FOR INTERNATIONAL DEVELOPMENT BUSINESS OPPORTUNITIES HANDBOOK
US Agency for International Development Handbook
US Agency for International Development Handbook
US Air Force Academy Handbook
US Air Force Academy Handbook
US Air Force Air University Handbook
US Air Force Air University Handbook
US Air Force Base Conversion Agency Handbook
US Air Force Base Conversion Agency Handbook
US Air Force Handbook
US Air force Handbook
US Air Force Handbook
US Air force Handbook
US Air force Handbook
US Air Force in Europe Handbook
US Air Force in Europe Handbook
US Air force or the Future Handbook Volume 1

For additional analytical, business and investment opportunities information, please contact Global Investment & Business Center, USA at (703) 370-8082. Fax: (703) 370-8083. E-mail: ibpusa3@gmail.com Global Business and Investment Info Databank - www.ibpus.com

Title
US Air force or the Future Handbook Volume 1
US Air Force or the Future Handbook Volume 1
US Air force or the Future Handbook Volume 2
US Air force or the Future Handbook Volume 2
US Air Force or the Future Handbook Volume 2
US Air force or the Future Handbook Volume 3
US Air force or the Future Handbook Volume 3
US Air force or the Future Handbook Volume 3
US Air Force or the Future Handbook Volume 4
US Air force or the Future Handbook Volume 4
US Air force or the Future Handbook Volume 4
US Air Force Special Operations School Handbook
US Air Force Special Operations School Handbook
US Air Transportation Business Law Handbook - Strategic Information and Basic Laws
US Air Transportation Business Law Handbook - Strategic Information and Basic Laws
US Air Transportation Handbook: Regulations and Business Opportunities
US Air Transportation Handbook: Regulations and Business Opportunities
US Airport Improvement Program Handbook
US Airport Improvement Program Handbook
US Airports Handbook: Regulations and Business Opportunities
US Airports Handbook: Regulations and Business Opportunities
US Airpower and Space Security Doctrine Handbook
US Alabama Business Registration and Incorporation Guide
US Alabama Investment & Business Guide
US Alabama Small Business Assistance and Programs Handbook
US American Indians Business Opportunities Handbook
US American Indians Business Opportunities Handbook
US American Indians Business Opportunities Handbook
US and Canada Literary Agents and Publishers Handbook
US Anti SPAM Laws and Regulations Handbook
US Anti SPAM Laws and Regulations Handbook
US Anti Terrorism Handbook: Strategy, Operations, Programs
US Anti Terrorism Handbook: Strategy, Operations, Programs
US Anti-Gambling Laws and Regulations Handbook
US Arms Control and Disarmament Agency Handbook
US Arms Control and Disarmament Agency Handbook
US Arms Control and International Security Policy Handbook
US Arms Control and International Security Policy Handbook
US Arms Export Policy and Control Procedures Handbook
US Arms Export Policy and Control Procedures Handbook
US Arms Export Policy and Control Procedures Handbook
US Arms Export Policy and Control Procedures Handbook
US Arms Sales to Foreign Countries Handbook
US Arms Sales to Foreign Countries Handbook
US Army Future Combat Systems Handbook
US Army Future Combat Systems Handbook
US Army Future Combat Systems Handbook
US Army Handbook

For additional analytical, business and investment opportunities information, please contact Global Investment & Business Center, USA at (703) 370-8082. Fax: (703) 370-8083. E-mail: ibpusa3@gmail.com Global Business and Investment Info Databank - www.ibpus.com

Title
US Army Handbook
US Army Handbook
US Army Modernization Plans Handbook
US Army Modernization Plans Handbook
US Army Modernization Plans Handbook
US Army National Guards Handbook
US Army National Guards Handbook
US Army New Weapon Systems Handbook
US Army New Weapon Systems Handbook
US Army New Weapon Systems Handbook
US Army Security Assistance Command Handbook
US Army Security Assistance Command Handbook
US Army Security Assistance Training Management Organization Handbook
US Army Security Assistance Training Management Organization Handbook
US Army Weapon Systems Handbook
US Army Weapon Systems Handbook
US Assistance to Afghanistan Handbook
US Assistance to Afghanistan Handbook
US Assistance to Albania Handbook
US Assistance to Albania Handbook
US Assistance to Angola Handbook
US Assistance to Angola Handbook
US Assistance to Armenia Handbook
US Assistance to Armenia Handbook
US Assistance to Azerbaijan Handbook
US Assistance to Azerbaijan Handbook
US Assistance to Bangladesh Handbook
US Assistance to Bangladesh Handbook
US Assistance to Belarus Handbook
US Assistance to Belarus Handbook
US Assistance to Benin Handbook
US Assistance to Benin Handbook
US Assistance to Bolivia Handbook
US Assistance to Bolivia Handbook
US Assistance to Bosnia-Herzegovina Handbook
US Assistance to Bosnia-Herzegovina Handbook
US Assistance to Brazil Handbook
US Assistance to Brazil Handbook
US Assistance to Bulgaria Handbook
US Assistance to Bulgaria Handbook
US Assistance to Burundi Handbook
US Assistance to Burundi Handbook
US Assistance to Cambodia Handbook
US Assistance to Cambodia Handbook
US Assistance to Colombia Handbook
US Assistance to Colombia Handbook
US Assistance to Croatia Handbook
US Assistance to Croatia Handbook

For additional analytical, business and investment opportunities information,
please contact Global Investment & Business Center, USA
at (703) 370-8082. Fax: (703) 370-8083. E-mail: ibpusa3@gmail.com
Global Business and Investment Info Databank - www.ibpus.com

Title
US Assistance to Cuba Handbook
US Assistance to Cuba Handbook
US Assistance to Cyprus Handbook
US Assistance to Cyprus Handbook
US Assistance to Czech Republic Handbook
US Assistance to Czech Republic Handbook
US Assistance to Dominican Republic Handbook
US Assistance to Dominican Republic Handbook
US Assistance to DR Congo Handbook
US Assistance to DR Congo Handbook
US Assistance to East Timor Handbook
US Assistance to East Timor Handbook
US Assistance to Ecuador Handbook
US Assistance to Ecuador Handbook
US Assistance to Egypt Handbook
US Assistance to Egypt Handbook
US Assistance to El Salvador Handbook
US Assistance to El Salvador Handbook
US Assistance to Eritrea Handbook
US Assistance to Eritrea Handbook
US Assistance to Ethiopia Handbook
US Assistance to Ethiopia Handbook
US Assistance to FYR of Macedonia Handbook
US Assistance to FYR of Macedonia Handbook
US Assistance to Georgia Handbook
US Assistance to Georgia Handbook
US Assistance to Ghana Handbook
US Assistance to Ghana Handbook
US Assistance to Guatemala Handbook
US Assistance to Guatemala Handbook
US Assistance to Guinea Handbook
US Assistance to Guinea Handbook
US Assistance to Guyana Handbook
US Assistance to Guyana Handbook
US Assistance to Haiti Handbook
US Assistance to Haiti Handbook
US Assistance to Honduras Handbook
US Assistance to Honduras Handbook
US Assistance to India Handbook
US Assistance to India Handbook
US Assistance to Indonesia Handbook
US Assistance to Indonesia Handbook
US Assistance to Indonesia Handbook
US Assistance to Indonesia Handbook
US Assistance to Ireland/Northern Ireland (UK) Handbook
US Assistance to Ireland/Northern Ireland (UK) Handbook
US Assistance to Jamaica Handbook
US Assistance to Jamaica Handbook

For additional analytical, business and investment opportunities information, please contact Global Investment & Business Center, USA at (703) 370-8082. Fax: (703) 370-8083. E-mail: ibpusa3@gmail.com Global Business and Investment Info Databank - www.ibpus.com

Title
US Assistance to Jordan Handbook
US Assistance to Jordan Handbook
US Assistance to Kazakhstan Handbook
US Assistance to Kazakhstan Handbook
US Assistance to Kenya Handbook
US Assistance to Kenya Handbook
US Assistance to Kosovo Handbook
US Assistance to Kosovo Handbook
US Assistance to Kyrgyzstan Handbook
US Assistance to Kyrgyzstan Handbook
US Assistance to Laos Handbook
US Assistance to Laos Handbook
US Assistance to Lebanon Handbook
US Assistance to Lebanon Handbook
US Assistance to Liberia Handbook
US Assistance to Liberia Handbook
US Assistance to Lithuania Handbook
US Assistance to Lithuania Handbook
US Assistance to Madagascar Handbook
US Assistance to Madagascar Handbook
US Assistance to Malawi Handbook
US Assistance to Malawi Handbook
US Assistance to Mali Handbook
US Assistance to Mali Handbook
US Assistance to Mexico Handbook
US Assistance to Mexico Handbook
US Assistance to Moldova Handbook
US Assistance to Moldova Handbook
US Assistance to Mongolia Handbook
US Assistance to Morocco Handbook
US Assistance to Morocco Handbook
US Assistance to Morocco Handbook
US Assistance to Morocco Handbook
US Assistance to Mozambique Handbook
US Assistance to Mozambique Handbook
US Assistance to Myanmar Handbook
US Assistance to Myanmar Handbook
US Assistance to Namibia Handbook
US Assistance to Namibia Handbook
US Assistance to Nepal & Pakistan Handbook
US Assistance to Nepal & Pakistan Handbook
US Assistance to Nicaragua Handbook
US Assistance to Nicaragua Handbook
US Assistance to Nigeria Handbook
US Assistance to Nigeria Handbook
US Assistance to Panama Handbook
US Assistance to Panama Handbook
US Assistance to Paraguay Handbook

For additional analytical, business and investment opportunities information, please contact Global Investment & Business Center, USA at (703) 370-8082. Fax: (703) 370-8083. E-mail: ibpusa3@gmail.com Global Business and Investment Info Databank - www.ibpus.com

Title
US Assistance to Paraguay Handbook
US Assistance to Peru Handbook
US Assistance to Peru Handbook
US Assistance to Philippines Handbook
US Assistance to Philippines Handbook
US Assistance to Poland Handbook
US Assistance to Poland Handbook
US Assistance to Romania Handbook
US Assistance to Romania Handbook
US Assistance to Russia Handbook
US Assistance to Russia Handbook
US Assistance to Rwanda Handbook
US Assistance to Rwanda Handbook
US Assistance to Senegal Handbook
US Assistance to Senegal Handbook
US Assistance to Serbia and Montenegro Handbook
US Assistance to Serbia and Montenegro Handbook
US Assistance to Sierra Leone Handbook
US Assistance to Sierra Leone Handbook
US Assistance to Slovak Republic Handbook
US Assistance to Slovak Republic Handbook
US Assistance to Somalia Handbook
US Assistance to Somalia Handbook
US Assistance to South Africa Handbook
US Assistance to South Africa Handbook
US Assistance to Sri Lanka Handbook
US Assistance to Sri Lanka Handbook
US Assistance to Sudan Handbook
US Assistance to Sudan Handbook
US Assistance to Tajikistan Handbook
US Assistance to Tajikistan Handbook
US Assistance to Tanzania Handbook
US Assistance to Tanzania Handbook
US Assistance to Turkey Handbook
US Assistance to Turkey Handbook
US Assistance to Turkmenistan Handbook
US Assistance to Turkmenistan Handbook
US Assistance to Uganda Handbook
US Assistance to Uganda Handbook
US Assistance to Ukraine Handbook
US Assistance to Ukraine Handbook
US Assistance to Uzbekistan Handbook
US Assistance to Uzbekistan Handbook
US Assistance to Vietnam Handbook
US Assistance to Vietnam Handbook
US Assistance to West Bank/ Gaza Handbook
US Assistance to West Bank/ Gaza Handbook
US Assistance to Yemen Handbook

For additional analytical, business and investment opportunities information, please contact Global Investment & Business Center, USA at (703) 370-8082. Fax: (703) 370-8083. E-mail: ibpusa3@gmail.com
Global Business and Investment Info Databank - www.ibpus.com

Title
US Assistance to Yemen Handbook
US Assistance to Yemen Handbook
US Assistance to Yemen Handbook
US Assistance to Zambia Handbook
US Assistance to Zambia Handbook
US Assistance to Zimbabwe Handbook
US Assistance to Zimbabwe Handbook
US Aviation and Aerospace Industry Handbook Vol 2 Military Equipment
US Aviation and Aerospace Industry Handbook Volume 1 BASIC TRENDS AND REGULATIONS
US Aviation and Aerospace Industry Handbook Volume 1 BASIC TRENDS AND REGULATIONS
US Aviation Industry Strategic Developments and Statistics Yearbook
US Banking & Financial Market Handbook
US Bankruptcy Regulations and procedures Handbook
US Bankruptcy Regulations and procedures Handbook
US Banks Handbook
US Banks Handbook
US Book Distributors Directory vol2
US Book Distributors Directory vol2
US Brazil Diplomatic and Political Cooperation Handbook
US Budgeting Process Handbook
US Business and Investment Opportunities Yearbook
US Business and Investment Opportunities Yearbook
US Business for Sale and Franchises Opportunities Handbook: Information by State
US Business Intelligence Handbook
US Business Intelligence Handbook
US Business Intelligence Report - Practical Information, Opportunities, Contacts
US Business Intelligence Report - Practical Information, Opportunities, Contacts
US Business Law Handbook - Strategic Information and Basic Laws
US Business Law Handbook - Strategic Information and Basic Laws
US Buying and Financing Residential Real Estate in the US Handbook
US Buying or Selling a Business in the US Handbook
US California Business Registration and Incorporation Guide
US California Government Handbook - Practical Information and Contacts
US California Investment & Business Guide
US California Small Business Assistance and Programs Handbook
US Catalog of Federal Domestic Assistance Handbook
US CENTRAL INTELLIGENCE AGENCY (CIA) HANDBOOK
US CENTRAL INTELLIGENCE AGENCY (CIA) HANDBOOK
US Chambers of Commerce Directory, Vol.1 Alaska, Arkansas, Arizona
US Chambers of Commerce Directory, Vol.3 Florida
US Chambers of Commerce Directory, Vol.3 Florida
US Chemical and Biological Weapon Strategy Handbook
US Chemical and Biological Weapon Strategy Handbook
US Chemical and Biological Weapon Strategy Handbook
US Citizenship, Naturalization Regulation and Procedures Handbook: Practical Information and Contacts
US Civil Rights Policy Handbook
US Civil Rights Policy Handbook
US Clothing & Textile Industry Handbook

For additional analytical, business and investment opportunities information, please contact Global Investment & Business Center, USA at (703) 370-8082. Fax: (703) 370-8083. E-mail: ibpusa3@gmail.com Global Business and Investment Info Databank - www.ibpus.com

Title
US Coastal Guards Handbook
US Coastal Guards Handbook
US Commercial insurance Modernization Handbook
US Commercial insurance Modernization Handbook
US Commercial insurance Modernization Handbook
US Commodity Futures Trading Commission Handbook
US Commodity Futures Trading Commission Handbook
US Companies in Russia Directory
US Companies in Russia Directory
US Company Laws and Regulations Handbook Volume 1 Corporate Laws and Regulations Basics
US Company Laws and Regulations Handbook Volume 2 Non Profits
US Congress Guide
US Congress Guide
US Congress Guide
US Congress Joint Committee on Printing Handbook
US Congress Joint Committee on Taxation Handbook
US Congress Joint Economic Committee Handbook
US Congressional Budget Office Handbook
US Congressional Budget Office Handbook
US Counterintelligence Handbook
US Counterintelligence Handbook
US Counterintelligence Operations against Cuba Handbook
US Counterintelligence Operations against Cuba Handbook
US Country Study Guide - Strategic Information and Developments
US Country Study Guide - Strategic Information and Developments
US Customs Broker Handbook: Regulations, Procedures, Opportunities
US Customs Brokers Directory
US Customs Regulations Handbook
US Customs Regulations Handbook
US Customs, Trade Regulations and Procedures Handbook
US Customs, Trade Regulations and Procedures Handbook
US Defense Advanced Research Projects Agency Handbook
US Defense Advanced Research Projects Agency Handbook
US Defense Agencies and Organizations Handbook
US Defense Agencies and Organizations Handbook
US Defense and Intelligence Abbreviations and Acronyms Handbook
US Defense and Intelligence Abbreviations and Acronyms Handbook
US Defense and Military Strategy Handbook
US Defense and Military Strategy Handbook
US Defense and Military Strategy Handbook
US Defense Information Systems Agency Handbook
US Defense Information Systems Agency Handbook
US Defense Intelligence Agency Business Guide
US Defense Intelligence Agency Business Guide
US Defense Intelligence Agency Handbook
US Defense Intelligence Agency Handbook
US Defense Policy Handbook
US Defense Policy Handbook

Title
US Defense Security Service Handbook
US Defense Security Service Handbook
US Defense Threat Reduction Agency Handbook
US Defense Threat Reduction Agency Handbook
US Department of Agriculture Business Opportunities Handbook
US Department of Agriculture Business Opportunities Handbook
US Department of Agriculture Handbook
US Department of Commerce Handbook
US Department of Commerce Handbook
US Department of Defense Handbook
US Department of Defense Handbook
US Department of Energy Business Opportunities Handbook
US Department of Energy Business Opportunities Handbook
US Department of Energy Handbook
US Department of Energy Handbook
US Department of Health and Human Services Handbook
US Department of Health and Human Services Handbook
US Department of Homeland Security Handbook
US Department of Homeland Security Handbook
US Department of Housing and Urban Services Handbook
US Department of Housing and Urban Services Handbook
US Department of Interior Handbook
US Department of Interior Handbook
US Department of Justice Handbook
US Department of Justice Handbook
US Department of Labor Handbook
US Department of Labor Handbook
US Department of State Handbook
US Department of State Handbook
US Department of the Air Force Handbook
US Department of the Air Force Handbook
US Department of the Army Handbook
US Department of the Army Handbook
US Department of the Navy Handbook
US Department of the Navy Handbook
US Department of the Treasury Handbook
US Department of the Treasury Handbook
US Department of Transport Handbook
US Department of Transport Handbook
US Department of Veteran Affairs Handbook
US Department of Veteran Affairs Handbook
US Diplomatic Handbook - Strategic Information and Developments
US Diplomatic Handbook - Strategic Information and Developments
US Drug and Medical Devices Export-Import Regulations Handbook
US Drug and Medical Devices Export-Import Regulations Handbook
US Ecology & Nature Protection Handbook
US Ecology & Nature Protection Laws and Regulation Handbook
US E-Commerce Business Guide

For additional analytical, business and investment opportunities information, please contact Global Investment & Business Center, USA at (703) 370-8082. Fax: (703) 370-8083. E-mail: ibpusa3@gmail.com Global Business and Investment Info Databank - www.ibpus.com

Title
US E-Commerce Business Guide
US E-Commerce Business Law Handbook - Strategic Information and Basic Laws
US E-Commerce Business Law Handbook - Strategic Information and Basic Laws
US Economic and Political Assistance to Macedonia Handbook
US Economic and Political Assistance to Macedonia Handbook
US ECONOMIC ASSISTANCE TO RUSSIA Handbook
US Economic Assistance to Russia Handbook
US Education System and Policy Handbook
US El Salvador Diplomatic and Political Cooperation Handbook
US Emission Trading Laws, Regulations and Programs Handbook
US Energy Policy, Laws and Regulation Handbook
US Energy Policy, Laws and Regulations Handbook
US Environmental Protection Agency Handbook
US Environmental Protection Agency Handbook
US Export Guide: How to Export Products and Services from the United States
US Export Guide: How to Export Products and Services from the United States
US Export Programs Guide
US Export Programs Guide
US Export-Import Bank Handbook
US Export-Import Bank Handbook
US Export-Import Trade and Business Directory
US Export-Import, Investment & Financial Assistance Handbook
US Export-Import, Investment & Financial Assistance Handbook
US Farmers Markets Directory
US Farmers Markets Directory
US Farmers Markets Directory
US Farmers Markets Directory – Volume 2 Ohio-Wyoming
US FDA Cosmetics Products Control and Regulations Handbook
US FDA Cosmetics Products Control and Regulations Handbook
US FDA Drug Products Control and Regulations Handbook
US FDA Drug Products Control and Regulations Handbook
US FDA Food Products Control and Regulations Handbook
US FDA Food Products Control and Regulations Handbook
US FDA Medical Devices Control and Regulations Handbook
US FDA Medical Devices Control and Regulations Handbook
US Federal Bureau of Investigation (FBI) Academy Handbook
US Federal Bureau of Investigation (FBI) Business Opportunities Handbook
US Federal Bureau of Investigation (FBI) Business Opportunities Handbook
US Federal Bureau of Investigation (FBI) Handbook
US Federal Bureau of Investigation (FBI) Handbook
US Federal Business Opportunities Handbook
US Federal Business Opportunities Handbook
US Federal Communication Commission Handbook
US Federal Communication Commission Handbook
US Federal Depository Libraries Directory
US Federal Depository Libraries Directory
US Federal Election Commission Handbook
US Federal Election Commission Handbook

For additional analytical, business and investment opportunities information, please contact Global Investment & Business Center, USA at (703) 370-8082. Fax: (703) 370-8083. E-mail: ibpusa3@gmail.com Global Business and Investment Info Databank - www.ibpus.com

Title
US Federal Energy Sector Regulations Handbook
US Federal Energy Sector Regulations Handbook
US Federal Executive Government Handbook
US Federal Executive Government Handbook
US Federal Government Directory
US Federal Government Directory
US Federal Grant Management Handbook
US Federal Grant Management Handbook
US Federal Law Enforcement Training Center Handbook
US Federal Law Enforcement Training Center Handbook
US Federal Maritime Commission Handbook
US Federal Maritime Commission Handbook
US Federal Maritime Commission Handbooks
US Federal Maritime Commission Handbooks
US Federal Mine Safety and Health Commission Handbook
US Federal Mine Safety and Health Commission Handbook
US Federal Reserve System Handbook
US Federal Reserve System Handbook
US Federal Trade Commission Handbook
US Federal Trade Commission Handbook
US Financial Crimes Enforcement Regulations Handbook
US Financial Crimes Enforcement Regulations Handbook
US Financial Crimes Enforcement Regulations Handbook
US Financial Crimes Prevention Handbook for Everybody
US Financial Crimes Prevention Handbook for Everybody
US Financial Crimes Prevention Handbook for Everybody
US Fire-Safe Hotels Directory: Fire-Safe Hotels by States
US Food and Drug Administration Handbook
US Food and Drug Administration Handbook
US Food Assistance to Russia Handbook
US Food Assistance to Russia Handbook
US Foreign Embassies, Representations and Consulate Offices in the US Handbook
US Foreign Policy & Government Guide
US Foreign Policy & Government Guide
US Foreign Trade Sanctions Handbook
US Foreign Trade Sanctions Handbook
US Foreign Trade Zones Handbook
US Foreign Trade Zones Handbook
US Free Trade Agreements with Foreign Countries Handbook
US Free Trade and Investment Agreements and Associations Handbook
US Free Trade and Investment Agreements and Associations Handbook
US Free Trade and Investment Agreements and Associations with Foreign Countries Handbook
US Free Trade and Investment Agreements and Associations with Foreign Countries Handbook
US Future Combat & Weapon Systems Handbook
US Future Combat & Weapon Systems Handbook
US Gabling Industry Investment and Business Guide - Strategic and Practical Information
US Gabling Industry Investment and Business Guide - Strategic and Practical Information
US Gaming Industry Investment and Business Guide - Strategic and Practical Information

Title
US Gaming Industry Investment and Business Guide - Strategic and Practical Information
US Gaming Industry Investment and Business Guide - Strategic and Practical Information
US Gaming Industry Investment and Business Guide - Strategic and Practical Information Volume 1
US Gaming Industry Law and Regulations Handbook
US Gaming Industry Law and Regulations Handbook
US Gaming Industry Laws and Regulations Handbook
US Gaming Industry Laws and Regulations Handbook
US General Service Administration Handbook
US General Service Administration Handbook
US George W. Bush President of the US (Leadership Vision Reforms)
US Gourmet Food Distributors Directory vol 1
US Gourmet Food Distributors Directory vol 2
US Gourmet Food Distributors Directory vol 3
US Gourmet Food Distributors Directory vol 4
US Gourmet Food Distributors Directory vol 5
US Gourmet Food Distributors Directory vol 6
US Gourmet Food Distributors Directory Volume 1
US Gourmet Food Distributors Directory Volume 2
US Gourmet Food Distributors Directory Volume 3
US Gourmet Food Distributors Directory Volume 4
US Gourmet Food Distributors Directory Volume 5
US Gourmet Food Distributors Directory Volume 6
US Government and Business Contacts Handbook
US Government and Business Contacts Handbook
US Government and Special Subsidized Housing Buying Programs Handbook
US Government and Special Subsidized Housing Buying Programs Handbook
US GOVERNORS FEDERAL LEGISLATIVE AGENDA HANDBOOK
US GOVERNORS FEDERAL LEGISLATIVE AGENDA HANDBOOK
US GOVERNORS GUIDE
US GOVERNORS GUIDE
US GOVERNORS STATE-TO-THE STATE ANNUAL ADDRESSES AND BUDGET PRESENTATIONS YEARBOOK
US GOVERNORS STATE-TO-THE STATE ANNUAL ADDRESSES AND BUDGET PRESENTATIONS YEARBOOK
US Green Card" How to Become US Permanent Resident Handbook"
US Hedge Finds Handbook
US Hedge Finds Handbook
US House Committee on Agriculture Handbook
US House Committee on Agriculture Handbook
US House Committee on Appropriations Handbook
US House Committee on Appropriations Handbook
US House Committee on Armed Services Handbook
US House Committee on Armed Services Handbook
US House Committee on Education and the Workforce Handbook
US House Committee on Education and the Workforce Handbook
US House Committee on Energy and Commerce Handbook
US House Committee on Energy and Commerce Handbook
US House Committee on Financial Services Handbook

For additional analytical, business and investment opportunities information, please contact Global Investment & Business Center, USA at (703) 370-8082. Fax: (703) 370-8083. E-mail: ibpusa3@gmail.com Global Business and Investment Info Databank - www.ibpus.com

Title
US House Committee on Financial Services Handbook
US House Committee on Government Reform Handbook
US House Committee on Government Reform Handbook
US House Committee on House Administration Handbook
US House Committee on House Administration Handbook
US House Committee on International Relations Handbook
US House Committee on International Relations Handbook
US House Committee on Resources Handbook
US House Committee on Resources Handbook
US House Committee on Rules Handbook
US House Committee on Rules Handbook
US House Committee on Science Handbook
US House Committee on Science Handbook
US House Committee on Small Business Handbook
US House Committee on Small Business Handbook
US House Committee on Standards of Official Conduct Handbook
US House Committee on Standards of Official Conduct Handbook
US House Committee on Taxation Handbook
US House Committee on Taxation Handbook
US House Committee on the Budget Handbook
US House Committee on the Budget Handbook
US House Committee on the Judiciary Handbook
US House Committee on the Judiciary Handbook
US House Committee on Transportation and Infrastructure Handbook
US House Committee on Transportation and Infrastructure Handbook
US House Committee on Veterans Affairs Handbook
US House Committee on Veterans Affairs Handbook
US House Committee on Ways and Means Handbook
US House Committee on Ways and Means Handbook
US House Joint Committee on Printing Handbook
US House Joint Committee on Taxation Handbook
US House Joint Economic Committee Handbook
US House of Representatives Ethics Manual
US House Permanent Select Committee on Intelligence Handbook
US House Permanent Select Committee on Intelligence Handbook
US Idaho Business Registration and Incorporation Guide
US Idaho Investment & Business Guide
US Idaho Small Business Assistance and Programs Handbook
US Illinois Business Registration and Incorporation Guide
US Illinois Investment & Business Guide
US Illinois Small Business Assistance and Programs Handbook
US Immigration Policy and Programs Handbook Vol. 1 Basic Information and Legislation
US Immigration Policy and Programs Handbook Vol. 1 Basic Information and Legislation
US Immigration Policy and Programs Handbook Vol. 2 Procedures, Regulations, Application Forms
US Immigration Policy Handbook
US Immigration Policy Handbook; Strategic and Practical Information
US Importing Products into the US Market Guide
US Income Tax Treaties with Foreign Countries Handbook

Title
US Income Tax Treaties with Foreign Countries Handbook
US Income Tax Treaties with Foreign Countries Handbook. Vol 2
US Income Tax Treaties with Foreign Countries Handbook. Vol 3
US Income Tax Treaties with Foreign Countries Handbook. Vol 4
US Income Tax Treaties with Foreign Countries Handbook. Vol 5
US Income Tax Treaties with Foreign Countries Handbook. Volume 2
US Income Tax Treaties with Foreign Countries Handbook. Volume 3
US Income Tax Treaties with Foreign Countries Handbook. Volume 4
US Income Tax Treaties with Foreign Countries Handbook. Volume 5
US Indian Gaming Laws and Regulations Handbook
US Indian Gaming Laws and Regulations Handbook
US Indian Gaming Laws and Regulations Handbook
US Indian Reservations Casino Gaming Industry Investment and Business Guide - Strategic and Practical Information
US Indian Reservations Casino Gaming Investment and Business Guide - Strategic and Practical Information
US Indian Reservations Casino Gaming Investment and Business Guide - Strategic and Practical Information
US Indian Tribal Leaders Directory
US Indian Tribal Leaders Directory
US Indiana Business Registration and Incorporation Guide
US Indiana Investment & Business Guide
US Indiana Small Business Assistance and Programs Handbook
US Industrial and Business Directory
US Industrial and Business Directory
US Information Agency Handbook
US Information Agency Handbook
US Initial Public Offering Regulations Handbook
US Initial Public Offering Regulations Handbook
US Intelligence and Counterintelligence History Handbook Vol.1 American Revolution, Civil War, World War 1, Between the Wars
US Intelligence and Counterintelligence History Handbook Vol.1 American Revolution, Civil War, World War 1, Between the Wars
US Intelligence and Counterintelligence History Handbook Vol.2 World War 2
US Intelligence and Counterintelligence History Handbook Vol.2 World War 2
US Intelligence and Counterintelligence History Handbook Vol.3 Cold War Counterintelligence, 1960s,70s,80s, end of 20th Century
US Intelligence and Counterintelligence History Handbook Vol.4 Military and Nuclear Technology, Russian Spies in the US, Defense Industry
US Intelligence and Counterintelligence History Handbook Vol.4 Military and Nuclear Technology, Russian Spies in the US, Defense Industry
US Intelligence and Counterintelligence Laws and Regulations Handbook
US Intelligence and Counterintelligence Laws and Regulations Handbook
US Intelligence and Counterintelligence Laws and Regulations Handbook
US Intelligence Community Handbook
US Intelligence Community Handbook
US Intelligence Community Legal Reference Book
US Intelligence Community Legal Reference Handbook
US Intelligence Policy Handbook

For additional analytical, business and investment opportunities information, please contact Global Investment & Business Center, USA at (703) 370-8082. Fax: (703) 370-8083. E-mail: ibpusa3@gmail.com Global Business and Investment Info Databank - www.ibpus.com

Title
US Intelligence Policy Handbook
US Internal Revenue Service Handbook
US Internal Revenue Service Handbook
US International Telephone Traffic Report
US Internet and E-Commerce Investment and Business Guide - Strategic and Practical Information: Regulations and Opportunities
US Internet and E-Commerce Investment and Business Guide - Strategic and Practical Information: Regulations and Opportunities
US Internet and E-Commerce Investment and Business Guide - Strategic and Practical Information: Regulations and Opportunities
US Investment and Business Guide - Strategic and Practical Information
US Investment and Business Guide - Strategic and Practical Information
US Investment and Trade Laws and Regulations Handbook
US Investment and Trade Laws and Regulations Handbook
US Investors' Fraud Prevention Handbook
US Investors' Fraud Prevention Handbook
US Iowa Business Registration and Incorporation Guide
US Iowa Investment & Business Guide
US Iowa Small Business Assistance and Programs Handbook
US Iraq Strategy Handbook: new developments
US Iraq Strategy Handbook: new developments
US Iraq Strategy Handbook: new developments
US Justice System and National Police Handbook
US Largest Commercial Banks Handbook (Banks with 300+ Mill Dol. Assets)
US Largest Commercial Banks Handbook (Banks with 300+ Mill Dol. Assets)
US Laws for Regulation of Therapeutic Goods in the United States Handbook
US Legislative Process Handbook Vol. 1 House of Representatives
US Legislative Process Handbook Vol. 2 Senate
US Libraries and Information Science National Commission Handbook
US Libraries and Information Science National Commission Handbook
US Marine Corp Handbook
US Marine Corp Handbook
US Marine Corp Handbook
US Marketing and Advertising Regulations Handbook
US Marketing and Advertising Regulations Handbook Volume 1 Ecommerce and Internet Marketing Regulations
US Medical & Pharmaceutical Industry Handbook
US Medical Drugs Development and Approval Process Handbook
US Michigan Life Sciences Business Opportunities and Programs Handbook
US Military Base Structure and Location Handbook
US Military Base Structure and Location Handbook
US Military Base Structure and Location Handbook
US Military Cooperation with African Countries Handbook
US Military Cooperation with African Countries Handbook
US Military Cooperation with Asian Countries Handbook
US Military Cooperation with Asian Countries Handbook
US Military Cooperation with China Handbook
US Military Cooperation with China Handbook

Title
US Military Cooperation with Eastern European Countries Handbook
US Military Cooperation with Eastern European Countries Handbook
US Military Cooperation with Russia Handbook
US Military Cooperation with Russia Handbook
US Military Forces Recruitment Handbook
US Military Forces Recruitment Handbook
US Military Forces Recruitment Handbook
US Military Intelligence Handbook
US Military Intelligence Handbook
US Military Intelligence Interrogation Techniques Handbook
US Military Intelligence Interrogation Techniques Handbook
US Military Policy Toward Iraq Handbook
US Military Policy Toward Iraq Handbook
US Mineral & Mining Sector Investment and Business Guide - Strategic and Practical Information
US Mining Industry Technology, Equipment and Financial Services Directory
US Mining Industry Technology, Equipment and Financial Services Directory
US Mining Laws and Regulations Handbook
US Missile Defense Agency Handbook
US Missile Defense Agency Handbook
US Missile Defense Glossary Handbook
US Mobile Telecom & Data Companies Directory
US Mobile Telecom & Data Companies Directory
US Mortgage and Financial Companies Directory
US Mortgage Market Handbook
US Mortgage Market Handbook
US Mortgage System Handbook Vol.1 : How to Obtain Mortgages for Foreigners
US Mortgage System Handbook Vol.1 : How to Obtain Mortgages for Foreigners
US Mortgage System Handbook Vol.1 : How to Obtain Mortgages for Foreigners
US Mortgage System Handbook Vol.2 : How to Obtain Mortgages in the US
US Mortgage System Handbook Vol.2 : How to Obtain Mortgages in the US
US Mortgage System Handbook Vol.2 : How to Obtain Mortgages in the US
US National Academy of Science and Research Policy Handbook
US National Academy of Science and Research Policy Handbook
US National Academy of Science Handbook
US National Academy of Science Handbook
US National Aeronautics and Space Administration Handbook
US National Aeronautics and Space Administration Handbook
US National Border Protection Strategy Handbook
US National Counter Terrorism Center Handbook
US National Counter Terrorism Strategy Handbook
US National Counterterrorism Center Handbook
US National Counterterrorism Center Handbook
US National Counterterrorism Strategy Handbook
US National Counterterrorism Strategy Handbook
US National Cyber Security Strategy and Programs Handbook - Strategic Information and Developments
US National Drug Control Policy Handbook
US National Drug Control Policy Handbook
US National Educational & Social Development Policy Handbook

For additional analytical, business and investment opportunities information, please contact Global Investment & Business Center, USA at (703) 370-8082. Fax: (703) 370-8083. E-mail: ibpusa3@gmail.com Global Business and Investment Info Databank - www.ibpus.com

Title
US National Educational and Social Development Policy Handbook Volume 2 Social Policy
US National Emergency Response and Rescue Training Programs Handbook
US National Emergency Response and Rescue Training Programs Handbook
US National Export Strategy and Regulations Yearbook
US National Fire Fighting Training Handbook - Strategic Information and Contacts
US National System of Fire Fighting Handbook - Strategic Information and Contacts
US National Governors Association Handbook
US National Governors Association Handbook - Organization, Strategy, Contacts
US National Guard and Reserve Management Policy Handbook
US National Guard and Reserve Management Policy Handbook
US National Guard and Reserve Management Policy Handbook
US National Guard Handbook
US National Guard Handbook
US National Guard Handbook
US National Homeland Security Strategy Handbook
US National Homeland Security Strategy Handbook
US National Homeland Security Strategy Handbook
US National Import Strategy and Regulations Yearbook
US National Import Strategy Handbook
US National Institute of Health Handbook
US National Institute of Health Handbook
US National Plan of Integrated Airport Systems Handbook
US National Plan of Integrated Airport Systems Handbook
US National Science Foundation Handbook
US National Science Foundation Handbook
US National Security Handbook
US National Security Handbook
US National Security Policy Handbook
US National Security Policy Handbook
US National Security Strategy Handbook
US National Strategy on Combating Terrorism Handbook
US Naval Intelligence Handbook
US Naval Intelligence Handbook
US Naval Postgraduate School Handbook
US Naval Postgraduate School Handbook
US Navy Defense Industry Handbook
US Navy Defense Industry Handbook
US Navy Enlisting Handbook Vol 1 Navy Enlisted Occupational Standards
US Navy Enlisting Handbook Vol 2 Navy Enlisted Classifications
US Navy Handbook
US Navy Seals Handbook
US Navy Seals Handbook - Strategic Information and Contacts
US Navy Total Manpower Requirements Handbook
US Nonproliferation, Arms Control, and International Security Handbook
US Nonproliferation, Arms Control, and International Security Handbook
US Nuclear Energy Development Strategy: Programs and Projects Handbook
US Nuclear Energy Sector Laws and Regulations Handbook
US Nuclear Industry Handbook

For additional analytical, business and investment opportunities information, please contact Global Investment & Business Center, USA at (703) 370-8082. Fax: (703) 370-8083. E-mail: ibpusa3@gmail.com Global Business and Investment Info Databank - www.ibpus.com

Title
US Nuclear Industry Handbook
US Nuclear Industry Investment and Business Guide - Strategic and Practical Information
US Nuclear Industry Investment and Business Guide - Strategic and Practical Information
US Nuclear Power Facilities and Power Stations Handbook
US Nuclear Power Facilities and Power Stations Handbook
US Nuclear Power Facilities Handbook
US Nuclear Power Facilities Handbook
US Nuclear Regulatory Commission Handbook
US Nuclear Regulatory Commission Handbook
US Ocean Transportation Companies Directory
US Ocean Transportation Companies Directory
US Office of Management and Budget Handbook
US Office of Management and Budget Handbook
US Office of Personnel Management Handbook
US Office of Personnel Management Handbook
US Oil & Gas Companies Directory
US Oil & Gas Sector Business & Investment Opportunities Yearbook
US Oil and Gas Exploration Laws and Regulation Handbook
US Overseas Private Investment Corporation Programs Handbook
US Overseas Private Investment Corporation Export Subsidies System Handbook
US Pacific Air Force Handbook
US Pacific Air Force Handbook
US Pacific Regional Strategy Handbook
US Pacific Regional Strategy Handbook
US Paging and Messaging Telecom Companies Directory
US Paging and Messaging Telecom Companies Directory
US Payphone Telecom Service Providers Directory
US Payphone Telecom Service Providers Directory
US Peace Corp Handbook
US Peace Corp Handbook
US Policy and Legislation on Cuba Handbook
US Policy and Legislation on Cuba Handbook
US Political Intelligence Handbook
US Political Intelligence Handbook
US Ports Handbook: Structure, Location, Operation
US Ports of Entry Handbook: Airports and Ports
US Postal Service Handbook
US Postal Service Handbook
US President George W. Bush Handbook
US President George W. Bush Handbook
US Presidential Doctrines Handbook - Reagan, Carder, Clinton, Bush, Obama
US Prison Privatization Handbook: Strategic Information, Regulations, Developments
US Private Security Contractors in Afghanistan and Iraq Handbook - Strategic Information and Regulations
US Private Security Forces Regulations Handbook - Strategic Information, Basic Laws and Regulations
US Privatization Programs and Regulations Handbook
US Privatization Programs and Regulations Handbook
US Privatization Programs and Regulations Handbook
US Privatization Yearbook: Major Programs and Projects

For additional analytical, business and investment opportunities information, please contact Global Investment & Business Center, USA at (703) 370-8082. Fax: (703) 370-8083. E-mail: ibpusa3@gmail.com Global Business and Investment Info Databank - www.ibpus.com

Title
US Privatizations Consulting Companies Directory
US Professional Internet Advertising Handbook
US Professional Internet Advertising Handbook
US Racing Industry Laws and Regulations Handbook
US Racing Industry Laws and Regulations Handbook
US Radio Broadcasting Business Opportunities and Regulations Handbook
US Radio Broadcasting Business Opportunities and Regulations Handbook
US Real Estate Market Business Law Handbook - Strategic Information and Basic Laws
US Real Estate Market Business Law Handbook - Strategic Information and Basic Laws
US Real Estate Markets Analysis and Investment Opportunities Yearbook
US Real Estate Markets Analysis and Investment Opportunities Yearbook
US Recent Economic and Political Developments Yearbook
US Recent Economic and Political Developments Yearbook
US Research & Development Policy Handbook
US Research & Development Policy Handbook
US Residential Real Estate Investment Guide for Everybody
US Residential Real Estate Investment Guide for Everybody
US Residential Real Estate Investment Guide for First Time Buyers
US Residential Real Estate Investment Guide for First Time Buyers
US Residential Real Estate Investment Guide for Foreigners
US Residential Real Estate Investment Guide for Foreigners
US Residential Real Estate Investment Guide for Permanent Residents
US Residential Real Estate Investment Guide for Permanent Residents
US Satellite Communication Companies Directory
US Satellite Communication Companies Directory
US Science and Technology Policy Handbook
US Science and Technology Policy Handbook
US Sea and River Ports Handbook
US Sea and River Ports Handbook
US Sea And River Ports Handbook Vol. 2 North Carolina-Wisconsin
US Secret Service Handbook
US Secret Service Handbook
US Securities and Exchange Commission Handbook
US Securities and Exchange Commission Handbook
US Security and Anti Terrorism Legislation Handbook
US Security and Anti Terrorism Legislation Handbook
US Security Cooperation Agency Handbook
US Security Cooperation Agency Handbook
US Security Cooperation Education and Training Center Handbook
US Security Cooperation Education and Training Center Handbook
US Senate Agriculture, Nutrition, And Forestry Committee Handbook
US Senate Agriculture, Nutrition, And Forestry Committee Handbook
US Senate Appropriations Committee Handbook
US Senate Appropriations Committee Handbook
US Senate Armed Services Committee Handbook
US Senate Armed Services Committee Handbook
US Senate Banking, Housing, And Urban Affairs Handbook
US Senate Banking, Housing, And Urban Affairs Handbook

For additional analytical, business and investment opportunities information, please contact Global Investment & Business Center, USA at (703) 370-8082. Fax: (703) 370-8083. E-mail: ibpusa3@gmail.com Global Business and Investment Info Databank - www.ibpus.com

Title
US Senate Budget Committee Handbook
US Senate Budget Committee Handbook
US Senate Commerce, Science, And Transportation Handbook
US Senate Commerce, Science, And Transportation Handbook
US Senate Committee On Indian Affairs Handbook
US Senate Committee On Indian Affairs Handbook
US Senate Energy And Natural Resources Committee Handbook
US Senate Energy And Natural Resources Committee Handbook
US Senate Environment And Public Works Committee Handbook
US Senate Environment And Public Works Committee Handbook
US Senate Finance Committee Handbook
US Senate Finance Committee Handbook
US Senate Foreign Relations Committee Handbook
US Senate Foreign Relations Committee Handbook
US Senate Governmental Affairs Committee Handbook
US Senate Governmental Affairs Committee Handbook
US Senate Guide vol1
US Senate Guide vol1
US Senate Guide VOLUME 2. United States Senators Biographic Information and Contacts
US Senate Health, Education, Labor And Pensions Committee Handbook
US Senate Health, Education, Labor And Pensions Committee Handbook
US Senate Joint Committee On Taxation Handbook
US Senate Joint Committee On Taxation Handbook
US Senate Joint Economic Committee Handbook
US Senate Joint Economic Committee Handbook
US Senate Judiciary Committee Handbook
US Senate Judiciary Committee Handbook
US Senate Rules And Administration Committee Handbook
US Senate Rules And Administration Committee Handbook
US Senate Select Committee On Ethics Handbook
US Senate Select Committee On Ethics Handbook
US Senate Select Committee On Intelligence Handbook
US Senate Select Committee On Intelligence Handbook
US Senate Small Business Committee
US Senate Small Business Committee
US Senate Special Committee On Aging Handbook
US Senate Special Committee On Aging Handbook
US Senate Veterans' Affairs Committee Handbook
US Senate Veterans' Affairs Committee Handbook
US Small Business Administration Handbook
US Small Business Administration Handbook
US Small Business Support Guide: 50 States of the United States
US South Africa Diplomatic and Political Cooperation Handbook
US Space Programs and Exploration Handbook
US Space Programs and Exploration Handbook
US Spain Diplomatic and Political Cooperation Handbook
US Special Combat Forces Handbook
US Special Combat Forces Handbook

For additional analytical, business and investment opportunities information, please contact Global Investment & Business Center, USA at (703) 370-8082. Fax: (703) 370-8083. E-mail: ibpusa3@gmail.com Global Business and Investment Info Databank - www.ibpus.com

Title
US Special Operations Command Handbook
US Special Operations Command Handbook
US Special Operations Forces Handbook vol 1
US Special Operations Forces Handbook vol 2
US Special Operations Forces Handbook vol 3
US Special Operations Forces Handbook vol 4
US Starting Business (Incorporating) in the US Guide
US Starting Business (Incorporating) in....Guide
US Starting Business (Incorporating) in....Guide
US STATE GOVERNMENTS KEY ECONOMIC AND POLITICAL ISSUES AND PROGRAMS HANDBOOK
US STATE GOVERNMENTS KEY ECONOMIC AND POLITICAL ISSUES AND PROGRAMS HANDBOOK
US Stem Cell Research Policy & Programs Handbook
US Stem Cell Research Policy & Programs Handbook
US Submarine Force Handbook
US Submarine Force Handbook
US Subsidized Housing Buying Programs Handbook
US Subsidized Housing Buying Programs Handbook
US Tax Guide - Corporate Taxation
US Tax Guide-Corporate Taxation
US Taxation Laws and Regulations Handbook
US Telecom Companies Directory
US Telecom Laws and Regulations Handbook vol 1
US Telecom Laws and Regulations Handbook vol 2
US Telecommunication Industry Business Opportunities Handbook
US Telecommunication Industry Business Opportunities Handbook
US Telecommunication Industry Business Opportunities Handbook
US Terrorism Prevention Regulations Handbook
US Trade & Export Sanctions Handbook
US Trade & Export Sanctions Handbook
US Trade and Development Agency Handbook
US Trade and Development Agency Handbook
US Trade Industrial and Business Show Handbook
US Trade Industrial and Business Show Handbook
US Trade Representative Office Handbook
US Trade Representative Office Handbook
US Transportation Policy and Regulations Handbook
US TV Broadcasting Business Opportunities and Regulations Handbook
US TV Broadcasting Business Opportunities and Regulations Handbook
US War Against International Terrorism Handbook
US War Against International Terrorism Handbook
US War Against Iraq Handbook: Political Strategy and Operations
US War Against Iraq Handbook: Political Strategy and Operations
US War on Terror" Military Strategy Handbook"
US Wine Industry Investment and Business Opportunities Yearbook
US Wireless Telecom & Data Companies Directory
US Yugoslavia Economic and Political Cooperation Handbook
US: Importing into the Unites States Practical Guide
US: State of Georgia Business Financial Assistance Programs Handbook

For additional analytical, business and investment opportunities information, please contact Global Investment & Business Center, USA at (703) 370-8082. Fax: (703) 370-8083. E-mail: ibpusa3@gmail.com
Global Business and Investment Info Databank - www.ibpus.com

Title
USA Constitution and Citizenship Laws Handbook - Strategic Information and Basic Laws
USA Immigration Laws and Regulations Handbook - Strategic Information and Basic Laws
USA Insolvency (Bankruptcy) Laws and Regulations Handbook - Strategic Information and Basic Laws
USA Labor Laws and Regulations Handbook - Strategic Information and Basic Laws
USA Land Ownership and Agriculture Laws Handbook
US-Argentina Diplomatic and Political Cooperation Handbook
US-Argentina Diplomatic and Political Cooperation Handbook
US-Argentina Economic and Political Cooperation Handbook
US-Argentina Economic and Political Cooperation Handbook
US-Armenia Diplomatic and Political Cooperation Handbook
US--Armenia Diplomatic and Political Cooperation Handbook
US-Armenia Economic and Political Cooperation Handbook
US--Armenia Economic and Political Cooperation Handbook
US-Australia Diplomatic and Political Cooperation Handbook
US-Australia Diplomatic and Political Cooperation Handbook
US-Australia Economic and Political Cooperation Handbook
US-Australia Economic and Political Cooperation Handbook
US-Austria Diplomatic and Political Cooperation Handbook
US-Austria Diplomatic and Political Cooperation Handbook
US-Austria Economic and Political Cooperation Handbook
US-Austria Economic and Political Cooperation Handbook
US-Azerbaijan Diplomatic and Political Cooperation Handbook
US-Azerbaijan Economic and Political Cooperation Handbook
US-Azerbaijan Economic and Political Cooperation Handbook
US-Belgium Diplomatic and Political Cooperation Handbook
US-Belgium Diplomatic and Political Cooperation Handbook
US-Belgium Economic and Political Cooperation Handbook
US-Belgium Economic and Political Cooperation Handbook
US-Bosnia & Herzegovina Diplomatic and Political Cooperation Handbook
US-Bosnia & Herzegovina Diplomatic and Political Cooperation Handbook
US-Bosnia & Herzegovina Economic and Political Cooperation Handbook
US-Bosnia & Herzegovina Economic and Political Cooperation Handbook
US-Brazil Diplomatic and Political Cooperation Handbook
US-Brazil Economic and Political Cooperation Handbook
US-Bulgaria Diplomatic and Political Cooperation Handbook
US-Bulgaria Diplomatic and Political Cooperation Handbook
US-Bulgaria Economic and Political Cooperation Handbook
US-Bulgaria Economic and Political Cooperation Handbook
US-Canada Diplomatic and Political Cooperation Handbook
US-Canada Diplomatic and Political Cooperation Handbook
US-Canada Economic and Political Cooperation Handbook
US-Canada Economic and Political Cooperation Handbook
US-Chile Diplomatic and Political Cooperation Handbook
US-Chile Diplomatic and Political Cooperation Handbook
US-Chile Economic and Political Cooperation Handbook
US-Chile Economic and Political Cooperation Handbook
US-Chile Free Trade Agreement Handbook
US-China Diplomatic and Political Cooperation Handbook

**For additional analytical, business and investment opportunities information,
please contact Global Investment & Business Center, USA
at (703) 370-8082. Fax: (703) 370-8083. E-mail: ibpusa3@gmail.com
Global Business and Investment Info Databank - www.ibpus.com**

Title
US-China Diplomatic and Political Cooperation Handbook
US-China Economic and Political Cooperation Handbook
US-Costa Rica Diplomatic and Political Cooperation Handbook
US-Costa Rica Economic and Political Cooperation Handbook
US-Costa Rica Economic and Political Cooperation Handbook
US-Croatia Diplomatic and Political Cooperation Handbook
US-Croatia Diplomatic and Political Cooperation Handbook
US-Croatia Economic and Political Cooperation Handbook
US-Cuba Political and Economic Relations Handbook
US-Czech Republic Diplomatic and Political Cooperation Handbook
US-Czech Republic Diplomatic and Political Cooperation Handbook
US-Czech Republic Economic and Political Cooperation Handbook
US-Czech Republic Economic and Political Cooperation Handbook
US-Egypt Diplomatic and Political Cooperation Handbook
US-Egypt Diplomatic and Political Cooperation Handbook
US-Egypt Economic and Political Cooperation Handbook
US-El Salvador Diplomatic and Political Cooperation Handbook
US-El Salvador Economic and Political Cooperation Handbook
US-El Salvador Economic and Political Cooperation Handbook
US-Estonia Diplomatic and Political Cooperation Handbook
US-Estonia Diplomatic and Political Cooperation Handbook
US-Estonia Economic and Political Cooperation Handbook
US-Estonia Economic and Political Cooperation Handbook
US-Finland Diplomatic and Political Cooperation Handbook
US-Finland Diplomatic and Political Cooperation Handbook
US-Finland Economic and Political Cooperation Handbook
US-Finland Economic and Political Cooperation Handbook
US-France Diplomatic and Political Cooperation Handbook
US-France Diplomatic and Political Cooperation Handbook
US-France Economic and Political Cooperation Handbook
US-Georgia Diplomatic and Political Cooperation Handbook
US-Georgia Diplomatic and Political Cooperation Handbook
US-Georgia Economic and Political Cooperation Handbook
US-Georgia Economic and Political Cooperation Handbook
US-Germany Diplomatic and Political Cooperation Handbook
US-Germany Diplomatic and Political Cooperation Handbook
US-Germany Economic and Political Cooperation Handbook
US-Germany Economic and Political Cooperation Handbook
US-Greece Diplomatic and Political Cooperation Handbook
US-Greece Economic and Political Cooperation Handbook
US-Greece Economic and Political Cooperation Handbook
US-Hungary Diplomatic and Political Cooperation Handbook
US-Hungary Diplomatic and Political Cooperation Handbook
US-Hungary Economic and Political Cooperation Handbook
US-Hungary Economic and Political Cooperation Handbook
US-India Diplomatic and Political Cooperation Handbook
US-India Economic and Political Cooperation Handbook
US-India Economic and Political Cooperation Handbook

For additional analytical, business and investment opportunities information, please contact Global Investment & Business Center, USA at (703) 370-8082. Fax: (703) 370-8083. E-mail: ibpusa3@gmail.com Global Business and Investment Info Databank - www.ibpus.com

Title
US-Indonesia Diplomatic and Political Cooperation Handbook
US-Indonesia Diplomatic and Political Cooperation Handbook
US-Indonesia Economic and Political Cooperation Handbook
US-Indonesia Economic and Political Cooperation Handbook
US-Iran Political & Economic Relations Handbook
US-Iran Political & Economic Relations Handbook
US-Iraq Political & Economic Relations Handbook
US-Iraq Political & Economic Relations Handbook
US-Israel Diplomatic and Political Cooperation Handbook
US-Israel Diplomatic and Political Cooperation Handbook
US-Israel Economic and Political Cooperation Handbook
US-Israel Economic and Political Cooperation Handbook
US-Italy Diplomatic and Political Cooperation Handbook
US-Italy Diplomatic and Political Cooperation Handbook
US-Italy Economic and Political Cooperation Handbook
US-Japan Diplomatic and Political Cooperation Handbook
US-Japan Diplomatic and Political Cooperation Handbook
US-Japan Economic and Political Cooperation Handbook
US-Jordan Free Trade Agreement Handbook
US-Kazakhstan Diplomatic and Political Cooperation Handbook
US-Kazakhstan Diplomatic and Political Cooperation Handbook
US-Kazakhstan Diplomatic and Political Relations Handbook
US-Kazakhstan Diplomatic and Political Relations Handbook
US-Kazakhstan Economic and Political Cooperation Handbook
US-Kazakhstan Economic and Political Cooperation Handbook
US-Korea South Diplomatic and Political Cooperation Handbook
US-Korea South Economic and Political Cooperation Handbook
US-Kuwait Diplomatic and Political Cooperation Handbook
US-Kuwait Diplomatic and Political Cooperation Handbook
US-Kuwait Economic and Political Cooperation Handbook
US-Kyrgyzstan Diplomatic and Political Cooperation Handbook
US-Kyrgyzstan Diplomatic and Political Cooperation Handbook
US-Kyrgyzstan Economic and Political Cooperation Handbook
US-Kyrgyzstan Economic and Political Cooperation Handbook
US-Latvia Diplomatic and Political Cooperation Handbook
US-Latvia Diplomatic and Political Cooperation Handbook
US-Latvia Economic and Political Cooperation Handbook
US-Latvia Economic and Political Cooperation Handbook
US-Lithuania Diplomatic and Political Cooperation Handbook
US-Lithuania Diplomatic and Political Cooperation Handbook
US-Lithuania Economic and Political Cooperation Handbook
US-Lithuania Economic and Political Cooperation Handbook
US-Mexico Diplomatic and Political Cooperation Handbook
US-Mexico Diplomatic and Political Cooperation Handbook
US-Mexico Economic and Political Cooperation Handbook
US-Mexico Economic and Political Cooperation Handbook
US-Moldova Diplomatic and Political Cooperation Handbook
US-Moldova Diplomatic and Political Cooperation Handbook

Title
US-Moldova Economic and Political Cooperation Handbook
US-New Zealand Diplomatic and Political Cooperation Handbook
US--New Zealand Diplomatic and Political Cooperation Handbook
US-New Zealand Economic and Political Cooperation Handbook
US--New Zealand Economic and Political Cooperation Handbook
US-Norway Diplomatic and Political Cooperation Handbook
US-Norway Diplomatic and Political Cooperation Handbook
US-Norway Economic and Political Cooperation Handbook
US-Norway Economic and Political Cooperation Handbook
US-Peru Diplomatic and Political Cooperation Handbook
US-Peru Diplomatic and Political Cooperation Handbook
US-Peru Economic and Political Cooperation Handbook
US-Peru Economic and Political Cooperation Handbook
US-Philippines Diplomatic and Political Cooperation Handbook
US-Philippines Economic and Political Cooperation Handbook
US-Poland Diplomatic and Political Cooperation Handbook
US-Poland Diplomatic and Political Cooperation Handbook
US-Poland Economic and Political Cooperation Handbook
US-Poland Economic and Political Cooperation Handbook
US-Portugal Diplomatic and Political Cooperation Handbook
US-Portugal Diplomatic and Political Cooperation Handbook
US-Portugal Economic and Political Cooperation Handbook
US-Portugal Economic and Political Cooperation Handbook
US-Russia Cooperation Against Terrorism Handbook
US-Russia Cooperation Against Terrorism Handbook
US-Russia Diplomatic and Political Cooperation Handbook
US-Russia Diplomatic and Political Cooperation Handbook
US-Russia Economic & Financial Cooperation Handbook
US-Russia Economic & Financial Cooperation Handbook
US-Russia Economic and Political Cooperation Handbook
US-Russia Economic and Political Cooperation Handbook
US-Russia Military Cooperation Handbook
US-Russia Military Cooperation Handbook
US-Russia Political Cooperation Handbook
US-Russia Political Cooperation Handbook
US-Russia Scientific & Technological Cooperation Handbook
US-Russia Scientific & Technological Cooperation Handbook
US-Russia Scientific Cooperation Handbook
US-Russia Scientific Cooperation Handbook
US-Russia Space Cooperation Handbook
US-Russia Space Cooperation Handbook
US-Saudi Arabia Diplomatic and Political Cooperation Handbook
US-Saudi Arabia Diplomatic and Political Cooperation Handbook
US-Saudi Arabia Economic and Political Cooperation Handbook
US-Saudi Arabia Economic and Political Cooperation Handbook
US-Serbia Diplomatic and Political Cooperation Handbook
US-South Africa Diplomatic and Political Cooperation Handbook
US-South Africa Economic and Political Cooperation Handbook

For additional analytical, business and investment opportunities information, please contact Global Investment & Business Center, USA at (703) 370-8082. Fax: (703) 370-8083. E-mail: ibpusa3@gmail.com Global Business and Investment Info Databank - www.ibpus.com

Title
US-South Africa Economic and Political Cooperation Handbook
US-South Korea Diplomatic and Political Cooperation Handbook
US-South Korea Economic and Political Cooperation Handbook
US-Spain Diplomatic and Political Cooperation Handbook
US-Spain Economic and Political Cooperation Handbook
US-Spain Economic and Political Cooperation Handbook
US-Sri Lanka Diplomatic and Political Cooperation Handbook
US-Sri Lanka Diplomatic and Political Cooperation Handbook
US-Sri Lanka Economic and Political Cooperation Handbook
US-Sweden Diplomatic and Political Cooperation Handbook
US-Sweden Economic and Political Cooperation Handbook
US-Sweden Economic and Political Cooperation Handbook
US-Switzerland Diplomatic and Political Cooperation Handbook
US-Switzerland Diplomatic and Political Cooperation Handbook
US-Switzerland Economic and Political Cooperation Handbook
US-Switzerland Economic and Political Cooperation Handbook
US-Taiwan Diplomatic and Political Cooperation Handbook
US-Taiwan Economic and Political Cooperation Handbook
US-Taiwan Economic and Political Cooperation Handbook
US-Turkey Diplomatic and Political Cooperation Handbook
US--Turkey Diplomatic and Political Cooperation Handbook
US-Turkey Economic and Political Cooperation Handbook
US--Turkey Economic and Political Cooperation Handbook
US-Turkey Economic and Political Relations Handbook
US-Turkey Economic and Political Relations Handbook
US-Turkmenistan Diplomatic and Political Cooperation Handbook
US-Turkmenistan Diplomatic and Political Cooperation Handbook
US-Turkmenistan Economic and Political Cooperation Handbook
US-Turkmenistan Economic and Political Cooperation Handbook
US-UK Diplomatic and Political Cooperation Handbook
US-UK Diplomatic and Political Cooperation Handbook
US-UK Economic and Political Cooperation Handbook
US-UK Economic and Political Cooperation Handbook
US-Ukraine Diplomatic and Political Cooperation Handbook
US-Ukraine Economic and Political Cooperation Handbook
US-Ukraine Economic and Political Cooperation Handbook
US-Ukrainian Business Contacts Directory
US-Uruguay Diplomatic and Political Cooperation Handbook
US-Uruguay Diplomatic and Political Cooperation Handbook
US-Uruguay Economic and Political Cooperation Handbook
US-Uruguay Economic and Political Cooperation Handbook
US-Uzbekistan Diplomatic and Political Cooperation Handbook
US-Uzbekistan Diplomatic and Political Cooperation Handbook
US-Uzbekistan Economic and Political Cooperation Handbook
US-Venezuela Diplomatic and Political Cooperation Handbook
US--Venezuela Diplomatic and Political Cooperation Handbook
US-Venezuela Economic and Political Cooperation Handbook
US--Venezuela Economic and Political Cooperation Handbook

Title
US-Vietnam Diplomatic and Political Cooperation Handbook
US-Vietnam Economic and Political Cooperation Handbook
US-Vietnam Economic and Political Cooperation Handbook
US-Yugoslavia Diplomatic and Political Cooperation Handbook
US-Yugoslavia Economic and Political Cooperation Handbook
Utah Business Registration and Incorporation Guide
Utah Business Registration and Incorporation Guide
Utah Investment & Business Guide
Utah Small Business Assistance and Programs Handbook

WORLD TRANSPORTATION SYSTEM, POLICY AND REGULATIONS LIBRARY

(PRICE $99.95)

Afghanistan Transportation System, Policy and Regulation Handbook
Albania Transportation System, Policy and Regulation Handbook
Algeria Transportation System, Policy and Regulation Handbook
Angola Transportation System, Policy and Regulation Handbook
Antigua and Barbuda Transportation System, Policy and Regulation Handbook
Antilles (Netherlands) Transportation System, Policy and Regulation Handbook
Argentina Transportation System, Policy and Regulation Handbook
Armenia Transportation System, Policy and Regulation Handbook
Aruba Transportation System, Policy and Regulation Handbook
Australia Transportation System, Policy and Regulation Handbook
Austria Transportation System, Policy and Regulation Handbook
Azerbaijan Transportation System, Policy and Regulation Handbook
Bahamas Transportation System, Policy and Regulation Handbook
Bahrain Transportation System, Policy and Regulation Handbook
Bangladesh Transportation System, Policy and Regulation Handbook
Barbados Transportation System, Policy and Regulation Handbook
Belarus Transportation System, Policy and Regulation Handbook
Belgium Transportation System, Policy and Regulation Handbook
Belize Transportation System, Policy and Regulation Handbook
Benin Transportation System, Policy and Regulation Handbook
Bermuda Transportation System, Policy and Regulation Handbook
Bhutan Transportation System, Policy and Regulation Handbook
Bolivia Transportation System, Policy and Regulation Handbook
Bosnia and Herzegovina Transportation System, Policy and Regulation Handbook
Botswana Transportation System, Policy and Regulation Handbook
Brazil Transportation System, Policy and Regulation Handbook
Brunei Transportation System, Policy and Regulation Handbook
Bulgaria Transportation System, Policy and Regulation Handbook
Burkina Faso Transportation System, Policy and Regulation Handbook
Cambodia Transportation System, Policy and Regulation Handbook
Cameroon Transportation System, Policy and Regulation Handbook
Canada Transportation System, Policy and Regulation Handbook
Chile Transportation System, Policy and Regulation Handbook

To order and for additional analytical and marketing information, please contacrt
International Business Publications, USA at:
P.O. Box 15343, Washington, DC 20003, USA. Phone: (202) 546-2103. Fax: (202) 546-3275.
E-mail: rusric@erols.com

China Transportation System, Policy and Regulation Handbook
Colombia Transportation System, Policy and Regulation Handbook
Comoros Transportation System, Policy and Regulation Handbook
Costa Rica Transportation System, Policy and Regulation Handbook
Croatia Transportation System, Policy and Regulation Handbook
Cuba Transportation System, Policy and Regulation Handbook
Cyprus Transportation System, Policy and Regulation Handbook
Czech Republic Transportation System, Policy and Regulation Handbook
Denmark Transportation System, Policy and Regulation Handbook
Ecuador Transportation System, Policy and Regulation Handbook
Egypt Transportation System, Policy and Regulation Handbook
El Salvador Transportation System, Policy and Regulation Handbook
Estonia Transportation System, Policy and Regulation Handbook
Fiji Transportation System, Policy and Regulation Handbook
Finland Transportation System, Policy and Regulation Handbook
France Transportation System, Policy and Regulation Handbook
Georgia (Republic) Transportation System, Policy and Regulation Handbook
Germany Transportation System, Policy and Regulation Handbook
Ghana Transportation System, Policy and Regulation Handbook
Gibraltar Offshore & Transportation System, Policy and Regulation Handbook
Greece Transportation System, Policy and Regulation Handbook
Haiti Transportation System, Policy and Regulation Handbook
Honduras Transportation System, Policy and Regulation Handbook
Hungary Transportation System, Policy and Regulation Handbook
Iceland Transportation System, Policy and Regulation Handbook
India Transportation System, Policy and Regulation Handbook
Indonesia Transportation System, Policy and Regulation Handbook
Iran Transportation System, Policy and Regulation Handbook
Iraq Economic Sanctions, Transportation System, Policy and Regulation Handbook
Ireland Transportation System, Policy and Regulation Handbook
Israel Transportation System, Policy and Regulation Handbook
Italy Transportation System, Policy and Regulation Handbook
Jamaica Offshore Transportation System, Policy and Regulation Handbook
Japan Transportation System, Policy and Regulation Handbook
Jordan Transportation System, Policy and Regulation Handbook
Kazakhstan Transportation System, Policy and Regulation Handbook
Kenya Transportation System, Policy and Regulation Handbook
Korea, North Transportation System, Policy and Regulation Handbook
Korea, South Transportation System, Policy and Regulation Handbook
Kuwait Transportation System, Policy and Regulation Handbook
Kyrgyzstan Transportation System, Policy and Regulation Handbook
Laos Transportation System, Policy and Regulation Handbook
Latvia Transportation System, Policy and Regulation Handbook
Lebanon Transportation System, Policy and Regulation Handbook

To order and for additional analytical and marketing information, please contacrt
International Business Publications, USA at:
P.O. Box 15343, Washington, DC 20003, USA. Phone: (202) 546-2103. Fax: (202) 546-3275.
E-mail: rusric@erols.com

Libya Transportation System, Policy and Regulation Handbook
Lithuania Transportation System, Policy and Regulation Handbook
Macao Transportation System, Policy and Regulation Handbook
Macedonia Transportation System, Policy and Regulation Handbook
Madagascar Transportation System, Policy and Regulation Handbook
Malaysia Transportation System, Policy and Regulation Handbook
Malta Transportation System, Policy and Regulation Handbook
Mauritius Transportation System, Policy and Regulation Handbook
Mexico Transportation System, Policy and Regulation Handbook
Moldova Transportation System, Policy and Regulation Handbook
Mongolia Transportation System, Policy and Regulation Handbook
Morocco Transportation System, Policy and Regulation Handbook
Myanmar Transportation System, Policy and Regulation Handbook
Nepal Transportation System, Policy and Regulation Handbook
Netherlands Transportation System, Policy and Regulation Handbook
New Zealand Transportation System, Policy and Regulation Handbook
Nicaragua Transportation System, Policy and Regulation Handbook
Nigeria Transportation System, Policy and Regulation Handbook
Norway Transportation System, Policy and Regulation Handbook
Oman Transportation System, Policy and Regulation Handbook
Pakistan Transportation System, Policy and Regulation Handbook
Panama Transportation System, Policy and Regulation Handbook
Peru Transportation System, Policy and Regulation Handbook
Philippines Transportation System, Policy and Regulation Handbook
Philippines National Police Force Handbook
Poland Transportation System, Policy and Regulation Handbook
Portugal Transportation System, Policy and Regulation Handbook
Qatar Transportation System, Policy and Regulation Handbook
Romania Transportation System, Policy and Regulation Handbook
Russia Transportation System, Policy and Regulation Handbook
Saudi Arabia Transportation System, Policy and Regulation Handbook
Scotland Transportation System, Policy and Regulation Handbook
Singapore Transportation System, Policy and Regulation Handbook
Slovak Republic Transportation System, Policy and Regulation Handbook
Slovak Republic Transportation System, Policy and Regulation Handbook
South Africa Transportation System, Policy and Regulation Handbook
Spain Transportation System, Policy and Regulation Handbook
Sri Lanka Transportation System, Policy and Regulation Handbook
Sudan Transportation System, Policy and Regulation Handbook
Suriname Transportation System, Policy and Regulation Handbook
Sweden Transportation System, Policy and Regulation Handbook
Switzerland Transportation System, Policy and Regulation Handbook
Syria Transportation System, Policy and Regulation Handbook
Taiwan Transportation System, Policy and Regulation Handbook

To order and for additional analytical and marketing information, please contacrt
International Business Publications, USA at:
P.O. Box 15343, Washington, DC 20003, USA. Phone: (202) 546-2103. Fax: (202) 546-3275.
E-mail: rusric@erols.com

Tajikistan Transportation System, Policy and Regulation Handbook
Thailand Transportation System, Policy and Regulation Handbook
Tunisia Transportation System, Policy and Regulation Handbook
Turkey Transportation System, Policy and Regulation Handbook
Turkmenistan Transportation System, Policy and Regulation Handbook
Ukraine Transportation System, Policy and Regulation Handbook
United Arab Emirates Transportation System, Policy and Regulation Handbook
United Kingdom Transportation System, Policy and Regulation Handbook
United States Transportation System, Policy and Regulation Handbook
Uzbekistan Transportation System, Policy and Regulation Handbook
Vietnam Financial and Trade Policy Handbook
Yugoslavia Transportation System, Policy and Regulation Handbook

To order and for additional analytical and marketing information, please contacrt
International Business Publications, USA at:
P.O. Box 15343, Washington, DC 20003, USA. Phone: (202) 546-2103. Fax: (202) 546-3275.
E-mail: rusric@erols.com

www.ingramcontent.com/pod-product-compliance
Ingram Content Group UK Ltd.
Pitfield, Milton Keynes, MK11 3LW, UK
UKHW051458290926
15471UKWH00008B/1273

9 781438 75435